Coaching
Canadian
Football

Football Canada

With Ryan Hall

HUMAN KINETICS

Library of Congress Cataloging-in-Publication Data

Title: Coaching Canadian Football / Football Canada ; With Ryan Hall.
Description: Champaign, IL : Human Kinetics, [2018]
Identifiers: LCCN 2017023252 (print) | LCCN 2017031511 (ebook) |
    ISBN 9781492558743 (ebook) | ISBN 9781450442619 (print)
Subjects: LCSH: Canadian football—Coaching. | Canadian football. |
    Football—Coaching.
Classification: LCC GV948 (ebook) | LCC GV948 .C55 2018 (print) |
    DDC 796.335—dc23
LC record available at https://lccn.loc.gov/2017023252

ISBN: 978-1-4504-4261-9 (print)

The web addresses cited in this text were current as of September 2017, unless otherwise noted.

Acquisitions Editor: Diana Vincer
Senior Developmental Editor: Cynthia McEntire
Managing Editor: Ann Gindes
Cover Designer: Keri Evans
Cover Design Associate: Susan Allen
Photograph (cover): Football Canada
Photo Production Manager: Jason Allen
Senior Art Manager: Kelly Hendren
Illustrations: © Human Kinetics
Production: Westchester Publishing Services
Printer: Versa Press

Human Kinetics books are available at special discounts for bulk purchase. Special editions or book excerpts can also be created to specification. For details, contact the Special Sales Manager at Human Kinetics.

Printed in the United States of America

10   9   8   7   6   5   4   3   2   1

The paper in this book is certified under a sustainable forestry program.

Human Kinetics
P.O. Box 5076
Champaign, IL 61825-5076
Website: www.HumanKinetics.com

In the United States, email info@hkusa.com or call 800-747-4457.
In Canada, email info@hkcanada.com.
In Europe, email hk@hkeurope.com.

For information about Human Kinetics' coverage in other areas of the world, please visit our website: **www.HumanKinetics.com**

E5860

Contents

◆ PART ONE ◆

FUNDAMENTALS OF COACHING

◆ PART TWO ◆

INDIVIDUAL SKILLS AND TEAM TACTICS

◆ P A R T   F I V E ◆

PROGRAM BUILDING AND MANAGEMENT

Foreword

I am both pleased and proud to introduce *Coaching Canadian Football* to the coaching community and the greater football family. This comprehensive compilation of content specific to Canadian football is unprecedented. It is only appropriate to extend my gratitude to the titanic team of contributors who have immeasurably enhanced this volume with topics from leadership to safe contact and player development to significantly more complex systems, strategies, and tactics. Football is a complicated game and this book is intended to be a resource and guide for both the seasoned coach and the beginner.

The fact is, the player experience is inextricably tied to the coach's leadership capacity and core competence. It's important for coaches to embody the traits we desire to see in our players. Steward your influence so that you can maximize your impact. My hope for you as coaches is that success won't pacify you and failure will not define you. The heartbeat of champions and the melody of excellence are grounded in perseverance and continuous improvement. Simply put, keep going and keep growing. In the succinct, poignant prose of the brilliant Winston Churchill, "Success is not final and failure is not fatal."

More personally, words are insufficient to quantify the immense impact coaches breathed into my life—ultimately facilitating a university scholarship, an ever-evolving career in sport, and more importantly, a team mindset. This ethos has positively influenced my 25-year marriage, loving and nurturing my three daughters and prioritizing community over self. In the words of the venerable Nelson Mandela, "Sport has the power to change the world." Coaches, you govern this process and you foster that change! Thank you for your time, your energy, and your sacrifice. Now let's GO and let's GROW!

Congratulations Football Canada.

Mike "Pinball" Clemons

Acknowledgments

Creating a uniquely Canadian coaching resource is crucial for the development of our coaching community, and this amazing resource would not have been possible without the tireless effort of Ryan Hall. Ryan's dedication and hard work have ensured that coaches across the country will be able to interact with some of the greatest coaching minds this sport has to offer, helping to develop the next generation of great coaches.

Football Canada

This book was a labour of love. Imagine trying to compile a book that takes in all the Canadian aspects of a sport, with contributions from writers speaking French and English and living in regions from the Pacific to the Atlantic.

I want to say a very sincere thank-you to the coaches who contributed chapters for this book. Some of you I know, and many of you I have never met in person, but your passion for the game and your commitment to its growth are evident in every word you wrote. Thanks for patiently going back and forth with me via e-mails and phone calls to try to make the book the best it could be. Thanks for the years of your life that you have invested to gain significant levels of football expertise that you willingly shared with our readers.

I have always wanted to write a book, and while *Coaching Canadian Football* is far from mine alone, I am very proud to have been a part of it in a variety of ways: author, editor, reviser, recruiter, collaborator, and coordinator. I have a lot of people to thank for allowing me to do what I do in contributing to football in Canada, and specifically to this book.

For the book, thank you to Rick Sowieta and Aaron Geisler of Football Canada for believing in the importance of a uniquely Canadian book for our uniquely Canadian game, and for making it happen. Thank you to Diana Vincer and Cynthia McEntire of Human Kinetics, two ladies I have never met, but with whom I've exchanged hundreds of e-mails and phone calls while making this book a reality. Thanks to Debbie Masi from Westchester Publishing Services for all of her collaboration on the copyediting process.

From my football life, thanks to the thousands of young people I have coached over the years. Whether you went on to playing postsecondary or professional football, to coaching at the youth or high school level, or to finishing your education, getting a meaningful job, and becoming a responsible, loving spouse and parent, thank you for allowing me to be a part of your life, even though I was far from perfect as a coach.

Thank you to the coaches and teachers who had a formative impact on my development as an athlete and later as a coach. Thanks to my minor fastball coach, Wilf Friesen. Thanks to my grade 12 English teacher, Jack Bradley. Thanks to my high school football coaches, Lloyd Friesen and Tim Herr. Thanks to my junior football coaches Frank McCrystal, Rick Seaman (Geno Fracas Award winner!), and Bernie Schmidt.

Thank you to the many coaches who have helped me grow in our time together during my coaching career. I learned something valuable from each one. Thanks to the men I coached high school football with: Wes Olmstead, Cal Macfarlane, Ken Guenter, Frank Spinozzi, Ron Cherkas, Jes Atchison, Rob Hartman, Kelly Adams, Cory Jones, Brent Glen, Jeff Stusek, Gary Bresch, Jeff Hagerty, Ryan Weir, Will Redl, Wil Putland, Tim McFadden, and Olivier Eddie. Thanks to the men I worked with in the early years of the Regina Thunder junior team: Randy Shaw, Sheldon Neald, Dwayne Masson, Sean Reader, Al Johns, Josh Shaw, and Craig Hammond. Thanks to the men I coached with for the first six years of the Team Saskatchewan under-19 program: Scott Hundseth, Blake Buettner, Scott MacAulay, Lonnie Horan, Jud Heilman, Mike Hummeny, Curtis Bulych, and Scott Farmer, and also Kevin Pierce with the inaugural under-16 program; thanks to Jeff Yausie and Mike Thomas for giving me that opportunity. Also, thanks to the coaches of the junior national team for their influence: Warren Craney, Kevin MacNeill, Brian Guebert, Justin Ethier, Brad Collinson, Kamau Peterson, Marcello Lio, and Samir Chahine. Thanks also to tackling guru Thurmond Moore, who greatly expanded my coaching competency. Thanks to Doug Krochak for his mentorship as a National Coaching Certification Program master learning facilitator.

I would also like to thank the great people of Regina Minor Football, who provide a youth football league for all of the right reasons. Thank you, Len Antonini, Kelly Hamilton, Grant Nicurity, and all of the other incredible board members that I have worked with over the years who give so much of themselves so that other people's kids can have a fun and fair developmental football experience.

Most importantly in my football life is Tony Agresta, a coach from Ohio who organized a Christian football outreach trip to Norway in 1999, and who brought me along as the only Canadian coach. Tony taught me that I could indeed perfectly integrate my passion for coaching football with my relationship with Jesus, and could coach for Him. That transformed my life and made me a much better coach (and person). From that experience came the concept of "Life Talks," a feature part of every program I have coached with since that experience.

I have mentors and friends who have influenced me in very significant ways, and have been with me through the ups and many downs of my coaching life. Thanks to my first principal, Bob Adam, and the many other school administrators who have supported me in many practical ways: David Frostad, Dwight Olney, Dr. Ivan Yakel, Howard Jesse, Bruce Pierce, Todd Edwards, Cindy Hock, and the many vice principals who gave me a teaching timetable that would coordinate with coaching football. Thanks to spiritual mentors Dr. John Barkman and

Larry Ballantyne. Thanks to friends and coworkers like Rodd Sawatzky, Barret Kropf, Rod Appleby, John Bechtold, Gib Hinz, Cal Carter, Jody Lehmann, Roger Morgan, Kevin Vollet, Darren Olsen, Glenn Szabo, Tom McGowan, Terry Pon, Karen MacDonald, Debbie Le Dressay, Aaron Anderson, Joan McCusker, Debbie Teece Nieblas, Brendan Stevens, Russ and Deidre Baird, Scott Peters, Greg Nesbitt, Glen Joorisity, Dave Bojic, Robin McDowell, Jeff Taylor, and Brent Adam, all of whom have been huge encouragers in my coaching life.

Thanks to the most significant mentor and encourager of my life: my dad, Danny. Thanks to my mom, Joy, who has become a lifetime sports fan of me and now my sons. Thanks to my parents-in-law Ramesh and Connie Jattansingh for supporting our family through the chapters of our family's football life. Thanks to the pride and joy of my life, my sons Marcus and Payton. Nothing in my life can compare to the years that they played together and played for me; I always think I couldn't be more proud of them, and then they go and achieve things to make me swell even more. Most importantly, thank you to my beautiful wife, Jody, who gladly and sacrificially became a lifetime coach's wife and football mom. I almost lost her when I put too much of myself into coaching and not nearly enough of myself into my relationship with her, but God is good and brought us through (thus my advice at the end of chapter 1, Responsibilities of a Coach).

By naming individuals, I have certainly left out dozens of other people. To the people I have coached with, coached against, or worked with in other ways in the football world, thank you for everything you have done for me, and more importantly, for the participants of our game in Canada.

Football has been a blessing in my life in so many ways. I hope this book is a small part of your football life that makes you a better person, and helps you more effectively lead and mentor young people to be a blessing in their life.

Go Canada!

Ryan Hall

Introduction: Football for Life

Tim Enger

In 1976, one of the top box office draws in movie theaters was *The Bad News Bears*, a satirical look at Little League baseball. A group of misfit 12-year-olds had to get a court order to allow them to play in their local league. The team turned out to be just as bad as the elitists running the league had predicted. That is, until a couple of ringers turned things around and led them to the championship game. In that game, Coach Morris Buttermaker, played by the legendary Walter Matthau, was suddenly faced with the dilemma of going for the win with his best players or playing everyone who had fought so hard to sign up in the first place.

In the end, Coach Buttermaker made what was portrayed as the right decision and played his bench, even though they wound up losing the game. The catch by the incredibly untalented Timmy Lupus and the efforts the other benchwarmers showed in trying to catch the evil Yankees in the last inning were heartwarming moments. Then consider the behavior of the Yankees coach, who struck his own son for not following instructions. It's pretty easy to see the filmmakers' intent.

The movie sent shivers through the minor sports scene in North America. What were we really doing for kids in sport? What was the intent, and who were we allowing to play? The on-screen efforts of Amanda Whurlitzer, Kelly Leak, and the other Bears, all strangely but effectively backdropped by an Italian operatic soundtrack, created a lot of nervous laughter in minor athletic boardrooms.

Since World War II, minor sports programs have exploded across the continent, with younger ages being added all the time. But most of these opportunities were being run with the sole goal of having the best athletes focused on winning as the only acceptable outcome. Kids as young as eight were being cut from programs or told that even though they wanted to play, they weren't good enough. For those who did make the cut, the high stakes in each competition relegated a lot of them to the bench or greatly limited their participation in competition. The final issue was that, with the notable exception of baseball (which is played on a smaller field with modified pitching rules), most sports expected kids to play the same game or competition the adults did, with similar size competition sites and rules.

On the other side of the ledger, what happens to athletes at the other end of the spectrum when they are in senior high school? The cuts come around when 15- to 18-year-olds try out for an elite high school, college, or community team, and they are left off the roster. What happens to them? Is there another outlet for them? What do you do with athletes who are deemed not ready for prime time but still love their particular sport and want to continue with it? What do you do with adults in their 20s and 30s who feel the same way?

Then there is the issue of how sports, especially at the younger levels, are being offered and whether they meet the needs of the participants and the needs of the sport at the same time. In the decades since the movie's premiere, *The Bad News Bears* is still seen as the starting point for discussions on how to offer youth sports. In many ways, the elitist league administrators had it half right in the movie. Timmy Lupus didn't belong on the same field as Joey Turner, the Yankees' talented pitcher. The half they got wrong was not endeavoring to find an outlet for Timmy and a different one for Joey. The idea is to help each boy find the level of play that works for him; that gives him enjoyment and challenges suitable to his abilities.

And what of Amanda Whurlitzer? The young female pitcher, portrayed by Tatum O'Neal, could sure bring the heat and struck out most of the boys she faced, but for how long would it be appropriate for her to play what was essentially baseball for boys? How do you handle the genders throughout the sporting experiences in all activities?

Obviously (or not so obviously, since it has taken a while), a holistic, big-picture view of sports in general was necessary, and that is where the concepts of Canadian Sport for Life (now named Sport for Life Society, or S4LS) and long-term athlete development (LTAD) have come into play in recent years. What was needed was some serious thought put into a person's wishes to be involved in one or more activities "from the cradle to the grave." The benefits of sport and general fitness to society are well known, especially in the areas of reducing health-related issues clogging up our hospitals. But it was very apparent that those activities needed to reach a larger audience for a longer period of time. With apologies to Vince Lombardi, winning *wasn't* the only thing when dealing with sport. There had to be a better way. Thus, the creation of LTAD planning for sports in Canada through S4LS.

S4LS was a movement created from observing what other countries, mainly European, were doing for their athletes at all levels of participation. Long-term athlete development was the most consistent finding. Out of this movement came a commitment for all sports in Canada to look at themselves with the stages of LTAD in mind, to take into account all the potential stages of sports experience throughout the lives of the participants.

The main concepts worked in an understanding of growth and maturation combined with what sport and recreation should be providing athletes as they move through their sporting lives. In reality, the vast majority of participants in sport will never get beyond a house league or high school level of play, and if elite sports are the main focus in Canada going forward, it's going to leave behind a lot of unhappy customers who left their activities way too soon. This isn't to say there shouldn't be an elite component to sport in Canada, but as part of a more balanced approach in which elite focus is just one part of keeping people engaged in sport for as long as they like.

LTAD points up certain realities that coaches and administrators need to know before designing programs for youth and adults. For instance, there's the "10-year rule" theory, which holds that becoming an expert at something takes at least

10,000 hours of practice over a 10-year period. And there's the need to focus on a player's physical literacy when starting out, with the basic components of movement (such as running, jumping, and throwing) all needing to be secured before any other skills can be imparted.

Specialization is another issue central to LTAD. Too many people think that a young athlete who shows ability at a particular sport should focus solely on that sport and build toward greatness. In reality, only some sports demand this kind of early focus for a shot at international or professional success. Those that do are body-control sports, such as gymnastics, figure skating, and diving. A childhood commitment isn't required in hockey, soccer, and football, to name some examples. But there's a creeping push by parents and coaches to act as if it were. In football, specialization is definitely not advisable, given the dangers of participating in a contact-type sport for more than a few months. Meanwhile, football players who take part in other sports can reap benefits. Skill-position players can run track to build their speed, and linemen can do weightlifting, wrestling, or basketball (for footwork).

Then there's developmental age. Since the beginning of youth sports, most young athletes have been slotted in with those who shared a similar age or grade. But maturation levels are never the same for everyone. Some kids may have the same birth date or be in the same class in school but be vastly different in size, shape, and the ability to learn skills, all because of their bodies' different maturation levels. Some potentially good athletes may be turned off early because they can't keep up with their larger, stronger, faster classmates. By the time they catch up to or surpass their contemporaries in athleticism, it might be too late to entice them back to sport.

LTAD asks sports to look at different ways to select competition levels, such as skills or developmental age. This is all well and good, but it opens the door to subjective evaluation (i.e., expert opinion) on who should go where, which can lead to hard feelings. In addition, you need a significant number of athletes in order to offer different groupings based on skill. In major centres in Canada, hockey and soccer are often, though not always, able to provide multiple skill level opportunities due to their large participation numbers. In smaller towns, you will get a limited number of participants and may have only one hockey, baseball, or soccer team. Joey Turner and Timmy Lupus will wind up on the same field. But if skill-based division of competition can be done, it's definitely a better option for the continuation of sport participation.

Other issues that need serious consideration from coaches and administrators according to LTAD include trainability (what athletes are able to learn), physical, cognitive, mental, and emotional development (what is appropriate for their age), and periodization and calendar planning (how to divide the year and how much practice and competition are appropriate). One of the most daunting aspects of LTAD is system alignment and integration, in which all levels within a sport work together and work with other sports and the core providers of funding. Obviously, this is easier said than done.

FOOTBALL'S LONG-TERM ATHLETE DEVELOPMENT

For football, LTAD has meant a comprehensive look at all levels of the game. Tackle football is not necessarily an early-entry game for youngsters, with the earliest entry into the game usually being at age eight or nine; other team sports, such as hockey or soccer, deal with kids as young as four or five. With the advent of flag or touch noncontact options, the age level can come down to include six-year-olds. But even at its simplest levels, the game of football requires a concentration level most kids don't display until at least grade one. Also, contrary to other sports, football still has the majority of its participants enter at the junior high or high school level (ages 14 to 18).

Therefore, while football does lay out planning for its LTAD model in stages based mainly on age, it also adds two more stages to better reflect realities for the critical ages of 14 to 18. The following information is taken from the Football Canada LTAD model.

Active Start (0 to 6 Years)

This stage represents entry into physical activity and sport, including the development of physical literacy. Athletes develop basic physical literacy and enjoy their first participation in organized games. Guiding principles for this stage include:

 ◆ Use safe, community-based programs (flag or touch).
 ◆ Ensure equal participation for all.
 ◆ Focus on the development of skills such as throwing, catching, attacking the flag, and running, not on competition.
 ◆ Provide broad-based, stage-appropriate development that includes football and other sports and activities.
 ◆ Never forget the need for social development and fun.
 ◆ Don't think it's necessary to separate the genders.

FUNdamentals (Girls, 6 to 8; Boys, 6 to 9)

This stage represents entry into physical activity and sport, including the development of physical literacy. The guiding principles are similar to the ones presented in active start. Touch and flag options are preferred at this stage, but a modified tackle version with reduced rosters (six-on-six) and rule modifications may be offered at the latter part of this stage. A smaller ball and smaller field are musts. If playing tackle football, participants should have the opportunity to play a variety of positions on both offense and defense to develop a variety of skills (blocking, tackling, ballhandling, etc.).

Learn to Train (Girls, 9 to 11; Boys, 10 to 12)

This stage represents development of a well-rounded set of football skills, complemented by participation in other sports. There is still an emphasis on using the touch and flag options for those just beginning their participation, but the tackle version can be offered with either a modified roster (6 a side, 9 a side) or the full 12 a side. There are still restrictions and modifications to the tackle game (i.e., only man-to-man coverage allowed) to make it easier for both players and coaches to adapt to the game at this level. The guiding principles of participation, however, encourage providing an opportunity for players to experience a variety of offensive and defensive positions. Training and competition should be appropriate to the development and maturation of the athletes.

Train to Train (Girls, 11 to 15; Boys, 12 to 16)

This stage resembles the last one in the way it's offered. But an introduction to training the physical body, keeping in mind the maturation levels of the participants, comes into play. It is now appropriate to consider off-field conditioning and opportunities to develop speed, aerobic power, and (in the stage's later years) the beginnings of strength building. Touch and flag programs may still be offered to newcomers and those who choose to stay in that stream. On the tackle side, modifications may still be suggested depending on circumstances (i.e., number of registrants), but the full game normally comes into play at this stage. Should numbers warrant, tiering or dividing players into teams based on skill and maturation should be considered to enhance the enjoyment of the game. A separation of genders should also be explored, if the number of registrants allows.

Learn to Compete (Girls, 15 to 17; Boys, 16 to 18)

At this level, a serious commitment to competition comes into play, coinciding with high school, midget, and CEGEP programs. Entry-level options of all versions of the game (flag, touch, and tackle) are still offered, but so are highly competitive options of each version. At this stage, all of the on- and off-field training elements (speed, strength, agility, flexibility, etc.) come into play. Player involvement in the tactical planning for upcoming games (i.e., film work) is introduced. Opportunities for provincial, national, and international competitions are often available for top-tier players and teams.

Train to Compete (Ages 17-Plus)

This stage focuses on athletes who are facing the biggest step in their journey though football. They may want to make a highly competitive football program at the postsecondary level (i.e., U Sports, CEGEP, or CJFL) or provincial or national representative teams. Annual training plans and position specialization come into play at this stage, all directed toward excellence. Programs supporting athletes to learn from victory and defeat, to live balanced lives, and to always compete in a fair, honest, and clean way are introduced. In particular, athletes should be educated on healthy nutrition (including supplements), the rules, ethics, and health risks of performance-enhancing drugs, use of prescription and over-the-counter drugs, and the health risks of alcohol and recreational drugs.

Learn to Win (Ages 18-Plus)

The objectives of this stage are not only to make and be retained on an elite post-secondary team, but to become a starter or a major contributor to the outcome of the game. All athletes are provided with optimal annual training, competition, and recovery programs. Tactical planning and a focus on physical excellence are primary objectives at this stage.

Train to Win (Ages 21-Plus)

The objectives at this stage focus on becoming a starter or a major contributor at the professional or national team levels. Every aspect of physical and mental development within the context of fair, drug-free living, training, and competition is considered. Specialization of position as well as sport is important at this level, and continuous work is put into maintaining the highest level of skill.

Football for Life (Any Age)

As early as the "train to train" stage, football participants may choose to opt out of the competitive stream but still wish to be involved in the game. Options such as recreational tackle, flag and touch programs, or giving back to the game via officiating or coaching can happen at any age. From a pick-up game in the park to volunteering as a minor official for a local association, there are plenty of chances to keep alive the principles of fun and respect for the game and its participants.

CONCLUSION

To follow the LTAD structure, football in Canada must look at the big picture and provide a meaningful, consistent developmental plan for all participants who choose to enter the sport. Although *The Bad News Bears* is a baseball example, any sport will have a lot more Timmy Lupuses than Joey Turners. All sports need to ensure that all children, wherever they fall in the spectrum of talent, may stay involved in the game for as long as they like. Those who seek excellence should have a way to do that as well. As Coach Mike Leak, portrayed by William Devane, said in his famous rant during *The Bad News Bears in Breaking Training*, "Let them play!"

Sport builds character and gives people of all ages, genders, and cultures a chance to experience fun and challenge not found in many other experiences. Winning is a laudable goal; goodness knows we want our bridge builders and heart surgeons to grow up knowing how to succeed every time. But winning can't be the only goal in sports, because then only a small group of individuals will ever participate. Excellence can be managed and encouraged in an atmosphere that takes in everyone, and the outcomes will be a healthier sports community for everyone.

Key to Diagrams

BC	Boundary cornerback
BE	Boundary end
BH	Boundary halfback
BS	Boundary safety
BT	Boundary tackle
FC	Field-side cornerback
FE	Field-side end
FH	Field-side halfback
FS	Field-side safety, free safety
FT	Field-side tackle
SS	Strong safety
W	Will (weak-side) linebacker
M	Mike/Mac (middle) linebacker
S	Sam (strong-side) linebacker
Z	Zeke linebacker
Q	Quick/Weak-side defensive end
R	Rush/Strong-side defensive end
DE	Defensive end
N	Nose tackle
T	Tackle
R	Rover
RET	Returner
HB	Halfback
CB	Cornerback
R,W,X,Y,Z	Wide receivers
TB	Tailback
QB	Quarterback
SB	Slotback
RB	Running back
FB	Fullback
TE	Tight end
O	Offensive player
⊠	Centre
◖ ◗	Shade/Alignment side
⟶	Run path
⟶⊣	Block path
- - -➤	Optional route
- - - -	Presnap key
∿∿➤	Presnap motion

PART ONE

FUNDAMENTALS OF COACHING

Responsibilities of a Coach

Ryan Hall

No leadership position in sport is more diverse and demanding than head coach of a football team. Regardless of the level of play—from youth football to the pros—the array of responsibilities characteristic of the head coaching position are vast due to the size of the team and coaching staff and the specialized units within the team (offense, defense, and special teams). For that reason, a head football coach must be highly organized, a strong communicator, and knowledgeable in all aspects of the game.

Several chapters in this book were written specifically for postsecondary coaches, but this chapter is written with the whole spectrum in mind. The topics in this book should be a great resource to help coaches get a handle on everything they need to do; hopefully, this chapter provides a strategy for turning an intimidating responsibility into a manageable and rewarding task.

ORGANIZATION

Organization of details is foundational to being a successful coach at any level. The second habit in *The 7 Habits of Highly Effective People* by Stephen Covey is "put first things first." Before you start worrying about playbooks, equipment, or practice fields, you should take some time to establish a firm foundation for your team. These are the first things that you should put first.

Develop a Coaching Philosophy

Before you can effectively lead a team, you need to take some time to articulate what you are all about as a coach. What are your values and goals as a coach, and what is your purpose for coaching this team? Make sure those things coordinate with the stated values and goals of your organization. If your goal is to win every game on the way to a championship so that you can move up to the CFL, but you are coaching for a minor football organization whose purpose is to develop the skills of all players in a fun environment, you are asking for conflict with league officials, players, parents, and possibly assistant coaches.

A valuable investment of time is to create a document such as a player's manual, a code of conduct, a set of team guidelines—whatever you want to call it. Put things in writing for all of your team stakeholders, such as league officials, administrators, coaches, players, and parents. Include things like your team purpose or mission statement, team goals and objectives, team expectations and standards of behavior, and perhaps some details about the consequences of not meeting the expectations.

Chapter 3, Establishing a Coaching Philosophy, provides ideas on how to put together a well-developed purpose for your coaching and your team.

Surround Yourself With Good People

A football team is much too big a responsibility for one person. The first group you should focus on is your coaching staff. As you recruit or select coaches, make sure they are on the same page with you philosophically so that everyone is pulling in the same direction. They definitely don't have to have the same personality as you (in fact, it is probably better if they don't), and you don't have to agree on everything. Some excellent advice comes from John Wooden, the top coach of the 20th century: "Surround yourself with smart people who will argue with you." Ideally, it would be great if all of your coaches are knowledgeable in at least one aspect of football (coaching a position group or coordinating offense, defense, or special teams), but it is more important to have a coaching staff of people who work hard to learn and improve, and people who are skilled, enthusiastic, and passionate teachers. Of course, their style of coaching and their knowledge of the game should be appropriate for the age and developmental stage of the athletes.

Another key person is a manager. To lighten the load of your responsibilities, you will want an organized and trustworthy person to take care of off-field responsibilities such as completing paperwork and registration forms, reserving practice and game fields, booking officials, arranging transportation, organizing road trip meals, ordering team clothing, arranging team photos, ordering team awards, coordinating a windup, and communicating with parents. If your team needs to do fundraising, your manager can take a huge load off your back by coordinating that task. Your manager can also be a buffer between you and the parents if problems arise.

A treasurer is also important to have. The manager could oversee the money or you could have a different individual responsible for taking care of money matters. You will need someone to handle team fees and bill payments. He may have to coordinate finances between the team and the league as well. A parent with an accounting background might be a natural choice. For accountability, it is a good idea to require a second person, such as an assistant coach, team manager, or a parent, to sign cheques and to be involved in all financial transactions.

Player safety is crucial, so equipment manager is another key role. The equipment manager's responsibilities include making sure all players have properly fitted equipment and that they're wearing the equipment properly. (Look for upside-down knee pads, underinflated helmets, chin straps outside of the cage, chewed-up mouth guards, etc.). The equipment manager's job does not end once the players have been given the equipment; the equipment manager should have a weekly routine of checking pads, mouth guards, and helmet inflation.

A trainer helps maintain player health. Ideally the trainer should have first-aid training, as well as some sports training experience so he can do basic tape jobs such as ankles and thumbs. Of course, it is very important that the trainer also knows how to recognize the symptoms of a concussion and is very familiar with the return-to-play protocol. Every team should have an emergency action plan (EAP), and the trainer is a key person for implementing the plan if a significant injury happens. An important element of an EAP is to have a form for each player showing important health information, such as previous injuries and allergies. Often leagues arrange for doctors, nurses, or first responders to be at games, but it is very important to have your trainer at all of your practices.

If you have the time and expertise to utilize video in your coaching, and your league does not record games for you, it is a great idea to have your own camera person. The camera operator can record not only games but also drills in practice, which is very helpful. This is a great job for a parent who maybe gets a little too vocal and critical; if the parent has to focus on looking through a camera screen and capturing useful footage, he won't have time to yell at refs, coaches, or players.

Another good job for an "overly enthusiastic" parent is statistics. Many coaches value having statistics from their games to help analyze the team's performance.

Because most of these people will be operating in positions of trust (either with young people or with money), it is a good idea for everyone to have a criminal record check. Most volunteer organizations can get a check done for free at their local police detachment.

Make a Calendar

For all levels of football, it is important that everyone understands the time commitments required. Your league or organization may have rules or guidelines for the number of practices, meetings, and games you can schedule. There may also be mandatory days off. Make sure to educate yourself on those details before you plan your season. It is also important to consult with your team staff to find out if there are any significant scheduling conflicts during the season.

As you plan your season, remember that there are other things going on in the lives of your team members. Young kids will have a hard time staying focused and energetic if you are going six days a week. If you are coaching high school students, you need to be mindful of school demands and possibly part-time jobs.

Depending on the level you are coaching, you may have to arrange preseason or exhibition play with other teams. It works best to find teams that are similar to yours in skill level and philosophy. Options for the preseason include joint practices (as you sometimes see in the NFL), controlled scrimmages (with or without special teams plays), or full exhibition games. If you have a midseason bye week, you may want to consider scheduling an exhibition game to keep your team focused in practice, and perhaps to give extra playing time to players on your team who aren't getting as many repetitions in regular season games.

Consistency in scheduling helps players and their families. If practices are generally on the same days and at the same time, you have far less chance of players missing them because someone misread the schedule. Consistency also helps families coordinate their commitments with the demands of the team. For example, a high school coach who never practices on weekends allows his players to schedule part-time jobs on those days, and allows families to schedule birthday parties and other gatherings on days when there is no football. The other benefit of taking weekends off is that it allows a high school coach to have all meetings and practices during the week, when the players are at school anyway.

Make Sure Your Team Is Well Equipped

Depending on the level at which you coach, your league may handle all equipment needs, or you may have to take care of it. There are three main categories of equipment: player equipment, field equipment, and game equipment.

Players will need helmets with chin straps, mouth guards, shoulder pads, practice pants, belts, leg pads (hip, knee, thigh, tailbone), girdles, practice jerseys, and cleats. In almost every organization, shoulder pads and helmets are supplied, so either your league will carry an inventory (especially in minor football) or your team will have to carry an inventory (high school and above). With helmets, it's good to have a variety of sizes and styles, but try not to have too many different brands—each brand has unique parts that need to be replaced. Players can be expected to purchase a number of items on their own, such as mouth guards, girdles, leg pads, and practice pants. With mouth guards, it is a good idea to recommend dentist-fitted versions. The $2 dip-in-boiling-water mouth guard rarely fits well, is often chewed up, and is seldom in the player's mouth properly. Most dental plans will cover the cost of custom mouth guards which fit much better and therefore protect better and are more comfortable, allowing players to talk or drink while they are in.

Of course, your team also needs uniforms to play. If these aren't provided by your organization, you will be responsible for ordering, laundering, maintaining, and inventorying them. Uniform care is a great job to delegate to your equipment manager or maybe even to some parents who are looking for ways to help. Practice jerseys are also great to have, as they make your team feel and look like more of a team. Ideally, get contrasting colours for the offensive and defensive players, or you could have pullover mesh pinnies for your defensive players to wear. (If offensive players wear them, they will probably get ripped up more easily.) You may also want your manager to order matching socks for game days if the budget allows.

Field equipment includes footballs, cones, hitting bags, step-over bags, hand shields, stand-up dummies, kicking tees, and blocking or tackling sleds. There are many options for these types of equipment, as well as some newer types of equipment, such as Shadowman tackling dummies or rugby tackling rings. Other helpful accessories are helmet pinnies, speed ladders, and kicking nets. You should also decide how you will manage water for players; will everyone bring an individual bottle, will the team purchase bottles, or will the team provide a hydration station? Remember that illnesses spread very quickly on a football team if water bottles are shared in an unhygienic way or if bottles are not regularly sanitized.

The game field will also need to be properly equipped if your league does not have a central playing field. You will need goalpost pads, a scoreboard and time clock, and first-down chains. It is also helpful to have yard markers, especially if you play on a grass field and are trying to keep stats. Of course, your field also needs lines. In many schools or in rural areas, the responsibility for painting the field ends up on the coach's shoulders. And you thought head coaching was all about the glory of being the fearless leader!

Build Your Playbook

If possible, it is best to have three coordinators on your team: offense, defense, and special teams. Especially at younger levels of football, the head coach is often the most knowledgeable and experienced coach, and will take at least one coordinator position. A head coach who takes the role of offensive or defensive coordinator runs the risk of focusing on only half the team and neglecting the other half. He may also tend to view the performance of the team, in practice or competition, on the performance of the area he is coordinating. This can cause players to feel neglected or underappreciated if they are not part of the group that the head coach coordinates. If the head coach is going to coordinate, special teams might be the perfect role. It allows the head coach to be involved with players from all positions on the team and emphasizes the importance of the kicking game.

A crucial habit of successful head football coaches is delegation. For one thing, it cuts your responsibilities so you can do your job very well rather than doing everyone else's job in a mediocre manner. Empowering good people is energizing to them, and if you have keen, hardworking assistants, they will put a lot of effort into validating your trust by doing a great job in their role. Of course, this means that things will not always be done the way you would do them. Make sure to be involved with the coordinators and give them input so that everyone is working in the same direction. It is a delicate balance between abdicating too much authority to assistants and being a control freak. You will definitely screw up at some point, but working through it with your assistants should improve your working relationships and strengthen your team.

As your coaches develop their playbooks and establish the important skills required, try to get everyone on the same page with their terminology. Great coaches use language very efficiently. For example, if all of your coaches have taken Football Canada's Safe Contact training (or read chapter 4), you have a great base of terminology that can be applied to a wide variety of football skills related to blocking and tackling. You may have players switching positions on your team, so it is much easier on them if coaches on both sides of the ball use the same words for the same things.

Plan Your Practices

Like many things in life, planning a football practice is about balance. A valuable aspect of football is routine; coaches can operate with increased efficiency if they take advantage of routine schedules and procedures in practice. The downside of routine is that it can become . . . routine; players might start getting bored. Strive for the balance of using routine to increase efficiency, but change things up enough to add energy to practice through variety.

The overall purpose of practice plans is to focus on the current priority of the team. In training camp, practice plans should focus on skill development and system introduction, as well as beginning to get players conditioned for the season. In the regular season, practice plans should focus on the skills and system emphasis that are needed to help players develop and be as effective as possible on game day. Bye weeks are great times to evaluate where the team is at in their skill development and to take the time to drill areas of needed improvement. In the playoffs, practice plans should focus on consolidating the crucial skills and systems needed to go as far as possible.

It is the head coach's responsibility to establish the practice plans, but it will work best if this is done in consultation with the coordinators. They will have some specific ideas of what their side of the ball needs in terms of drills and time allocations. Chapter 18 details planning a practice, so read through that for some ideas of how to organize your practices (though that chapter is written from a postsecondary perspective). Keep in mind that there are different priorities and limitations depending on the age and developmental stage of your athletes. Ten-year-olds will not be able to focus and perform effectively for a two-hour practice. Elite or all-star teams likely won't need to spend as much time on skill development as a youth or high school team will.

Practice planning should not be done day to day. It is better to plan the practices for the whole week at the same time. This allows all of your coaches to know how much time they have for their skill and system periods, and to plan an appropriate progression of teaching and drilling throughout the week. Of course, practice plans are not carved in stone. If you get partway through your week and realize you need more time on one priority and less time on another, you can make adjustments. If these changes affect only one side of the ball (for example, if the defensive coaches want to spend a little less time on individual skills so they can spend a bit more time on pursuit skills), that can be decided by the coaches involved. If the changes involve the whole team, the head coach must make the final decision.

Staying on schedule is also the head coach's responsibility. Be aware of the time left in each period of practice. If possible, give the assistant coaches a two-minute warning when each period is almost done. This will allow them to come to a suitable conclusion for that period, send the players for a drink, and have them ready for the next period without delay. Practice periods should never go overtime unless the head coach makes the decision. (Offensive coaches are notorious for "one more" so they can finish with a positive play!)

Control the Contact

A crucial aspect of Football Canada's Safe Contact training is controlling the levels of contact in practice. This does not necessarily mean having no contact in practice; it simply means thinking about the purpose of the drill or practice period, and matching it with a suitable level of contact. If the players are working on tackling skills in a circuit or positional drill, contact will be important, but you can set up the drill to reduce the chance of injury. Modify the drill to limit the speed of the players or the distance between players. Have players carry a hand shield so the contact is not body-on-body. Do not have players going to the ground unless it is necessary. Take advantage of sleds and tackling dummies to do full-speed tackling without risking an injury to a ball carrier. The Safe Contact program has many other ideas for modifying drills to reduce the risk of injury from contact.

If you are doing one-on-ones between receivers and defensive backs, do you need contact? The purpose of the drill is for the receivers to run good routes and catch the ball, and for the defensive backs to use good technique to cover the receivers. Tackling in a drill like that serves no purpose and increases the chance of unnecessary injury.

If you are practicing run plays with the offensive line and running backs going against the defensive line and linebackers, do you need to go live? The purpose of the drill is for the offensive players to properly execute their plays (blocking and timing) and for the defensive players to go to their proper run fit or gap responsibility. Again, going live in a drill like that increases the risk of unnecessary injury. If you think the players need to work on tackling or fighting through tackles, do a one-on-one drill in which the coaches can control the drill and give individual feedback.

If you are practicing short-yardage or goal-line plays, do you need to go full out? The purpose of the drill is for the offense to earn the most important yard on the field, and for the defense to defend the most important yard on the field. It is an all-out effort. In this case, it may be appropriate to go live. Of course, you probably shouldn't run 15 short-yardage plays in a practice.

Plan Your Game Day

Even though game day is the focal point of your week, it isn't uncommon for coaches to neglect planning their game day routine. As much as possible, control what you can control. If you only get a 15-minute warm-up because there is a game on before you, find another space close by where you can do your dynamic warm-up and positional drills so that, by the time you get onto the playing field, you can focus on running through systems and plays.

If you coach a high school team in an urban centre, you may be able to begin your warm-up on your home field prior to getting on the bus to the game field. Again, this allows you to conduct your warm-up in a way that isn't rushed. Players won't cool down that much after a 15-minute bus ride, and should be able to easily conclude the last part of the team warm-up at the game field.

Don't forget to take into account your specialists. Make sure your punters and kickers get to warm up their legs, and that the returners get to field some kicks. Get some repetitions for your long and short snappers as well.

COMMUNICATION

It's true of any organization, from a football team to a family to a company: the effectiveness of your communication will dictate the effectiveness of your group. There are very few examples of too much communication leading to problems, but thousands of dysfunctional teams, broken families, and failed businesses have fallen victim to insufficient or ineffective communication. These modes of communication should help your team operate much more productively and positively.

Administration and Organization Support

No matter what level of football you are coaching, you will find that having the support of those above you, such as school administrators, athletic directors, and league directors or board members, will always be a benefit. Make sure to get to know them personally, share your philosophy, team goals, and expectations, and ask them questions to help you work effectively under their leadership. If you keep those people updated with highs and lows of your season, they will very likely be allies to you when you need them.

Player Recruitment and Retention

At every level of football, coaches need to have a strategy to find and keep athletes. If you coach minor football, you usually get the kids who are registered by their parents, but maybe some of those kids have friends who should play football. Encourage players to do some recruiting for you, or contact the parents and see if they are interested in letting their child play. If you coach high school, you may need to scan the hallways and gym to find players. Talk to the physical education teachers and get leads on athletic or big kids who could be good players. Collaborate with coaches from other school sports (especially basketball, wrestling, soccer, and track) or community sports (like hockey or baseball) to encourage multisport participation. Of course, that goes both ways. There is tremendous benefit to having your football players participate in other sports in order to develop overall athleticism and to contribute to the school programs.

Retaining your players is also a challenge. Formal and informal communication through the season and beyond will show that you are invested in each individual and are developing a relationship with them. Those connections and relationships are often the keys to keeping athletes engaged with the sport and your team.

Coaches Meeting

As you gather your staff prior to the season, it is important to start with the basics of your coaching philosophy and the goals and purposes for the team. Getting everyone on the same page (even if you have been coaching together for years) is always worth the time. This is a very important opportunity to establish how the staff will work together. Specify and delegate roles and responsibilities for practices and games. Establish an effective chain of command by reminding position coaches that they aren't coordinators. Set norms for how coaches will communicate with each other on the practice field or the game sideline. Disagreements in opinion or approach will happen, so how do you want them to be verbalized? A little rule that I like for my coaching staff is "Praise the other coaches in front of the team, but deal with problems and mistakes in private."

Once you have dealt with these big-picture issues, you can deal with details. Be clear on things like how you want the coaches to dress, what kind of language you want them to use (or not use), and even how you want them to use whistles in practice. Let them know if you expect them to have a written practice plan each day. Talk about trying to maximize player activity and minimize coach talking in practice. Delegate responsibilities such as setting up field equipment, leading the warm-up or cooldown, or taking charge in certain periods of practice.

Continue by going through the season schedule and upcoming practice plans. It is important for the head coach to come up with a starting point in the form of a tentative season schedule and practice plans, but a head coach who surrounds himself with good people will be open to feedback and making adjustments.

A high-functioning coaching staff will meet throughout the season to evaluate their processes and plans and look for ways to improve. These can be formal meetings or they can be done in a more casual setting over a meal or at someone's deck. You can also watch film together. This can be a great learning experience for young coaches and can help everyone on the staff to be on the same page in the analysis of your team or the opposition. At the end of the season, conduct another formal coaches meeting to evaluate the season and begin planning for the future.

Parents Meeting

Holding a preseason parents meeting gives you a chance to introduce yourself and your staff to the parents, as well as outline your coaching philosophy and the mission, goals, expectations, and standards of the team. Make sure to give parents a copy of your team's manual or code of conduct for players so that they have things in writing. It is a good idea to include the players in this meeting, so that everyone is receiving the same message at the same time.

At this meeting, give parents a copy of the season schedule and emphasize your expectations regarding player attendance at practices and games, and how you want communication to take place relating to parents, players, and coaches. This is also a perfect time to distribute the player health forms and, if possible, to collect them right away.

Players Meeting

While it is beneficial to have players attend the parents meeting, you will want to have a meeting with the players as well. At this time, you can go over the parts of the player's manual or code of conduct that are more specific to them and their participation on the team. Remember that youth and high school athletes are not at an adult level of psychological development, so they tend to take things quite literally. Be clear in your verbal communication and make sure it matches up with what you have in writing. Often younger athletes will not pick up on things such as sarcasm or allusion.

Other Sports

One of the big frustrations for football coaches is players who are involved in other sports that conflict with a full commitment to the team. Football is a practice sport. For individual player safety and overall team performance, it is vital that players attend all practices. In your parents meeting, emphasize the importance of practice participation in football, and caution parents against overcommitting their children by having them involved in more than one sport in a season. (Let's be honest—more often than not, it is the parents who are pushing this, not the kids.) Taking part in more than one sport is great, but the two sports shouldn't fall during the same months.

Of course, the biggest problem relates to hockey, as that sport's season significantly invades the fall season of football, even at youth levels that wrap up in early October. Many parents seem to look at the financial investment they make in each sport and deem hockey to be more important because it is far more expensive. Make sure you have thought about how you will deal with this reality, and communicate that clearly to the parents and the players. I try to remind parents and players that football starts first and ends first, so it should be the first priority.

Sideline

Just as the pregame routine is an often-neglected detail in planning, so are sideline responsibilities for coaches during the game. Make sure that every coach has established roles or else you will have a bunch of coaches doing nothing to help the team, or all of them sharing their opinion about what should or shouldn't be done by the head coach and coordinators.

Who will make the decision about whether to accept or decline penalties? Who is allowed to call a time-out? Who is allowed to talk to the officials? (Hopefully, no one except the head coach!) Who will decide when to gamble on third down, or when to make an aggressive play call on special teams? Who will manage substitution of players, especially due to injury? Who will be the get-back coach (making sure the players stay back from the sideline)? Who will be in the spotter's booth and on the headsets?

Ongoing Coach–Player Communication

A good coach will make sure that players always have a clear idea of their standing on the team. In fact, this should be the responsibility of all the coaches, not just the head coach. Make sure your assistant coaches know what you expect from them in the way of conversations with their players about the players' current status on the team.

Depending on the age and maturity of the athletes, it can be a good conversation starter to ask them how they think they are doing, and for them to give specific examples to support their self-evaluation. Make sure to be clear about what athletes are doing well, and what they should improve. Ensure that they know why they have their current roles on the team, and what they need to do to keep them or to earn more significant roles.

The football season is not very long. If you don't make time for this type of reality check communication, you can easily go through the season missing huge opportunities for the athletes to grow and improve.

KNOWLEDGE

A great coach has an in-depth knowledge of the nuances and details of the game. Like most of us, you probably aren't at that point yet, and that is why you are reading this book! Theodore Roosevelt is quoted as saying, "People don't care how much you know until they know how much you care." This is a great starting point for you as a coach. The requisite element of coaching is love of the game, genuine interest and care for the players as people, and the effort to invest significant time planning and coaching the football season. If you do those things and have a basic understanding of the techniques and systems of football, you can be an effective coach. Of course, most of us want to go beyond the basics, so here are a few ideas to increase your football IQ.

Understand the Rules

It is very important for the head coach to be well acquainted with the rules and expectations of the league. At every level of football from minor to university, specific rules and standards must be followed. It is the head coach's responsibility to know these rules and to communicate them to the assistant coaches and support staff.

It is also incumbent on the head coach to be familiar with the rules of the game. In Canada, most levels of football follow *The Canadian Amateur Rule Book for*

Tackle Football, which is typically updated every two years. Don't be that person who shows his ignorance by basing his football acumen on Sunday afternoon NFL games or football street knowledge. Any credible league should supply you with a copy of the rulebook at their expense, or you could look it up online. Some provincial football governing bodies publish the current Canadian rulebook on their websites. Some leagues and organizations also offer meetings with football officials to get updates on rule changes and interpretations, and for coaches to ask rule-related questions; make sure to take advantage of those opportunities.

Coaching Development

Some more great words of wisdom from John Wooden: "It's what you learn after you know it all that counts." As coaches, we expect our players to constantly learn and improve, so we will be much more effective if we model that in our own approach to the game. Even if you have been coaching for years, there is always something you can pick up at a coaches clinic or by collaborating with a peer or mentor coach. Many local and provincial football organizations host annual coaching clinics. The National Coaching Certification Program has revamped its football certification program in recent years to better suit it to the different goals of individual coaches. There is also the option of attending the wide variety of excellent coaching clinics south of the border. While the X's and O's may not transfer directly, U.S. clinics often have a strong emphasis on coaching philosophy and leadership that is not specific to four-down football. You can even learn good coaching principles from coaches in other sports.

Another way to develop as a coach is to gain practical experience working with a mentor coach on-field. Take advantage of opportunities to guest coach at your local high school, Canadian Junior Football League, CEGEP, or U Sports program, or to work with coaches from those programs at youth football camps.

Off-Season Training

Depending on the level at which you coach, you may have access to your players well beyond the football season. These days it is becoming very common for players at the high school level to begin off-season training focusing on strength, power, speed, quickness, and agility. Many high schools have satisfactory facilities for physical training, so that is a great opportunity to improve the level of performance of your players, and to build team morale throughout the off-season.

Make sure you find or develop a program that is suitable to the physical and mental maturity level of your athletes. So many coaches lose buy-in and participation by presenting their players with complicated programs that take hours to complete. High school–aged athletes should be able to complete a well-rounded and intense workout in around an hour if they go hard. Of course, if they spend time talking and visiting it will take longer, but just consider that an investment in team building.

Don't feel that you have to be all things to your team. If you don't have the expertise to put together a program, consult with a local fitness expert (from the school or a local gym) who can put something together, and learn from the results. This could also be a good responsibility for a knowledgeable assistant coach or trainer.

If you want the players to get the maximum benefit from an off-season program, you need to be with them, supervising and coaching, joining them in the workout, or both. If you just tell them to go do it, they probably won't work nearly as hard nor will they follow the program correctly. Again, it doesn't always have to be you; this is a great way to involve assistant coaches.

CONCLUSION

Now that you have read this chapter, are you sure you still want to be a head coach?

While the responsibilities are numerous and sometimes exhausting, I hope you will find that the rewards of working with young people make the effort fully worthwhile. Football is all about relationships, and most of my best friends are the men that I coach with, and nearly all of the close relationships I have with students exist because I am not only their teacher but, more importantly, their football coach.

With the importance of relationships in mind, please take this final piece of advice to heart. I have attempted to give you a detailed overview of the immense number of responsibilities you have as a head football coach. These responsibilities will take a massive amount of time and effort to do with excellence. Please keep your role as a coach in proper perspective. While being a head coach is a significant and honorable responsibility, it is not nearly as significant and honorable as being a loving spouse and parent (if those roles are part of your life). To be a football coach, you will need the support of your spouse and children; make every effort to give them the time, energy, and attention they deserve as the most important "team" in your life.

2

Leading a Team

Joe D'Amore

By definition, a leader is a person who rules, guides, or inspires others. But merely being in charge of a team doesn't make you a leader. What matters is how you carry out this charge.

In football, the head coach is always seen as a leader. When I took over at the University of Windsor in 2011, I had no experience as a coordinator or a head coach at the Canadian Interuniversity Sport (now U Sports) level. Many felt that I was not qualified for my new post. But leadership isn't about how long you have been there; it's about getting your players to do the things necessary to be successful and to be better than they thought they could be. Leading is about setting a good example, outlining goals and objectives, holding firm to your beliefs, and being flexible enough to evaluate and positively change areas of your team, as needed.

Whether coaching at the high school level, in the CJFL, or in U Sports, there are eight key areas that will help coaches lead and build an environment for team success. Focusing on these areas will lead to success at any level.

ESTABLISH SMART GOALS

Whether you are leading a team for the first time or have been doing it for years, first you need to establish SMART goals for your team. The acronym SMART can be used to provide a more complete definition of goal setting.

S: specific

M: measurable

A: attainable

R: realistic

T: timely

Specific goals in relation to football are defined very clearly to players and coaches. These goals can be short-term, long-term, or lifetime goals. Specific goals should be well defined and easily understandable. Goals such as "rush for 100 yards a game" or "win 4 games this season" are specific and clear.

To measure goals, establish specific criteria that reflect your progress in reaching your goals. If your goal is to rush for 100 yards a game, you might say that you need to run the ball 25 times in order to attain this goal. This is a great way to help you achieve your goal.

One of the most important aspects of developing goals is that the goals you set for your team must be attainable. It doesn't make any sense for you to set a goal of going undefeated for a season if you were zero for eight the previous year. You are more likely to achieve these goals and to get buy-in from your players if they are seen as realistic and attainable.

For goals to be realistic, players must be *willing* and *able* to reach them. A goal can be both high and realistic; you and your players are the only ones who can decide just how high your goal should be.

Finally, in order for your goals to be achieved, they must be attained in a timely manner. Let's say your goal is to win a national championship in 10 years. Players, knowing they will never see the results, may not work toward that goal. The goals you set with your players must be reached during their time with you.

Once you have clearly defined your SMART goals, make sure you review them every week or two throughout the year. That way you can make sure you are staying on the right track and everyone on the team is working toward these goals. Have the goals posted somewhere visible for your players to see, such as a locker room or bathroom mirror or on the bus, as a continual reminder of what you as a group have set out to accomplish.

BE PREPARED AND ORGANIZED

A coach may have many of the tools necessary to be a great leader; a coach may be educated and knowledgeable in X's and O's. But leave out preparation and organization, and the coach will never be as effective as necessary. True leaders rigorously plan their course of action. This requires careful attention to detail and effective planning. Otherwise, there is a greater likelihood of forgetting or overlooking a play or a game situation that could be the difference between winning and losing. It is important for players to see how organized and prepared you are. Yearly schedules, practice plans, and play scripts are all valuable ways to stay organized and prepared. One thing I have learned as a coach is that, if you come to practice or a meeting unprepared, the players will notice and lose confidence in you. If they see that you are invested in the process of success, they will buy in.

BE WILLING TO MAKE THE TOUGH DECISION

It is inevitable that at some point a coach will have to make tough decisions, whether sitting a player, cutting someone from the team, or replacing a current staff member. Coaches are forced to make decisions that are not only difficult but sometimes unpopular. No matter what the decisions are, make decisions that are best for the team as a whole by referring to your coaching philosophy, team code of conduct, and team goals. Then stand behind those decisions even if they are not popular with those they might affect. When I am forced to make a decision that may get some negative response, I always use the following three steps before the decision is made.

Set Aside Your Emotions

The worst thing a coach can do is make a tough decision in the heat of the moment. Often coaches make rash decisions based on a specific moment without looking at the future consequences of their decision. For example, a player might have an uncharacteristic and unacceptable serious outburst, and your reaction might be to cut him immediately. Maybe there was more to his actions than you might see on the surface (like he is going through something unrelated to football that is affecting him emotionally). Take time when deciding and consider the ramifications of the outcome. Wait until emotions have subsided before you look at the situation.

Look at the Big Picture

When making a tough decision, always look at everyone involved. Quite often, discipline decisions affect not only the people involved, but the team and program as a whole. Sit down and look at the pros and cons of your decision, who it will affect directly, and who will be affected indirectly. For example, benching the starting quarterback for a minor discipline infraction will affect the whole team, and maybe there is an alternative. But a quarterback who is disregarding team expectations or undermining the culture should be disciplined, or even removed from the team, for the sake of the program's long-term health. If you can still find merit behind the decision after looking at the big picture, then your choice will be much easier to make and much easier to explain.

Seek Out Opinions of Others

Even though you may be responsible for making a final decision in a tough situation, it is very important to seek advice from others, whether assistant coaches, mentors, or even current players. Never make a tough decision on your own. Often you can gain insight that you may not have been aware of that could change the way you look at the situation. Just because you are responsible for making a difficult decision doesn't mean you have to make it alone.

SURROUND YOURSELF WITH THE RIGHT PEOPLE

Of course, every coach wants to stack the team with blue-chip players. But that isn't a realistic situation. Finding the right blend of talent and character will go a long way in determining the success of your program. Players who want to succeed, and who have the work ethic to achieve success, will usually get there if they are supported with the right leadership and environment. I have always lived by the philosophy "Never sacrifice character for talent." If you fill your locker room with character players, you will be able to get through the difficult times over the year and you will avoid many difficult times that come from within the team. It is easy to be a leader when things are going well, but when adversity arrives you may see the true colours of individuals within the group. By surrounding yourself with good character, you are more likely to get through the tough times more quickly and more easily.

Don't forget the staff. When it comes to team success, they'll be just as important as the players. A big mistake many coaches make is to surround themselves with yes-men for fear of dealing with someone who has just as much or more football knowledge than themselves. Football is a unique sport where you rely so much on others for the success of your team. I have never heard of a head coach getting let go because a smart and talented assistant coach helped him win. I take a lot of pride in seeing my assistant coaches move on to other jobs within the game, because it showed they were a vital part of our success. That means hiring qualified assistant coaches who believe in you and your system and philosophy, but who bring their own unique style and ideas to the team.

BE DEMANDING

Simply put, you must demand excellence from your players and coaches by having high expectations in all areas of being a member of the team. Anything less cannot be accepted. The minute a coach allows players to slack off and do their own thing, the coach's leadership is tested. Everyone involved with the team must be held accountable for everything they do. Beyond setting an example, leadership is about staying consistent with your message. In *How Good Do You Want To Be?*, Nick Saban spoke about a phrase that he constantly used with his staff: "If you're not teaching it that way, you must be allowing it to happen that way." If the coach does not demand a certain expectation, then how can it be reached?

Leaders and coaches cannot accept anything but the best. A leader must insist that each area of the team and organization performs to its potential and exhibits the qualities that best represent the team. This does not mean just excellence from the players, but from the assistant coaches, the medical staff, the video coordinators, and equipment staff—from anyone involved in the success of the team. A leader cannot accept mediocrity.

And for all of this to happen you must first insist on excellence in yourself. This does not mean you need to work long hours or take on every issue. The head coach must demonstrate to the team that he is invested in the success of the program and that his pursuit of success is in line with the team's goals and objectives. Show this with what you do, not just with what you say.

BELIEVE IN YOUR SYSTEM

One of the biggest mistakes coaches make is they abruptly change what they are doing because of a loss. Often it is not the plan that failed, just the implementation. How often do you hear coaches on television say, "We just didn't execute" or "We had a good game plan; we just missed some opportunities"? In football, if you run an aggressive style of offense and like to throw the ball downfield, and you lose a few games, do you then change to a more conservative style? History has shown that if you believe in what you are doing, and stick to it, your approach will eventually pay dividends. Immediately after failure is not always the best time to make adjustments. Be patient and be prudent. Always evaluate, but drastic changes are rarely called for. Look at what went wrong, look at why it happened, and then put a plan into place to rectify the situation and minimize the possibility of it occurring again.

DEFINE ROLES CLEARLY

One of the important aspects of leading a team is making sure that all players and coaches clearly understand their roles and responsibilities. A key aspect of role acceptance is clearly defining roles for each player and coach. Role definition means that each player knows what is expected of him to help the team be successful. One way to make sure players understand their roles on the team is to conduct weekly individual meetings—weekly because roles can change that often due to injury or performance. Have your positional coach sit with each member of the position group and clearly define roles for that week. It is usually best to begin by asking the players how they feel about their present role. Find out how satisfied each player is with his role, as well as determining any future roles he might like to play. Either the player sees things the way you do, or you need to bring in your perspective as a coach to help clarify matters for him. If a player would like to play a greater role, discuss what you think it will take for him to have that chance. The key is to have honest and open communication between the coach and each player. When I took over the University of Windsor, the first thing I told my players was that I would never lie to them about their role on this team. They may not always agree with you or like what you have to say, but they will respect you.

Role clarification is also important for assistant coaches. Everyone should know what areas of planning, preparation, coaching, and input are their responsibilities and which areas are not. A clear chain of command from the head coach to the coordinators to the position coaches is very useful in avoiding unnecessary conflict. It is also helpful to delegate responsibilities so that all coaches feel that they are making significant contributions to the team in their areas of expertise. A common tendency is for head coaches to be control freaks; you can lose good people because they end up feeling undervalued and underutilized.

BE A COACH

What may be the most important tool in leading your team is to remember that you are a coach. Webster's Dictionary defines *coach* as "a person who teaches and trains the members of a sports team and makes decisions about how the team plays during games." True, but being a coach and a leader is also much more.

Teach

Everyone has heard the line "Don't tell them how to do it, but show them." When a coach treats the player as a student, players and the team show tremendous improvement. Coaching is about teaching players the skills necessary for a system to be effective. It is easy to stand back and yell at players, telling them they did things wrong. But a player will never really understand what you are asking of him unless you teach him what to do, how to do it, the reason you are asking him to do it, and why it is important to do it this way. Treat players like students by teaching them, helping them improve, and making sure they are always working toward seeing the results of that improvement.

Stay Positive

Being positive might be one of the most challenging aspects of being a coach. When players are not doing what you have asked, it can be very easy to yell and scream and be negative in your approach. Providing positive feedback to your players (when it is earned) makes them more receptive to negative or corrective feedback. When you are constantly giving negative feedback, players become defensive or tune you out and your voice becomes noise. No, you don't need to avoid negative or corrective feedback altogether. But practice, not a game, is the time and place for that feedback. Use game day to build confidence, not anxiety. You need to get the most out of players, and breaking them down will not get you there.

Lead by Example

One of the worst things a head coach can do is to practice the "Do as I say, not as I do" philosophy. Players need to know they can trust you. When you don't lead by example, you are creating a double standard, which will eventually lead to conflict. The head coach is responsible to his players and fellow coaches. A big part of that responsibility is to lead by your own actions. Telling players not to be late, and then showing up late yourself, shows players that you don't believe in what you are preaching. That will quickly lead to defiance. Good leaders push people forward with excitement, inspiration, trust, and vision. If you lead a team that doesn't trust you, success will be hard to come by. Learn to lead by example and you will find your players will begin to move toward the same goals, with you leading the way!

Care

Caring is really what coaching football is all about, and one of the reasons why I love it so much. The young men under our guidance are just beginning their lives. They are often full of questions, face challenges daily, and have big dreams. Our goal as coaches is not just about winning football games, but helping these young men answer those questions, face those challenges, and achieve their dreams. One of the best ways to motivate players is to show that you care about them outside of the football field. This will show them that you really care about them and will help you build a better relationship. Once they believe you truly care, they will go to war for you!

Every player is different, motivated in unique ways, learning at different speeds, and engaging in social settings in their own unique ways. Get to know your players as individuals. Spend time talking to them one-on-one. It doesn't have to be for hours; a couple of minutes will reap dividends. The point is to let them know that their lives are important to you, and that you want them to succeed as people as much as you want them to succeed as players.

CONCLUSION

Whether you have been coaching football for a year or 30 years, leading your team is about getting your players to do the things necessary to be successful and to become better than they thought they could be. No matter what your philosophy is, remember that you do not have all the answers. Be willing to grow as a coach and a leader, and find what works for you. Believe in your system, demand excellence from everyone involved, be open and honest with your players, and above all care about them as individuals. This will help you lead and build an environment for team success.

3

Establishing a Coaching Philosophy

Ryan Hall

As a younger coach, I had the opportunity to go to the American Football Coaches Association Coaches Conference. I went to Orlando expecting to attend many sessions where I could improve my skills at coaching specific football techniques or get some innovative systems that I could adapt from American to Canadian football. I got almost none of that. Instead, I found the conference sessions to be focused on coaching philosophy, not the pragmatic details of systems and skills.

The keynote speaker was the late Zig Ziglar, a famous motivational speaker and best-selling author whose messages focused on goal setting, healthy lifestyles, a positive attitude, and living with a purpose. His delivery was captivating, but more importantly I felt the impact of his message, one of living with a purpose within the context of a life coaching football. It seemed that he set the tone for the conference, as the big-name, successful coaches I heard (including the late Bo Schembechler, national champion Steve Spurrier, and longtime NCAA coaches Hayden Fry and Bill Snyder) built their presentations around the importance of an introspective approach to developing a personal coaching philosophy. This was one of the transformational experiences of my coaching career; it shifted my focus from winning to a grander purpose that I could achieve regardless of the scoreboard from week to week and my team's record from season to season.

We all have a coaching style and a coaching philosophy, even if we don't realize it. When we don't clarify and articulate our philosophy, we make short-sighted decisions based on pragmatic decisions that we often regret. All teams have a culture, and if the head coach isn't purposeful in establishing a desired culture, he abdicates control of the team. If it is true that we all have a coaching philosophy (whether we realize it or not) and we all set a team culture (whether we realize it or not), wouldn't it be wise to consciously establish a sound philosophy, and in turn establish a positive and purposeful team culture? Some of the important steps in developing, articulating, and applying an effective coaching philosophy are to develop a mission statement, state your values, and apply them to team goals and expectations. This chapter is a guide to strategically controlling your leadership role as a coach.

IT STARTS WITH YOU

One of the consistent messages of wise and experienced coaches is that you have to be yourself when you coach, and that includes developing your coaching philosophy. That doesn't mean that you can't be influenced and mentored by other coaches or learn from reading books, but filter the ideas through your own personality and life experience. Throughout this chapter, I reference several great coaches from whom I have borrowed philosophies, ideas, and practices, but I have always tailored these things to fit my personality and coaching context.

Most modern psychologists would tell us that we are all products of our environments, and in particular they would emphasize the significance of our formative years. When you think about who you are now, look back on your life to consider how you became the way you are. Certainly, parenting and family dynamics are central to any individual's growth and development. Other factors include your community, schools, faith, and friends. Take note of the crucial experiences in your life as a child and adolescent, and how you were formed through successes and failures, good decisions and bad mistakes.

As you think back over your football life, many influential coaches will come to mind. Hopefully, many of them were people who molded, guided, challenged, and encouraged you to be the best player or coach you could be. A few of them, unfortunately, may have been people who took the joy and enthusiasm of football out of you. Some of them probably seemed to have no recognizable impact on your life at all. The truth is, all of them are an important part of your life and who you are as a coach. Take time to reflect on what you appreciated about those positive people, or the things that were done to you that you hope you'll never do to anyone else. Most of us have heard about a child who had an abusive or dysfunctional family (or we lived that situation ourselves), and we've promised ourselves to never be like that to our own kids, but people often find that they've broken that promise. Changing from how we were molded as children does not happen by accident; it has to be done intentionally, with thought, planning, and support.

In his outstanding book *InSideOut Coaching*, former NFL player and longtime high school coach Joe Ehrmann presents four foundational questions that coaches should ask themselves in order to develop a solid coaching philosophy and have a positive, transformative effect on their athletes:

- Why do I coach?
- Why do I coach the way I do?
- What does it feel like to be coached by me?
- How do I define and measure success?

As you can see, these are not simple questions, and if you are honest with yourself, you may not like your answers. But this step is crucial to developing your coaching philosophy and to moving beyond what Ehrmann calls transactional coaching, coaching driven by egotistical motivations such as winning and notoriety. Do not hurry through this step. Get out a pen and notepad (or smartphone or tablet) and write down your responses to those questions for further reflection.

The fourth question addresses the mammoth topic of success, a word that has so many different connotations and definitions. A helpful perspective on success comes from the greatest coach of the 20th century, John Wooden. He defined success as "peace of mind, which is a direct result of self-satisfaction in knowing you made the effort to become the best you are capable of becoming" (www.coachwooden.com/pyramid_of_success). As you think about success and how you measure it as a coach, both on and off the field, this definition adds significant breadth of perspective to all of the energy you put into coaching.

As well as considering Ehrmann's questions, take time to write down your values. Don't limit it to values within your football context (winning, working hard, team culture, playing fair, etc.); make sure to include values from all areas of your life (family, friends, health, love, patience, honesty, etc.). In order to develop a sound coaching philosophy, you have to know what is important to you in life, and to integrate those values into everything you do. Your list of values will be a key aspect of any philosophical foundation you have for your coaching.

While you consider wisdom from your personal mentors or the great coaches of our game, make sure to remain true to who you are as an individual. Your coaching personality must be genuine if you want to be respected by your co-coaches as well as your players and their parents. There is no such thing as an ideal coaching personality that you need to try to mimic. Football has seen winning and positive influence achieved by coaches as different as Tony Dungy, Vince Lombardi, Bill Walsh, and Pete Carroll. The world doesn't need another Wally Buono, Hugh Campbell, Cal Murphy, or Bob O'Billovich; it needs your best version of you.

BEGIN WITH THE END IN MIND

In one of the best-selling self-help books of all time, *The 7 Habits of Highly Successful People*, Stephen Covey stated that the second habit of highly successful people is to "begin with the end in mind." If we get into a car with no clear idea of where we are going, we are certain to not get anywhere! Before dwelling on day-to-day details, it is crucial to think about the ultimate destination. This step is important for life in general, and it's also important in your coaching context. Where do you ultimately want to go with your life? With your coaching? A helpful exercise for some people is to write their own eulogy. While it seems morbid, it gets you to think about what you want people to say about you when you die (assuming they will be telling the truth!). In the coaching context, what would you want your current and former athletes to say about you at your funeral? That can be an enlightening task to help you think about your destination as a coach and as a person.

As you begin with the end in mind, you will be confronted with the most important philosophical question: why? Simon Sinek's book *Start With Why* outlines the thought process that an organizational leader needs to focus on at all times. Why do you coach? Starting with why is implicit in some of Joe Ehrmann's questions. It also provokes big-picture thinking. Unfortunately, many coaches skip this question and go straight to "How?" and "What?" (playbook systems, practice schedules, game film software, etc.). These pragmatic details are important, but still secondary to a solid coaching philosophy.

Now it is time for the foundation of your coaching philosophy: your coaching mission statement. The thesis statement of an essay is typically one sentence and provides an overview of what you want to say. Similarly, a mission statement provides the overview of what you want to do. A mission is a calling for your life. It is the most meaningful purpose for which you have been created. As you begin to consider your mission statement, go back to your list of values and choose the ones that are the most important to you (as a person and as a coach). For most of us, a big part of our life mission statement would be our role within our family, especially as a spouse and parent. In the football context, our mission should be similar, but will be more focused on the context of coaching. As an example, here is my coaching mission statement:

> To use the pursuit of excellence in the great sport of football to help young men develop positive character traits that will facilitate a happy and productive life in the home, community, and work place.

This mission statement includes the essential values of my coaching life: excellence, positive character, and mentoring young people to become the best that they can be. Those values can also be applied to my life as a teacher, husband, and dad, but would be stated a bit differently in a life mission statement. I also have a mission statement that I use for my football team, a statement that provides everyone in our organization with a clear idea of what we are all about:

> To use the experience of preparing for and competing in high school football to develop the football skill and aptitude, personal character, and life experience of all team members in the pursuit of excellence.

It is no coincidence that the values of my coaching mission statement are clearly reflected in our team mission statement. As the leader of the team, it is vital that my team mission is consistent with my coaching and personal missions.

Let's talk some more about character. Conflicting quotations say that "Sport builds character" and "Sport does not build character, it reveals it." I don't think either claim covers the whole truth. First, sport does not build character unless the coaches make specific efforts to teach character through the day-to-day training process and the triumphs and failures of competition. I have heard coaches from championship teams rave about the high character of their players, when all I see is a group of very talented individuals who trash-talk, showboat, talk back to officials and even their own coaches, and show no sportsmanship or grace when things don't go their way. Only the second part of the second statement is

100 percent true: sport does reveal character. But again, I strongly disagree with the first part. Sport does build character, but only if the coaches are deliberate and purposeful in teaching, modeling, and demanding positive character traits.

Now back to mission statements. A mission statement is important for yourself, but it will also be very important to everyone with whom you work as a coach: assistant coaches, league or school administrators, players, parents, and other team supporters. You are the leader, and it is vital that everyone you are leading knows where you are taking them. Everyone needs to understand your mission statement so that they understand why you coach the way you do and why your team runs the way it does. Just as it is crucial for your players to all be operating from the same playbook when they are on the field, your program needs to be operating from the same playbook (or mission) in everything you do on and off the field. This does not mean that you have a team of clones who all think and act like you, but it does mean that everyone has to buy into and support the values that you have articulated in your mission statement. They then apply that mission statement with their individual personalities and gifts. As John Wooden wisely advised, "Surround yourself with smart people who'll argue with you." Hammering through hard conversations about philosophy and mission can be a great unifying experience for a coaching staff or other important team stakeholders.

A big part of being a successful coach or teacher is to be a strong salesman. In particular, you need to sell everyone on your coaching philosophy and your team philosophy. Take the time to memorize your coaching and team mission statements, and make reference to them when you are speaking to administrators, parents, or your team. When you are interviewed, take the opportunity to outline your team's mission. When you award or recognize outstanding team members, describe how they have contributed to accomplishing the mission of the team. Another idea for an early-season team meeting, especially if you are coaching more mature athletes, is to ask the players how they could see themselves living out and contributing to the mission of the team this season (this could be done as individual reflection as well). This will increase their buy-in because they will feel part of the process of developing the team culture. If you neglect the aspect of selling your big ideas, your coaching philosophy and mission statement become lost and forgotten on pieces of paper everyone loses after the first meeting of training camp.

Once you have a mission statement, you have a guide for all of the pragmatic details of your coaching and how you operate your team. Your mission statement should guide you through player discipline issues, planning and organizing practices and meetings, setting team expectations, and even keeping your locker room and equipment shed organized. It should also guide you through rare, big decisions you may encounter. For example, our team was invited to participate in an American football weekend in Ireland. As we considered this opportunity with our coaches, players, school administrators, and parents, we filtered everything through our mission statement. Would the opportunity to play football against a team from another part of the country, or from the United States, help us to develop our football skill and aptitude? Would it give us opportunities to develop the positive character traits we wanted our players to exhibit? Would it be a unique life experience? Would it help us to pursue excellence as individuals? We felt the answer to all of those questions was yes, so we explored the opportunity until we came to the point of narrowly deciding against it due to cost and the pressures it would put on our team as we entered a very competitive season. More recently, we pursued an opportunity to travel to a remote northern community in our province to do an exchange camp where we would provide football instruction to the teams in the area and they would provide us with education and experiences from their Dene culture. Again, everything in our mission statement said that this was a good fit for our program, so the Friendship Camp is something we hope will become an annual part of our football program tradition.

A complement to your coaching mission statement could be a team vision statement. A vision statement provides a description of what other people will see if your mission statement is accomplished. Again, your personal and team values should be represented in a vision statement. Here is an example:

> Our team will improve every week as we compete to win every game, because all team members will make every effort to be the best that they can be as players, coaches, and people.

With this vision statement, our values are emphasized in a way that opponents, fans, and others would be able to see as they watched us from week to week in the season.

BREAK IT DOWN

Mission and vision statements provide the big picture of your coaching philosophy. From there, you can formulate other tools to communicate the kind of coach you want to be and the kind of program you want to lead. These are more specific and tangible, so are often easier to understand and latch on to, especially for younger people like your players.

The first option is a motto. A motto is a concise, punchy statement that gives a sense of direction to your team. Some well-known examples include "Win the day" (Oregon Ducks), "Always compete" (USC Trojans and Seattle Seahawks under Pete Carroll), and "Play like a champion today" (Notre Dame Fighting Irish). A motto makes a great banner in your dressing room, a great design for a team T-shirt, and a great sign on your field.

Another option is a short list of your key values or, as some people describe them, pillars. The key values that are the foundation for my program are discipline, intensity, enthusiasm, poise, and grit. Each of those traits is described in our player manual, and they provide a foundation for our team expectations, specifically how we act and perform in games, practices, meetings, classes, and the community. Scott MacAulay, head coach of the CJFL's Regina Thunder, uses these pillars: aggressive, united, well prepared, and accountable. Again, these pillars are developed into slogans, descriptions, and a team ethic for everyone to follow.

Many coaches find value in quotations to communicate the key values and philosophies of their team. The quotes may come from many areas of life:

- ◆ Football: "Winning is not a sometime thing; it is an all the time thing. You don't do things right once in a while . . . you do them right all the time" (Vince Lombardi). "Played wholeheartedly, football is a soul-satisfying outlet for the rugged, courageous type of boy who likes physical contact. Played half-heartedly, football is a waste of time and energy. Football is no halfway game. To play it, you have to get wet all over" (Dana X. Bible).
- ◆ Other sports: "Champions aren't made in the gyms. Champions are made by something they have inside deep them: a dream, a desire, a vision" (Muhammad Ali). "Love is playing each game as if it's your last" (Michael Jordan).
- ◆ Movies: "Do or do not; there is no try" (Yoda). "The needs of the many outweigh the needs of the few . . . or the one" (Mr. Spock).

GETTING PRACTICAL

Younger athletes may struggle to relate to philosophical mission statements, but they should be able to grasp the more tangible process of goal setting. Goals can be set by the head coach or the coaching staff, but you will probably get more buy-in from your team if players have a role in the process. The other great thing about including players (team leaders if it is too difficult to include the entire roster) is that you can teach and guide them through the process with the focus on your mission statement and team values.

As well as making reference to the philosophy you and the program have, you will also have to educate players on making good goals. One of the most common strategies for making effective goals is using the acronym SMART: specific, measurable, attainable, relevant, and timely (see chapter 2 on team leadership, and chapter 13 on gaining a competitive mental edge). While setting goals is important, it is even more important to establish an action plan for every goal. The old saying holds true: "If you fail to plan, you plan to fail." As you make your plan, you can consider long-term goals (months or more into the future), medium-term goals (weeks into the future), and short-term goals (day-to-day). Once team goals are set, groups and individuals within the team can focus on their own goals and action plans to contribute to the team goals.

The first goal almost every team and athlete will want to set is to win. Sports are meant to be competitive, and there is always a winner and a loser, but make sure to bring everything back to your philosophy and mission statement. The younger the athletes, the less important winning should be. If you are a minor or high school football coach, you are probably not being paid, and your athletes aren't either. In professional football, where livelihoods are on the line, winning is much more central than it is in a youth sport setting. When your athletes say that they want to win the championship, make sure that the goal fits as a SMART goal. Yes, winning the championship is a specific goal. It is definitely measurable. Is it attainable? That may require an honest look at your team and your competi-

---

Learn From the Best

Several influential books have helped me develop my coaching philosophy or have confirmed I'm on the right track. You may find these works inspirational and challenging:

Win Forever: Live, Work, and Play Like a Champion by Pete Carroll, Yogi Roth, and Kristoffer A. Garin, Portfolio, 2011.

The 7 Habits of Highly Effective People: Powerful Lessons in Personal Change by Stephen R. Covey, Simon and Schuster, 2013.

Quiet Strength: The Principles, Practices, and Priorities of a Winning Life by Tony Dungy and Nathan Whitaker, Tyndale Momentum, 2008.

The Mentor Leader: Secrets to Building People and Teams That Win Consistently by Tony Dungy, Tyndale Momentum, 2011.

Uncommon: Finding Your Path to Significance by Tony Dungy and Nathan Whitaker, Tyndale Momentum, 2011.

InSideOut Coaching: How Sports Can Transform Lives by Joe Ehrmann and Gregory Jordan, Simon and Schuster, 2011.

The Lombardi Rules: 26 Lessons From Vince Lombardi, the World's Greatest Coach by Vince Lombardi Jr., McGraw-Hill Education, 2004.

Bo's Lasting Lessons: The Legendary Coach Teaches the Timeless Fundamentals of Leadership by Bo Schembechler and John U. Bacon, Hachette Book Group, 2008.

Start With Why: How Great Leaders Inspire Everyone to Take Action by Simon Sinek, Penguin Books, 2009.

The Score Takes Care of Itself: My Philosophy of Leadership by Bill Walsh with Steve Jamison and Craig Walsh, Penguin Books, 2010.

A Game Plan for Life: The Power of Mentoring by John Wooden and Don Yaeger, Bloomsbury Press, 2009.

Coach Wooden's Pyramid of Success by John Wooden and Jay Carty, Baker Publishing Group, 2014.

Wooden: A Lifetime of Observations and Reflections On and Off the Court by John Wooden and Steve Jamison, McGraw-Hill, 1997.

Wooden on Leadership by John Wooden and Steve Jamison, McGraw-Hill, 2005.

tion. Winning the championship is timely, because you will know by the end of the season. But is it relevant to your mission statement and your other team goals? That is a big question.

Another consideration for setting goals is to try to focus as much as possible on things that are within your control. Winning has a lot to do with things that are out of your control, such as the health of your athletes, the level of your competition, and the unpredictable bounces of a pointed ball. Make sure to devote considerable attention to goals that are mostly or completely within your control.

Assuming that the goal of winning has passed the SMART standard, it is now time to set short- and medium-term goals. The short-term goal would probably be winning your first game, and the medium-term goal might be winning at least three of your first four games to put yourself in a favourable position to make playoffs at the end of the season.

Your action plans should focus mainly on your short-term goals. In order to win this week's game, how do we need to practice? How do we need to prepare mentally by studying game film and learning game plans? How do we need to manage our rest, hydration, and nutrition to make sure we are at our physical best on game day? How do we need to take care of our school and family responsibilities to make sure we are eligible to play on game day? As you can see, these are all things within the control of your team and its individuals. Answering these questions should give you a measurable plan to follow and to keep each other accountable as you strive to reach your short-term goal.

From there, players can set individual goals for practices. If ball security is one of your performance goals, the quarterbacks may make the goal of avoiding poor decisions that lead to interceptions by throwing the ball away when they are under extreme pressure in practice. If mental execution is one of your performance goals, your receivers may set the goal to run the correct route on every play in practice this week. If gang tackling is one of your performance goals, your defensive backs may set the goal of pursuing the ball on every play in pass skeleton and team periods. Players can also identify specific technical goals for themselves in practice. Your centre may put extra practice and focus into his shotgun snaps, or your defensive linemen may work on their rip and sit technique in order to control and squeeze gaps. As you can see, we are now focusing on things that even young athletes can easily manage, and these goals are all within the control of the individual.

If you set goals, make sure to devote time to evaluating them. Did you achieve your goals? Why or why not? This process is important because you want to celebrate successes, both small and large. If you did not achieve your goal, you want to make adjustments if your plan or effort was not sufficient to achieve the goal.

As mentioned earlier in the chapter, another pragmatic detail your mission and values can help you with is setting team expectations. "Expectations" seems to have more positive connotations than "rules," so that is the word I prefer. Many coaches believe in having as few rules or expectations as possible. While it is true that it is very cumbersome to make rules for every little thing, young athletes need to have specific guidance. Longtime NCAA coach Lou Holtz's dictum to "Do the right thing" may not be clear enough for athletes whose cognitive psychological development is still at the concrete operational stage. Making your expectations principle-focused is perhaps the most economical and effective way to communicate expectations. Rather than outlining the kind of effort you expect from players in practices, meetings, games, and in the classroom, your principle can focus on your team value of hard work: "Players are expected to give a full effort in both football and academic activities." That principle covers a lot of situations. Take time to define your values and principles in detail, and then it is easy to apply them to the wide variety of situations you will face as you work with young athletes.

CONCLUSION

Developing a coaching philosophy is a dynamic process. Every year, you learn a little more from experience, coaches clinics, and personal reflection, which should motivate you to hone your philosophy and skills. But your philosophy should be stable and strong throughout the season. It is quite unsettling to a team to have a radical change of philosophy in the middle of the season, whether it is a dramatic change in playbooks or an overhaul to the standards and functioning of the team. Change can be good, but it must be rational and carefully implemented in order for everyone to fully buy in to it.

Consistency is also crucial in the application of your philosophy, values, and expectations. Nothing can lower morale and tear a team apart faster than preferential treatment for star players who are not held accountable for going against the team's foundations. Even young athletes can see the hypocrisy of disciplining marginal players for breaking team rules while overlooking the same behaviors in the starting players. Poor leadership like this will undermine the respect your players (and their parents) have for you, and will destroy any efforts you make to teach positive character.

We all make mistakes. As the leader, it is vital to quickly admit to mistakes and take actions to make atonement. If your mistake was toward an individual, you only need to address it with that one person, but if it was to the whole team, or the whole team is aware of it, it is important to apologize to the whole group. Remember that an apology loses all effectiveness if it is followed with a "but" or any kind of excuse or blame on someone else. Take responsibility for your actions without excuse, just as you would expect your players to. Having a sound coaching philosophy, mission statement, and values will help guide you away from missteps, but we are all human and need to be ready and willing to seek forgiveness and make restitution when we step out of line from our ideals.

Developing a comprehensive coaching philosophy is a challenging process. Don't feel that you have to tackle it all at once. Start with one of the ideas that is most comfortable and natural to you; maybe it will be composing a mission statement or a motto, or it could be compiling your key values. Just start with something and then build on it from year to year as you gain experience, wisdom, and perspective.

Never underestimate the opportunity you have as a coach to positively affect the lives of the young people with whom you interact. Kids don't get to choose their parents. Generally, they don't get to choose their teachers, especially for required classes. But (hopefully) nobody is forcing them to play football; they have made the choice to be on your team. That gives you an amazing platform to affect their lives and be a positive influence on their development as people, not just as athletes. When looking at high school football, a retired English teacher from Erasmus High School in New York said, "Football is the best-taught subject in America, because it's the only one we haven't tried to simplify." Let's develop a solid, consistent coaching philosophy, and keep our standards high to bring out the very best in everyone we teach and mentor as football coaches.

CHAPTER

4

Safe Contact

Tom Annett

On September 21, 2002, I experienced a major life-changing event. I was playing middle linebacker for the Wilfrid Laurier University Golden Hawks in an important week 3 matchup against our conference rivals, the Western Mustangs. In the third quarter, the Western offense was in a crucial second-and-short situation and called an inside run. I recall reading the play perfectly and attacking the line of scrimmage to meet the running back in the hole. It was a violent head-on-head collision that echoed throughout the stadium and knocked the Western ball carrier back a couple yards. As I ran off to the sideline pumping my fist in excitement, I felt a sharp piercing pain at the base of my neck.

That game versus Western was the last time I played competitive football. The outcome of that violent head-on-head collision was a fractured cervical vertebra and a blown disc in my cervical spine. I had spinal-fusion surgery a few days after the game. I was extremely fortunate to have a nearly full recovery.

While in the hospital awaiting the surgery, I engaged in deep self-reflection. I must have revisited that career-ending tackle hundreds of times in my mind. A split-second lapse in judgment led to flawed tackling technique that almost paralyzed me for life. I asked myself questions. Why me? What kind of long-term effects would this injury have? How did it even happen? Could it have been prevented? Was playing football worth it?

When my mind finally cleared, I realized how important football was to me. It hurt deeply to realize I'd never play competitive football again, but I had no regrets about my football career. The memories, life lessons, and relationships I made through football were priceless. I wanted to give back to the game, and coaching was my calling.

From the start of my coaching career, I made a commitment to teach safe and effective tackling technique. I wanted to do everything in my power to prevent one of my players from suffering a career-ending injury like mine. I also wanted my players to be highly skilled and proficient tacklers. I read books, watched videos, attended clinics, and spoke to as many coaches as I could about tackling technique. Some of the coaches who have had the greatest influence on the way

I teach tackling are Bill Williams and his son Kyle Williams of the Football Coaches Professional Growth Association, Chris Ash (Ohio State University), Chuck Clemons (University of Central Missouri), Rick Ponx (North Central College), Hugh Wyatt (North Beach High School, Washington), Kevin Bullis (University of Wisconsin at River Falls), and my university coach, Ron VanMoerkerke (Wilfrid Laurier University). Here I'll share the most effective tackling coaching strategies that these great coaches taught me.

OVERVIEW

Every football coach knows that tackling is one of the most important fundamental skills in the sport, yet few coaches know how to properly teach tackling. In this section, I cover some of the main reasons teams struggle with tackling, along with my thoughts on each issue.

Coaches Assume Players Already Know How to Tackle

In minor or high school football, many players show up to tryouts who have never played the game before. Whether you're coaching minor or professional football, tackling needs to be consistently coached and drilled in practice with proper progressions to ensure safe and sound technique. This will help build confidence in athletes, and it will develop muscle memory that will reduce the chances of flawed (and potentially dangerous) technique during competition.

Too many coaches introduce tackling with the phrase "Let's see who wants to hit!" They follow this up with a full-speed tackling drill. It's dangerous and counterproductive to have athletes participate in live-contact drills before they are ready. Even if players already know how to tackle properly, technique should be reviewed by starting with the preliminary progressions. Starting right from the basics can help correct any bad habits players may have developed, and it also helps players become more confident in their ability to tackle.

Coaches Fail to Recognize Tackling Proficiency

Coaches, fans, and the media often glorify a big hit even when the technique is flawed and potentially dangerous (e.g., lowered head, arm tucked into tackler's body). This misguided praise perpetuates unsafe and inconsistent tackling. Hard hits can be made with safe and sound technique. Recently the rules have expanded to further protect players from helmet-initiated contact. Leagues everywhere have made this a point of emphasis. It's a step in the right direction, but coaches, fans, and the media need to follow suit by discouraging these dangerous types of hits. Often, the most challenging and technical tackles made in a game don't involve the huge collisions that get fans out of their seats. It is our job as coaches to recognize when our players make fundamentally sound tackles and celebrate them.

Coaches Lack the Knowledge and Experience to Effectively Coach and Drill Tackling

We often hear coaching clichés like "Tackling is 80 percent desire and 20 percent technique." Yes, desire counts, but it is the coach's responsibility to help develop this desire. When a player is confident in his technique and assignments, he is more likely to play aggressively. A coach may label a player as "not tough enough" or "doesn't like contact" when in reality the coach hasn't taught the athlete how to tackle properly. Providing detailed coaching with proper progressions will instill confidence and ultimately the desire to make tackles.

A few years ago, I saw University of Miami offensive line coach Art Kehoe speak about offensive line fundamentals. I was blown away by the incredible precision that Coach Kehoe brought to teaching each type of block. Coach Kehoe dissected every step down to a fraction of an inch; he talked about weight distribution, where the offensive lineman's eyes should be focused, the spacing of the fingers, and more. The level of detail he provided was mind-blowing! In my opinion, all great position coaches teach the fundamentals in this manner, but for some reason defensive coaches tend to be vague and lacking in detail when teaching tackling. A second problem is that very few defensive coaches have the ability to identify, isolate, and correct mistakes in tackling. These two problems are interrelated; teaching the skill of tackling in greater detail and with appropriate progressions will allow coaches to more effectively identify and communicate breakdowns in technique. It allows coaches to correct mistakes by referencing drills and using buzzwords (handy terms) that emerge during drill work. For example, a coach can say, "Squeeze your clamp just like we do in our goalpost tackle drill."

Coaches Emphasize Schemes Instead of Tackling Fundamentals

It doesn't matter if you have the perfect schemes installed; if your players can't tackle, you won't win football games. I think that, now and then, just about every coach gets too caught up in schemes or blames his schemes for a poor performance. Usually, big plays are given up by a defense when tackles are missed, not because somebody thinks the 4-3 defense sucks. Anybody can draw up a defensive playbook or find one on the Internet, but few people can teach players how to execute the skills necessary to succeed in that defense. There are plenty of X-and-O coaches out there, but the great coaches are the ones who know how to coach the fundamentals and understand how fundamentals relate to schemes. Tackling is the most important fundamental skill in any defensive scheme. To be a great tackling team, you need to practice the fundamentals of tackling almost every day. Make sure that tackling gets the required attention in your practice plans.

Athletes Lack Speed or Strength to Be Proficient Tacklers

In Canada, the calibre of play at the high school level through to university has improved by leaps and bounds over the past 15 years. We are at the point now at which athletes need to participate in year-round strength and speed programs in order to compete at the highest levels. The bigger, stronger, and (most importantly) faster athletes have greater potential to succeed on the football field. An effective off-season strength and conditioning program not only increases players' potential to become better tacklers, it also protects players from injuries. I'm convinced that when I suffered my career-ending neck injury, my large muscular neck is what saved me from paralysis. After my spinal-fusion surgery, I recall the surgeon telling me that I had the largest sternocleidomastoid (a neck muscle) he had ever seen. He told me that the musculature in my neck acted as a natural brace and that it probably saved me from suffering a more severe injury. Be sure to include neck-strengthening exercises in your strength and conditioning program.

SAFETY CONSIDERATIONS

The increasing awareness of head and spinal injuries has had a profound effect on football. A greater understanding of concussions and their long-term effects has significantly reinforced the importance of teaching safe tackling technique. The most important fundamental aspect of teaching tackling is to *keep the top of the head out of contact*. You cannot stress this coaching point enough to your players. Even with perfect technique, often you will see some incidental contact with the face mask, but contact should never be initiated with any part of the helmet; the rules specify this and player safety demands it! All coaches should eliminate any language from their coaching that insinuates making contact with the helmet ("earhole him" or "crack his skull"). Not only will this protect your players, but it could save you from being liable for any injuries your players may suffer. Many coaches have gone so far as to film themselves teaching safe tackling during training camp to protect themselves from potential lawsuits.

Today's athletes are bigger, stronger, and faster than ever. Therefore, collisions are more violent and have greater potential to injure players. Coaches need to find ways to work on tackling throughout the year while minimizing the amount of contact players are exposed to. Many coaches still believe that the only way to improve tackling is by using full-contact drills. I strongly disagree. Tackling can be significantly improved through noncontact drills that require no equipment at all. An additional advantage of using non-equipped drills is that it allows teams to work on tackling throughout the off-season, when full-equipment practices may be restricted or limited by league rules. Noncontact drills are not only safer, but they also build player confidence by allowing players to be successful early in the learning process. The majority of the drills I discuss in this chapter require no contact or very limited contact. The bulk of our technical teaching takes place during these types of drills.

Also note that we rarely take ball carriers to the ground in practice. The risk of injury increases considerably when players are taken to the turf. Instead we require the tackler to drive the ball carrier back a specified distance or until the coach stops the drill. This strategy reduces the risk of injury but allows us to stress the importance of finishing tackles.

CHALLENGES

One of the most challenging aspects of coaching tackling is the dynamic and unpredictable nature of the act. Every tackle in a game is different because of the countless variables that can affect each tackle:

- ◆ Ball carrier's size compared to the tackler's size
- ◆ Angle at which the tackle is made
- ◆ Tackler chasing a ball carrier from behind
- ◆ Speed of the ball carrier and tackler before contact
- ◆ Tackler or ball carrier being off-balance or in an unfavorable body position before contact
- ◆ Tackler hitting a receiver in the act of catching a ball
- ◆ Tackler being the second or third man in to make contact
- ◆ Field location of the tackle (sideline, open field, in traffic, goal line, end zone)
- ◆ Tackler's help (inside-leverage defender versus outside-leverage defender)
- ◆ Ball carrier's skill set (agile scatback, speed back, big thumper, etc.)
- ◆ Game situation (need to keep ball carrier in bounds to keep the clock running, need a turnover, etc.)

When first introducing tackling, it would be overwhelming and counterproductive to address all of these scenarios. Fortunately, one tackling fundamental remains relatively constant regardless of the circumstances: the act of striking the ball carrier.

The remainder of the chapter will focus on striking fundamentals, coaching strategies for the strike, and drills to improve striking. The strike is the first phase of tackling to coach because there is great carryover to the many situational tackles taught later. The objectives of the strike are:

- ◆ Get the ball carrier on the ground.
- ◆ Knock the ball carrier backwards (i.e., no extra yards after contact).
- ◆ Tackle with violence and power to create fumbles.

When you think about some of the greatest tacklers to ever play the game (e.g., Mike O'Shea, Dick Butkus, Ray Lewis, etc.), they all excelled in this regard.

Again, coaches must stress the importance of keeping the top of the head out of contact during tackling. Strike-drill progressions and coaching cues help emphasize this coaching point. Coaching cues are one of the most overlooked aspects of coaching. Coaches need to find buzzwords that allow them to emphasize or even exaggerate coaching points. Using these terms—words or very short phrases that have precise meanings known to the staff and players—will also allow coaches to coach on the fly, which can improve practice tempo and maximize repetitions. Make sure that the coaches all use the same buzzwords. In the next section I present the exact coaching progression used to teach the striking phase of tackling.

STRIKE TEACHING PROGRESSION

Before drilling the strike progression, it is important to show your players what a well-executed tackle looks like. The Football Canada Safe Contact course (safe-contact.footballcanada.com) provides clear instruction on safe tackling.

In performing a perfect tackle, a player would:

- Be in an ideal pre-contact body position:
  - Feet staggered and about armpit-width apart
  - Ankles, knees, and hips flexed
  - Back flat, with a concave lower back arch
  - Body at approximately 45 degrees with the chin out in front of the toes
  - Hands back by the hips with elbows tight to the body
  - Neck bulled
  - Eyes up and at the level of the ball
- Position the head to slide to the side of the ball carrier's body.
- Make initial contact with the front top of the shoulder pad.
- On contact, fire both hands up explosively in an uppercut action.
- As the tackler extends into the ball carrier at the ankles, knees, and hips, body contact with the ball carrier should slide from the shoulder to the chest and abdomen. The tackler's neck remains bulled, which should result in him looking up with his head back.
- Drive the knees with a high, wide action to maintain power and drive the ball carrier back.

The series of drills used in the progression breaks down the tackle into stages to simplify teaching.

The Clamp

Begin the tackling teaching progression with the finish position, which we refer to as the clamp. This is the position the tackler is in after striking and driving the ball carrier back or to the ground. It helps to start with the finish position because that shows players the body posture they are striving to achieve in a successful tackle. Have players get in the finish body posture (figure 4.1) and hold it for approximately 10 seconds. Note that we exaggerate technique and form in many of these drills to emphasize coaching points. For example, athletes try to squeeze their elbows together and get their hands above their heads when they hold the finish position in this drill. It's highly unlikely that this exact body posture will be seen when a player executes an actual tackle, but the position stresses the importance of shooting the hands in an uppercut motion and squeezing the ball carrier after grabbing cloth.

Coaching Points for the Clamp

- ◆ Feet hip- to shoulder-width apart
- ◆ Feet slightly staggered (have players hold the finish with the right foot forward and the left foot forward)
- ◆ Hips extend through ball carrier (belt buckle forward)
- ◆ Hands above the head
- ◆ Claw the hands and squeeze the pinkies together (this simulates grabbing high cloth on the back of the ball carrier's jersey)
- ◆ Eyes focused on the pinkies ("sky the eyes")
- ◆ Squeeze the elbows (think of the movement on the old pec-deck strength-training machines)

FIGURE 4.1 Clamp finish position.

Holding the finish position appears relatively easy, but when it's done properly, every muscle in the body should be tensed (just like when finishing a tackle). That makes it challenging to hold the position for extended time.

To maximize repetitions, we usually line players up in a grid format (players spread out 5 × 5 yards), as shown in figure 4.2. Coaches circulate to ensure that players have the proper body posture and that they are maintaining muscle tension.

X	X	X	X	X	X
X	X	X	X	X	X
X	X	X	X	X	X
		Coach			

FIGURE 4.2 Drill grid alignment.

Finish Position March and March on Partner

Once players master the clamp body posture, add the drive phase. Players get into the clamp finish position and advance at a marching pace while aggressively driving their knees high and wide to engulf the ball carrier. Exaggerate the height and width of the knee drive to stress the importance of aggressively driving the legs after contact. Players march in this manner for 10 yards. Next, speed up the drill from a march pace to full speed, with athletes explosively pumping the legs high and wide. We refer to this fast, high knee action as "double-timing the knees," or as Pete Carroll says, "Drive for five."

Next, players get into a fit position on the ball carrier (figure 4.3a):

- Tackler puts his chin on the ball carrier's right or left chest plate.
- Tackler's eyes are looking through the ball carrier's neck.
- Tackler's clamp is secured by clawing high cloth on the back of the ball carrier's jersey.

On the start command, the tackler simultaneously squeezes his pinkies and elbows, marches the knees high and wide around the ball carrier, brings the hips tight to the ball carrier (there shouldn't be any space between the tackler and ball carrier once the marching starts), and skies the eyes (figure 4.3b).

FIGURE 4.3 Finish position march on partner: (a) fit position, (b) march.

The tackler continues to march forward for 10 yards while maintaining a finish body posture. This drill gives tacklers the sensation of being properly "fit up" on a ball carrier and driving him back. It's important that players learn what a good fit and finish feels like before executing the skill at faster speeds.

HIT UP TEACHING PROGRESSION: STRIKING

After players learn the finish position, they learn the actual striking portion of the tackle. The tackler's ability to explosively bring his hips and arms into the tackle is paramount. My experience has led me to believe that the hardest hitters are the players who have the ability to generate the most explosive power through their hips. These are the players who make the great knockback tackles that excite the crowd and change the momentum in a game.

In order to develop this explosive hip power, an athlete first needs to have adequate hip mobility and sufficient strength relative to his body weight. Any athlete who cannot perform a proper body-weight squat below parallel will usually struggle with the mechanics involved in tackling and many other fundamental football skills. This issue is common among younger players, especially those who struggle with obesity. We incorporate a series of hip-mobility exercises (mostly variations of body-weight squats and lunges) into our warm-up and our off-season strength and conditioning program. Athletes who are unable to perform full squats or lunges will use a smaller range of motion for these movements until they improve mobility or get strong enough to progress. Advanced athletes with sufficient levels of strength and mobility can work to improve their explosive hip power. I have found that the best way to do this is through weighted jump variations or Olympic lifts such as squats, deadlifts, and cleans. Make sure your athletes receive proper instruction from a knowledgeable trainer before attempting any of these advanced exercises.

Pre-contact Body Position

Figure 4.4 shows the athlete's body position just before he initiates contact with the ball carrier. A player's ability to get into the proper pre-contact body position will reduce the risk of injury while significantly increasing his chances of making a successful tackle.

Coaching points for the pre-contact position:

- ◆ Feet staggered and at approximately armpit width
- ◆ Eyes on target (the football)
- ◆ Chin up and over the toes

* Head and shoulders square, not turned to one side
* Elbows high and tight to the sides
* Arms bent at approximately 90 degrees
* Hands at holsters (gunslinger)
* Eyes lowered to ball level by sinking the hips and bending the knees
* Butt back and upward to get a slight concave arch in the low back. This will help the tackler get his hips cocked and loaded (think of a slingshot pulled all the way back and ready to fire)
* Torso leaning forward at approximately a 45-degree angle
* Weight on the balls of the feet (body weight should be out in front of the base)

FIGURE 4.4 Tackling pre-contact body position.

Eyes Mirror Ball Level Drill

This drill teaches tacklers to hinge at the hips (not bend at the waist) and get in the proper body position to deliver a powerful strike. Ideally, tacklers will hit on the rise, which requires them to go into contact from a low coiled-up body position. As a general rule, we tell players to get their eyes at ball level when going into contact. This allows tacklers to hit on the rise and gain leverage when finishing the tackle.

The ball carrier and tackler stand approximately 3 yards apart. The ball carrier stands perpendicular to the tackler (i.e., not facing the tackler), holding a football in the arm closest to the tackler. The tackler begins the drill in the pre-contact position—head up, chin out, hands holstered—with his eyes at ball level.

On the start command, the ball carrier slowly rises and descends in a squat. The tackler mirrors the ball height with his eyes while maintaining pre-contact posture.

It's critical that the tackler alter his depth by hinging the hips and bending the knees, not bending at the waist. The tackler's torso angle should remain at approximately 45 degrees throughout the drill. The drill should last approximately 10 seconds.

Striking the Ball Carrier

To stress the importance of keeping the top of the helmet out of contact, we tell players to lead with the chin and the chest and to strike with the chest. Ideally, the chest and the front of the shoulder pads initiate contact during a tackle.

It's important that players do not initiate the act of striking (i.e., bringing the hips and arms) until the tackler is close enough to the ball carrier to step on his toes. Initiating the strike too soon results in less force being generated during contact. Players who strike too soon are unable to hit through the ball carrier and as a result they are less likely to get knockbacks.

Once close enough to strike the ball carrier, the tackler learns to:

- Shoot violent double uppercuts while keeping the arms tight to the sides. I tell them to "scrape paint" (their ribs) with their elbows.
- Explosively pop the chest and thrust the hips through the ball carrier. If the uppercuts are violent, the hip thrust and chest pop should happen naturally. If the hips do not fully thrust, it is because the uppercuts were not violent.
- Sky the eyes (look through the ball carrier's neck to the sky).
- Secure the clamp by grabbing high cloth on the back of the ball carrier's jersey.
- Squeeze the pinkies and elbows and don't let go until the echo of the whistle.
- Drive the back knee through the ball carrier. Continue to rapidly and aggressively drive the knees high and wide until the ball carrier is on the ground or until the echo of the whistle.

Overemphasizing the violent double-uppercut action and bringing the eyes to the sky are the two most effective coaching points for preventing the top of the helmet from being involved in contact. A common mistake that should be avoided at all costs is using a horizontal hugging or wrapping action with the arms. This leads to head-down posture and it is an opposing force to the upward hip thrust required. Many coaches have gone so far as to eliminate the word *wrap* from their coaching buzzwords because they feel that it encourages an undesirable horizontal arm movement and dangerous head-down posture. Again, overemphasize shooting violent vertical uppercuts, not horizontal hugging.

The following drill progressions are used to teach synchronized explosive arm and hip movement.

Strike Up From Knee

Players start on one knee in a flat-back position with the chest over the front knee, chin up, and eyes looking straight ahead. The hands are holstered, with arms tight to the sides and elbows high and bent at approximately 90 degrees. The front foot is flat. The back foot should have the laces into the grass (athletes must not push

(continued)

off the back foot; all the force must be generated from the hips). Hips are cocked back and loaded (slingshot analogy).

On the hit command, players explosively thrust their hips forward and up (rolling motion) and shoot violent double uppercuts. Players claw the hands while squeezing the pinkies and elbows. The eyes look through the pinkies (sky the eyes). Players hold the tensed finish position until the coach releases them.

When players execute the drill with the proper level of power, they should get slightly airborne when they shoot their arms and hips.

This is another drill that can be run from a 5×5 grid format (figure 4.2) to maximize repetitions. Coaches should circulate throughout the grid to ensure proper technique. Be sure to run the drill with both the right knee down and the left knee down.

Strike Up From Knee to Finish

The next drill in the progression starts off the same, but the drive phase is added. In this drill, the drive phase is simulated by having the tackler double-time the knees high and wide at full speed. The tackler should be in the clamp finish position while driving upfield for 10 yards.

Players start the drill in the same way as the strike up from knee drill: on one knee in a flat-back position with the chest over the front knee, chin up, and eyes looking straight ahead. The hands are holstered with arms tight to the sides and elbows high and bent at approximately 90 degrees. Hips are cocked back and loaded.

Make sure the back foot has shoelaces on the ground, not the sole of the shoe. This forces the tackler to use explosive hips and arms to propel his movement instead of pushing off the back foot. As the athlete explosively shoots his hands and hips, he rises and transitions into the drive phase of the tackle. When done properly, the transition should look fluid.

Players simulate engulfing the ball carrier with a high-and-wide knee drive (i.e., double-time the knees). Players squeeze the pinkies and elbows while keeping the eyes focused on the pinkies (sky the eyes). Players maintain this clamped finish posture while double-timing the knees for 10 yards or until the coach ends the drill.

Strike Up From Pre-contact Position

Next, athletes execute the same drill except they start from the pre-contact position.

Athletes start in a proper pre-contact position with the eyes at ball level and the hips cocked back. As they explosively shoot the uppercuts and hips, athletes transition into the drive phase of the tackle. Players simulate engulfing the ball carrier with a high-and-wide knee drive (i.e., double-time the knees). Players squeeze the pinkies and elbows while keeping the eyes focused on the pinkies (sky the eyes).

Players maintain this clamped finish posture while double-timing the knees for 10 yards or until the coach ends the drill, finishing the drill in the same manner as the strike up from knee to finish drill.

Goalpost Pop

One of the best pieces of equipment for developing the striking phase of the tackle is the goalpost pad. Many teams have spent thousands of dollars on tackling sleds, when something they already have in their football shed can often teach tackling more effectively. The goalpost pop and goalpost strike and drive are two goalpost pad drills that we include in our tackling teaching progression.

In the goalpost pop drill, the focus is strictly on hip explosion and knee drive. For that reason, the arms are eliminated by having the tackler hold his hands behind his back.

The player starts in the pre-contact position with both hands behind his back and his chin on the goalpost pad. On the hit command, the tackler drives his back knee forward and up, explodes his hips through the pad, pops the chest, and skies his eyes. He is required to freeze for a second in the finished position. The hips should be tight against the pad, the eyes should be up, and the knee should be high. Change the stagger foot throughout the drill. Players must be able to initiate contact with either foot back.

Goalpost Strike and Drive

Next, the arms are added to the drill and the tackler will be required to double-time his knees after contact for approximately five seconds.

The tackler starts in the pre-contact position with his chin on the goalpost pad and his hands holstered. On the hit command, the tackler rips the hands up with violent double uppercuts, drives the back knee forward and up, explodes the hips through the pad, pops the chest into the pad, and skies the eyes. The tackler must attempt to sink his clamp deep by trying to get his pinkies to touch around the pad. He may not get his pinkies to touch if the goalpost pad (or ball carrier) is too big, but it is the intent to sink the clamp deep that enables the tackler to initiate contact with the chest. Once the clamp is secure, the tackler squeezes his pinkies and elbows while double-timing the knees high and wide. The tackler continues to aggressively squeeze and drive his knees for approximately five seconds. Change the initial stagger foot throughout the drill.

Strike and Drive on Handshield

The next drill in the progression involves striking a player holding a handshield and driving him backward. This drill will give the tackler the sensation of striking

(continued)

Strike and Drive on Handshield   *(continued)*

and driving against some resistance. It's an important step for easing players into live contact and building confidence. Remember to emphasize eyes at ball level.

Coach players on how to hold the handshield. Players should grab the top edge of the pad and keep their elbows high and flared out. The shield should be tight against the player's body with the top of the bag protecting the player's chin (see figure 4.5a). This allows the ball carrier to protect his head from contact. It also helps the tackler sink the clamp deep on the ball carrier's upper back to simulate a perfect fit up.

The tackler starts in the pre-contact position with his chin on the handshield and his hands holstered. On the hit command, the tackler executes a proper strike and drives the ball carrier back approximately 7 yards while double-timing the knees (figure 4.5b). Make sure the tackler is grabbing high cloth on the ball carrier's upper back while squeezing the pinkies and elbows. Emphasize sinking the clamp deep by trying to get the pinkies to touch behind the ball carrier.

FIGURE 4.5   Strike and drive on handshield: (a) start position, (b) drive.

After a few successful repetitions, increase the space between the tackler and the ball carrier by up to 4 yards and have the ball carrier slowly advance toward the tackler. In this case, the tackler will take a few steps before getting into the pre-contact position and striking.

An agility drill or an up-down can be added before the tackler strikes the player holding the handshield. This develops body awareness and teaches players how to get into a proper pre-contact position from various game-like situations.

This drill can also be run without the handshields to give tacklers a more realistic feel. When eliminating the handshield from the drill, have the ball carrier advance at about 70 to 90 percent effort and then stop his feet after he feels the tackler initiate contact. This allows tacklers to experience game-like speeds while also ensuring that they will get the sensation of driving the ball carrier backward after contact.

Variations of the strike and drive drill are the most frequently used tackling drills at our in-season practices. It can easily be added as a finish to any block-shedding drill or agility drill. The strike and drive drill is critical for developing perfect-technique muscle memory. It is also a great drill for helping coaches identify breakdowns in tackling technique.

Splatter Drill

The final drill we do before introducing full live contact is the splatter drill. In this drill, the tackler actually takes the ball carrier to the ground, but we use a crash mat to soften the landing. We like to use the school's high-jump mat, but you can also use a pile of agility bags and handshields if you don't have access to a large crash mat. It is a good idea to fasten the bags together with duct tape so they don't come apart when players fall on them.

The player being tackled should hold a handshield tight to his body as described for the strike and drive on handshield drill. The player being tackled stands with his back to the mat approximately 2 yards away from the mat. The ball carrier does not move for this drill; he is basically a tackling dummy.

The tackler stands approximately 3 yards away from the ball carrier in an athletic stance. On the hit command, the tackler attacks the ball carrier. He sinks into a pre-contact position, strikes the ball carrier, and drives him back into the crash mat. This is all done at full speed in one fluid motion. The tackler stays locked in a tight clamp (even after the ball carrier has been taken down to the mat) until the whistle or release command.

After each repetition, players switch lines (i.e., tackler goes to ball carrier line and vice versa). Two groups can alternate repetitions (group 1 repetition, followed by group 2 repetition) to increase the tempo and maximize repetitions (figure 4.6). For safety purposes, don't have both groups going at the same time on the same crash mat.

(continued)

Splatter Drill   *(continued)*

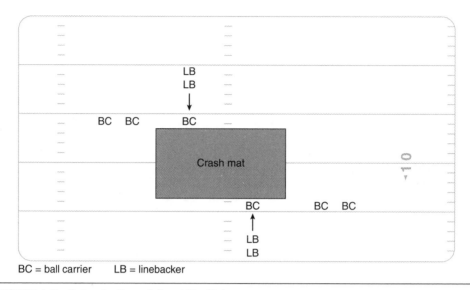

BC = ball carrier   LB = linebacker

FIGURE 4.6   Setup for the splatter drill with two groups.

We also like to perform this drill with the ball carrier standing perpendicular to the crash-mat area to simulate a profile tackle (i.e., angle tackle).

Players love the splatter drill because they get full-speed collisions, but the impacts are significantly softened by the crash mat and handshield. This is a great drill for teaching players how to hit through the ball carrier and finish tackles. It's important that your players get the sensation of running through an opponent rather than just catching and lifting him.

Correcting Specific Technical Flaws in the Strike

The previous drills are the foundation of our strike teaching progression. Athletes complete most of these drills before advancing into live contact. We use several other strike drills to add variety or to address specific technical flaws. Usually, when a flaw is found in tackling technique, it can be categorized in one of three areas:

1. *Arms*. The tackler isn't properly shooting uppercuts or isn't securing a proper clamp

2. *Hips*. The tackler does not bring his hips when tackling or is not generating enough force with his hips when tackling (uppercuts aren't violent)

3. *Feet.* The tackler stops his feet on contact or unnecessarily leaves his feet to make contact

Here are some additional drills we use to address these flaws in the strike.

Uppercut and Clamp Drill (Arms)

This drill teaches players to shoot proper uppercuts and secure a deep clamp. This is another drill that can be executed in grid format (figure 4.2) to maximize repetitions.

Players partner with somebody approximately the same height. Players face each other and then get down on one knee. Both players should be down on the same knee (i.e., tackler on right knee and ball carrier on right knee). The knee that isn't on the ground should be beside the partner's hip. Players start very close together. The tackler's face mask should be touching the ball carrier's upper chest. The ball carrier tries to stretch taller than the tackler and extends his arms out to the sides in a T shape (figure 4.7a).

This is an upper body–only drill. Focus strictly on the arm and hand action. For safety purposes, it's important that players do not use their hips or legs in this drill. The tackler should

FIGURE 4.7 Uppercut and clamp drill: (a) start, (b) uppercut and clamp.

(continued)

Uppercut and Clamp Drill *(continued)*

have his hands holstered while maintaining a 90-degree bend at the elbow. Arms should be tight to the torso. Make sure the tackler's chest and eyes are up before starting.

On the hit command, the tackler explosively rips up with violent double upper-cuts (figure 4.7b). He grabs high cloth on the back of the ball carrier's jersey and attempts to sink the clamp deep by getting the pinkies to touch behind the ball carrier's upper back. The tackler aggressively squeezes the pinkies and elbows and skies the eyes.

Coaches can circulate through the grid to make sure the clamp is secured. We like to try to pull the tackler's hands off the ball carrier's upper back to make sure he has a tight grip.

Spin Drill (Arms)

Every football coach has witnessed a tackler make great contact and then have the ball carrier slip away for a big gain. When this happens, it's demoralizing for the defense. The spin drill emphasizes the importance of securing and maintaining a tight clamp until the whistle. Coaches must constantly preach to their players that there is no shame in getting run over, but there is shame in letting go. If players are unable to take the ball carrier down, we at least expect them to hold on until help comes.

The drill starts with the tackler locking up on the ball carrier in a fit position (i.e., chin on ball carrier's right or left chest and a secured clamp). On the start command, the ball carrier aggressively torques and twists his body to try to free himself from the tackler's clamp. The tackler must work to stay locked in the clamp position for the full duration of the drill; the coach usually ends the drill after five to seven seconds.

This drill can get very competitive and aggressive. We tell ball carriers to try to stay on their feet but sometimes players go down to the turf. When this happens, we expect the tackler to stay locked up, but we usually stop the drill when players go down. Players with strong grip strength tend to do well in this drill.

Side note: In my opinion, grip strength is the most overlooked aspect of strength training for football. A strong grip will significantly improve an athlete's ability to execute many of the fundamental skills in football, especially tackling. Some of our favorite exercises to improve grip strength include timed holds with heavy dumbbells or barbells, towel pull-ups, and regular pulling exercises using fat bars. Be sure to incorporate grip-strengthening exercises in your strength-training program.

Superman Drill Without Arms (Hips)

This drill teaches players to shoot their hips explosively through the ball carrier.

Place a pair of agility bags flat on the ground. The tackler kneels approximately 1 yard away from the bags. The tackler places his hands behind his back and his butt back on his heels (figure 4.8a) to ensure that his hips are cocked back and loaded (use the slingshot analogy). Eyes and chin are up.

On the "hit" command, the tackler explosively pops the chest and thrusts the hips forward and up in a rolling motion (figure 4.8b). He skies the eyes. When performed properly and with sufficient force, the tackler should get airborne. The agility bags provide a soft landing.

FIGURE 4.8 Superman drill without arms: (a) start, (b) rolling motion.

Superman Drill With Arms (Hips)

We add the arms to the Superman drill to teach synchronized explosive arm and hip movement. This drill is set up and executed the same as the Superman drill without arms. The only difference is that the player will now add a violent double-uppercut movement (figure 4.9) on the hit command.

FIGURE 4.9 Superman drill with arms.

Strike Handshield From Knees (Hips)

This is another drill that teaches synchronized hip and arm explosion. We add a handshield with some resistance behind it to give tacklers the sensation of hitting a ball carrier.

A coach or player holds a handshield in front of the body at around belly height. The tackler is down on his knees, facing the handshield. The tackler should be approximately half a yard away from the pad. The tackler pulls his arms as far back as possible while maintaining a 90-degree bend at the elbows. The tackler's butt should be back on his heels to ensure that his hips are cocked back and loaded (use the slingshot analogy). Eyes and chin are up.

On the "hit" command, the tackler explosively pops the chest and thrusts the hips forward and up in a rolling motion. He shoots violent double uppercuts and skies the eyes. He clamps down on the handshield.

Sometimes we run this drill against players instead of handshields to give the sensation of striking an actual ball carrier and grabbing a jersey.

Tackling Sled (Feet)

The tackling sled is a good tool for teaching players to run their feet through contact. The sled gives players the sensation of hitting something with significant weight behind it and driving it backward. When using the tackling sled, a group of players are lined up in single file about 5 yards away from the sled and then take turns hitting it, driving it backward, and taking it to the ground. The technique used to hit the sled should be the exact same as hitting a ball carrier. We've found that the self-pop-up style of sled allows us to get more repetitions because players aren't wasting time lifting the sled up after each repetition.

Strike From Pre-contact Position With Resistance Band

Over the past couple years, more band work has been incorporated into our drills. Resistance bands are a great tool for adding resistance while having minimal impact on form and technique. This drill was discussed earlier in the chapter but without the resistance band. The band forces the tackler to explosively drive his knees forward in order to advance. The band will also allow the tackler to have a forward lean while executing the movement; this better replicates the body position a tackler will be in when making tackles at game speed.

The partner secures a resistance band around the tackler's waist. You may have to tie two bands together. Make sure the band is stretched and providing some resistance before the drill starts to ensure that the tackler will be working against tension immediately (figure 4.10). When the repetition is finished, the player holding the band slowly returns the band to the slack position.

FIGURE 4.10 Strike from pre-contact position with resistance band.

These are the drills we use to teach the fundamentals of striking the ball carrier. Do not allow athletes to progress to full-speed, live-contact drills until coaches and players are fully confident in their technique and ability.

Full-Contact Drills

When introducing live full-contact drills, it is important to match up players according to physical ability and football experience. This is important for safety, but it also provides inexperienced players with a greater opportunity to be successful, which will build confidence.

Goal-Line Tackle

This is the first competitive live-contact drill that we do. The distance between the ball carrier and the tackler is very small and we don't take the ball carrier to the ground.

The ball carrier and tackler stand approximately 1.5 yards apart, facing each other. The ball carrier positions his arms to receive a handoff from a coach or other player standing beside him with a football. The tackler is in the pre-contact position with eyes at ball level. When the ball is handed to the ball carrier, the drill begins.

The ball carrier attempts to get across the goal line but he cannot juke or spin; he must try to run through the tackler. The tackler executes a proper strike and

(continued)

Goal-Line Tackle *(continued)*

drives his feet in an attempt to keep the ball carrier from crossing the goal line. The drill ends when any of the following occur:

- ◆ The ball carrier crosses the goal line.
- ◆ The tackler drives the ball carrier back a few yards.
- ◆ There is an extended stalemate that lasts longer than four seconds.
- ◆ One or both players go to the ground.

We want players to stay on their feet in this drill, but if they do accidentally go to the ground, end the drill immediately. This is a great competitive drill to introduce live contact.

Third and Goal

As part of our live-contact progression, we use a variation of the goal-line tackle drill that we call third and goal. This drill increases the starting distance between the ball carrier and the tackler, and we allow the ball carrier to break to his right or left. The premise is the same as the previous drill in that the tackler is trying to keep the ball carrier out of the end zone, while the ball carrier is trying to cross the goal line.

Set up a 5×5 yard box with cones or use the yard line stripes as your boundaries and the sideline as your goal line. Place an agility bag in the middle of the 5×5 box. The ball carrier and tackler line up approximately 4 yards apart and face each other. The tackler's heels are on the goal line (or the sideline simulating the goal line as in figure 4.11). The agility bag should be between the tackler and the ball carrier.

FIGURE 4.11 Third and goal drill starting setup.

On the start command, the ball carrier breaks right or left of the agility bag and tries to run into the end zone. The ball carrier cannot juke or spin; he must run through the tackler to get into the end zone. The ball carrier must also remain within the drill boundaries to win. (At the beginning, it may be good to have the ball carrier put out 80 percent effort rather than making it a competitive drill.)

The defender attacks the ball carrier and tackles him. The defender's goal is to keep the ball carrier from crossing the goal line. The drill ends when any of the following occur:

- The ball carrier crosses the goal line.
- The tackler drives the ball carrier back a few yards.
- The tackler knocks the ball carrier out of bounds.
- There is an extended stalemate that lasts longer than four seconds.
- The players go to the ground.

We want players to stay on their feet in this drill, but if they do accidentally go to the ground, end the drill immediately. This is a great crossover drill that allows the offense to compete against the defense. We like to keep score in this drill and offer some sort of reward to the winners.

10 Most Common Mistakes in the Strike Phase

Table 4.1 lists the most common technical errors made in the strike phase of tackling and the best drills for correcting those errors. After the table, I've provided some tips and coaching cues that can be used to correct mistakes as well.

TABLE 4.1 Common Mistakes in the Strike Phase and Corrective Drills

Mistake	Corrective drills
Tackler is too high	Eyes mirror ball level drill
Tackler hits up too soon	Third and goal drill
Tackler's feet stop on contact	Goalpost strike and drive Strike from pre-contact position with resistance band Tackling sled
Tackler waits for the ball carrier instead of attacking and initiating contact	Third and goal drill
Tackler does not clamp down and grab cloth	Clamp finish position hold Uppercut and clamp drill Spin drill Goalpost strike and drive

(continued)

Table 4.1 *(continued)*

Mistake	Corrective drills
Tackler does not thrust his hips through the ball carrier	Strike up from knee Strike and drive on handshield Strike handshield from knees Strike player from knees Superman drill without arms (hips) Superman drill with arms (hips) Splatter drill Strike and drive
Tackler turns sideways or isn't squared up	Strike and drive
Tackler does not sink the uppercuts and clamp deeply enough	Uppercut and clamp drill Goalpost strike and drive Spin drill
Tackler horizontally wraps his arms instead of ripping up with the arms	Strike and drive on handshield Strike handshield from knees Strike player from knees Superman drill with arms Strike up from knee drill Strike and drive
Tackler's head is down	All tackling drills

Tackler Is Too High

The tackler must sink his hips and get his eyes at ball level before striking. The tackler's descent is done through hip hinge, not knee bend. His torso angle should never drop below a 35-degree angle. Athletes need to work on hip mobility all year to ensure that they can get into the proper pre-contact position. Emphasizing a proper pre-contact position in drill work is paramount. The best drill for teaching tacklers to get low is the eyes mirror ball level drill.

Tackler Hits Up Too Soon

The tackler should not bring his hips and arms into the tackle until he's close enough to step on the ball carrier's feet. The timing of the strike usually improves with increased repetitions in tackling drills in which the ball carrier and tackler start from greater than 2 yards apart (e.g., strike and drive from increased distances or with an agility movement added prior to contact).

Tackler's Feet Stop on Contact

Emphasize knee drive and accelerating the feet after contact. We frequently yell "feet, feet, feet" after contact is made during drills. Most of the tackling drills in the progression provide opportunities to develop leg drive and running the feet through contact, although three of our favorites are the goalpost strike and drive, strike from pre-contact position with resistance bands, and tackling sled.

Tackler Waits for the Ball Carrier

The tackler needs to attack and initiate contact. Coaches need to develop an attack mentality in their defensive players by constantly preaching that there are no free yards for the offense. A phrase my high school coach used that stuck with me was "Be the hammer, not the nail."

Use the lines on the field during tackling drills to show players where contact was made relative to where they started. Contact should be made at least at the halfway mark between the ball carrier's and tackler's starting points. The third and goal drill is a great drill for teaching defenders how to attack the ball carrier.

Tackler Does Not Clamp Down and Grab Cloth

Players must secure their tackles by grabbing jersey and clamping down on the ball carrier. Failure to do so will result in inconsistent tackling. We preach that there is no shame in getting run over, but there is shame in letting go. Developing upper-body strength, especially grip strength, will significantly improve a tackler's ability to secure his clamp. The best drills for developing the clamp are clamp finish position hold, uppercut and clamp drill, spin drill, and goalpost strike and drive.

Tackler Does Not Thrust His Hips Through the Ball Carrier

Tacklers who have the ability to explosively bring their hips through contact are able to generate greater force when they strike. Their tackles are more likely to generate knockbacks, create turnovers, and change the momentum of a game.

This problem is easily identifiable: if there is a substantial amount of space between the tackler's hips and the ball carrier, the tackler isn't striking with maximal force. Emphasizing a violent double-uppercut arm action and making players sky their eyes after contact will significantly improve their ability to extend their hips forcefully when they hit.

Athletes should focus on improving explosive hip power during off-season strength and conditioning programs. Hip mobility should be worked on year-round. The best drills for developing explosive hips: strike up from knees, strike and drive on handshield, strike handshield from knees, strike player from knees, Superman drill with arms (hips), Superman drill without arms (hips), splatter drill, and strike and drive. The strike and drive drill is also the best drill for identifying this problem.

Tackler Turns Sideways or Isn't Squared Up

When a tackler turns sideways to shoulder check the ball carrier, he can't wrap up and secure a clamp. This leads to missed tackles. Tacklers are more vulnerable to jukes made by the ball carrier when they aren't squared up. Almost all of the drills in this chapter stress striking with the chest and the front of the shoulder pads from a squared-up position. Exposing athletes to numerous repetitions of the strike and drive drill will usually resolve this issue.

Tackler Does Not Sink Uppercuts and the Clamp Deeply Enough

When players make this mistake, we jokingly tell them that they have T-rex arms. Tacklers must attempt to get their pinkies to touch behind the ball carrier's upper back when striking. Sinking the clamp deeply secures the tackle and allows the tackler to strike with his chest and the front of the shoulder pads. Some drills to teach players to sink their clamp deep include the uppercut and clamp drill, goalpost strike and drive, and the spin drill.

Tackler Wraps Instead of Rips

When the tackler horizontally wraps with the arms (i.e., hugging) instead of ripping up, it leads to a head-down posture and is an opposing force to the upward hip thrust required. Teach athletes to rip up their arms with a violent double-uppercut motion when hitting. When we see players using a horizontal wrapping motion, we remind them that they aren't trying to hug their grandmother when they tackle. The rip-up action of the arms facilitates a head-up posture and helps bring the hips through the ball carrier. The best drills for developing explosive hips are strike and drive on handshield, strike handshield from knees, strike player from knees, Superman drill with arms, strike up from knee, and strike and drive.

Tackler's Head Is Down

Keeping the top of the head out of contact is the number-one priority when teaching tackling. Tacklers must keep their heads and eyes up for safety and performance. We emphasize this key coaching point with "Lead with the chin and chest and strike with the chest." Another popular cue is "See what you hit."

Never allow a player to advance through the tackling progression until he can clearly and consistently demonstrate the ability to keep his head up when tackling. All of the tackling drills stress this critical coaching point.

ADDITIONAL CONSIDERATIONS

The tackling techniques and drills outlined in this chapter are an essential part of coaching, but they are just the tip of the iceberg. Tackling drill progressions advance well beyond what was discussed in this chapter to address the wide range of situational tackles that can arise in a game (e.g., open field or shimmy tackle, profile or angle tackle, gator roll tackle, sideline tackle, etc.). The emergence of spread offenses in recent years has forced defenses to make more tackles in space. This is especially true on our larger Canadian fields. Additionally, a greater emphasis on kicking and punting in the Canadian game demands that extra attention is paid to the specialized tackling techniques used when covering kicks. Simply drilling the basic form tackle in a confined area is not enough to prepare athletes for competition.

The majority of our coaching for situational tackles occurs during position work or special-teams periods. The types of tackles a defensive lineman makes in a game are noticeably different than the types of tackles a corner has to make. As a result, coaches should devote positional drill time accordingly. Situational tackles that overlap all positions (e.g., angle or profile tackle, gator roll tackle) can be drilled during defensive tackling circuits that all positional groups participate in.

Tackling circuits are a great way to maximize repetitions in a short amount of time. We try to schedule at least two tackling circuits per week. Usually we divide the defense into three groups (e.g., defensive line, linebackers, defensive backs) and have them rotate through three drill stations. Each station typically lasts around three minutes. We have approximately 10 drills that we choose from for our weekly tackling circuits. Table 4.2 shows a sample circuit.

Another crucial element of tackling success is pursuit. All great tackling teams are also great pursuit teams. In fact, great pursuit can mask or compensate for poor tackling. Defenses that have the ability to swarm the ball carrier and gang-tackle will typically record more tackles for losses, create more turnovers, and have fewer big plays run against them. Players must have a strong understanding of angles, leverage, and assignments for a defense to excel in pursuit. That being said, the most important factors for determining success in pursuit are team speed and hustle.

TABLE 4.2 Sample Tackling Circuit

Station	Drill
1	Goalpost strike and drive
2	Spin drill
3	Gator roll tackle

CONCLUSION

In closing, I'd like to reemphasize the importance of teaching tackling using safe and fundamentally sound drill progressions. Beginning the tackling teaching progression with the act of striking allows coaches to stress the importance of keeping the top of the head out of contact. Additionally, strike fundamentals provide a solid foundation for tackling technique, a foundation that carries over to numerous situational tackles. Tackling is a complex athletic skill that requires tremendous attention to detail and extensive drill work to master. Teaching players how to tackle properly will improve your team's performance and it will significantly reduce the risk of injury.

INDIVIDUAL SKILLS AND TEAM TACTICS

CHAPTER

5

The Running Game

Neil Lumsden

When you look at Canadian football, the running game is a big part of championship football teams. That's the case at any level of play, and in any region of this great country. Given that most of Canada starts to get a bit chilly and wet in October, ball control is a vital strategy that has been implemented as far back as I can remember. Weather conditions aside, the run game should be a vital part of your offensive game plan because of what it offers to your overall team success. It is always tough for an offensive team to have success in difficult conditions, but if you run the ball effectively, you have a better chance to control the pace of the game, wear down the defense, set up your play-action game, and gain other important tactical advantages.

CANADIAN FOOTBALL AND THE RUNNING GAME

Some coaches south of the border have referred to Canadian football as a pass-happy game. I like to think of it as run-and-gun football. It's an explosive game that can change in a matter of seconds and that needs athletes at every position. The old expression "If you live by the sword (the passing game), you'll die by the sword (incompletions and interceptions)" can still be heard across the country, usually echoed by fans of losing teams with a pass-happy coordinator. So how do you fix that? Carry a different sword—the running game. Football is like the music business: there are plenty of styles and artists who present a wide range of music, but the one style that lives on is rock and roll. The rock and roll of Canadian football is the running game: dynamic, reliable, and incredibly entertaining. Establishing a successful running game is the key foundation to your offense and is now more than ever complementary to your passing attack. The two together will create big plays whether the ball is handed off or delivered through the air.

The installation of synthetic field surfaces over the past 10 years has dramatically cut the concern of having to play on a field in poor condition. But the turning of the weather in Canada hasn't changed, and that means a solid running game is vital to team success.

RUNNING-GAME STRUCTURE IN MODERN OFFENSES

The offensive system should have the flexibility to adapt and be complementary to the athletes' skills. If you are able to recruit players, target and secure players to fit your system. If you're in a situation that is not recruiting-based, such as high school, rep, or house league football, your system needs to be flexible enough to fit the skill level of your athletes. An effective and complementary running game should be able to attack a defense in a multitude of ways. It is no longer only about outmanning or strong-arming a defensive unit; it's about putting a segment of the defense in a situation in which players have to make split-second decisions based on the formation and the action between the tailback and quarterback that create mismatches. An example of this is a run-pass option play, called a zone read by some coaches.

The ace tailback with a five-receiver set, having evolved from the two-back set, is now common. But I am happy to see that the tight end and fullback still find their way into a number of offensive sets. Spreading out the defense—not only with offensive linemen splits, but with motion and receiver sets—can really put a defense in a bind, and from there weaknesses and mismatches can be exploited. The fullback in the two-man backfield set has really been a victim in the metamorphosis of the passing game. We now see the H-back play a very large role in the offensive design. The H-back is really a hybrid of the fullback, tight end, and wide receiver, and when the right player is identified, he can really serve as a difference maker in the running game. The H-back's skill set demonstrates toughness, great feet, and agility. The H-back possesses a physical stature and strength that will allow him to block a defensive end or linebacker, while having the quickness and ball-catching skills of a wide receiver. He can even line up as a fullback and lead block for the tailback, so the H-back truly is a jack-of-all-trades in offensive football skills.

I do not think the running game should be limited to either a one- or two-back set, and the H-back can give you the option of multiple sets with the same play. The tailback comes in all shapes and sizes, and it has been proven that, at the pro level, this player can be a 6'2", 225-pound player with great vision, feet, speed, and agility, or the diminutive 5'8", 160-pound guy who can make you miss in a phone booth.

In many cases, I find that the tailback position in youth football is the most undercoached position on the field when it comes to blocking techniques, steps, defensive sets, and running routes. Coaches often take the fastest, most instinctive player, give him the ball on almost every play, and let him go. The development of this position should start with learning techniques, ball security, footwork, and body position, as well as understanding what the offensive line does on each and every play. Some coaches might think this material can be introduced and worked on in training camp and then omitted in the regular season. Not so. Watch a great running team in their individual periods at practice, and you'll see the running back coach drill the basic steps and pass protection techniques every day. The running back in Canadian football must also be very skilled when it comes to pass protection, and like all the other elements of the game, technique is very important and must be coached and practiced.

CHOOSING A RUNNING GAME PHILOSOPHY

Coaches come from varied backgrounds and tend to gravitate to the running system they either played in or coached in, but the good ones continue to advance their knowledge by attending clinics and taking advantage of guest coaching opportunities with programs at a higher level. The coaching at the U Sports level is second to none, not only at the head coach level but at the position coach level. I strongly recommend that high school, rep, house league, or beginning coaches contact the local university and ask about any opportunity to be a guest coach. There are also some tremendous coaching tools, programs, and seminars offered by Football Canada and the provincial football associations. If you're a coach who wants to get better and help make a difference in the lives of those who play the game, register for a National Coaching Certification Program course or a coaching clinic.

Choosing how to incorporate the running game into your offense is a complex decision and requires that you look at the whole picture of your offense. To decide on the type of running game you want to employ, you must first understand the types of runs you can employ.

INSIDE RUN VERSUS OUTSIDE RUN

Typically, the inside run attacks the defense between the tackles, and that can be done in a variety of ways using the ace set, two backs, or ace with the fullback or H-back in motion to give different looks. The outside run attacks the defense outside the defensive end and stretches the field horizontally. The outside run uses the same formation and personnel as the inside run.

All running plays require great technique from the tailbacks when it comes to the lead step sequence from the stance. This needs to be coached with the backs every practice during either an individual period or an offensive installation period. All of the running plays that follow have the tailback leaving on the snap count; no early motion or steps are required.

Search Series (Inside Run)

The target of the attack is between the tackles (figure 5.1). Though it can look like a straight power or lead run, the zone-blocking technique employed gives the ball carrier a number of options with or without the lead back.

One of the main keys to success in the search series is that the tailback sets his depth with his heels 7 yards from the line of scrimmage and takes the lead step to his landmark, which is targeted at the middle of the tackle's rear. This first step is

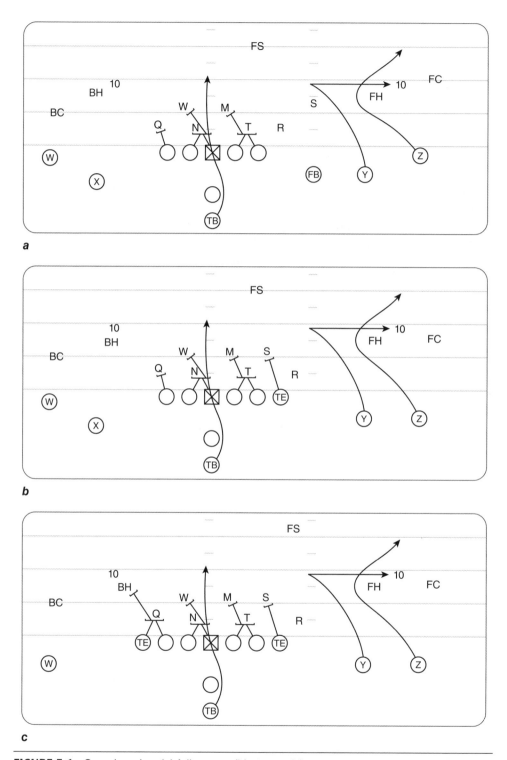

FIGURE 5.1 Search series: (a) full or ace, (b) strong, (c) cannon.

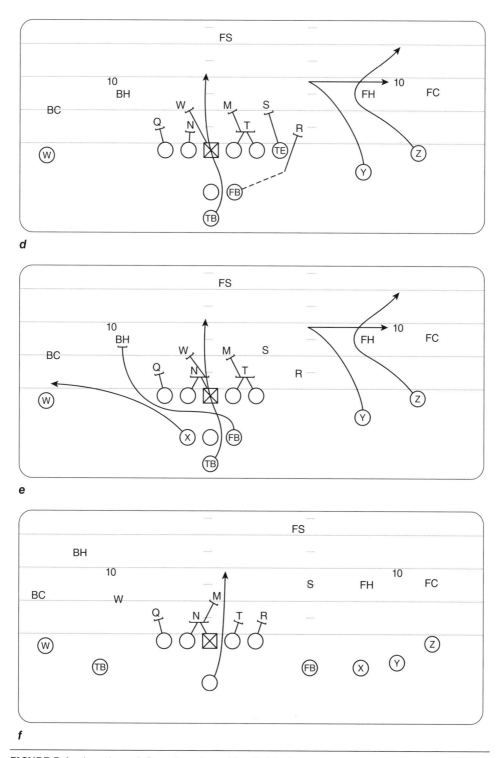

FIGURE 5.1 (*continued*) Search series: (d) tuff, (e) diamond search, (f) gryphon QB search.

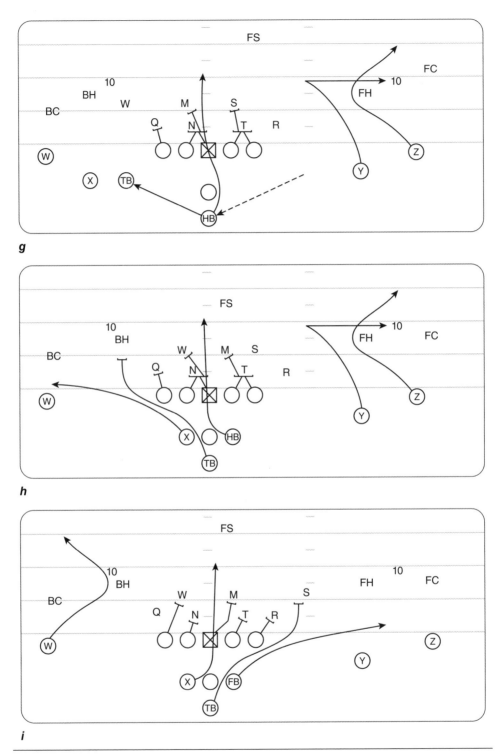

FIGURE 5.1 (*continued*) Search series: (g) ace hammer search, (h) diamond hammer search, (i) diamond axe search.

the key so that the tailback's hips and shoulders are almost square to the line of scrimmage once the handoff is complete. This body position allows the tailback to make an effective cut with his outside foot into three potential zones. The mechanics of this cut are vital because, once the decision is made, the cut is executed with the outside leg. That means the result translates into a power step, not just a change of direction.

The search series looks very much like a power run, but the options for the tailback are expanded based on early success at the initial point of attack. Once the Mac linebacker and defensive tackle react to the flow of the tailback, options for a cutback open up (figure 5.2). The quarterback must also follow through on his play-action fake to hold the defensive end and to develop the play-action pass progression.

Using an ace back formation presents an opportunity to really create some running lanes for the tailback, and in the next step of the play progression, the

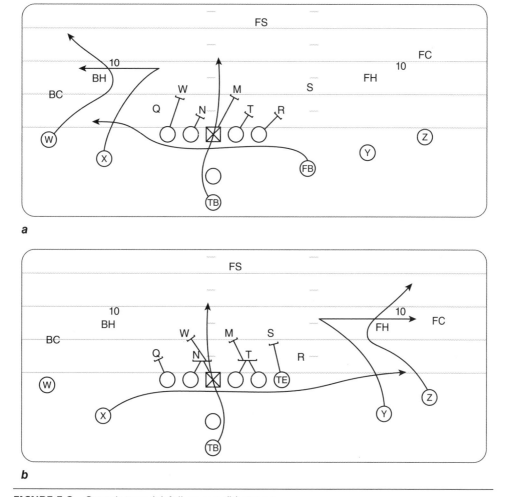

FIGURE 5.2 Search trap: (a) full or ace, (b) strong.

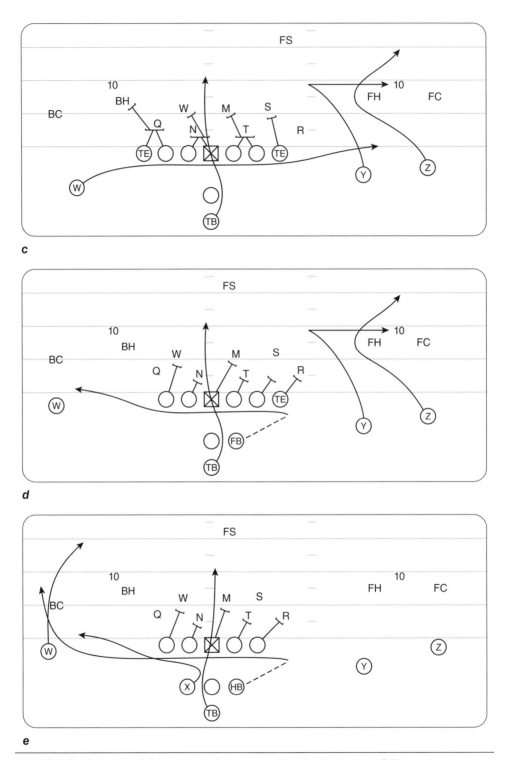

FIGURE 5.2 (*continued*) Search trap: (c) cannon, (d) tuff, (e) diamond S.T.

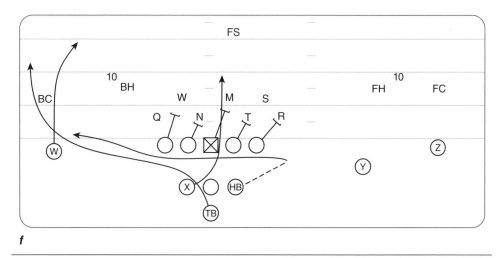

FIGURE 5.2 *(continued)* Search trap: (f) diamond axe S.T.

play-action backside to W and X and the throwback option to X can really open up. The same can be said for the two-back set with the X motion to the boundary and Y running the post on the play-action throwback.

Power Weak or Strong From Ace Set (Inside Run)

Again, the tailback needs to be exact with the lead step. It is the same as the search step, with the heels at 7 yards from the line of scrimmage. It is important to note that timing with the fullback or H-back's motion and arriving to the block-point landmark is key to the success of the play (figure 5.3). If the tailback too soon arrives at the landmark, the middle of the B gap, he loses his leverage point and blocking angle for the kick out; if he arrives late, the defensive end can keep his leverage on the perimeter and close on the tailback.

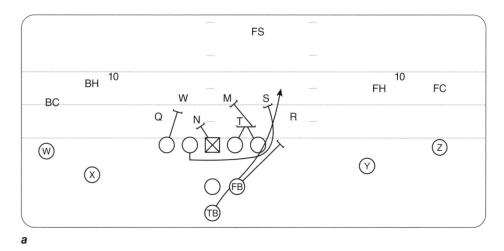

FIGURE 5.3 Power: (a) full.

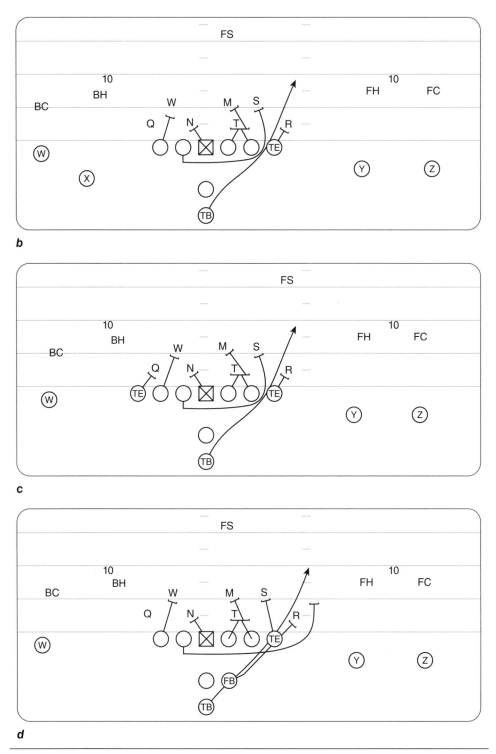

FIGURE 5.3 (*continued*) Power: (b) strong, (c) cannon, (d) tuff.

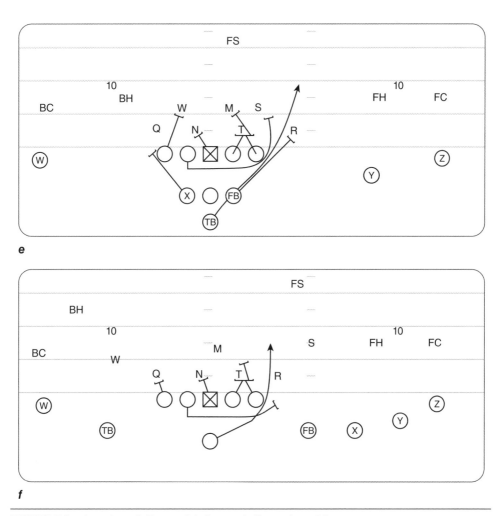

FIGURE 5.3 (*continued*) Power: (e) diamond, (f) gryphon QB power.

The tailback's read is off the kick-out block with a vertical cut, and then he must gain some width as he gets into the open field (figure 5.4). Timing is vital for the tailback as well because his lead step will force the defensive end to honor his perimeter responsibility and give the fullback or H-back that split second to cross the defensive end's face and kick out the end.

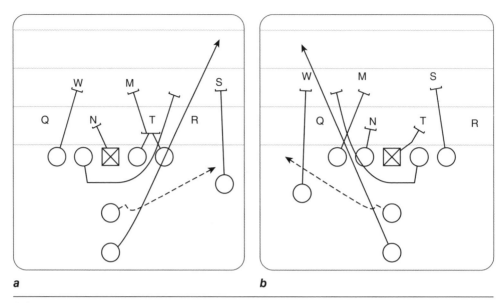

FIGURE 5.4 Power read: (a) 43 strong, (b) 43 weak.

If the defensive end and linebacker have a stunt on and the end crosses the offensive tackle's face hard into the B gap, the tackle blocks the defensive end down, and the lead blocker (fullback or H-back) looks for the linebacker and kicks him out (figure 5.5).

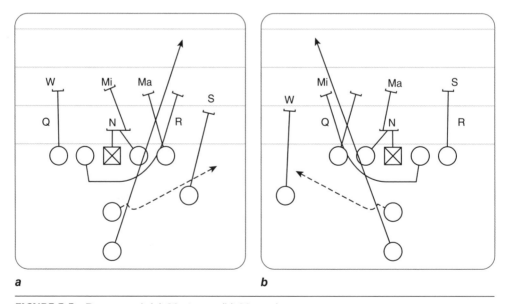

FIGURE 5.5 Power read: (a) 30 strong, (b) 30 weak.

Frontside

Tackle: Zone double #2 to #3.

Guard: Zone double #2 to #3.

Tailback: Open to the 3 gap and follow the pull and read blocks.

Fullback or halfback: Block the linebacker or player lined up on top of you.

Wide receivers (W, X, Y, Z): Tagged routes.

Quarterback: Pop hips to playside 3 gap, riding the tailback. Read the frontside defensive end; if he crashes, pull with the run or pass option.

Backside

Tackle: If #6 tries to cross your face, take him; if not, climb to #5.

Centre: Down block #4.

Guard: Skip pull up into the playside hole and lead onto most dangerous man.

Wide receivers (W, X, Y, Z): Block most dangerous man.

When the play is run to the strong (wide) side, the weak-side guard pulls up into the hole off the tail of the down block by the tackle, looking for the Sam linebacker. The fullback or H-back has the same assignment with the kick-out block on the defensive end.

Stretch Series (Outside Run)

I hear the word *finesse* used a fair bit when talking about the execution of the stretch play (figure 5.6), and I think that comes from the way it's blocked. Zone blocking is not often referred to as an aggressive style of blocking, but it is. To me, the stretch play is the ultimate power run that could rival the old Lombardi sweep that the Packers employed so successfully in the 1960s.

The objective of this play is simply to attack the edge of the defense and make them defend the wide side of the field. The landmark or target for the tailback is a yard outside the tight end, where the fullback/H-back and tight end are creating a double team. A lead step is key; otherwise the tailback gets too tight to the landmark and will be unable to make an effective and explosive cut. The tailback should have his heels at 8 yards, not 7 yards, from the line of scrimmage, and he needs to use controlled speed on his path to the landmark. Once the decision is made, the tailback explodes up into the lane, and at the linebacker level gains width on a 45-degree angle.

Again, this is a play that can be run from multiple sets for diversity. The tight end and fullback or H-back motion to the play side signals the defense "Here we come; try to stop us." Once the defense adjusts to that set, it's not over—that adjustment plays into the tailback's option read for the cutback. The offensive line and the point-of-attack blockers must stay on their defenders. A quick vertical cut

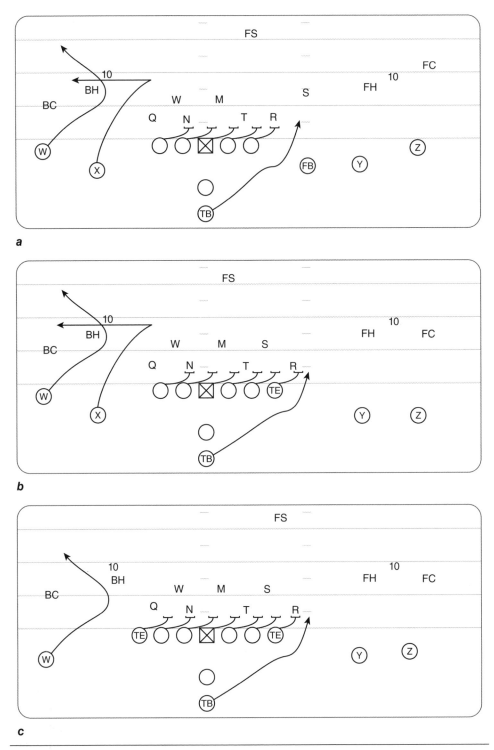

FIGURE 5.6 Stretch series: (a) full or ace, (b) strong, (c) cannon.

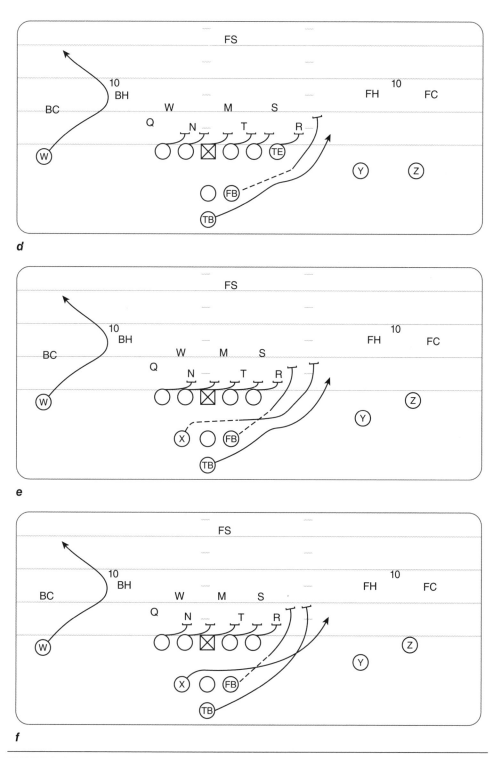

FIGURE 5.6 (*continued*) Stretch series: (d) tuff, (e) diamond stretch, (f) diamond axe stretch.

by the tailback as the play expands in width can result in a very effective run. When the play is run without the tight end, some of the blocking responsibilities change, but the rules for the tailback stay the same regarding steps and landmarks. Discipline and hard work are the main ingredients for success on all fronts when running the ball, especially in zone blocking scenarios.

CONCLUSION

No matter how you incorporate the running game or which schemes you use, running the ball is a priority—even in the highly pass-oriented Canadian version of football. My hope is that this brief summary provides some insight and possibly a different approach to the running game. Many of the formulas and principles presented have been used by some of the highest-powered U Sports and CFL teams, both past and present. It would be easy to cite specific accomplishments of running backs who have had these plays in their playbooks, but football has never been and should never be about one or two players. This is the ultimate team sport, played and coached by passionate and emotional people; it is an examination of one's character and will to succeed for all the right reasons. I thank my lucky stars for what the game has given me, both on and off the field, and now it's my turn, and your turn, to pass on what we have learned and will continue to learn to the next group of kids who choose to play our game.

6

The Passing Game

Jay Prepchuk

The quarterback position is one of the most demanding positions in all of sport. The quarterback must communicate with the coach, call the proper formation, play, and snap count, and manage a group of 11 other players, all while getting the play off in only 20 seconds! Once at the line of scrimmage, the quarterback must quickly analyze the defense and attempt to run a successful play. The coach's job is to properly prepare the quarterback for success. This is a challenging task, whether you coach flag football, high school, CJFL, U Sport, or in the Canadian Football League. This chapter will assist you in effectively coaching the quarterback and give you some ideas to run a potent and efficient passing game.

CHOOSING AND DEVELOPING QUARTERBACKS

Developing quarterbacks is a year-round job. Not only should they be doing the regular workouts with their teammates (lifting weights, speed work, etc.) but they also should continue to improve their throwing mechanics, become familiar with any changes made in the offense, and study the opponent's defenses. Sometimes doing all these things just isn't possible. Like all athletes, the quarterback must put a priority on family and academics. Many quarterbacks are multisport athletes (which I have always promoted), so their time to train in the off-season may be limited. I strongly recommend that quarterbacks attend camps with a specialized quarterbacks coach. Team coaches should attend along with their quarterbacks so the coaches can learn the position as well.

Choosing the quarterback is not always an easy task. At the university, junior, and pro levels, coaches have the luxury of recruiting a quarterback to fit the needs of the offense. Coaches at the lower levels do not have the good fortune of recruiting a quarterback, so they must coach-up and develop their own players based on who is on the team. There are many variables and questions to be answered when making this decision. Do you choose the player based on his physical attributes, such as arm strength and quickness, or do you look at intangibles such as coachability and leadership? I feel it is a combination of both physical and mental characteristics. Consider the following characteristics of a top quarterback.

Commitment

The quarterback needs to be committed to the football program for the team to be successful. The committed quarterback will do what it takes to be successful. Working out regularly, studying film, throwing in the off-season, and going to football camps are just a few things that a committed player will do.

Leadership

The quarterback does not have to be a rah-rah type of person, but should have strong leadership skills. These characteristics can be taught to any athlete. Being a leader these days is about giving, about having the attitude "What can I do to make my teammates better?" and "What can I do to make this team better?" A regular meeting with all of your captains (including your quarterback) is an important way to keep in tune with the pulse of the team.

Over the years, I have found that a player's peers may be more powerful than a coach. An example of strong leadership may be having your quarterback welcome a new player to your program by inviting him to a team function, or encourage a player who is having a bad day on the football field. A pat on the back or some positive words goes a long way to making other players feel better about themselves.

Attitude

Whether a quarterback likes it or not, he is constantly under the scrutiny of others. Teammates, fans, teachers, and scouts alike are constantly focusing on the quarterback. When a quarterback makes a mistake, everybody sees it. A quarterback with a positive attitude will go a long way to building a football team that can succeed through adversity. Sooner or later, every quarterback is going to have a bad play—throw an interception, get sacked, or fumble the ball away. The way the quarterback reacts to these moments are the real revelation of character and attitude. Again, teaching a positive attitude is something that a coach should attempt to focus on with all players. Enthusiasm is contagious!

Passion for the Game

The quarterback must have a love for the game, and must be willing to learn the intricacies of the game and game strategy. Quarterbacks have technological advantages these days, as they have a variety of tools. They can learn the game from playing video games, watching football on the NFL Network 24/7, or using online game-film services. Players really have football at their fingertips at any time. The quarterback must fully understand the rules of the game, especially when it comes down to the clock in the last three minutes of a half (see chapter 16 for more on clock management).

Fundamentals

Like in any sport, mastering the fundamentals of the position is paramount to succeeding. Depending on the offense, there are many skills to master: taking a snap from centre, handing the ball off properly, executing an option or shovel pass, and such fundamentals as throwing the football from a stationary position and throwing the ball on the run.

Knowledge of the Game

Quarterbacks must not only understand their own offenses and the opposing defenses, but also the rules of the game of football. The timing rules in Canadian football can be extremely tricky; as Coach Marc Trestman says, "There are two games to be played: one is 57 minutes long, and the other is the last 3 minutes of a game." The quarterback must be alert at all times and pay attention to defensive personnel, alignments, substitutions, the play clock, the game clock, and down and distance. At a high school semifinal playoff game at BC Place one year, the quarterback spiked the ball to stop the clock; little did he know that it was fourth down (British Columbia high schools play U.S. rules)!

QUARTERBACK CHALLENGES IN CANADIAN FOOTBALL

Playing quarterback in Canadian football definitely has its challenges. With only 3 downs to make 10 yards, the quarterback really has to be a playmaker.

Another major challenge is the weather. When faced with wind and cold and poor playing surfaces, the quarterback must focus on time management and must also know his limitations. With only 20 seconds to get the ball into play, there is not a lot of room for error. Once a play is completed, the quarterback must quickly communicate with the coach for the next play to be run. This takes discipline, since a quarterback usually wants to watch the completion of a play and often will congratulate a teammate for making a great catch or busting a long run. It is a luxury for fields to have a 20-second clock in both end zones. If there isn't a 20-second clock, the quarterback should communicate with the referees as to which one of them will have his hand up once there's five seconds left on the play clock.

Field size is also a major factor for a quarterback, as throwing a wide-side-out pattern is a tremendous challenge. Another challenge facing quarterbacks in the Canadian game is the lack of quarterback coaches. This is by no means a criticism of Canadian football programs; it is just a reality. Many programs have a difficult time fielding enough coaches to coach the other positions, let alone having a quarterbacks-only coach. I do feel it is advantageous for a quarterback to have a coach who has played the position before.

The quarterback position is one of the most unique and demanding positions in all of sport. Unfortunately, not a lot of Canadian quarterbacks play professional football. Many great athletes playing at a high level of football do not continue playing the quarterback position because they know the difficulty of playing at the pro level. Instead they switch to a receiver or defensive back position in the hopes of fulfilling their dreams of playing pro football. Not many athletes have the talent and ability of a Mathieu Bertrand, a CFL fullback who started as a quarterback with the Laval Rouge et Or.

In a personal conversation, Shawn Olson, the former head coach of the University of British Columbia Thunderbirds, and I discussed the fact that a key challenge of playing quarterback in Canada is getting your head around how these four things affect the play at the position:

1. 3 downs or 2 downs to get 10 yards,
2. the size of the field, especially the width,
3. the extra defender normally in the defensive secondary, and
4. the effect that motion from multiple receivers has on defenses and, in turn, reads.

These rule differences, in isolation or combination, drastically affect the way you have to approach the game as a quarterback. For example, the width of the field makes arm strength or moving the quarterback essential if a team is to access the 12 yards outside the numbers to the wide side of the field. The two playable downs really force a quarterback to get the ball down the field at some point for chunks of yardage if the offense is consistently going to put up points. The extra receiver and defensive back even up the field for a quarterback, and defenses don't necessarily declare a strong side of their secondary, presenting a much more balanced approach to the skill set of the back-end players, equivalent to a nickel or dime defense in the American game. The amount and use of motion in the Canadian game puts extra pressure on postsnap reads for a quarterback in Canada, forcing him to recognize coverage and get his feet set a little later.

In a personal conversation, Travis Lulay, the quarterback for the BC Lions, who played his high school football in Oregon and his college ball at Montana State University, described a number of challenges to playing quarterback in Canadian football. First, managing a game with three downs takes a completely different mindset. There are fewer opportunities to waste a down, so you have to think twice about throwing the backside go route too often or you will be punting all day. That being said, you still have to take some chances to make a play, because maintaining long drives is tougher to do. So you have to be selective about when to take chances, and you have to make them count when you do.

The motion rules give you tons of flexibility on the offensive side of the ball. You can soften up defensive backs with speed downhill, and you can run rub routes and gain presnap leverage more effectively. The defense has to move around more presnap to adjust to motion, which means the quarterback has to rely more on information gathered after the snap in this league.

The field size definitely plays a part in learning the 12-man game. Most guys think that a bigger field will mean bigger passing windows. What people fail to realize is that the hashes are wider in this league, meaning the boundary side of the field is similar in dimension to that of 11-man ball, and the side of the field that has bigger windows also requires more distance to access those open spots. Passes to the wide side of the field must be thrown on time and accurately because the ball is in the air long enough that the defender can see it and react.

The other thing we discussed, one that many people don't think about, is that— because the ratio of pass plays to run plays is generally higher in Canada—the defensive linemen are much more pass rush–oriented. They pin their ears back and rush passing lanes more often than in 11-man football. So the quarterback takes a few more hits in Canada. You have to be tough and stand in there to throw!

READING DEFENSES

This is one of the most difficult tasks a quarterback has. It can also be one of the most difficult things that a football coach has to teach. Before a quarterback can learn to read defenses, he must fully understand how defenses operate. He must understand the responsibilities of each defender and be able to decipher the coverage. As a player, I spent countless hours visiting with the defensive coordinator to learn about the defensive side of the ball. We would go over the responsibilities and assignments of primarily the linebackers and defensive backs. I learned names of the pass drop zones so I could properly communicate with my offensive coordinator and be on the same page as he was. I would sit in on defensive player meetings to get the full grasp of what the defense was doing, and I had many discussions with my defensive teammates about their responsibilities.

Here are some suggestions to help your quarterback read defenses:

◆ *Do your homework.* Nothing beats proper preparation! Watch film and get the tendencies of the opponent's defense. What defense do they run on first and 10 when you have the ball on your 40-yard line? What are their favorite blitzes near their own goal line? What is their defensive philosophy: are they a pressure team or do they sit back and play a lot of zone coverage? I often do some research on the defensive coordinator to see what type of defense he has run in the past.

◆ *Check the defensive personnel.* How many defensive lineman do they have in? How many linebackers? How many defensive backs? Did they substitute a defensive back for a linebacker or a defensive lineman?

◆ *Start to set up and formulate part of your game plan based on mismatches.* Can you isolate a receiver or a running back on a linebacker who is a weaker cover player? Move your receivers and running backs around so you create mismatches.

◆ *At the line of scrimmage, the quarterback must quickly scan the defense.* Scan from left to right; are the defensive backs aligned evenly and are their eyes focused on the receivers? Do defensive backs follow the receivers across the formation when they go in motion? If so there is a good chance they are in man-to-man coverage.

If the defensive backs are staggered, there is a good chance they will be in zone coverage. Check the feet of the defensive backs: are they parallel or staggered? Often a defensive back squares his feet to the receiver if he is in man-to-man coverage. If the defensive back is head up with the receiver, that may also be a giveaway that he is playing man-to-man. Check the depth of the linebackers. Are they within 3 yards of the line of scrimmage? Are their feet staggered? Are their eyes focused on one of the offensive gaps or on one of the receivers or running backs or on the quarterback? If so, there is a good chance that one or more of them may be blitzing. The depth and the alignment of the free safety will tell you a lot about the coverage. During your week of preparation, you should try to determine what their alignment is when they play zone coverage or when they are in cover 1 or cover 0. In zone coverage, how does the free safety drop? Does he line up on the hash mark in some coverages and off the hash in other coverages? It is important to have your scout team simulate your opponent's coverage during your week of practice. If the free safety lines up 5 yards outside the hash mark and drops on a 45-degree angle to the field when your opponent plays cover 3, then make sure that your scout team safety does the same. Have your scout team study film to understand how your opponent plays various coverages.

◆ *In practice, run the passing plays with only one side of the receivers running the play.* It is less intimidating for the quarterback to read half of the scout defense, and it gets the receivers more action.

◆ *Make it simple for your quarterback!* Make it clear exactly who he is to read on each pass play.

◆ *In the game, have a coach in the press box who is able to see the drops of the linebackers and defensive backs.* If he sees a weakness in the secondary, make sure that he relays that information to the sidelines. Have that coach be in regular communication with the quarterback during the game.

CHOOSING AN OFFENSE

Many factors should be considered when deciding on the type of offense to implement in your program:

- How many players do you have on your team? Do you have enough to go 12-on-12 in practice? Do you have enough players for two platoons? If so, you have the luxury of having more time to work on your offense.

- How often do you practice? How often do you meet? Are you able to record practice and watch it with your coaches and players? Do you have rules on how many hours you can spend with your players per week?

- How many returning players do you have? If you have a lot of returning experienced players, you may be able to run a more intricate system. In our program we have three teams: a grade 8 team, a junior team (grades 9 and 10), and a senior team (grades 11 and 12). All of our coaches run basically the same system, so our grade 12 players have run the same system since the eighth grade.

- How many coaches do you have? Do you have a quarterback coach? Do you have coaches for the seven different positions?
- How is the weather in your area, especially in the late fall, around playoff time? What is your playing surface like? Is it artificial turf or natural grass? On the west coast, we have the challenge of the rain and thus wet fields when playing on natural grass. Do you have lights on your practice field? Sometimes it gets dark at 4 p.m.!
- What type of defenses do you usually play against? Do you see a lot of pressure defenses? Do you see a lot of man-to-man or zone defenses?
- Make sure that your pass plays stretch the defense vertically and horizontally with your routes.

These are just a few of the factors that a coach must consider when making a decision on what type of offense he implements.

The following sections focus on a few passing plays I have selected to attack any defense. Please note that I will be focusing more on the play and reads of the quarterback and not on the protection scheme, and so on. Feel free to incorporate motion with these plays.

Pass 30 Cross (Three-Step Drop; figure 6.1)

Offensive line: Block solid

TB: Check Will linebacker.

X and Z: Take outside release and run a three-step slant.

W and Y: Run flat route, make sure you go underneath the X and Z.

SB: Look hot, run seam route.

QB: Choose a side and determine which defender has the flat responsibility. For example, if you choose the boundary (narrow) side of the field (the

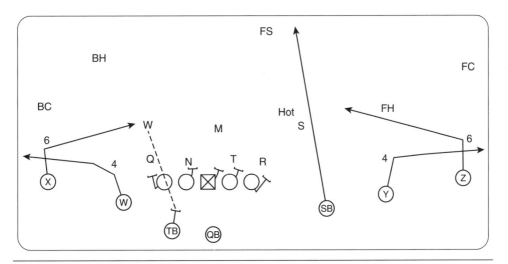

FIGURE 6.1 Trips RT Pass 30 Cross.

offensive left side in figure 6.1), which defensive back has the flat? Is the boundary cornerback (BC) playing cut coverage (corner in flat) or is the boundary halfback (BH) playing high/hold coverage (halfback in flat)? If you're throwing to the field (wide) side of the field, identify the flat defender and read his drop. If the flat defender flies out hard to the flat, look to hit the slant; if he does not, look to hit the W or Y on the flat route. If you choose to hit the slant route, do so before that route runs into the linebacker's drop. If you read man-to-man, work the mismatch you determined during the week and throw a strike!

Pass 30 Streak/Hook (Three-Step Drop; figure 6.2)

Offensive line: Block solid.

TB: Check Will linebacker.

X and Z: Hook at 6 yards; if you read man coverage or cut coverage, run a break-in.

W and Y: Look hot, run seam route inside defensive halfback. Be alert that you will probably get jammed by the halfback.

SB: Look hot, run seam route; bend it slightly in, attacking the free safety's shoulder closest to the middle of the field.

QB: On your presnap routine, you may find one of your inside receivers is open hot. If so, quickly throw a firm, hard pass just below the receiver's inside shoulder. If no one is open hot, pick a side and determine who the flat defender is. If, for example, you choose the wide side of the field and the field halfback (FH) is that flat player (which is the case in many coverages), then

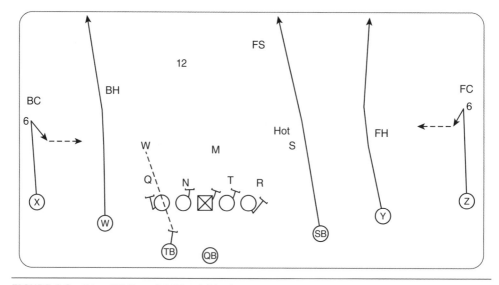

FIGURE 6.2 Trips RT Pass 30 Streak/Hook.

read his drop. Because halfbacks are taught to jam inside receivers who run vertical routes, they often do not get to the flat or get there late. If the halfback backpedals and runs with the inside receiver (W or Y), then look to hit X or Z, who has converted his hook route into a break-in. If the halfback flies to the flat and does not jam the inside receiver, throw a firm, hard pass to him once he clears the halfback. The quarterback must make sure that he does not lob this pass as the free safety (FS) comes into play. The quarterback must throw this pass before the X or Z run into linebackers taking their drops.

80/70 Corner/Out (Sprint Out; 80 Sprint Right; 70 Sprint Left; figure 6.3)

Offensive line: Sprint out protection.

TB: Waggle up and reach the rush end.

X and W: Run backside catch-up routes (for a catch-up route, the backside receivers, away from the quarterback's roll, run an in-breaking route to catch up to the quarterback, usually in or post routes).

SB: Take an inside release and run an 8-yard bang route.

Y: Run a 10-yard corner route; versus cut coverage, Y may curl to the outside.

Z: Run a 16-yard comeback route.

QB: Full sprint out; read the play-side corner. If the corner bites on the comeback route, then hit the corner route. If the corner drops deep (which he usually does in zone coverage), then hit the Z on the comeback route. If the field-side halfback (FH) drops underneath the comeback route, then look to the

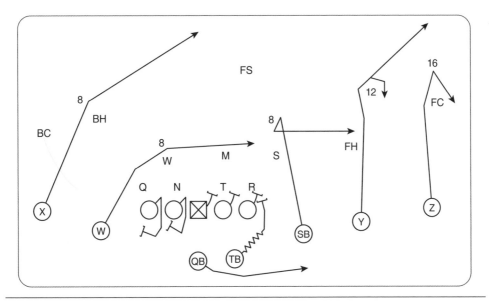

FIGURE 6.3 Trips RT 80/70 Corner/Out.

SB running the bang route. One phrase to use to remember the read on this play is "Read the corner, to throw the corner." If the free safety (FS) flies to the sprint-out side, then stop and hit the backside X on a post route. This is something the coach in the press box and the backside receivers should look for.

This play also may be run with a run fake (play-action pass).

80/70 Flood (Sprint Out; figure 6.4)

Offensive line: Sprint out protection.

TB: Waggle up and reach the rush end.

X and W: Run backside catch-up routes.

SB: Outside release, run a 10-yard corner route.

Y: 10-yard out route.

Z: Streak route.

QB: Full sprint out; read the defender covering the flat. If that defender (often the field halfback, FH) has a shallow drop and covers Y on the breakout, then look to hit the slotback (SB) on the corner route. If the flat defender drops deeper and covers the corner route, then look to hit Y on the breakout. If the free safety (FS) flies to the sprint outside, then stop and hit the backside X on a post route.

For this play to be successful, the Z receiver must sprint hard and run the play-side corner off.

This play also may be run with a run fake (play-action pass).

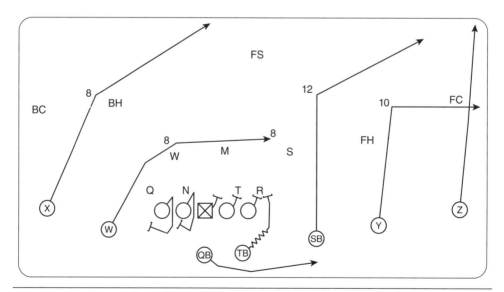

FIGURE 6.4 Trips RT 80/70 Flood.

50 Middle (Five-Step Drop; figure 6.5)

Offensive line: Five-step protection

TB: Check Will linebacker, swing.

X: Streak.

W: 8-yard break-in.

SB: 4-yard break-in; look hot.

Y: 12-yard break-in.

Z: 10-yard post.

QB: Five-step drop. Presnap read the free safety (FS); if he has moved up and looks to be playing man-to-man (cover 0), then look to hit the deep post to Z. Be alert for two more defenders blitzing on this coverage. If they are in zone coverage posture, read the Mac linebacker (M). If the defender blitzes, look to hit the slotback hot as he runs the break-in. If the Mac drops, read his depth. If he drops deep, look to hit the crossing slotback. If the Mac has a shallow drop, look to hit the crossing W receiver.

This can also be an effective play versus a cover 2 man-coverage scheme (two deep safeties), as the Y receiver is often open versus this coverage, especially if the offense is in a second-and-long situation. This is also a good pattern combination versus man-to-man coverage, as the defenders are often in a chase position. It is important for the quarterback to lead the receivers and not have them break stride so they have the opportunity to outrun the chasing defenders.

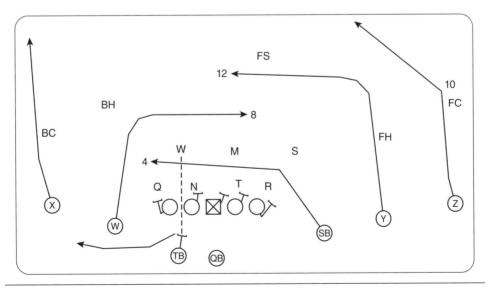

FIGURE 6.5 Trips RT Pass 50 Middle.

Pass 50 Seam In (figure 6.6)

Offensive line: Five-step drop protection

TB: Check Will linebacker, swing.

X and Z: 12-yard break-in.

W and Y: Seam route, release outside of the halfbacks.

SB: Fake bubble screen.

QB: Five-step drop. On the drop, read the free safety (FS). If FS drops straight back, then look to the wide side of the field and attempt to hit Y on the seam route. If the FS does not open, look to hit Z on the break-in route. If the field halfback (FH) takes the break-in away, look to hit the slotback on the bubble route. If the FS drops to the field, then immediately look to W running the seam route; if W is not open (the boundary halfback, BH, may be in cut coverage and have deep third responsibility), then look to X on his break-in.

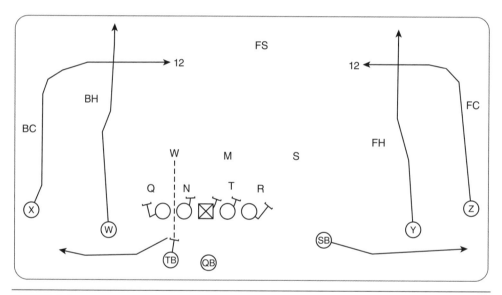

FIGURE 6.6 Trips RT Pass 50 Seam In.

Pass 50 Wheel (figure 6.7)

Offensive line: Five-step protection

TB: Check Will linebacker, swing.

X: 12-yard post; if boundary halfback (BH) drops deep (cut coverage), then convert to a 12-yard break-in.

Z: 12-yard post.

W and Y: Run an 8-yard wheel route.

SB: Run a 6-yard curl route.

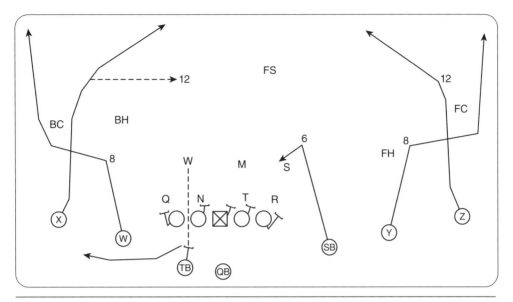

FIGURE 6.7 Trips RT Pass 50 Wheel.

QB: Five-step drop. Presnap read the free safety (FS); if he has moved up and looks to be playing man-to-man (cover 0), then look to hit the deep post to Z or X. The wheel route may also be open versus man-to-man coverage. If the FS drops straight back, look to hit Z on his post route with a firm, hard pass, so the FS is not able to make a play on the ball. If the Sam linebacker (S) drops deep and gets under the post route, then look to hit the slotback on his curl route. If your game preparation showed you that the field corner (FC) has a tendency to take a hard inside release to the field and follow the post on his drop, then you may want to look to the Y wheel route. If the FS drops to the field, look for the X post route. If he is covered by the boundary half (BH, playing cut coverage), then look to W on the wheel route.

SCREENS

Receiver screen plays (with pump options) can be very effective plays. For a screen play, your quarterback does not need to have a strong arm, and you do not need big, powerful offensive linemen. These are easy reads for the quarterback, and he will gain confidence as he runs these plays. Screen plays open the quarterback draw play, but still allow a deep threat. Screen plays open up the running game (zone read plays) and provide a play-action look.

Offensive linemen like running these plays because screen plays get them moving and give them a chance to hit some defensive backs! Screen plays provide a chance to tire out the defensive linemen.

Screen plays are easy plays for check-with-me or audibles. You can run these plays from a quads formation (4×1) to outman the defense if they do not adjust (play 12).

To run screen plays successfully, receivers must take pride in their blocking assignments. They also must be able to communicate effectively.

30 Double Bubble (figure 6.8)

Offensive line: Give the defensive linemen a shot and work upfield to linebackers, defensive backs, or both.

TB: Fake zone play, check Will linebacker.

X: Block most dangerous man (MDM), either the boundary corner (BC) or boundary halfback (BH).

Z: Block field halfback (FH).

Y: Block field corner (FC).

W and SB: Run bubble screen.

QB: Presnap read the Will (W) and Sam (S) linebackers. Determine which of the two is tighter to the ball. Take shotgun snap, fake zone run play, and throw to SB or W based on your presnap read.

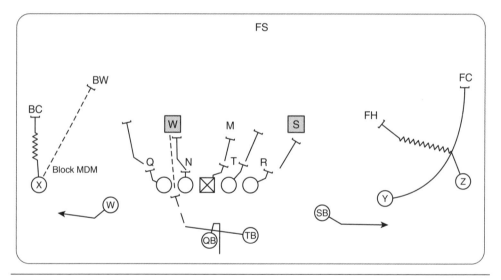

FIGURE 6.8 Trips RT 30 Double Bubble.

30 Double Bubble Pump (figure 6.9)

Offensive line: Block solid, do not release.

TB: Fake zone run play, check Will linebacker.

X and Y: Run at the corners, break down like you are going to block them, and sprint down the sideline (once you see the defender drive down on the bubble), ready to catch the pass.

Z: Run at the FH, break down like you are going to block him, and sprint up the hash mark and look back for the football.

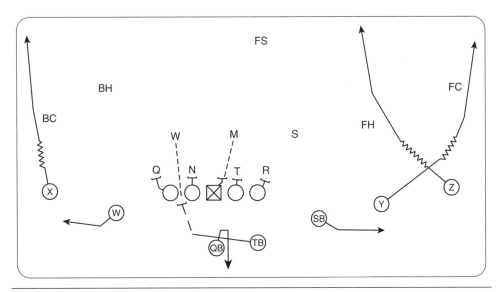

FIGURE 6.9 Trips RT 30 Double Bubble Pump.

W and SB: Run bubble route.

QB: Fake the zone play to the tailback (TB), pick a side, pump-fake to W or SB, and throw to X or Y. If the FS is in cover 0, then you have the option to hit Z up the hash mark.

Pass 30 X/Z Screen (figure 6.10)

Offensive line: Give the defensive linemen a shot and work upfield to the linebackers and/or defensive backs.

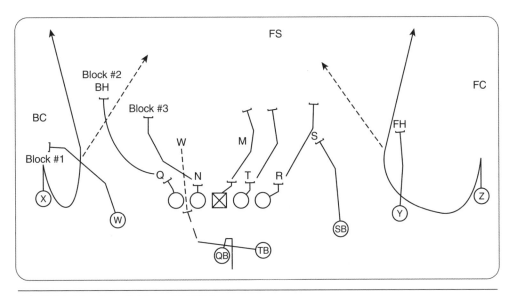

FIGURE 6.10 Trips RT Pass 30 X/Z Screen.

TB: Fake zone run play, check Will linebacker.

X and Z: Take three hard steps upfield and then work back to the quarterback; make the catch and burst upfield.

W: Block most dangerous man (MDM).

Y: Block most dangerous man (MDM).

SB: Block Sam linebacker.

QB: Presnap, read which side of the field has fewer defenders (read outside linebackers). Fake the zone play to the tailback (TB) and throw to the predetermined side. Throw a firm pass to X's or Z's upfield shoulder.

Pass 30 X/Z Screen Pump (figure 6.11)

Offensive line: Block solid, do not release.

TB: Fake zone run play, check Will linebacker.

X and Z: Run X/Z screen route.

W and Y: Run at the corners, break down as if you are going to block them, then sprint down the sidelines.

SB: Run at the FS, break down as if you are going to block him, then sprint upfield ready to catch the ball.

QB: Fake the zone play to the tailback (TB), pick a side, pump-fake to X or Z, and throw to W or Y. If the FS is in cover 0, then you have the option to hit the slotback (SB) up the seam.

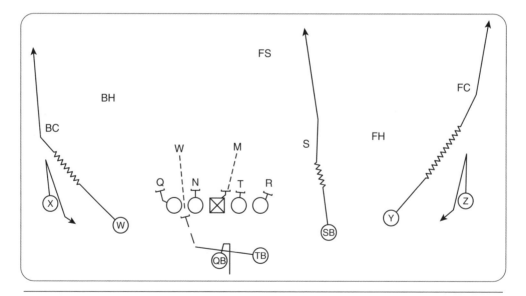

FIGURE 6.11 Trips RT Pass 30 X/Z Screen Pump.

Pass 30 Read Screen Quads Formation Wac Motion (figure 6.12)

Offensive line: Give the defensive linemen a shot and work upfield to linebackers and/or defensive backs.

TB: Fake zone, check Will linebacker.

X: Take three hard steps upfield and then work back to the quarterback; make the catch and burst upfield.

W: Motion across the formation and run bubble screen.

SB: Block Sam linebacker.

Y: Block field halfback (FH).

Z: Block field cornerback (FC).

QB: Motion W across, read the boundary halfback (BH); fake the zone play to tailback (TB). If the BH follows W or rotates to the quads side, then hit X; if the boundary cornerback (BC) stays on the boundary side, look to hit W on the bubble route.

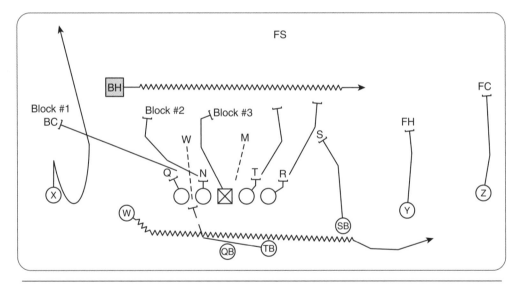

FIGURE 6.12 Pass 30 Read Screen Quads Formation Wac Motion.

CONCLUSION

At any level, playing quarterback or coaching the quarterback is a tremendous challenge. I hope that this chapter will assist you in determining who your quarterback will be, and has given you some ideas on developing this position. Our job as coaches is to give the quarterbacks confidence by putting them in positions where they can succeed. Keep things simple and sound, make this challenge a year-round process, and enjoy the journey!

CHAPTER

7

Offensive Play Calling

Scott Flory

Offensive play calling in football has so many aspects that it's hard to try to cover all the situations and scenarios that may present themselves. In this chapter I will give you my perspective, as both a coach and a player, regarding what helps bring about success on the football field.

I joined the University of Saskatchewan Huskies coaching staff in 2014, right after I retired from playing in the Canadian Football League for 15 years with the Montreal Alouettes. With the Huskies, I began as run game coordinator and offensive line coach and spent the year learning how to coach and formulate an offensive system. I took over as the play caller for the last third of the season in 2014 and then fully took over as offensive coordinator for the 2015 season. It was a great help to have the off-season to truly understand and formulate the offense, all the while thinking about the players first.

CREATING A SYSTEM

You have to have a foundation that is adaptable and that makes sense to both coaches and players. The coaches have to understand it to be able to teach it, and the players have to learn it to be able to execute it. The players are the ones who actually have to perform what you ask them to do, and the learning and understanding will happen faster with terminology that is consistent and makes sense to them. If the players don't understand what you want, they won't execute their jobs effectively. The deeper the level of understanding and comfort with what they have to do, the more effective they will be. For example, play-call names should follow a consistent structure. For us, a typical play call is structured using the following order:

1. Movement (if any), creating the desired formation
2. Formation and direction
3. Movement (if any) from the declared formation
4. Deployment (if any), such as tight ends, alignment switches, and so on
5. Play

6. Snap count

7. Ready . . . break

Movement refers to any motions to be incorporated. The motions can be on the part of one receiver or a collection of receivers moving together. If you want to move the Z receiver, maybe use a term such as "ZIP" (Z to inside position) that can easily be remembered by both players and coaches.

Formations generally are pretty basic and straightforward. *Trips* is often referred to as a three-receiver by two-receiver formation (3 × 2) in a one-back offense. Figure 7.1 shows the formation and motion portion of the play call.

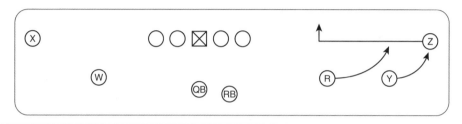

FIGURE 7.1 Trips RT ZIP.

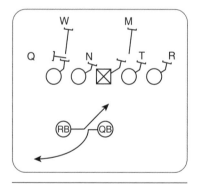

FIGURE 7.2 Trips RT 44.

There are a number of ways to structure actual play calls. Running plays can be designated either by the back and hole number or by names referring to the type of play and some way to indicate direction. If you use the hole numbering system, the running play 44 (figure 7.2) would be the #4 back (usually the running back, RB) toward the number 4 hole (between the right guard and right tackle). This is commonly known as inside zone; the quarterback reads the backside defensive end and decides whether to hand off the ball for a running play or pull the ball in and run or throw it.

When it comes to the passing game, you have protection and routes to call. A general rule for pass protection is to have a two-number system similar to the running game. Use numbers in the 50s when employing 5 blockers, numbers in the 60s when using 6 blockers, and numbers in the 70s when using 7 blockers. When it comes to receiver routes, basically the two systems are to use the route tree or to use names that describe the concept behind the patterns you want. If you use the route tree (figure 7.3) to tell each receiver what to do, a good way to do it is inside out from the called strength to the opposite side.

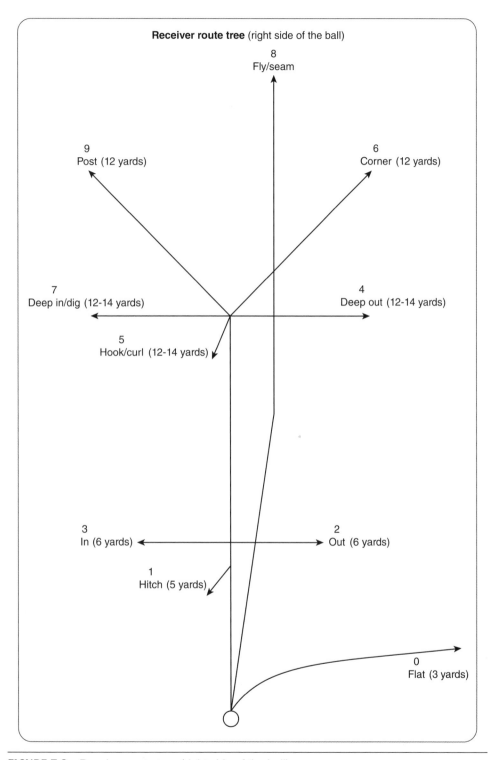

FIGURE 7.3 Receiver route tree (right side of the ball).

For example, Trips RT 60 633/48 (figure 7.4). The play is Trips right (3×2), the protection is 60 (6 blockers, the 5 offensive linemen, and the running back), and the routes are corner-in-in into the field, and out-fade to the boundary.

If you wanted to use concept names, the names would just replace the route combinations. In figure 7.5, for example, the corner-in combination is called Chicago and the out-fade combination is called Omaha. Thus, the play call is Trips RT 60 Chicago/Omaha.

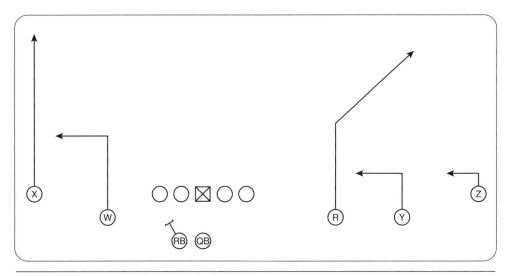

FIGURE 7.4 Trips RT 60 633/48.

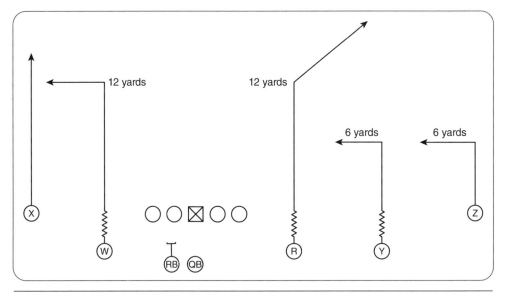

FIGURE 7.5 Trips RT 60 Chicago/Omaha.

TEACHING YOUR SYSTEM

The better that things are taught, the better they can be understood, which will lead to better production. As much as coaches are people managers, therapists, and mentors, they are teachers first and foremost. It's no simple task to have each player understand his role within the team and be comfortable in doing his job. There are a lot of moving parts in a football play, and the best coaches get them all moving in sync. Being a great teacher of the game of football is no different than teaching anything else. You need to have great communication skills and to be patient, compassionate, empathic, organized, trustworthy, and inspiring.

Consistency and rules within your structure are crucial as well. From week to week, you must be able to vary route depths, stems, timing, blocking assignments against certain defenses, and so on, all depending on your opponent's scheme and athletes. That is game planning. The problem is, if you don't have clear and consistent rules for your plays, and a defense shows a look that you haven't prepared for, chaos ensues and your play fails.

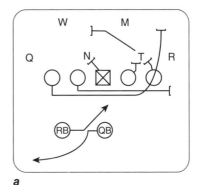

When you teach rules, be consistent. When an athlete is tired and can't think straight or when defenses give a different look than anticipated, athletes need to be able to revert to their rules to perform their jobs. A consistent set of rules is necessary, especially in times of duress.

For example, if you are running a counter play and your rule for the first puller is to pull for the end man on the line of scrimmage, then the front side of the offensive line has to know that and adjust the blocking scheme accordingly, as shown in figure 7.6.

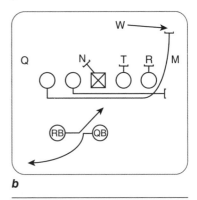

FIGURE 7.6 Counter play with adjustment by offensive line.

CHARACTERISTICS OF AN EFFECTIVE OFFENSIVE PLAY CALLER

Some of the same factors are necessary for success as a player or a coach. Here are the characteristics an offensive coordinator and offensive play caller need.

Identity

What is the basis of your success? Know your foundation, your bedrock principles. Then you know what to resort to when things aren't going as planned. When your offense struggles and things aren't going in your favor, which inevitably will happen, you have to know what call will lead to success. What's your best stuff?

In building the structure of an offense, you need to know your identity. You can have a multitude of formations, motions, plays, and so on, but your base system must be built around something, and that something has to be your most efficient and successful play. I've been in offenses that were a vertical, quick-strike passing game; when all else failed, we reset to that. Other offenses are based around a fullback with a downhill, power-running game, and everything else flows from that. Some are two-back offenses, tight-end offenses, or five-receiver and one–running back offenses. Whatever yours is, your foundation needs to be your focus every week.

Preparation

To me, as both a player and a coach, preparation is the key to success. As a player, if I had done everything I could during the week to be ready to play, both physically and mentally, I knew I would do well. If I had difficulty falling asleep, that usually meant I didn't think I was truly prepared. It is the same for me as a coach.

My preparation mainly comes through film study. It's impossible to watch too much film, because each time you learn something new or see something you missed the 10 times before that. "Paralysis by analysis" isn't something I worry about when it comes to me, though I am careful not to overwhelm my players with excessive information. In football there are so many moving parts that it takes watching the same play 20 times or more to see all the nuances of that play—body position, feet placement, hand placement, linebacker depth, defensive lineman alignment, defensive back eyes, presnap communication. A coach can always use more information. The key is what he does with that information and how much of it he gives to his players. Chapter 12 on scouting the opposition provides more details for doing film analysis.

Don't overload players with data. The offensive line probably doesn't care what coverage they're in; they care about what blitz the opposition may bring. The play caller needs to study and analyze every possible situation to put players in the best position possible to execute the play.

The game plan grows as I watch film. This is when I analyze the strengths and weaknesses of the opposing defense and formulate the plan of attack. Every defense has weaknesses on every play, and you have to be able to exploit those weaknesses. For example, if we are playing a defense that likes to use a three-man line (3–4), we'll probably lean toward running the ball because of the two natural bubbles created over the offensive guards. If a team likes to play a lot of man-to-man coverage in the back end, we will run crossing patterns and also try to isolate our best receiver in what we deem to be a favorable matchup.

When analyzing film, I often look at how defenses try to defend certain formations, and then I try to match that with their tendencies based on field position. For example, a defensive coordinator might be in man coverage 55 percent of the time versus a 3-by-2 formation, but once an offense gets inside the 15-yard line and is about to try to score, that number goes up to 100 percent. Not only are there formation and field-position tendencies that should be studied, you need to factor in down and distance, drive length, time on the clock, score, and other game scenarios. All situations should be accounted for. Generally, when I break down a defense I look at how the players defend an offense based on the offensive formation, the down and distance for a first down, and the field position the offense is scrimmaging from. Field position can be broken up into three zones:

1. Backed up (between your own goal line and the 25-yard line)
2. Middle of the field (between the 25-yard lines)
3. Red/score zone (25-yard line to the opposition's goal line)

The field-position analysis can change depending on the defense and how they treat situations. Each defense is different depending on their philosophical approach.

The analysis then becomes specific to the position groups, yet it all factors into the game plan and the play caller has to know it all. The offensive line does not care about coverage in the defensive backfield; they want to know what the defensive front is. Conversely, the receivers don't care how many defensive linemen are in the game; they care what coverage they will face and how that will affect the routes they run.

The play caller needs to take all of this information into account when building the weekly game plan. Try to match your strengths against their weaknesses and have a plan for each scenario in the game. The big things to analyze when breaking down a defense are:

Defensive Front

- ◆ Number of linemen in the game (generally three, four, or five) and their alignment. The defensive line's alignment can have a huge effect on how the offensive line blocks a particular play.
- ◆ What, if any, stunts or twists they run and when they run them.

Linebackers

- ◆ Alignment and depth. Usually their alignment will fit within the defensive structure but if it varies, that could be an indicator for blitzes and so on.
- ◆ Do they dog or blitz any of their linebackers, and who do you have to watch out for?

Defensive Backs

- Coverage (how many deep zone players, followed by whether it's man or zone underneath them) and alignment. As with the defensive line, the technique or shade a defender will play on a receiver could alter his route, his release, or both, depending on the concept of the play.
- Depth can also indicate possible coverage or tendencies. Teams try to disguise coverages and roll down into zones or man-to-man coverage, but deep zone defenders generally start deep. When close to the line of scrimmage, it's tough to bail to a deep zone spot fast enough and then attempt to locate receivers and the ball.
- Do they like to bring secondary blitzes?

Opening the Game

The first play of the game usually gets a lot of attention, probably without much reason. The opening few series will give an indication of exactly what the defense has in mind for stopping you. The questions really are these: what do you want to see from the defense, and how have they departed, if at all, from their usual structure or tendencies? The key is to know what you are looking for. If your game plan is to attack the short side halfback, then what, if anything, is the defense going to do to protect and help him? Structure your plays and calls to get the info as quickly as possible, and file it away. Football is definitely a game of patience, knowing that when an opportunity presents itself and you get the look you want, you have to exploit it and execute.

Early in the game, using multiple formations and personnel packages will give you a lot of information and will be a great indicator of any changes the defense has made in trying to stop you. Use four-, five- and six-receiver sets deployed in 3×2, 2×3, 3×3, 4×2, and 4×1 formations. Are they going to substitute when you bring in a tight end or a sixth offensive lineman? Do they run with motions across the ball or just bump their zone coverage responsibilities? Again, knowing what you want to accomplish and getting predictors on how the defense plans to stop you will give you the chance to call the right plays, which gives your players an opportunity to succeed. That's great coaching.

Don't Search for the Perfect Play

Many coaches are always searching for the perfect play, every play, depending on what the defense is about to do. This is incredibly difficult and usually requires calling multiple plays in the huddle, with the ability to audible at the line of scrimmage. I've always felt it is easy for coaches to see and to know how to get to the perfect play. But an athlete has so many things going on, not to mention he may be eight plays into a drive. Usually he's just trying to identify the defense and not go offside, let alone remember three plays that were called in the huddle. I try to build enough diversity and options into each play to protect us for the what-if scenario. I try to structure and teach that each play can, more often than not, be a successful play because defenses can't stop everything. This can get complicated, but simplicity comes through understanding, and that's where teaching and communication come into play.

Steps Ahead

When it comes to calling a game, one thing I learned very quickly was just how far ahead you have to be. Play calling is definitely a cat-and-mouse game of strategy and timing. Throughout the game I note possible adjustments that can be made before the game's end, and I scratch plays off the call sheet that I won't call or don't want to go back to. I'm always thinking several plays and series ahead.

If you have the luxury of assistant coaches in the spotter's booth, make sure you decide on what each coach will watch and chart. Ideally, one coach will chart coverages, another coach will chart fronts, stunts, and blitzes, and another will look for specific things during each specific play (as requested by the offensive coordinator). As a play caller on the sidelines, your down, distance, and hashmark information should come from upstairs, as it can be difficult to see from the sidelines.

Figure 7.7 is an example of a call sheet I use. It's a basic spreadsheet in which I can separate all plays into their own category, as well as situations and scenarios that may occur during a game. One thing I found early was I would sometimes get lost in my call sheet, always staring at it and looking for the next play. When setting up the call sheet, you have to trust your game plan as well as have a feel for the flow of the game.

From the time the play is called until the end of that play, I am constantly running situations and scenarios to get the next play called. As a play caller, you can't get caught up being a spectator and watching the game. After every play is called, I usually have two or three plays cued up depending on the possible scenarios that may unfold. I'll have a second and medium, a second and long, and my next first down all ready to go. If the result of the play happens to be second and short, I'll resort to my call sheet. There I'll have my top six or eight second and short plays in the order I want them called.

Home vs visitor

Game plan passes	Situational passes	Run game

Quick game | **2nd and short** | **Inside zone**

Game plan passes — Quick game:
#		
1		
2		
3		
4		
5		
6		
7		
8		
9		
10		
11		
12		
13		
14		
15		

Base passes:
#		
1		
2		
3		
4		
5		
6		
7		
8		
9		
10		
11		
12		
13		
14		
15		
16		
17		
18		
19		
20		
21		
22		
23		
24		
25		

Deep passes:
#		
1		
2		
3		
4		
5		
6		
7		
8		
9		
10		

Situational passes — 2nd and short:
#		
1		
2		
3		
4		
5		
6		
7		
8		
9		
10		

2nd and medium:
#		
1		
2		
3		
4		
5		
6		
7		
8		
9		
10		

2nd and long:
#		
1		
2		
3		
4		
5		
6		
7		
8		
9		
10		

Notes

Run game — Inside zone:
#		
1		
2		
3		
4		
5		
6		
7		
8		
9		
10		
11		
12		
13		
14		
15		

Outside zone:
#		
1		
2		
3		
4		
5		
6		

Counter:
#		
1		
2		
3		
4		
5		

Iso lead:
#		
1		
2		
3		
4		
5		

2nd and medium runs:
#		
1		
2		
3		
4		
5		

2nd and short runs:
#		
1		
2		
3		
4		
5		

Short yardage:
#		
1		
2		
3		
4		
5		

FIGURE 7.7 Sample call sheet.

Home vs visitor

1st half openers				Red zone				Play action		
1				1st down				Speed sweep		
2				1				1		
3				2				2		
4				3				3		
5				4				4		
6				5				5		
7				6				6		
8				7				7		
9				8				8		
10				9				9		
				10				10		

2nd half openers				2nd down				Naked boots		
1				1				1		
2				2				2		
3				3				3		
4				4				4		
5				5				5		
6				6				6		
7				7				7		
8				8				8		
9				9				9		
10				10				10		

Move the pocket				Notes	In the pocket play action		
1					1		
2					2		
3					3		
4					4		
5					5		
6					6		
7					7		
8					8		
9					9		
10					10		

Screens				Off-tackle/hitch screens		
1				1		
2				2		
3				3		
4				4		
5				5		
6				6		
7				7		
8				8		
9				9		
10				10		
2-point plays				11		
1				12		
2				13		
3						

FIGURE 7.7 (continued)

111

Stick to the Game Plan

Throughout the game, I constantly remind myself to stick to the plan. Putting together the game plan takes hours of thought and consideration on the part of all the coaches. It shouldn't be thrown out on a whim. That's not to say adjustments don't need to be made, but if the plan is to use your short passing game on first down because the opponent has a very big and out-of-shape defensive line, then stick to it. If the plan is to wear down the opponent by pass rushing and running to the ball, then don't lose sight of that because of some struggles early on. More often than not, consistency will pay dividends as the game progresses.

Finish the Game

Near the end of the game, a lot of coordinators lose sight of their game plan. If winning, they go ultraconservative; if losing, they just start airing the ball out. Don't hit the panic button. As the game gets near the end, coaches and players need to operate with a sense of urgency but also a calm, controlled, and composed demeanor.

CONCLUSION

A lot of elements go into calling plays. If you properly and diligently prepare, trust your game plan, and make any necessary adjustments, you will no doubt have success. As a coach, you make supper and set the table, but it's the players who eat.

8

Run Defense

Clint Uttley

Defending the run at any level of football is the foundation for playing great defense. A football team's ability to stop the run will determine the overall success of that football team. Defense wins championships. Generally, the number-one goal for most defensive football teams is to stop the run; I personally put that ahead of creating turnovers and pressuring the quarterback. Your defense's ability to control the line of scrimmage and win short yardage and goal-line situations will have a direct impact on the outcome of a football game.

By stopping the run and controlling the line of scrimmage, you will also neutralize a team's play-action passing game and will force teams to drop back and throw the football in situations when they wanted to run the ball. At this point the defense has taken control of the game.

COACHING RUN DEFENSE

Having a great run-stopping defense starts with preaching mental and physical toughness. Players must be willing to do the necessary physical competing along the line of scrimmage to control the run. The defensive linemen need to be committed to physically dominating the offensive linemen, and the linebackers must be prepared to take on linemen and running backs to stop the run. This attitude must be preached and prioritized in practice.

Early in the week we commit time to showing players how they fit versus the opponent's top five run plays. *Fit* means to fulfill the responsibilities that a given player has for stopping the opponent's plays. Defensive practices also feature pursuit, tackling circuit, and turnover circuit. Once everyday drills are finished, individual position group periods begin to focus on schemes. Players must embrace these principles:

- Applicability to base defense (ways to be successful playing the usual scheme)
- Outstanding technique (reacting to blockers, defeating blocks, and making tackles)

- ◆ Great pad level (stay in a low, stable athletic position).
- ◆ Leverage (keep the ball contained)

PRINCIPLES OF RUN DEFENSE

Regardless of scheme, several principles of defending the run must be applied.

First, control all of the gaps. A gap is a running lane that can develop between two offensive blockers. *A gaps* are between the centre and guards. *B gaps* are between the guards and tackles. *C gaps* are between the tackles and the next offensive player (tight end, wingback, slotback, etc.), and *D gaps* are outside of the tight end, wingback, and slotback. The gaps are also designated by whether they are on the strong or weak side of the line (weak A gap, strong C gap, etc.).

Next contain the ball carrier. Because of the width of the Canadian field, most defenses emphasize keeping the ball from getting outside; they have players designated to contain the ball carrier and force him back to the interior of the defense.

Designate the roles of the defensive linemen. Defensive linemen can use different techniques in a run defense system. One is to take on the offensive lineman across from him. When doing this, the defensive lineman should keep his body in the gap for which he is responsible, squeeze the adjacent gap by preventing the offensive lineman from pushing him back, and keep the offensive lineman away from the linebackers. Ideally the defensive lineman should push his offensive lineman back behind the line of scrimmage. With this system, the linebackers should make the majority of tackles on run plays.

Another technique is for the defensive linemen to penetrate the line of scrimmage through their assigned gaps. This increases their opportunity to disrupt the running play in the backfield, and it allows the defensive linemen to get to the ball carrier more quickly. The liabilities are overpenetrating and leaving gaps wide open, and leaving the offensive linemen free to block the linebackers.

Designate flow responsibilities to the linebackers. The principle of flow is that the linebackers must fill the gaps that are not filled by the defensive linemen, prioritizing the gaps in the direction of the offense's flow. With a two-back offense (I formation or fullback in a wing position), the fullback typically designates flow. If the fullback lines up or motions to the strong side, the linebackers go to their strong flow gaps and responsibilities. If the fullback lines up or motions to the weak side, the linebackers go to their weak flow gaps and responsibilities.

Designate run-support responsibilities to the defensive backs. Depending on your level of football or your opposition, you may need your defensive backs more or less involved in run support. Typically, defensive backs are pass-first players: their eyes and minds should be on their pass responsibilities, especially if you are playing man-to-man coverage. When you play zone defense, the defensive backs do not have their eyes locked on a receiver, so they are more available to provide run support. But this should apply only to players responsible for short zones. Deep-zone players must keep everything in front of them until there is no chance of a run (once the ball has crossed the line of scrimmage).

Carefully consider other options to make it more difficult for the offensive linemen to make their blocks. You can stem the defensive linemen (change alignment once the quarterback starts his cadence), stunt the defensive linemen (angle left or right, or attack a predetermined gap), and force fit the linebackers (blitz through a predetermined gap). You can line up in a lot of fronts and do a few things well enough to win, or you can line up in few fronts and do lots of things well.

Designate pursuit responsibilities for all players. Pursuit means that after every player has done his designated responsibility, he must chase the ball carrier if he runs to a different gap.

Determine what type of athletes you have and what gives them the best tools to succeed. As a coordinator, my greatest success came when we had three fronts, one run stunt, and one run blitz. Aside from that, we based our defensive front on the offensive backfield and put our best defensive lineman over their best offensive lineman on run downs, and against their worst offensive lineman on passing downs. Remember: keep it simple and let the kids play fast.

BASE DEFENSE

The base defense is the system you practice and play the majority of times. There are many schools of thought when it comes to implementing a base defense. As a coach, consider what type of athletes you have and then decide what scheme best fits your personnel.

The two most common schemes in Canada are the 4-3 defense (figure 8.1), which features four defensive linemen and three linebackers, and the 3–4 defense (figure 8.2), which features three defensive linemen and four linebackers. (Another version of the 3–4 has Will and Sam at the same depth as the inside linebackers.)

It's important to determine what scheme will best fit your athletes. Both schemes have advantages and disadvantages. The 4-3 is effective for occupying most or all of the offensive linemen blocking defensive linemen so the linebackers are free to make tackles. If you have a group of good-size defensive linemen, the 4-3 is a good option. The

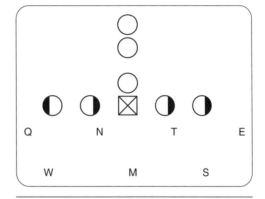

FIGURE 8.1   4-3 Base.

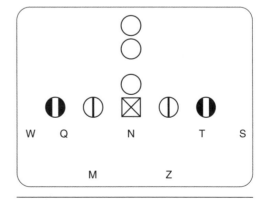

FIGURE 8.2   3–4 Base.

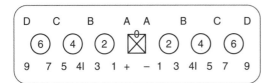

FIGURE 8.3 Defensive linemen and linebacker alignments.

3–4 can be a more dynamic system because the offensive linemen do not know which linebackers will attack gaps or where they will come from. If you have a strong and athletic group of linebackers and a big-bodied nose tackle who can fill both A gaps, the 3–4 is a good option.

Regardless of scheme, the starting point of any defense is teaching players how and where to line up on the football field. You also need to have a system so you can communicate with your players. Figure 8.3 explains in great detail how and where defensive linemen and linebackers line up. Lining up correctly on defense is half the battle.

For linebacker alignments (5 yards from line of scrimmage), add a zero (1 = 10, 3 = 30).

Defensive Alignment and Responsibility

0: Head up on centre

-/+: Outside shoulder of centre (split crotch of centre).

1: Inside shoulder of guard (split crotch inside)

2: Head up guard

3: Outside shoulder of guard (split crotch outside)

4I: Inside shoulder of tackle (split crotch inside)

4: Head up on tackle

5: Outside shoulder of tackle (split crotch outside)

7: Inside shoulder of tight end (split crotch inside)

6: Head up on tight end

9: Outside shoulder of tight end (split crotch outside)

General

Even-numbered alignment: nose to nose

Odd-numbered alignment: split crotch inside or outside

A gap: Between centre and guard

B gap: Between guard and tackle

C gap: Between tackle and tight end or slotback

D gap: Outside tight end or slotback

4-3 DEFENSIVE SYSTEM

The rest of the chapter will teach the base 4-3 defense. Included will be the teaching progression that provides the best results for instructing the front seven: the defensive linemen, and linebackers:

- *Assignment.* Know responsibilities: which gap, player, or zone.
- *Alignment.* Know precisely where to line up.
- *Stance.* Know what stance will best allow the execution of the assignment.
- *Visual key.* Know who on the opposition to look at and what to look for to provide the best chance to make a good reaction.
- *Response.* Know how to defeat various blocks and finish the tackle.

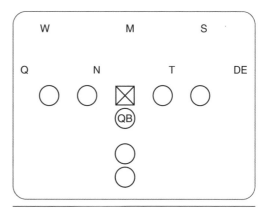

FIGURE 8.4 4-3 defensive system.

The 4-3 defensive system (figure 8.4) is designed so that each front seven player is responsible for a single gap (table 8.1). Defensive linemen learn to key

TABLE 8.1 Defensive Alignments, Keys, and Responsibilities for the 4-3

Position	Alignment	Keys and responsibility			Coaching points
		Flow to	Flow away	Pass rush or pass	
End	6	C gap	50/50	C gap/box QB	50/50 = Play away; stay square and shuffle; play contain or boot and reverse
Tackle	3 strong	B gap	B gap	A or B gap strong	Never get cut off by the guard. Pass rush = Two-way go
Nose	1 weak side	A gap	A gap	A gap	Never get cut off by the guard or hooked by the centre. Do not cross the centre on pass rush
Quick	6	C gap	Bend	C gap/box QB	Bend = If play goes away, pursue flat down the line of scrimmage and exchange with Will

(continued)

Table 8.1 *(continued)*

Position	Alignment	Keys and responsibility			Coaching points
		Flow to	Flow away	Pass rush or pass	
Sam	40	Mirror RB	Cutback	Cover call	Opened/closed with flow to you. Coverage dictates alignment
Mike	+	A gap strong	Mirror RB	Cover call	Attack gap according to flow
Will	50	B gap	Shuffle	C gap/box QB	Opened/closed with flow to you. Coverage dictates alignment

the foot or shoulder of the offensive lineman inside them. Linebackers learn to key the running back's flow.

Defensive Linemen

The starting point for the defensive lineman is reaction. Use drills to teach defensive linemen how to defend these blocks:

- Base block (man inside of defensive player blocks him)
- Down block (man outside of defensive player blocks him)
- Reach block (man inside of defensive player attempts to get outside of defensive player to block him)
- Double team (two offensive players block one defensive player)
- Traps/pulls (man moves horizontally behind other offensive players to block the side of a defensive player)
- Pass block (man is pass protecting)

See figure 8.5 for the blocks for the defensive end and figure 8.6 for the blocks for the nose tackle.

DE	**Defeating the base block, inside** • Attack V of neck. • Create separation. • Squeeze offensive man into opposite gap. • Play square to line of scrimmage. • After ball has crossed face, disengage and make the tackle.

DE	**Defeating the down block, outside vs. TE or FB**
	• Attack V of neck.
	• Jam offensive man to the inside
	  (get hands on him).
	• Keep shoulders square to line of scrimmage.
	• Eyes inside. Look for the ball carrier. Be alert for a kick-out
	  (trap) block.
	• Cutback, counter, reverse.

DE	**Defeating the reach block, outside** • Attack V of neck. • Redirect footwork with offensive man to the outside. • Create separation. Could use push-pull rip technique. • Play square to line of scrimmage. • Maintain leverage on ball carrier. Disengage (rip) and make the play.
DE	**Defeating the double team, outside vs. TE or FB** • Attack V of neck. • Maintain gap leverage. Keep shoulders square to line of scrimmage. • When feeling second man, drop and pop. Drop inside knee and pop up, ripping with inside arm to split the double team. • This has to happen fast. Do not be driven to LB depth.
DE	**Defeating the trap block** • Attack V of neck. • Jam offensive man to the inside (get hands on him). • Eyes inside. Look for the ball carrier. Look for the trap blocker. • Use wrong-arm technique or rip-and-sit technique on trap blocker. • Make the play bounce to the outside.
DE	**Defeating pass protection** • Attack V of neck. • React to pass set and use a pass rush move (push/pull, rip, speed rush, quick swim). • Maintain pass rush lanes.

FIGURE 8.5 Blocks for the defensive end.

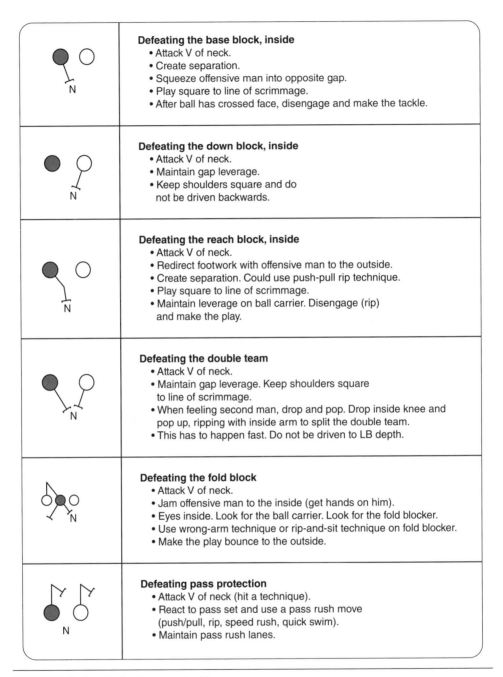

Defeating the base block, inside
- Attack V of neck.
- Create separation.
- Squeeze offensive man into opposite gap.
- Play square to line of scrimmage.
- After ball has crossed face, disengage and make the tackle.

Defeating the down block, inside
- Attack V of neck.
- Maintain gap leverage.
- Keep shoulders square and do
  not be driven backwards.

Defeating the reach block, inside
- Attack V of neck.
- Redirect footwork with offensive man to the outside.
- Create separation. Could use push-pull rip technique.
- Play square to line of scrimmage.
- Maintain leverage on ball carrier. Disengage (rip)
  and make the play.

Defeating the double team
- Attack V of neck.
- Maintain gap leverage. Keep shoulders square
  to line of scrimmage.
- When feeling second man, drop and pop. Drop inside knee and
  pop up, ripping with inside arm to split the double team.
- This has to happen fast. Do not be driven to LB depth.

Defeating the fold block
- Attack V of neck.
- Jam offensive man to the inside (get hands on him).
- Eyes inside. Look for the ball carrier. Look for the fold blocker.
- Use wrong-arm technique or rip-and-sit technique on fold blocker.
- Make the play bounce to the outside.

Defeating pass protection
- Attack V of neck (hit a technique).
- React to pass set and use a pass rush move
  (push/pull, rip, speed rush, quick swim).
- Maintain pass rush lanes.

FIGURE 8.6 Blocks for the nose tackle.

Linebackers

For linebackers, the starting point is teaching proper reaction to the four different types of flow (figure 8.7):

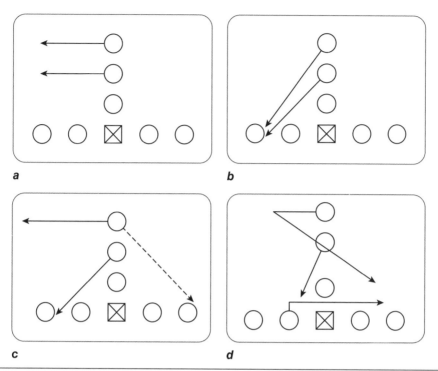

FIGURE 8.7 Keys for linebackers versus four types of flow: (a) fast flow—both backs going outside the offensive tackle immediately, (b) hard flow—both backs attacking the line of scrimmage in the same flow, (c) split flow—one back attacking the line of scrimmage and the other going on a pitch path, or backs going in opposite directions, (d) counter flow—backs starting in one direction and the ball ultimately going in the opposite direction.

- Versus fast flow, shuffle laterally, and mirror the inside shoulder of the ball carrier.
- Versus hard flow, shuffle and scrape hard downhill to meet the ball carrier at the line of scrimmage.
- Versus split flow, key the fullback.
- Versus counter flow, shuffle, read, and react. (The outside linebacker away from the initial flow should be patient before reacting.)

The fullback typically dictates flow, so the Mike linebacker should key the fullback.

Game Planning and Practicing

When game planning for an opponent, you need to identify their base run plays. Make sure you dedicate enough practice time so that your players know exactly what gap they must fit into. On top of the time you spend doing this with the defense alone, you can also have an inside run period that operates at the same time as the pass-shell period. During inside run, diagram the opponent's top run plays and focus on defeating blocks and seeing the path of the running back.

To properly teach players where they fit in the run game, you have to show players video clips, diagram those plays on the whiteboard, walk through run fits, see the same run plays in inside run, and then see them in a team period as well. By taking these five steps, you cater to all of the ways in which a player can learn and retain information.

Stopping the Run With Stemming: Stunts and Blitzes

In some games and situations, either you won't match up physically with your opponent or you'll be at an athletic disadvantage and have difficulty stopping the run out of your base defense. When these situations happen, respond following this sequence:

1. Stem or move the front or set the front based on the offensive backfield set (figures 8.8 and 8.9).

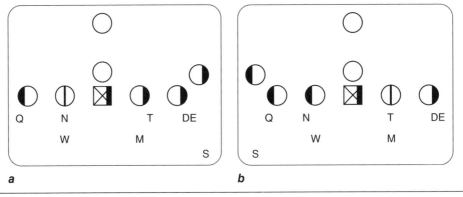

FIGURE 8.8 Setting the front versus two-back sets: (a) base versus fullback set strong, (b) base versus FB set weak.

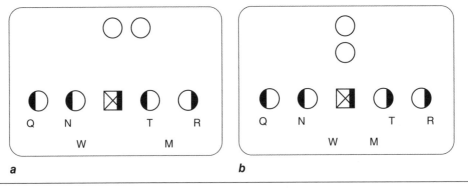

FIGURE 8.9 Setting the front versus one-back sets: (a) base versus gun strong, (b) base versus pistol.

2. Stunt the defensive line; give the defensive line predetermined movements (figure 8.10).

3. Force fit linebackers; linebackers automatically fit into a gap determined by flow or backfield set (figure 8.11).

4. Run blitz; pinch the defensive line and blitz the linebackers; play cover 0 behind it (figure 8.12).

We set the front to the fullback and have the Sam linebacker adjust to the fullback from 1 yard deeper than the Mike and Will linebackers. By doing this, our front, excluding the Sam, has minimal adjusting to do; they can simply align, get their eyes on their visual keys, and get ready to react.

For the base versus gun strong (figure 8.9a):

◆ Set the front opposite the running back (the nose and tackle switch their normal base gaps).

◆ The Sam linebacker is out of the box with the fullback/fifth receiver.

◆ The Mike linebacker and defensive end exchange depending on the right tackle's block.

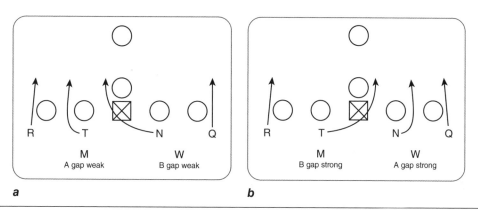

FIGURE 8.10 Defensive-line run stunts: (a) circle strong, (b) circle weak.

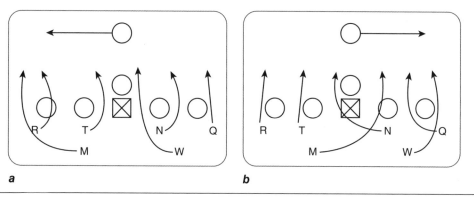

FIGURE 8.11 Hokie: (a) versus flow strong, (b) versus flow weak.

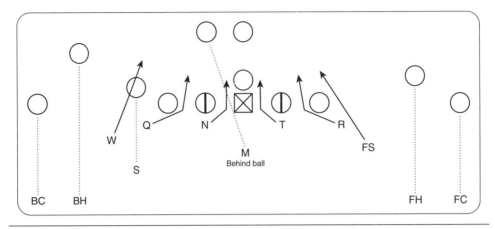

FIGURE 8.12 Run blitz: Devel cover 0.

For the base versus pistol (figure 8.9b):

- Set the front to double 3 techniques.
- These alignments will allow you to defend outside zone.
- The Mike and Will linebackers key the centre and fill the A gaps.

For the defensive-line run stunts (figure 8.10), the nose and tackle slant and penetrate while the linebackers fill the opposite A and B gaps.

On force fits (figure 8.11), the linebackers anticipate the ball spilling out. The linebacker fits into a designated gap of the flow of the backfield or reads out of the blitz and redirects to pursue the ball.

For the run blitz (figure 8.12), it is important that linebackers understand that they are run blitzing, not pass blitzing. When run blitzing, they should attack their gap, get across the line of scrimmage, and "sit down" (get under control so they can react to the ball carrier). If they go full speed through their gap and don't sit down, they will likely run past the ball carrier or will leave their gap wide open.

The strategies of stemming, stunting, and blitzing are important parts of a run defense. But I can't overstate the importance of teaching players how to hustle, pursue, defeat blocks, and tackle. There simply is no substitute for teaching players those skills every day in practice. From a scheme perspective, you must keep it simple and be gap sound. Your players need to know how and where to line up, and they need to understand blocking schemes and backfield flows.

CONCLUSION

Keep these points in mind as a guide for coaching players on defense. Let your personnel dictate the scheme. Make sure that your athletes have the appropriate physical traits to be able to play your scheme effectively. Put your players in a position to succeed and keep it simple. Examine your scheme and make sure the drills in individual periods match the scheme from a technique standpoint. This is where it is very important for all of the position coaches on defense to be consistent with the defensive coordinator and the techniques used on the team. Make sure you incorporate a pursuit period, tackling circuit, and turnover circuit into your defensive practice structure. Get to know your players! They all learn and retain information differently; it is your job as a coach to identify what type of learner each player is. Draw your scheme on the board, watch video, walk through the scheme, and then execute assignments at full speed.

Teach the game, respect the game, and be a mentor to your players.

9

Pass Defense

Scott Brady

Pass defense is an important part of coaching a successful Canadian football team. Many systems can be used, and a wise coach will match the system to the athletes on the team and to the opposition's system. A zone defense tends to be more conservative and makes it difficult for the offense to throw deep. A blitzing man-to-man defense leaves cover players matched one-on-one to the receivers and relies on the pass rushers to get to the quarterback quickly enough to rush the pass or cause a sack. Most defensive coaches use some of each scheme and possibly some other unique or specialized options.

It is important to remember that pass defense involves two distinct aspects: coverage and pressure. *Coverage* refers to the players and systems involved in covering the eligible receivers. *Pressure* refers to the players and systems involved in rushing the passer. I will summarize some common systems used in Canadian football, and then will outline some important principles to consider when designing and implementing a pass defense system.

While you probably have some options in your playbook for playing pass defense, it is very important to have one system that is your base, the one you practice and play the most and that you go to in any situation when players aren't sure how to react to the offense. Our unique base system at Mount Allison University is quarters coverage, and later in the chapter, I will go into that system in detail.

PASS COVERAGE PRINCIPLES

Cover all eligible receivers. Regardless of what system you use, and what situation you are in (including punt return or field goal or convert defend), account for all eligible receivers. This will include the two players at each end of the offensive line (tight end or split end), the player lined up behind the centre, and the four other players in the backfield (slotbacks, running backs, flankers).

Determine your matchups. Especially in man-to-man defense, you want athletes in favourable matchups. Usually defensive backs cover receivers, and linebackers cover running backs. Whatever your matchup rules, make sure they are consistent and that they will work when the offense does not line up in a balanced formation or when the receivers go in motion.

In zone defenses, the zones move. Players in zone defense should not cover grass; they should cover any receiver threats to their zones. The usual rule if you can't see a receiver in your short zone is to get deeper. The rule if you can't see a receiver in your deep zone is to "get your head on a swivel" (look to adjacent zones) to see if any receivers are coming your way. If the quarterback moves out of the pocket, the zones should move with him. If the quarterback is rolling to the defense's left, there is little chance that he can throw a pass to the right flats or deep outside third.

Coverage and pressure need to complement each other. Cover 3 and cover 1 have seven or eight players in coverage and only four or five players pressuring the quarterback. The coverage players must understand that they have to maintain their coverage longer because the quarterback will not be facing significant pressure. In cover 0, the 6 players pressuring the quarterback must have a sense of urgency in their rush because the 6 players in coverage can't maintain man-to-man coverage with no help for very long.

COVER 3

In cover 3 defense (figure 9.1), the field is divided into zones. Defensive backs and linebackers are assigned to each zone. There are 3 deep zones (deep outside thirds and deep middle third) that start approximately 15 to 18 yards from the line of scrimmage; this is why it is called cover 3. Each deep third must be covered by a player; usually the safety has the deep middle third and the corners cover the deep

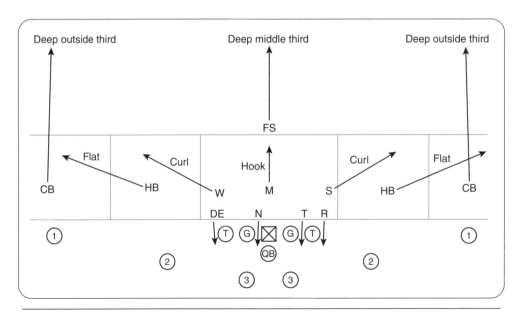

FIGURE 9.1 Cover 3 zones with the ball spotted in the middle.

outside thirds. There are five short or underneath zones (hooks, curls, and flats). The hook zone extends 15 to 18 yards from the line of scrimmage and is slightly wider than the width of the offensive tackles. The curl zones are on either side of the hook zone, and the flat zones are from the curl zones to the sidelines. The size of these zones depends on where the football is; if the ball is on the hash mark, the zones on the wide side will be larger (figure 9.2). Typically, the flat zones are covered by the halfbacks, the curl zones are covered by the outside linebackers, and the hook zone is covered by the middle linebacker.

A cover 3 defense provides several options:

◆ *Hold (halfbacks cover the flats) or cut (corners cover the flats)*. Hold (some coaches call it hail) is the usual way to play cover 3, but if you are playing an offense that likes to attack the flats with quick passes (hitches or screens) or likes to roll out, it may be advantageous to play cut (some coaches call it cloud). You can cut both sides, or you can play cut on one side and hold on the other side. The weak spots of a cover 3 hold coverage are the flats and the seams (the areas between the deep zones). The weaknesses of a cover 3 cut coverage are the curls and the outsides of the deep outside thirds.

◆ *Blitz a linebacker*. There are five short zones and five defenders covering those zones. An option to add pressure to the pass rush is to blitz a linebacker. If you blitz the middle linebacker, the hook zone is wide open, so the outside linebackers need to wall off the middle of the field and try to funnel the receivers outside. If you blitz an outside linebacker, the middle linebacker needs to push out wider to replace the blitzer. Again, both linebackers in coverage need to wall off the middle of the field.

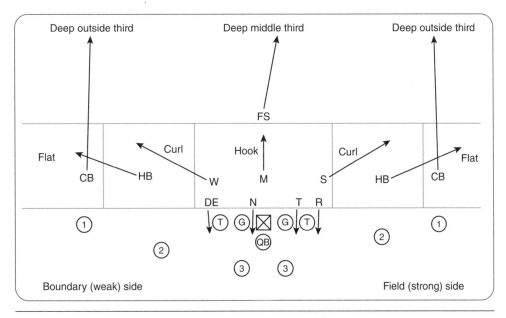

FIGURE 9.2 Cover 3 zones with the ball spotted on the left hash marks.

◆ *Blitz a defensive back.* If you blitz a short zone player, you are vacating a zone. The flats are the zones farthest from the quarterback, so blitzing the player that usually covers the flats leaves the offense with a long throw to make a completion.

COVER 1

Cover 1 is a man-to-man defense in which every eligible receiver is covered by a specific defender. There is also at least one free player, usually the safety, covering the deep middle of the field, which is why it is called cover 1. If you are playing with a four-player defensive line and are not blitzing an extra player, you will also have another free player, usually the middle linebacker, who can cover the short middle of the field.

With a man-to-man defense, eligible receivers are usually counted from the outside in on both sides of the offense. The widest receiver is #1, the next receiver is #2, and so on. (This includes the running backs.) Typically, cornerbacks cover the #1 receivers, halfbacks cover the #2 receivers, and outside linebackers cover the #3 receivers (running backs) in a balanced formation (same number of receivers on each side of the offense; figure 9.3).

Similar to cover 3, the coach has the option of blitzing a player to increase pressure on the quarterback. The blitzing player will almost always be a linebacker. Since the middle linebacker has no man-to-man responsibilities, he is an easy player to blitz. The outside linebackers and halfbacks need to know if the middle linebacker is blitzing because they won't have any help on an inside breaking pass route. An outside linebacker can also blitz, and then the middle linebacker would need to cover the open receiver.

The strengths of playing cover 1 are that all receivers are accounted for, and you have a free player who can help protect deep inside passes. (The safety probably

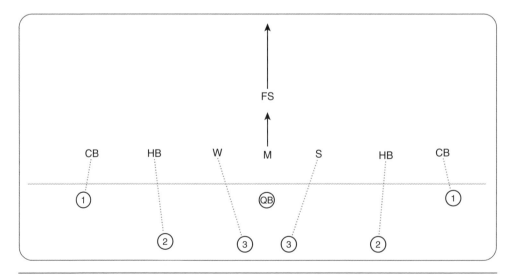

FIGURE 9.3 Cover 1 matchups.

will not be able to help much with deep outside passes.) A weakness of cover 1 is that six of the players in man-to-man coverage will have their eyes on their man (and often their backs to the offensive backfield), so they won't be able to provide run support. Another weakness could be if players in man-to-man coverage have a significant deficit of athleticism compared to the receivers they are covering.

COVER 0

Cover 0 is a man-to-man defense with no free players. Six players cover the six eligible receivers, and the other six players pressure the quarterback (instead of just the usual four defensive linemen pressuring the quarterback). Cover 0 is built off of cover 1. The six players in man-to-man coverage need to know who is blitzing, and then the players who would normally be free (the safety and one of the linebackers) need to cover the remaining receivers.

There are many combinations of cover 0 blitzes that can be run: two linebackers, a halfback and a linebacker, the safety and a linebacker, and so on. Figure 9.4 shows a 43 Base Cover 0 Mac and Will (MoW) blitz and illustrates the responsibilities of the coverage players.

Cover 0 is a very aggressive defense that provides opportunities to make a big play (sacking the quarterback) but also increases the risk of giving up a big play (a receiver beating a pass coverage player who has very little help to make the tackle). It also has the same liabilities as cover 1 in defending the run, though the blitzers may be able to make the tackle on a run play behind the line of scrimmage.

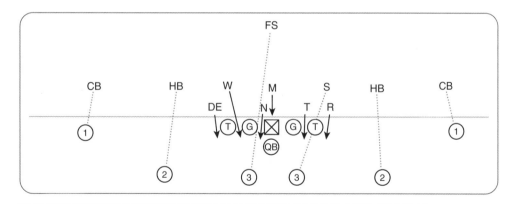

FIGURE 9.4   43 Base Cover 0 MoW matchups and blitz responsibilities.

QUARTERS COVERAGE

Mount Allison University is a base quarters coverage team within a 4-2-6 defensive structure. We play quarters coverage 60 to 65 percent of the time in base situations over the course of a season. While it is important to have changeups in the defensive package in order to keep the offense off-balance, it is crucial to the success of the defense that players develop a high level of understanding, confidence, and proficiency when playing the base defense. At Mount Allison, we believe that a dominating defense requires a simple and effective approach to attacking offenses. Our defensive philosophy is simple:

- ◆ Dominate the run.
- ◆ Eliminate the long pass.
- ◆ Create takeaways.

By focusing on these three goals, we have created a dominating defense that plays extremely fast, physically, and with maximum aggression.

Evolution of Quarters Coverage

In order to understand why we base out of quarters coverage at Mount Allison, it is important to examine the evolution of offensive football. Many defenses in both Canadian and American football have traditionally relied on some form of cover 3 as their base defensive coverage. Against the run, cover 3 allows the defense to maintain good run support for both sides of the formation while ensuring that a defender accounts for each gap in the running game. Against the pass, cover 3 divides responsibility for the deep pass zones among three defenders while having five defenders account for the underneath pass zones. This makes cover 3 a relatively balanced coverage that is solid versus both the run and pass.

The biggest limitation of cover 3 is its inability to consistently handle the four verticals route concept. The concept was designed specifically to combat three-deep coverage, with both outside receivers running go routes up the numbers while two inside receivers run go routes up the hash marks. The purpose of this concept is to create a horizontal stretch with the three deep-zone defenders by spacing four receivers evenly across the deep part of the field. While there are techniques within cover 3 that can help a defense defend the four verticals concept, a disciplined offense with good route spacing and timing should be able to defeat cover 3 every time.

A similar route concept that is equally difficult to defend in cover 3 is the divide concept. This is a variation of the four verticals concept with three vertical routes coming from one side of the formation. Again, the outside receivers will run landmark go routes up the numbers. One inside receiver will run a landmark go route up the near hash marks while another inside receiver from the same side of the formation will run a landmark go route crossing to the far hash marks. This creates a two-on-one horizontal stretch of the safety and places him in a very vulnerable situation. When installing cover 3, coaches will try to combat the four verticals and divide route concepts by teaching the underneath zone defenders to reroute the seams and by teaching the three deep-zone defenders to weave with the quarterback's eyes and to break on his throw. While this can be an effective strategy, it becomes extremely challenging against quarterbacks with excellent timing and a strong arm, especially those that are adept at looking off the deep-zone defenders.

With the proliferation of spread offenses, modern offenses present the threat of running four verticals and divide on the majority of snaps. This is especially true in the Canadian game, in which even two-back offenses are able to maintain the threat of four receivers running vertical routes. The ability of offenses to attack three-deep zone defenses with four verticals and divide requires that modern defenses find a solution to better defend the vertical passing game while maintaining sound run-support angles.

The most obvious answers to combat the problems created by modern offenses are either to play some form of man-to-man coverage or a four-deep zone coverage. Both of these strategies, while useful in certain situations, are problematic as solutions for every down. Man-to-man coverage eliminates perimeter run support entirely by requiring defenders to turn their backs to the play as they trail their receivers. Man-to-man coverage can also make the defense vulnerable to unfavorable one-on-one matchups, especially if the defense features lesser athletes than the opponent. Cover 4, meanwhile, leaves only 6 defenders in the box to defend the run against two-back offenses. Attempting to defend 7 run gaps with just 6 defenders is clearly a significant problem in base situations that are approximately 50–50 run-pass. Additionally, cover 4 leaves only 4 defenders to account for the 6 underneath pass zones, providing large windows in the underneath and intermediate passing game.

Strengths and Weaknesses of Quarters Coverage

This brings us to quarters coverage. At Mount Allison, we believe quarters coverage is the absolute best coverage in football for base situations. In order to effectively implement any coverage within a defensive system, it is important to first consider the specific strengths and weaknesses of each coverage.

Strengths of Quarters Coverage

- Strong perimeter run support to both sides of the formation; can play eight defenders in the box versus two-back offenses
- Strong versus quarterback run game; the eighth box defender helps maintain a numbers advantage against teams that run the quarterback
- Matches up against the four vertical passing game by placing a defender directly over the top of each vertical threat
- Perimeter run support by defensive backs allows linebackers to run and make plays without worrying about threat of cutback

Weaknesses of Quarters Coverage

- Vulnerable to quick passing game against an off-technique corner
- Play-action passes can be problematic if safeties are not disciplined in reading their keys
- Typically, no deep defender to provide help on post-breaking routes
- Isolates corners to play man-to-man coverage on outside receivers

Within our program, we believe the most important benefit that playing quarters coverage provides is that it allows us to get eight defenders in the box versus a two-back offense. Two-back offenses present seven gaps to defend versus the run. Putting eight defenders in the box gives the defense a numbers advantage. This is especially beneficial if the defense must rely on smaller players than the opponent. Having an extra run defender can allow smaller or more athletic defenders, who must rely on speed and instincts to defeat blockers, to run to the ball without having to worry about the ball carrier cutting back. In a traditional 4-3 cover 3 defense, the defense is able to get only 7 run defenders in the box versus a two-back offense, forcing each defender to account for a single gap. Only the middle linebacker is guaranteed support versus a cutback run.

The other great benefit to playing quarters coverage is that it allows us to eliminate the vertical passing game entirely. By placing a defender with vertical responsibility directly over the top of each eligible receiver, the offense cannot stress our deep-zone defenders or create two-on-one matchups in the downfield passing game. This eliminates many of the problem areas that exist within cover 3 and provides an immediate solution to the four verticals and divide route concepts discussed earlier.

Another important factor for us in choosing quarters as our base coverage is that we like to base from a two-high safety look. This has allowed us to use a greater variety of coverages within the system while simplifying and strengthening our effectiveness at disguising which coverage we are actually playing. Using a two-high safety look has also helped to simplify and vary the blitz package. It is easier to disguise pressure and coverage rotations from a deep alignment and to stem on the snap to an underneath position rather than the opposite.

A final benefit to using a two-high safety shell is that it is a novel concept within Canadian football. While many defenses in the United States use a two-high safety shell on the majority of snaps, most Canadian defenses play some form of cover 3 on base downs, and thus use a single-deep safety presnap. While this is not a crucial factor, there are advantages that come from providing a look to the offense that is unique and outside of what they prepare for in a typical week.

Teaching Quarters Coverage

Now that we have examined why quarters coverage is the ideal solution to the problems created by modern offenses, we can begin to explain quarters coverage in greater detail. Quarters is an often-misunderstood coverage. The most common misconception is that it is a soft, spot-dropping four-deep zone coverage similar to cover 4. This could not be further from the truth. Quarters coverage is a two-deep safety coverage with roots in the cover 2 coverage family. Quarters coverage relies on pattern reading by defenders to aggressively match up with the specific routes being run by receivers. This pattern-matching philosophy allows our defense to aggressively jump routes and to shrink passing windows for the quarterback.

The starting point for teaching quarters coverage to your players is to have them understand that each side of the secondary operates independently. Quarters coverage relies on a number of different coverage calls to communicate the coverage responsibility of each defender on one side of the formation. The specific coverage call that is used is determined by the number of receivers split to each side of the formation. This is one of the key reasons that we operate from a two-high safety shell: it allows each safety to communicate the specific coverage call to all of the defenders on his side of the formation. We teach safeties that they operate and are responsible for their sides of the formation.

The other key to simplifying the teaching process for implementing quarters coverage as much as possible is to begin by teaching every player five different techniques. Regardless of the formation presented by the offense, every coverage defender will use one of these five techniques on every snap. The specific technique used communicates each player's individual key and responsibility within the coverage on the particular play.

Quarters Coverage Techniques: Inside 1/4 Defender

The first technique we teach when installing quarters coverage is the inside 1/4 defender. The inside 1/4 defender is almost always the safety to his side of the formation. The only situation in which another defender will use the inside 1/4 technique is a corner to a single-receiver side of the formation.

The inside 1/4 defender aligns 10 yards from the line of scrimmage and splits the difference between the end man on the line of scrimmage and the nearest inside receiver. His primary responsibility is to maintain position directly over the top and inside of the inside receiver. It is crucial that the safety maintain inside position in order to protect the middle of the field. In quarters coverage, the inside 1/4 defender has no help to the middle of the field, and for this reason we teach the inside 1/4 defender to align up to 2 full yards inside the inside receiver.

The reads and route reactions for the inside 1/4 defender are:

- Inside receiver releases vertical.
- Inside receiver releases outside.
- Inside receiver releases inside.

(Note: In figure 9.5, the free safety is used to demonstrate the inside 1/4 technique.)

The inside receiver releases vertical (figure 9.5a): The inside 1/4 defender slowly backpedals off the ball while keying the inside receiver. Once the inside receiver clears the underneath portion of the coverage, the inside 1/4 defender matches the receiver's vertical release. He is now responsible for the receiver man-to-man for the remainder of the play.

The inside receiver releases outside (figure 9.5b): The inside 1/4 defender slowly backpedals off the ball while keying the inside receiver. When the inside receiver releases outside, the inside 1/4 defender opens his hips on a 135-degree angle and runs over the top of the outside receiver. He now matches the outside receiver's route all over the field. It is crucial that the inside 1/4 defender open on a deep angle before reacting to any intermediate break in order to maintain inside and on top position if the outside receiver runs a vertical route.

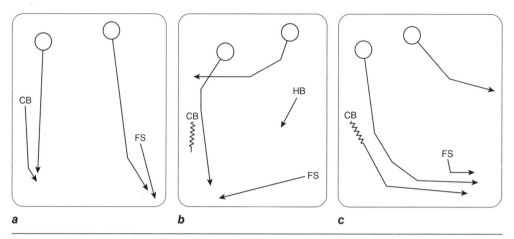

FIGURE 9.5 Inside 1/4 defender: (a) inside receiver releases vertical, (b) inside receiver releases outside, (c) inside receiver releases inside.

The inside receiver releases inside (figure 9.5c): The inside 1/4 defender slowly backpedals off the ball while keying the inside receiver. When the inside receiver releases inside, the inside 1/4 defender looks to rob any inside breaking route by the outside receiver. The inside 1/4 defender can aggressively jump any inside breaking routes by the outside receiver because the read defender is in position to control the outside receiver on any vertical route.

Quarters Coverage Techniques: Outside 1/4 Defender

The second technique to teach when installing quarters coverage is the outside 1/4 defender. The specific player who uses the outside 1/4 technique varies greatly based on the offensive formation.

The outside 1/4 defender aligns 5 yards from the line of scrimmage and 1 yard outside the leverage of the nearest receiver. His primary responsibility is to maintain position directly over the top of the outside receiver until the inside receiver attempts to cross his face. By maintaining position directly over the top of the outside receiver, we can successfully defend the four verticals and divide route concepts. By maintaining outside leverage on an inside receiver attempting to cross the face of the defender, we are able to keep our force player close enough to the box that we maintain a numbers advantage in the running game without risk of being outleveraged to the flat.

The outside 1/4 defender's keys are:

- ◆ Inside and outside receivers both release vertical.
- ◆ Inside receiver releases vertical, outside receiver stops or releases inside.
- ◆ Inside receiver releases outside.
- ◆ Inside receiver releases inside.

(Note: In figure 9.6, the cornerback, CB, is used to demonstrate the outside 1/4 technique.)

The inside and outside receivers both release vertical (figure 9.6a): The outside 1/4 defender shuffles while keying the inside receiver. Once the inside receiver clears the underneath portion of the coverage, the outside 1/4 defender moves his key to the outside receiver. When the outside receiver also continues vertical, the outside 1/4 defender must stay on top of the receiver and squeeze through his outside hip in order to defend against the vertical route concepts.

The inside receiver releases vertical while the outside receiver stops or releases inside (figure 9.6b): The outside 1/4 defender shuffles while keying the inside receiver. Once the inside receiver clears the underneath portion of the coverage, the outside 1/4 defender moves his key to the outside receiver. When the outside receiver stops or releases inside, the outside 1/4 defender must continue to shuffle and maintain outside position on the inside receiver in order to protect the

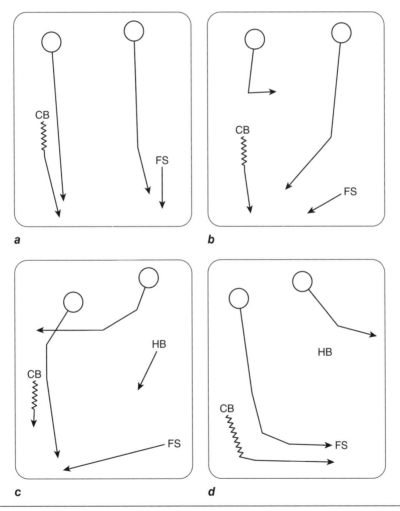

FIGURE 9.6 Outside 1/4 defender: (a) inside and outside receivers both release vertical, (b) inside receiver releases vertical, outside receiver stops or releases inside, (c) inside receiver releases outside, (d) inside receiver releases inside.

inside 1/4 defender against the corner route. To alert the curl defender to expand his drop, the outside 1/4 defender must give a "smash" call anytime the outside receiver stops his route in the flats.

The inside receiver releases outside (figure 9.6c): The outside 1/4 defender shuffles while keying the inside receiver. When the inside receiver releases outside, the outside 1/4 defender drops the outside receiver and maintains outside leverage on the inside receiver running to the flat. To buy time for the safety to run over the top of the outside route, it's crucial that the outside 1/4 defender jam and funnel the outside receiver toward the safety before leveraging the flat. If the inside receiver releases outside and then runs vertical, the outside 1/4 defender must carry the vertical of the inside receiver.

The inside receiver releases inside (figure 9.6d): The outside 1/4 defender shuffles while keying the inside receiver. When the inside receiver releases inside, the outside 1/4 defender moves his key to the outside receiver. If the outside receiver continues vertical, the outside 1/4 defender must stay on top of the receiver and squeeze through his outside hip in order to defend against any vertical route.

Quarters Coverage Techniques: Lock Defender

The lock defender plays an inside-leverage man-to-man technique on his receiver (figure 9.7). He can align as far inside the receiver as needed in order to maintain an inside-leverage position, and he is responsible for matching any route by his receiver all over the field.

Using the lock technique on outside receivers allows us to maintain our three-on-two pattern match rules on the inside receivers and helps eliminate any new learning for the secondary. In figure 9.7, the halfback (HB) becomes the outside 1/4 defender while the safety (FS) remains the inside 1/4 defender.

The game plan can dictate a lock technique on any receiver, but we most commonly apply the technique to the receivers farthest outside in a trips or quads set. The reason for this is simple: a lock technique places a defender in pure man-to-man coverage without any help, and we want to ensure that this throw is as far away from the quarterback as possible. This greatly reduces the completion percentage on any downfield throws, and often the lock defender is never challenged because of the length of the throw.

The inside 1/4, outside 1/4, and lock defenders are all primary deep responsibility defenders in quarters coverage. The other two techniques are used by the underneath coverage defenders. While all of our deep responsibility players are concerned with pass-first, all of our underneath defenders are run-first defenders and their coverage responsibility is lessened to allow them to focus on executing their run assignments first.

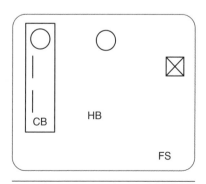

FIGURE 9.7 Lock defender.

Quarters Coverage Techniques: Curl Defender

The first technique taught for the underneath portion of the coverage is for the curl defender. The curl defenders are also our force players versus the run, and for this reason we always have a curl defender on each side of the formation. The curl defenders always play run-first and receive their initial key from the end man on the line of scrimmage. Their primary responsibility is to maintain outside leverage on any run block and keep the ball carrier from outleveraging us on the perimeter of the defense.

Once he reads a pass key, the curl defender is responsible for dropping to the inside receiver and matching the first inside breaking route to his side of the formation. The curl defender must also maintain leverage on any receiver attempting to cross his face from the backfield.

The curl defender's pass keys are:

- Inside receiver releases vertical.
- Inside receiver releases vertical while outside receiver stops or releases inside.
- Inside receiver releases outside.
- Inside receiver releases inside.
- Receiver who starts the play in the backfield releases outside.

(Note: In figure 9.8, the halfback, HB, demonstrates the curl technique.)

The inside receiver releases vertical (figure 9.8a): After reading pass, the curl defender drops on a 45-degree angle to the inside hip of the inside receiver. When the inside receiver continues to release vertical, the curl defender collides with the receiver to slow his release while maintaining inside leverage in order to protect the middle of the field.

The inside receiver releases vertical while the outside receiver stops or releases inside (figure 9.8b): After reading the pass, the curl defender drops on a 45-degree angle to the inside hip of the inside receiver. When the inside receiver continues to release vertical, the curl defender collides with the receiver while keying the release of the outside receiver. When the outside receiver either stops or releases inside, the curl defender expands his drop to the outside receiver and matches his route. Any time the outside receiver stops, the outside 1/4 defender should give a "smash" call in order to help the curl defender identify the route and expand his drop.

The inside receiver releases outside (figure 9.8c): After reading the pass, the curl defender drops on a 45-degree angle to the inside hip of the inside receiver. When the inside receiver releases outside, the curl defender must expand his drop to the inside hip of the next outside receiver. The curl defender must maintain inside position on the outside receiver in order to protect the middle of the field. It is crucial to teach players that anytime they identify an outside route, they should expect a complementary inside route from an outside receiver.

The inside receiver releases inside (figure 9.8d): The curl defender drops on a 45-degree angle to the inside hip of the inside receiver. When the inside receiver releases inside, the curl defender locates the route of the next outside receiver and maintains the inside position. It is important that players understand that anytime

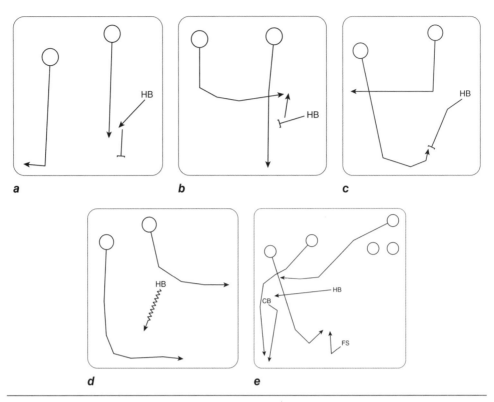

FIGURE 9.8 Curl defender: (a) inside receiver releases vertical, (b) inside receiver releases vertical while outside receiver stops or releases inside, (c) inside receiver releases outside, (d) inside receiver releases inside, (e) receiver who starts the play in the backfield releases outside.

a receiver releases inside and in front of the underneath portion of the coverage, they must anticipate an inside breaking route behind them.

A receiver who starts the play in the backfield releases outside (figure 9.8e): The curl defender drops on a 45-degree angle to the inside hip of the inside receiver. If any receiver leaving the backfield attempts to cross the face of the curl defender, the curl defender must maintain outside leverage on the route. If the receiver attempts to cross his face and then continue vertically upfield, the curl defender must match the route of the receiver all the way down the field.

Quarters Coverage Techniques: Vertical Hook Defender

The final job to teach when introducing the underneath portion of the coverage is that of the vertical hook defender. The vertical hook defender, nearly always a linebacker, is responsible for the vertical release of the near running back. The vertical hook defenders are also primary run defenders and will maintain inside leverage on any blockers. Against a two-back set, we use two vertical hook defenders, but just one vertical hook defender versus a one-back set.

The vertical hook defender's keys are:

- Key the triangle (guard-centre-guard) for run-pass key.
- If pass, key the near running back for pass responsibility.
- If the near back is vertical, open hips and maintain inside and on top position on the running back, with the responsibility of running with the back all the way down the field.
- If the near back is out, give a "push" call to the wall-flat player and replace the wall-flat player to that side of the formation.
- If the near back is under or stays in to pass protect, spot-drop 10 to 12 yards deep and mirror the quarterback.

Quarters Coverage Alignments

Before covering the alignments specific to quarters coverage, I quickly provide the base alignment rules for the secondary in the 4-2-6 defense.

Corners always align over the top of the #1 receiver to their side of the formation, with their heels 5 yards from the line of scrimmage. Their leverage on the receiver will be determined by the technique they are playing.

In alignment, safeties always split the difference between the end man on the line of scrimmage and the next inside receiver, with their heels 10 yards from the line of scrimmage. The safeties must align with enough depth to see the entire formation and to communicate the coverage responsibilities to their side of the ball.

Halfbacks are the primary adjusters against most formations and have the greatest variation in their initial alignment. Halfbacks align over the top of the #2 receiver to their side of the formation, with their heels 5 yards from the line of scrimmage. If there is no #2 receiver to his side of the ball, the halfback runs across the formation and aligns over the top of the #3 receiver to that side.

Linebacker base alignment is determined by the number of running backs in the offensive backfield. Versus a two-back set, both linebackers align in 30 technique (B gap) to their side of the ball, with their heels 5 yards from the line of scrimmage, and play a vertical hook technique. Versus a one-back set, the linebacker to the passing strength splits the distance between the end man on the line of scrimmage and the inside receiver and becomes the curl defender. The other linebacker must adjust his alignment to a 00 technique (head up on the centre) and remain a vertical hook defender.

The safety to each side of the formation must give a specific coverage call to all of the defenders to his side. The coverage call is determined by the number of receivers on each side of the formation and communicates which of the five coverage techniques should be used by each defender.

Defending Twin Sets

When we begin teaching players how to align to the wide variety of formations an offense can present, the starting point remains a two-receiver, or twins, set

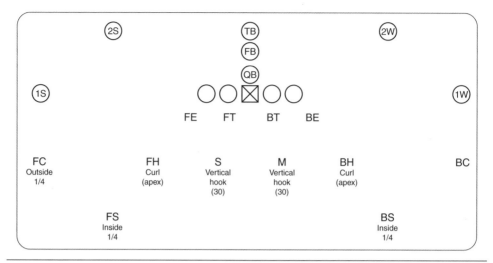

FIGURE 9.9 Quarters coverage versus a 2×2 formation: A deuce call is given to both sides of the formation.

(figure 9.9). Versus two spread receivers, the safety gives a "deuce" call to the cornerback and halfback to his side of the formation. A deuce call indicates that there are two receivers in position to run vertical routes. Any time a deuce call is made, the safety to that side of the formation plays an inside 1/4 technique while keying the #2 receiver. The corner now knows that he will use the outside 1/4 technique and will key the #2 receiver. Finally, a deuce call informs the halfback that he is the curl defender to his side of the formation. The halfback is now a primary run defender and has force responsibility versus the run. This allows the safety and cornerback to match the vertical threats to their side of the formation while allowing the halfback to remain close enough to the box to play run first.

Defending Trips and Quads Sets

Versus three detached receivers (figures 9.10 and 9.11), the safety gives a "trio" call to the cornerback and halfback to his side of the formation. A trio call indicates that there are three receivers in position to run vertical routes. Any time a trio call is made, the safety to that side of the formation plays an inside 1/4 technique and keys the #3 receiver. The halfback to that side of the formation uses the outside 1/4 technique and also receives his initial key from the #3 receiver. In order to maintain our base coverage rules on the inside receivers, the corner to a trips side will play a lock technique on the outside receiver. He is now responsible for him man-to-man all over the field. Depending on the number of running backs in the offensive backfield, the curl defender will either be a linebacker (versus a one-back set) or the opposite halfback (versus a two-back set).

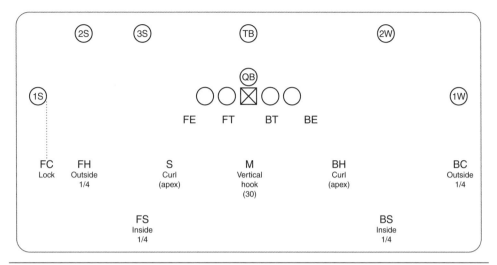

FIGURE 9.10 Quarters coverage versus a 3×2 formation: A trio call is given to the trips side of the formation while a duo call is given to the twins side. The Sam linebacker moves to an apex position versus a one-back set and becomes the curl defender.

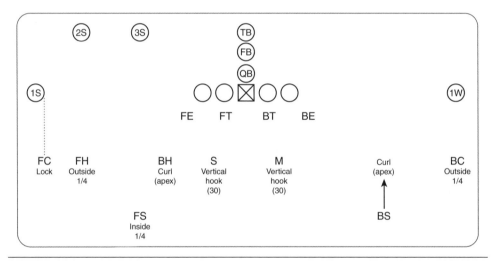

FIGURE 9.11 Quarters coverage versus a 3×1 formation: A "trio" call is given to the trips side of the formation while a "solo" call is given to the single side. The boundary halfback runs over to become the curl defender because there is no #2 receiver to his side.

When the offense presents a formation with four spread receivers (figure 9.12), the safety to that side of the formation will give a "quad" call to all of the defenders to that side. A quad call requires that the corner and halfback to that side of the formation both play a lock technique on the #1 and #2 receivers, respectively. The opposite halfback runs over and becomes the outside 1/4 defender over the top of the #3 receiver, while the safety remains the inside 1/4 defender and receives

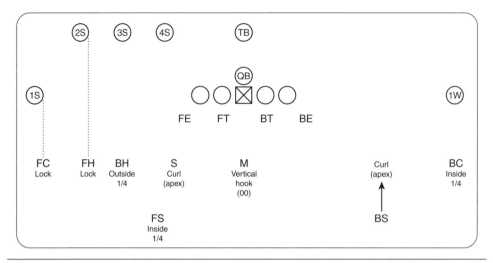

FIGURE 9.12 Quarters coverage versus a 4×1 formation: A quad call is given to the four-receiver side of the formation while a solo call is given to the single-receiver side. The boundary halfback runs over to become the curl defender because there is no #2 receiver to his side. The Sam linebacker moves to an apex position versus a one-back set and becomes the curl defender.

his key from the #4 receiver. The linebacker to the quad side must adjust his alignment to an apex position and becomes the curl defender to the four-receiver side.

Defending Single Sets

Versus a single detached receiver, the safety makes a solo call to the cornerback on his side of the formation. A solo call indicates that there is a single vertical threat to their side of the formation. This is the only situation in which the safety will not be the inside 1/4 defender. Versus one receiver, the corner becomes the inside 1/4 defender and receives his key from the #1 receiver. The safety becomes the curl defender and must now receive his key from the end man on the line of scrimmage because the safety is a run-first player. Depending on personnel, you can also switch jobs between the corner and safety in order to keep the safety as the inside 1/4 defender, provided your corner is physical enough to be a primary run defender.

CONCLUSION

The chapter provides an overview of how quarters coverage has evolved to combat the threats presented by modern offenses, and it provides ideas about how to implement quarters coverage as part of a defensive system. Quarters is a very time-intensive coverage to teach, but it's worth the investment for the many advantages that quarters coverage creates in defending both the run and pass. Perfecting our ability to play quarters coverage has been a critical factor in our program's recent success. We will continue to rely heavily on it as we seek to dominate opposing offenses in coming years.

10

Defensive Play Calling

Greg Marshall

Before discussing defensive play calling, we need to understand formulation of the game plan. How do coaches come up with these plays, and why do they believe they should call a given play at a particular time? What have they done during their preparations that have led them to believe they should make this call? These decisions, and the skill at which players execute these decisions, ultimately decide the outcome of the game.

There are three components to formulating the game plan:

1. Planning
2. Implementing
3. Executing

The better the coach does in the planning and implementing stages, the more opportunity players have to be successful in the execution stage. Throughout the whole process, the key isn't what the coach knows, it's what he can teach the players that will give them the confidence to successfully execute the game plan.

PLANNING

The planning stage begins with breaking down the opponent's game film. At the professional or U Sports levels, coaches usually break down at least the last three games played. Depending on the amount of time between games, which is not always a constant in the CFL, it may be ideal to add a game or two. Especially if we have played this opponent already, we will look at what they have done versus us in the past. A breakdown this in-depth may not be possible at the youth or high school levels. But at least be sure to study the opponent's last game and any previous games between their team and yours.

While breaking down the opponent's film, we gather information on backfield sets, the formations the team likes to use, the types of plays they like to run, where on the field they're likely to run certain plays or play types, and the team's play tendencies by down and distance. With the heavy emphasis on passing in the CFL, two vital components of our breakdown are the types of pass protection the opponent likes to use and the various route combinations in their passing game.

Once we finish gathering this data, the defensive staff puts together the scouting report that will be given to each player and coach. With all the technology that is available to analyze the information from film breakdowns, you have to decide what information is most useful to you and your players. Be careful of paralysis by analysis. Too much information can be confusing to players. Provide them with the main tendencies of your opponent and how you want them to react or adjust.

Two items should be part of the scouting report: a personnel sheet and an offensive summary sheet. The personnel sheet is basically a depth chart showing the opponent's starting lineup and backups by position. The information on each player can be as basic as his height, weight, and experience level, or you may wish to include some analysis of each player's strengths and weaknesses as well. Using this page as an introduction will help familiarize players with their opponent. Often they will have some information to add because they have faced this opponent before or may have previously played with some of your opponent's players somewhere before joining your team.

The offensive summary sheet is important in a couple of ways. First, studying this page should give the players a basic understanding of the opposing team's offense. By looking at the page's various sections, they should be able to tell if the opponent favors running or throwing the ball, the opponent's favorite plays, and the opponent's tendencies based on down and distance, field position, and formation.

Second, the defensive coaches should be able to take the information on this sheet and start to formulate their game plan. Figure 10.1 gives us material for a couple of great examples. By looking at the data found in the down and distance section for all second downs, a few important pieces of information can be gained. This opponent ran 53 total plays on second down with 4 or more yards to go for a first down, and 47 of those plays have been passing plays. Also, on second down and 3 yards or less for a first down, this opponent ran 18 total plays, with 15 of them being running plays. These are both strong tendencies that should influence the calls that the defensive coordinator would make in these situations. Another example of how the defensive coordinator could use this sheet is found in the backfield set tendencies section. This opponent ran a total of 64 plays with two–running back sets (Roger/Louie gun, Roger/Louie, I, and split gun), and 54 of those plays involved run action (42 runs and 12 play-action passes). Again, this is a strong tendency, and the defensive coordinator would probably make calls that are best designed to defend against these types of plays when there are two running backs in the game. If you use a video service like Hudl, you can run reports to generate this kind of data as long as you have tagged (entered) all of the information on your game film.

The next step is to look at the strengths and weaknesses of the opponent. How does our defensive package stack up against our opponent's offensive package in terms of physical and schematic matchups? What do they do offensively that

Offensive Stats	
Rushing yards per game: *156* Passing yards per game: *312* Total offensive yards per game: *460*	Second down conversion rate: *43/71 = 60%* Turnovers per game: *2.5* Scoring per game: *35.5*

Offensive Stats					
Run: *67* Pass: *82*		Play pass: *24* Screen: *6*		Draw: *2* Tricks: *0*	

Favourite protections	Favourite runs	Favourite play passes	Favourite screens	Favourite draws	Favourite tricks
1. 60s (45x) *2. Slide str (8x)* *3. 50s (7x)* *4. 70s (6x)* *5. Slide sprint str (5x)*	*1. Zone opp special str/wk (16x)* *2. Zone str/wk (15x)* *3. Zone opp wk/str (9x)* *4. Toss T str/wk (7x)* *5. Wham wk (3x)*	*1. Sally str (5x)* *2. Zone pass wk/str (5x)* *3. Zone opp pass str (4x)* *4. FB shovel str (3x)* *5. TB shovel str (3x)*	*1. Hitch screen wk (3x)* *2. Bubble screen str (2x)* *3. TB screen wk (1x)*	*1. QB lead draw (1x)* *2. QB draw (1x)*	

Players of note

Down and distance tendencies

Down	Total	Run	Pass	Play pass	Screen	Draw	Tricks
First play of the series	*14*	*6*	*5*	*3*			
First and 10	*76*	*29*	*24*	*18*	*4*	*1*	
First and other	*11*	*5*	*4*	*2*			
Second and 7 or more	*27*		*26*		*1*		
Second and 4 to 6	*26*	*3*	*21*		*1*	*1*	
Second and 3 or less	*18*	*15*	*2*	*1*			
Third down	*6*	*6*					

Backfield set tendencies

Backset	Total	Run	Pass	Play pass	Screen	Draw	Tricks
Zero gun	*53*	*14*	*29*	*9*	*1*		
Roger/Louie gun	*45*	*29*	*7*	*9*			
Weak gun	*26*		*22*	*1*	*2*	*1*	
Strong gun	*22*		*18*	*1*	*3*		
Roger/Louie	*10*	*7*	*1*	*2*			
Back zero	*10*	*9*		*1*			
1	*6*	*6*					
Split gun	*3*		*2*	*1*			
Empty gun	*3*		*2*			*1*	

FIGURE 10.1 Sample offensive breakdown.

could create problems? Have we learned anything about our opponent from other teams' successes or failures during our film study? By answering these questions, we can take the base defensive package we play every week and make the necessary adjustments, additions, and subtractions for this game. As a defense, we want to force the offense out of its comfort zone. We want to force them to get away from their bread-and-butter plays and make them operate from the back of the playbook or the bottom of the call sheet.

IMPLEMENTING

The next step is implementing the game plan. It is critical to decide what information the players should have, what they must learn and keep in mind about the opponent. You should plan out each film session, meeting, walk-through, and practice so you can maximize the teaching you want to get done.

During the practice week, challenge the players the way they'll be challenged in the game. Don't always script for success when drawing up your practice cards; put the players in some difficult situations. You will have the opportunity to make corrections in meetings, walk-throughs, or the next practice. Players will feel better prepared because you have controlled the environment and given them confidence that they can be successful if they pay attention to the game plan.

When teaching players about their opponent's offense, go beyond individual plays and underline concepts. It's common for an offense to change formations, thereby disguising their intentions while probably creating different matchups for the defense. But often the old and new formation will fall under the same play concept. If your players recognize the concept—say, a pass route combination—the switch shouldn't cause confusion. For them to recognize the concept, teach it to the entire secondary and linebacking corps.

In the example shown in figure 10.2, the offense is running a strong-side option route combination with the #3 receiver as the intended receiver to the field. In this example, the offense is forcing three different defenders to cover this route combination against three different offensive players. By changing their formation, the offense is forcing different positions to defend this route, but the offense's intent has not changed. By teaching this concept to the entire group, you have prepared them to succeed no matter what formation or alignment the offense uses to run this route combination.

It is important to identify and understand the type of pass protection the opponent is using. For defensive players to be successful rushing the passer (individually or as part of a stunt or blitz package), they need to know what type of pass protection they are working against. They should also know how mobile the quarterback is and if he is right- or left-handed. Most quarterbacks scramble to their throwing hand side when feeling pressure, so it is important for players to be aware of this tendency.

An example of this would be if the defensive coordinator called for a weak-side blitz versus a right-handed quarterback. With the wide side of the field to the quarterback's right, the contain player on the wide side should be aware that the quarterback is probably coming his way when pressured. Using this knowledge, the contain player should know that he must always maintain outside leverage on potential blockers so he will be able to contain the quarterback on this blitz. This would be the wrong time for the contain player to gamble and make a move to the inside!

Commit practice and meeting time to these areas as well: the red zone (when you are defending your own goal line area) and the green zone (when your opponent is coming off his own goal line area). Success in the red zone means you are limiting

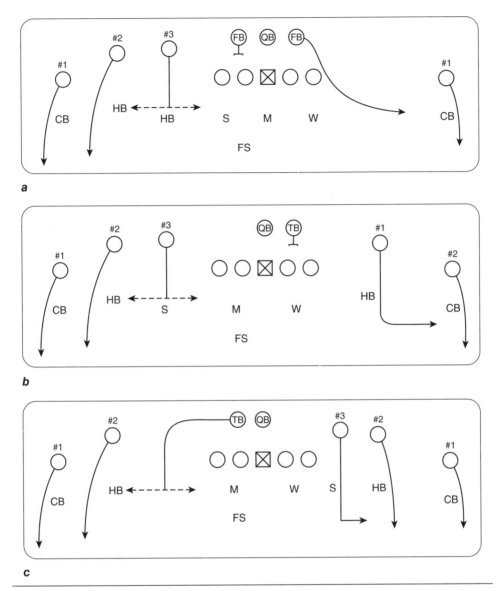

FIGURE 10.2 Strong-side option route: (a) versus 31 set, (b) versus 32 set, (c) versus 23 set.

your opponent's point total, and success in the green zone creates opportunities for your team to score. As your players get a better understanding of the types of plays they have to defend in these areas, their execution of your calls will improve.

It is important for players to be involved and engaged during meetings. Asking or answering questions as they watch film creates mental repetitions that play a big part in the learning process. Not only that, but coaches will get a good indication of how well players understand the opponent and the game plan. If you are using an online video service such as Hudl, you can expect the players to have studied some plays in advance and can give them study sheets or review quizzes to check their learning. You can also quiz their study of your opponent information sheet.

As you work through the week, the call sheet for the game is developed by watching more film, evaluating practice, and updating any injury concerns that affect your opponent or your team. (An example of an injury situation: will the opponent's starting quarterback be playing or not?) As you finalize your call sheet, how do you organize it to remind yourself which calls to make when certain situations arise during the game? Are the calls organized by down and distance, by personnel groups, by base calls and blitzes, or by special situations? Most likely by a combination of these and other factors, but the system, whatever it is, must allow the individual defensive coordinator to function as efficiently as possible.

EXECUTION

Finally, after many hours of film study, practicing, and meetings, it is game day and time to execute the game plan. As the defensive coordinator, it is your job to make the calls that will give the players an opportunity to use their abilities to make plays and play with great confidence. For the players, it comes down to knowing their job, doing their job, trusting their teammates, and making a play when they have the opportunity to make one.

During the course of the game, many factors can affect the calls made: field position, weather, score, injuries, time in the game, and offensive personnel. And you must be ready to adjust your calls as the game progresses, both to keep your opponents off-balance and to counter any new wrinkles they come up with.

You must also decide how you are going to communicate the defensive call to the players on the field, and which player or players are responsible to relay the call to the entire defensive group. Most often the call is communicated by hand signals or by numbers that match up with a list of calls on your defensive signal caller's wristband. The advantage of the wristband method is that the numbers can be changed at any time, throwing off your opponent (you would have to have a second set of wristband sheets to go with your second call sheet if you wanted to change your numbers within a game). The disadvantage is that your signal caller has to look at his wristband, which can mean a hesitation of a few seconds.

On-field play-calling responsibilities naturally fall to the middle linebacker or free safety because of their central location in the defense, which is a factor versus no-huddle offenses. When choosing which players to use, consider experience, reliability, willingness to take control, communication skills, and the simple ability to see. That last factor can be crucial. We had a middle linebacker who had a hard time seeing signals from the bench. Until we caught on to the problem and adjusted, there was more than one occasion when our defense played something totally different from what the defensive coordinator had signaled.

An option that is particularly effective against fast-paced offenses is the muddle, in which all of the players look to the sideline for the defensive call. The obvious benefit is that the call from the sidelines can be swiftly communicated to the defense on the field. But individual players may misread the signal or miss part of it. For this reason, get the players to verbalize the call to their teammates to verify that everyone is on the same page.

It is important for coaches and players to have procedures in place for the sidelines and halftime. When players come off the field after a series, they should go to a designated area on the bench (unless they have an equipment or injury issue). This way the coach doesn't have to hunt anyone down before going over whatever adjustments need to be made.

Communication between players and coaches, whether on the sidelines or in the spotter's booth, plays a vital role during the game. Encourage players to speak to you or their position coach about what is happening on the field. At halftime, be organized to maximize the time to address any concerns, talk about what to expect, tell the players what needs to be accomplished in the second half, and how you're going to do it.

The final piece to the puzzle when calling the game is to trust your preparation in the film room and on the practice field. This will allow you to be confident that you and your players are prepared for this challenge. As the defensive play caller, you must get a feel for the ebb and flow of the game so your decisions help the team.

CONCLUSION

Being effective as a defensive play caller starts and ends with detail. You must have an in-depth understanding of your opponent, with a special focus on their most effective plays and formations. From there, consider what information your players should learn and what information you have to keep in mind. Plan the meetings and practices needed during the week for your players to feel prepared and confident ahead of the game. Your knowledge of your opponent will also give you the confidence to lead your players through the week, and the ability to make the right calls at the right times during the game. The more prepared you and your players are, the "luckier" you will be on game day.

11

Special Teams

Patrick Tracey

At every level of competition, games are won or lost as a result of plays on special teams. If you approach the special teams as just another thing to do in practice, players will not respond at a championship level. This chapter will present several important aspects of coaching special teams, including coaching roles, basic rules, player assignments, weekly scheduling, and some basic systems.

Often television cameras will zoom in on the kicker, punter, or returner when there is a kicking situation, and most players and fans follow the ball in flight. Special-teams play involves so much more: player substitutions, presnap alignments, protection schemes, coverage and return calls, post-snap lanes, techniques, leverage, landmark drops, blocking, tackling, and sideline adjustments. Unlike offense (in which there is a designed call or a designated play side) or defense (in which you defend a specific area), a special-teams play involves more players and yardage because the trajectory of the football is often unpredictable.

COACHING SPECIAL TEAMS

The head coach decides who coaches the special teams, and he does so with an eye to maximizing resources for the good of the program. Many programs divide the special-teams units among the staff, others assign a coach to coordinate, and others let the defensive staff handle the returns and the offensive staff oversee the coverage units. The character of special teams often reflects the head coach's personality and commitment to the overall kicking game. His active involvement in setting practice schedules and depth charts, attending unit meetings, teaching skills, rewarding players, and developing the special-teams game plan sets the weekly tempo for everyone. Using assistant coaches to lead drills and teach individual skills will maximize the players' learning and execution, and will help keep the terminology consistent.

Many crucial game-time decisions occur on third down and involve the kicking game. "Should we go for the first down or kick the field goal?" "Should we punt for the single or try the long field goal?" "How much time can we run off the clock before we snap the football?" One question each coaching staff should consider before the playbooks are written is what the overall strategy is for blocking kicks, attempting fakes, and running trick plays or reverses. These situations are examples of why you need a head coach who is directly involved with special teams, possibly a coordinator who is responsible for all special teams, and regular game-planning meetings for coaching staff to help keep everyone on the same page with these decisions.

IMPORTANT RULES OF THE CANADIAN FOOTBALL KICKING GAME

Many players and coaches are more familiar with American football rules than Canadian football rules because of the extensive coverage that the NCAA and NFL have on television. For that reason, it is a good investment of time to review special-teams rules that are unique to the Canadian game.

On any kick or punt, anyone behind the kicker is onside and can recover the ball without penalty, but he must go for the ball and not interfere with the returner. An off-side player must allow 5 yards to an opponent who's attempting to gain possession of the ball on a punt or a missed field goal.

On punts, kickoffs, and missed field goals, no fair catches are allowed. Players on the covering teams must allow a 5-yard radius for the returning player to catch the ball. The penalty for violations is 5 yards if the ball is fielded off the ground, and 15 yards if it is fielded in the air. Missed field-goal attempts can be returned out of the end zone; if the recovering team gets the ball over the goal line, the ball is spotted at the 20-yard line (conference or league rules may apply) unless it is returned past the 20-yard line. The recovering team has the choice of which hash to place the ball.

After a punt, kick, or missed field goal downed in the end zone, a single point or rouge is awarded, and the team scored against puts the ball in play (first and 10) on their own 35-yard line, or on the previous line of scrimmage on a field-goal attempt if it was farther than the 35-yard line. The team in possession of the ball has the choice of which hash to place the ball. In amateur football, the line of scrimmage for a convert attempt is the 5-yard line. If a field goal is good, the team scored against has the option of putting the ball in play at their 35-yard line or they can have the scoring team kick off. It is not a blocked kick if the ball is touched by an opponent and then crosses the line of scrimmage; off-side players must give 5 yards.

PLAYER ALLOCATION

Successful teams (conference champions, statistical leaders) put a strong emphasis on player selection for special teams, and look for ones who have proven to be the very best at specific skills such as open-field blocking and tackling, understanding correct leverage or body control, and playing in space.

What makes special teams unique is the number of players that you can utilize on your team. Distributing talent can be an effective way to bond the team and to develop players' and staff members' appreciation of different skills. You can put offensive linemen on the kickoff return unit, defensive linemen on the field-goal unit, running backs and linebackers on the punt team, and use quarterbacks as holders or punters, and defensive backs or receivers as returners or gunners on punts or kickoffs.

In order to develop consistent and quality special-teams players, coaches must stress the same qualities they look for in offensive and defensive personnel: positive attitude, accountability, discipline, consistency, teamwork, mental awareness, passion for skill development, and belief in the system. Each member of the football team must have the belief "We can," especially that we can win games with our special teams. What can take a team to the next level are the players who play the system and take a leadership role in making it their identity.

Every player wants to be a starter. They must understand that everyone who is dressed for the game can be a starter in the kicking game. Special-teams play can be the link between offense and defense—a team within the team. The task of special-teams coaches is to get the players to understand the principles, concepts, rules, and game strategy within the overall structure of the football game.

Depending on roster sizes, each player can have a role on special teams if he believes in the overall team goals and wants to make a positive difference in the outcome of the football game. Coaches at every level like players who make intelligent decisions and limit penalties by practicing correct skills in game situations. Roughing the kicker, holding, clipping, and no-yards penalties can be avoided through repetition and positive reinforcement. It is also important to develop a player's game awareness. Players can anticipate game-changing situations, and they can alert their backups when there is an injury. What they shouldn't do is take themselves off the field without communication with the medical staff or their position coaches.

A good idea for your coaching staff is to keep updated charts that track how players are being used on offense, defense, and special teams. These distribution-of-labour charts help you to identify if any players are being over- or underutilized. The sample shown in table 11.1 has only five players on the list; yours would include the entire roster. The first column is for jersey number and name, and then the subsequent columns are for each special team. A 1 indicates a starter, 2 indicates a backup, and an X indicates that the player is not on the team in question. You could also include offense and defense if you wanted a complete representation of each player's involvement on the field.

TABLE 11.1   Special-Teams Distribution-of-Labour Depth Chart

Jersey and player	Punt cover	Punt return	Kickoff cover	Kickoff return	Field-goal protection	Field-goal defense	Hands protect	Onside recover
11. Name	1	2	1	1	X	X	X	2
18. Name	1	1	2	2	3	X	X	1
29. Name	X	X	2	2	1	2	2	X
57. Name	1	1	1	X	X	X	X	1
75. Name	2	2	X	1	X	1	1	X

To help organize yourself on game day (as well as during the practice week), it is very helpful to have your special-teams depth chart on an easy-to-read sheet. That way, if you are missing a player, it is simple to look on the sheet for the vacant position and find the player or substitute who belongs there. During the game, at least one coach on the sideline should have this depth chart to manage substitutions for injury, equipment repairs, player rest, and so on, and if you have a coach in the spotter's booth, he can help the sideline coach identify the missing player better from his vantage point. Figure 11.1 shows a sample template for a special-teams depth chart. This chart lists jersey numbers, but you can insert player names as well.

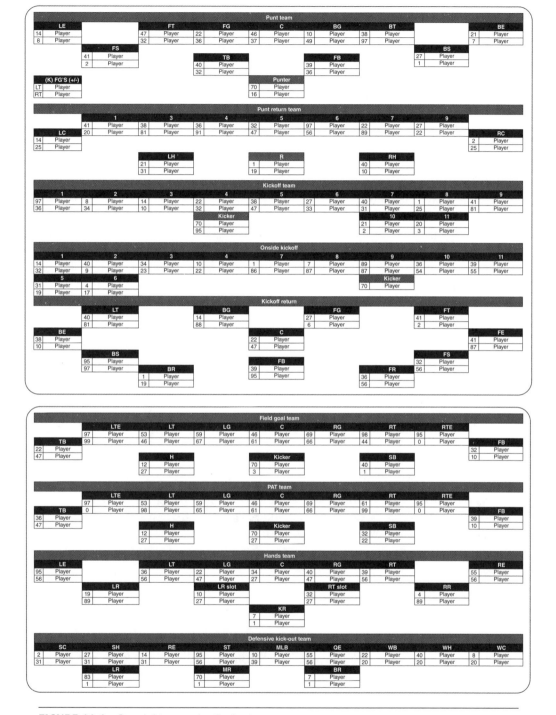

FIGURE 11.1 Special-teams depth chart.

WEEKLY PREPARATIONS

The kicking game starts every game, and games often end in a key kicking situation. Time invested on special teams must be equal or greater than the time invested in the two-minute offense, goal line defense, heavy or short-yardage offensive sets, the prevent coverage package, the red zone series, pass protection schemes, and defensive zone blitz concepts.

Weekly Special-Teams Practice Schedule

You will know the level of commitment in a football program by where the special-teams section is placed in the playbook, when it is scheduled in the daily practice plans, and the hustle on the field when a special-teams period is whistled in. To demonstrate this, a sample time period allotment for special-teams learning appears here. This is just one example; a coaching staff needs to decide where special-teams meetings, skill development, and systems practice fit best in the weekly schedule.

Day 1

This is the first day of the week, and likely the players have had a day off after the previous game, so they should be ready for some quality skill work. It is also a good opportunity to correct mistakes from the last game.

Practice includes:

- Ten-minute skill periods for the kickers, long snapper, holder, and returners prepractice
- Five-minute protection scheme practice and adjustments for the interior of the punt-cover team
- Five-minute protection scheme practice and adjustments for the field-goal and convert teams, and review huddle, cadence, fire calls (bad snaps), and coverage lanes for the field-goal unit
- Five-minute lane adjustments and corrections for the kickoff cover unit

Day 2

This is fast-paced practice for the field-goal, punt, and field-goal defense and return units:

- Five-minute period for the field-goal team, including three kicks from each hash mark (L/M/R), varying the yardage, and a full-team live rush versus the defense

- Review by the defense unit of the field-goal rush (blocks and returns) in the defensive team prep period, and execution of the full return in the live period. When rushing the protection team, it is more efficient to send only part of the unit (three or four players) while others step to gaps. This will focus all eyes on the execution at the point of contact and eliminate the confusion on the line of scrimmage.
- Five-minute period versus 10- or 11-man fronts, and a 5-minute period for coverage lanes
- Ten-minute period for man punt returns, including the field and boundary wall schemes
- Five-minute period to review the front-line landmark drops and the wedge and kick-out blocks for the kickoff return unit

Day 3

This is a regular practice for depth chart review, player substitutions, and returns units if you have only three practices prior to the next game. If you have a fourth, that fourth day can be for depth chart, player substitutions, and special-teams walk-throughs (slow-, medium-, or full-speed repetitions with no contact and sometimes with no opposition).

Practice includes:

- Ten-minute period for punt return divided into 10- and 11-man blocks and returns
- Ten-minute field goal and punt fakes or trick plays
- Five-minute kickoff return period reviewing the hands team
- Five-minute kickoff coverage period reviewing the onside kick

Day 4

This is a physically light practice that requires a high degree of mental focus and concentration. Practice includes:

- Five-minute walk-through for each special-teams unit
- Time to review depth chart and player substitutions

A good way to practice substitutions is to mix special-teams walk-throughs with offensive and defensive walk-throughs.

It is important that your special-teams unit captains meet weekly with the head coach and special-teams coordinator to review possible game scenarios, such as when to take a time-out or delay-of-game penalty if there are too many men on the field or not enough men on the field, or whether to concede a safety or punt from your end zone. All of these situations must be covered in weekly meetings and rehearsed in practice situations. Your team should plan to win every phase of the kicking game, not just play even or leave things up to your offense or defense.

Specialist Practice

Many teams find it difficult to allocate practice time to specialist skills, so these skills often must be worked on outside of the regular practice schedule. Again, this will need to be planned based on your team's situation and needs. Specialists often practice their skills just before or after practice, or sometimes they may have their own short practice during a school lunch hour. All of the specialists (kicker, long snappers, punter, holder, and returners) require a set routine and weekly schedule that allows for skill development and consistency.

Punt Long Snapper

Rules now limit contact on the third down long snapper, so the athlete who can consistently fire the ball back and cover downfield is coveted. The skill set requires flexibility in the hips, range of motion in the shoulders, handgrip strength, and a strong mental attitude. It is important that the long snapper have a set practice schedule and a routine for warming up. Depending on factors relating to the age of the athletes (depth of the punter, size of the football), the following drill protocol is effective:

- Seven- to 10-minute stretch and agility warm-up and 3 to 5 minutes of hand, shoulder, and forearm flexion.
- A balanced stance opposite a partner with the football raised overhead, gripped with both hands. The partners should stand 5 yards apart and release the ball forward, concentrating on the release and follow-through. Repeat 10 times, and with each repetition work toward hip acceleration and rotation of the ball.
- Advance to 10 yards apart for 5 repetitions.
- Go back to 5 yards apart and start throwing the ball backward between the legs from a narrow two-point stance; it is important that the receiving player gives a clear target and a cadence for the snapper.
- Extend the distance to 10 yards and then a maximum depth of 14 yards.
- Release and cover downfield for 15 yards; add step-over bags for agility or standing blocking bags for avoidance and lane integrity.
- Advance with the full punt unit for coverage lane responsibility.

The long snapper should vary his rhythm; he should not stay down in a ready position over the ball too long. When approaching the football, instruct him to take a look down the field; the number of returners (one or two) could indicate if he has a blocking assignment in the protection scheme. If the snapper is not playing another position, he can do some target work by aiming at the goalpost pads during the week. To develop strength in the arms and preparation for a heavy wet ball, use a weighted football for part of the warm-up period.

Field-Goal Long Snapper

A drill protocol similar to the one for the punt long snapper is effective. Repeat the drills described in that section, but use a wider stance to strengthen the centre of gravity; be aware that this also expands the lanes of the defensive rush team. Coverage is not as critical for the snapper on field goals. It is common for teams to use a larger athlete (offensive or defensive lineman) in this situation to maximize the protection.

The distance is usually 7 yards from the line of scrimmage to the holder; it is critical that the snapper, holder, and kicker are working together on timing, cadence, tilt of the ball, and angle of the kick.

Kicker and Punter

These specialists should practice with their holders (convert and field-goal kicker) and their snappers (convert and field-goal kicker, punter), but they should spend time on their own as well. For kickoffs, the kicker should practice his approach to the ball to establish consistency for his plant foot, as well as in the speed of his run-up so that the coverage team can time their approach. The kicker should always aim at a target instead of just kicking the ball aimlessly downfield. Special kicks such as onside kicks, squib kicks, and sky-ball kicks are needed at crucial points in the game, and these kicks require regular practice.

Punters should practice their grip on the ball and a proper drop to ensure consistent foot contact and to avoid shanking the ball. As they begin to make foot contact with the ball after practicing their drops, it's helpful for them to punt into a net so that they can get more repetitions without anyone having to chase the ball. Once they start full punts, they should always have a target; most coaches want the punter to aim the ball to a specific area of the field so that the coverage team's job is easier.

Returners

Returners can never practice catching kicks and punts too often. When you think of the huge field position and momentum swings that occur from a muffed kick or punt, it's clear that it's an important investment of time to have the returners fielding as many balls as possible. The trajectory of a kickoff in the air is generally fairly predictable, significant wind notwithstanding, but punts can be unpredictable even in perfect weather conditions. Fielding punts cleanly and consistently may be one of the most difficult individual skills in football, so make sure returners spend considerable time practicing with the punter.

Meetings and Goal Setting

If your team has weekly meeting times, make sure to schedule time for special-teams meetings. During these times, you can review the performance of the special-teams units in the previous game (including watching game film if it is available), update and review the depth charts, and begin to prepare each unit for the upcoming opponent. Chapter 12 on scouting the opposition has more detail describing all of the aspects of analyzing an opponent and making appropriate adjustments to prepare the team.

Many players and coaches find it motivational to set specific performance objectives for special teams. These give a more objective measure for game performance than how the coach or players feel about how things went. When setting objectives (goals), it is important to make them SMART: specific, measurable, attainable, relevant, and timely. Here are some examples and nonexamples of each aspect of SMART goals:

- S: "Our net punting average for this game will be at least 31 yards," not "We will improve our net punting average."
- M: "All players will be within 11 yards of the tackle on every kickoff coverage play," not "Everyone will give a full effort on every kickoff coverage play."
- A: "We will limit all kickoff returns of the opponent so that none of them get past their 35-yard line." This is probably not attainable if your kicker can kick the ball only to the opponent's 28-yard line.
- R: "We will block at least three converts." This goal is probably not relevant if your opponent is very weak and is unlikely to score three touchdowns on your defense.
- T: "We will lead the league in punting average this week." This is probably not a very timely goal if your regular punter is injured.

Here are some examples of SMART special-teams objectives:

- Allow no blocked punts or field goals by our opponents.
- Allow no successful fake punts or fake field goals by our opponents.

- Limit our opponents to less than an 8.0-yard average on punt returns.
- Have a 10-plus-yard average on punt returns and 25-plus yard average on missed field-goal returns.
- Limit our opponents to 25 yards or less on all kickoff returns.
- Start at least on our 45-yard line after a kickoff return.

Another area of focus for your players is to strive for momentum-changing plays, such as blocking a kick (punt, field goal, convert), returning a kick (punt, kickoff, or missed field goal) for a touchdown, recovering a fumble on a punt or kickoff, recovering an onside kick attempt, executing a successful fake punt or field goal, forcing a substitution error, or forcing a time-out. As mentioned in the introduction, the kicking game has a high potential for generating momentum-changing plays, so if your team is best able to take advantage of these opportunities, your chances of winning will increase significantly.

SPECIAL-TEAMS SYSTEMS

As with offense and defense, there are many ways to operate special-teams systems. In designing your special teams, it is very helpful to do so within the framework already established on offense and defense. When possible, try to use terminology and skills that are already being used by the players in their offensive and defensive roles. Often even position names can be consistent.

Another efficient teaching strategy is to use defensive principles for punt returns, convert defends, and field-goal blocks because the opponent is in an offensive formation. The main principle would be to make sure that all eligible receivers are accounted for. Similarly, use offensive principles when teaching punt covers, converts, and field-goal covers. An example would be that you always have to have seven players on the line of scrimmage, and that the two players on the ends of the line must be eligible receivers. Another point is that all players lined up on the interior five positions of the offensive line must be wearing ineligible numbers (league rules apply) or else report to officials.

Another similarity between special-teams systems and offensive or defensive systems is that they all have strengths and weaknesses. There is no right way to run a kickoff return or a punt cover. You have to decide which system best fits your athletes, is relatively easy for them to learn and implement, and is a sound football strategy. This section outlines some special-teams system ideas for you to consider.

Kickoff Cover

The objective on the kickoff cover unit is to limit the return of the opposition as much as possible. One part of the strategy is ball placement. The kicker should have a designated target area, and the coverage team should be designed to attack that part of the field. The ball can be spotted anywhere between the hash marks, so take advantage of that to help your kicker reach the target area and maximize distance. If you feel that kicking the ball from the hash gives your opponent too much of an indication of where the ball will be kicked, kick it from the middle of the field.

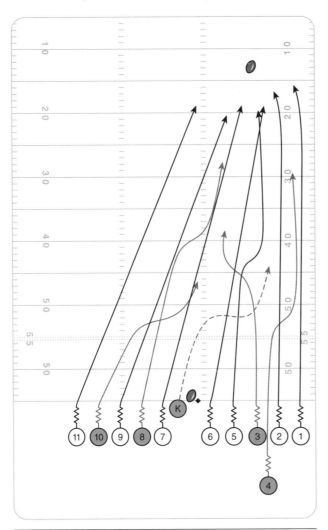

There are different skill sets and body types needed for kickoff cover. The players closest to the aiming point of the kick should be big, strong, fast, and tough, such as linebackers and defensive ends. They will need to run through blockers (who are probably bigger than they are) in order to make the tackle. Close to them would be other strong, fast, and tough players who are good tacklers, such as halfbacks and fullbacks. Other coverage team players who are farther from the aiming point of the kick should be fast and good open-field tacklers. Big, slow players will probably not fit on the kickoff cover team.

Figures 11.2 and 11.3 show two basic kickoff cover plays.

FIGURE 11.2 Kickoff cover deep right or left: A base landmark kick designed to land on the numbers and limit the return lanes. Seven force players, two fill players, and two third-level safeties. Can flip the formation to kick left (wind, kicker strength).

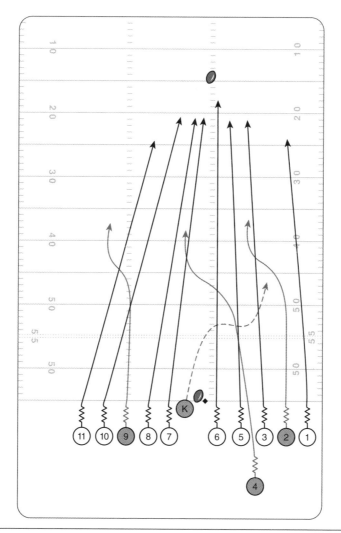

FIGURE 11.3   Kickoff cover deep right or left: A base hash-mark kick designed to land on the hash and limit the return lanes. Eight force players, three fill players, and one safety. Can flip the formation to kick left (wind, kicker strength).

Kickoff Return

The kickoff return has big-play potential because often the coverage team will run downfield in a wave. If you can create a small opening for the returner at the right time, he can run for big yards. Because the Canadian football field is wide, many coaches try to run their kickoff returns wide, but this often plays into the hands of the coverage team spread across the width of the field. Often a better strategy is to design the return to be more north-south and to attack a specific spot in the coverage team.

For personnel, it is a good idea to have mobile, tough athletes who are good blockers in the front row. These players have to be skilled at open-field blocking, but may also be required to field the ball if the opposition tries a short kick. Good-size running backs, slotbacks, linebackers, and defensive backs are good for the interior of the front row, and you may want some tall receivers on the ends of the front row to defend against onside kicks. The middle row of players should be big and tough, and good blockers with some mobility; typically, offensive and defensive linemen are well-suited. If you are running a north-south return, your returners do not need to have fancy moves; they need to be able to catch the ball cleanly, run hard, and make a decisive move as they approach their blocking.

Figures 11.4 and 11.5 show basic returns. In figure 11.4, on the boundary return, the alignment shifts versus the ball on the right hash. Set the three-man

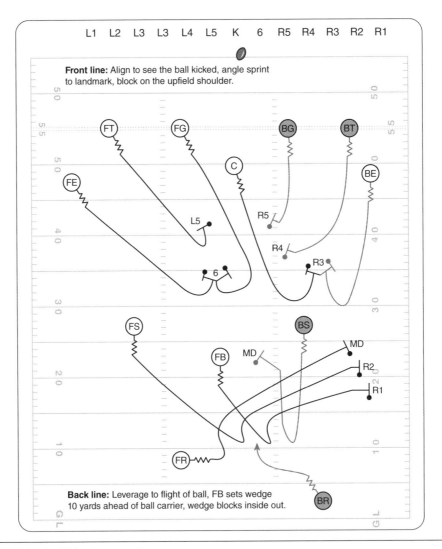

FIGURE 11.4 Kick return numbers veer.

wedge near the hash and bring it vertical for three steps, then veer to the boundary. The boundary slot looks for any inside threat to seal the veer and trap. Personnel along the front line must align to see the ball kicked, then angle sprint to their landmarks and block on the upfield shoulder. Personnel along the back line leverage to the flight of the ball. The fullback sets 10 yards ahead of the ball carrier. The wedge blocks inside out.

In figure 11.5 on the wedge or hash, the alignment is designed to defend all possible short, pop, or moon kicks. Players perform vertical drops versus a deep kick location and then convert the double team, set the two-man wedge to the ball, and lead up to the number-four cover player. Personnel along the front line align to see the ball kicked, angle sprint to their landmarks, and block on

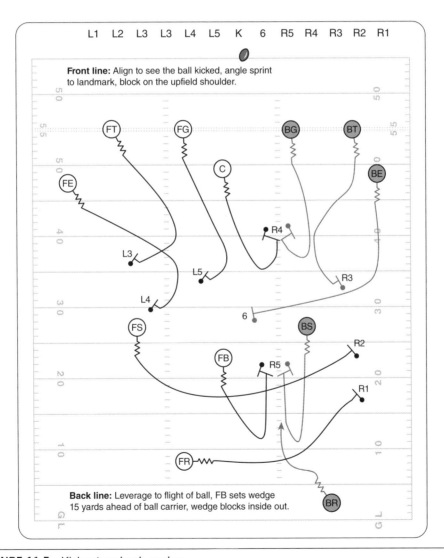

FIGURE 11.5 Kick return hash wedge.

the upfield shoulder. Front-line blockers must clear the seam inside the hash mark. Personnel along the back line leverage to the flight of the ball. The fullback sets the wedge 15 yards ahead of the ball carrier and the wedge blocks inside out.

Punt Cover

The punt-cover team is very dynamic. Because it is an "offensive" team, there's a wide variety of formations you can use and a plethora of options for fakes besides punting: run plays, pass plays, or onside punt plays. This section focuses only on punting the football. Make sure to emphasize to your players that the number-one objective for this team is to punt the ball safely without it being pressured or blocked. Protection comes before coverage.

When assigning personnel, the key player is the long snapper. Not only does the long snapper have to perform the very difficult task of getting the ball reliably to the punter, he also has to get downfield to help in coverage. The main requirement is skill at long snapping. After that, ideally you want a player who can possibly help block and then get downfield quickly to tackle the returner. Defensive ends and linebackers are often the kinds of athletes you want.

The rest of the players on the offensive line should be fairly big and strong so they can protect the punter, but they should also be quick so they can get downfield in coverage, and they should be good open-field tacklers. Again, defensive linemen and linebackers are often the best fit.

Outside players have the crucial responsibility of getting downfield and containing the returner so that the majority of the field width is cut off. Players such as defensive backs who are good at evading blocks and tackling in the open field are often a good fit. Upbacks are usually the "quarterbacks" of the punt-cover team, setting the blocking, making play calls, and calling audibles. For that reason, they need to be smart and decisive, as well as good blockers and open-field tacklers. Running backs often work best. Of course, with personnel you also have to consider the fakes you might want to run. Whoever will be trying to get open for a pass or running with the football should be good at those skills.

Figures 11.6 through 11.9 provide options for punt-cover plays, as well as some information about roles in protecting the punter and covering the punt downfield.

Figure 11.6 shows the punt-formation boundary twins. The boundary end is on the line of scrimmage to the boundary side. He splits the difference between the numbers and the sideline. In the middle of the field, he aligns at the bottom of the numbers. The fullback must take ownership of the unit, communicate on the fly, and be ready to quick snap. He's in command. The system cannot change or have multiple exceptions; this creates too many variables. The rules for counting and identifying the fronts must operate at 100 percent efficiency so we can manage any potential what-if scenarios.

When we want to punt into the boundary, we flip our personnel based on the hash. The protection rules and assignments are mirrored for the middle and a left

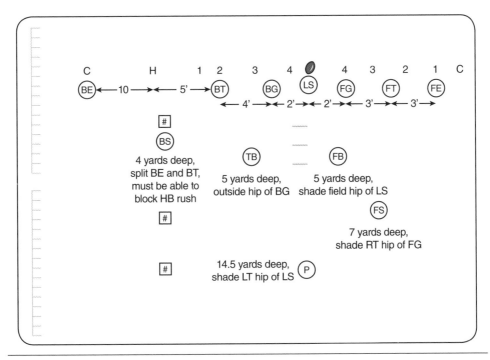

FIGURE 11.6 Punt-formation boundary twins.

hash Liz call. Each side of the punt unit is responsible for identifying the number of players on their side of the centre prior to the fullback's call. Always start the numbering from the outside in (D gap to A gap). All hard players are on the line of scrimmage. The basic count is 1, 2, 3, 4, up to a maximum of 6. The soft players are off the line of scrimmage. These off defenders can move and shift prior to the snap. The player over the centre is designated as 0 to balance the count. The fullback calls the operation signals.

Figure 11.7 shows a zone slide protection, or Liz call. To maintain our team philosophy of punting to the boundary, we flip our personnel based on the hash. The protection rules and assignments are mirrored for the middle and a right hash Rip call. If the corner creeps in to blitz, the boundary end tracks him and blocks the outside man between the halfback and corner. The boundary safety protects the boundary edge inside out. He must make the outside rusher go wide and block through the rusher. The tailback protects the kicking side B gap, blocking for the punt first, then scanning inside out on the kicking side. He must not widen, and instead allows the fullback to come to him. If there is no threat to the kicking side, the tailback checks the back side before releasing. After the snap, the fullback adjusts to the tailback and scans "eyes" to protect the inside gaps. If there is no threat of a blocked punt, he checks the backside A gap before releasing into a coverage lane. The free safety blocks the first threat backside, scanning from the A gap out. He always protects the punter's kicking leg.

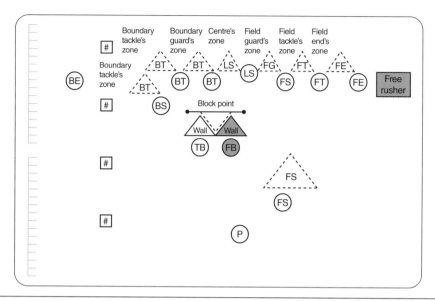

FIGURE 11.7 Zone slide protection (Liz).

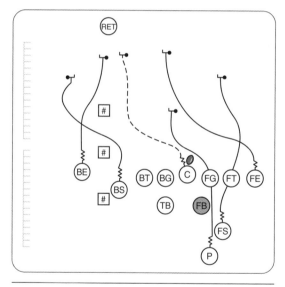

FIGURE 11.8 Coverage lanes: BE, BS, centre, FS, FE.

Figure 11.8 shows coverage lanes for the boundary end and slot, centre, and field slot and end. The centre runs a first-level arrow. He escapes, releases, and adjusts to the ball. The centre must make the returner restart his feet. If the ball is kicked outside the numbers, the centre gets to the returner's field shoulder. The boundary end also runs a first-level arrow. He leverages the boundary side shoulders. Against press coverage, the boundary end shortens his stance. He can use motion to avoid a jam and get to ball depth. The boundary slot plays second-level contain and leverages the boundary side shoulder. He acts as secondary contain 3 yards outside and behind the boundary end. He can motion sideways and toward the line of scrimmage. The field end runs first-level contain and goes as deep as the returner. He sets the edge and plays hard contain. The field slot plays second-level contain and leverages between the hash and the goalpost. He plays secondary contain 5 yards outside and 10 yards behind the field end. The punter acts as the fourth-level safety and maintains his depth and field hash leverage.

Win with your feet. Take the blocker away from the ball when he is close enough to step on, strike with your hands, and expand your separation. Interior players on the line of scrimmage should align on the heels of the centre to gain depth and vision. They key the ball movement for the start of play. Do not get jammed at the line of scrimmage. Players learn to knock the defenders' hands off and beat their assignments with speed. To eliminate blocking angles, players lean in and stack on top of their assignments.

Figure 11.9 shows the coverage lanes for the boundary tackle and guard, the tailback and fullback, and the field guard and tackle. This group carries out a second-level attack, leveraging the ball carrier with their inside shoulders. Lanes squeeze to 3 yards wide at the control point. Players must hit their lanes and then, when they get within 10 yards of the ball carrier, shorten their strides.

Defend one-third of the field (sideline to hash marks) with three levels of coverage. Approximately 10 yards in front of the returner is the collision point and lockout. Players must prevent blockers from grabbing them or

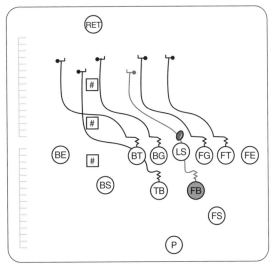

FIGURE 11.9 Coverage lanes: BT, BG, TB, FB, FG, FT.

running them beyond the ball. Keep the ball inside and in front.

Boundary and field guards protect, release, and widen to coverage lanes within the first 20 yards. They attack 5 yards outside their centre and the opponent's returner. They must keep the ball inside and in front. If double-teamed, they replace the tailback and fullback in coverage. The guards tackle with the inside shoulder and keep the outside arm free. As the second wave of tacklers, they rip the ball out.

Tailbacks and fullbacks are third-level, leveraging the ball carrier with the outside shoulder. They fill 8 to 10 yards behind the first wave through the open seams.

Boundary tackles and field tackles protect, release, and widen to coverage lanes within the first 20 yards. They attack 10 yards outside of the returner and replace the guard if he is not in his lane. They must keep the ball inside and in front. If double-teamed, they replace the tailback or fullback in coverage. The tackles tackle with the inside shoulder and keep the outside arm free.

Punt Return

Similar to players on defense, the players on the punt-return team must be ready for any kind of formation or play. Another similarity to defense is that there are different levels of aggression used with this unit. A conservative system would emphasize defending against a fake, making sure the ball is punted, and setting up a good return. A more aggressive approach would be to send extra pressure on the punter in an attempt to block the punt, leaving the returner with limited blocking. This section focuses on three conservative punt-return options using man blocking.

Because punt return is a "defensive" team, it is often helpful to use a lot of defensive players. The players along the line of scrimmage need to be strong and big enough to take on blockers, but also athletic enough to get downfield and block in open space. Usually defensive ends and linebackers fill these positions. The players on the outside of the line are often called on to pressure the punter or to cover or block eligible receivers. For that reason, they have to be explosive and athletic, such as running backs or defensive backs. The players in the middle of the team sometimes have to take charge if the punt-cover team lines up in an unusual way; smart players such as the middle linebacker or safety are usually competent doing that. The players out in space are required to be able to cover and block in the open field, so athletic players such as defensive backs or receivers can play those positions. Fielding a punt is one of the most difficult responsibilities in football, so returners have to be highly skilled. They also have to be elusive open-field runners and good open-field blockers (if they don't have the football).

There are two main types of punt return: man and zone. The system for a man return is the easiest to coach because the principle is very simple: block your man. The skill aspect of a man return is difficult because, in order to be successful, most or all of the players have to defeat their opponent in one-on-one battle. A zone punt return usually takes the form of a wall of blocking set up for the returner to run to one sideline or the other. The system is more complex to teach. In order to focus on simple systems, figures 11.10, 11.11, and 11.12 are examples of three man return options.

In figure 11.10, the front-line players align 1 yard off the line of scrimmage. They rush and jam their opponents to the field side, keep their leverage, and work their assignments away from the return.

The punt-return unit must be able to execute this

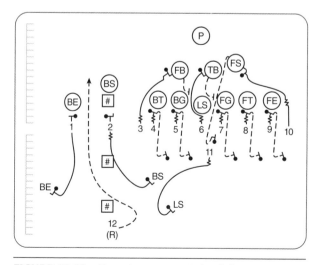

FIGURE 11.10 Boundary versus twins left.

return versus all formations. Numbers 1 and 2 have the option to wash their assignments based on the release lanes. An option is to double-team the boundary tackle or boundary guard, have #6 lock on the long snapper, or have 7, 8, and 9 rush while 11 picks up their man. Players can run from a two- or three-point stance. If the ball is caught on the numbers or close to the hash, the punt returner stems to the field then breaks to the boundary lane, taking as wide a path as needed to set up the blocks.

In figure 11.11, the front-line players align 1 yard off the line of scrimmage, rush, and jam their opponents to the boundary side. They keep leverage and work their assignments away from the return.

The punt-return unit must be able to execute this return versus all formations. Numbers 1 and 2 have the option to get depth before the snap and give up the boundary lanes. An option is to double-team a field tackle or field end, have #6 lock on the long snapper, or have 7, 8, and 9 rush while 11 picks up their man.

Players may use a two- or three-point stance. If the ball is caught outside the numbers, the punt returner takes it up the sideline.

In figure 11.12, the front-line players align 1 yard off the line of scrimmage, then rush and jam their opponents from the inside out. They keep leverage and work their opponents away from the return.

The punt-return unit must be able to execute this return versus all formations. Numbers 1 and 2 have the option to get depth before the snap and give up the boundary lanes. An option is to double team the most dangerous man, have #6 lock on the long snapper, or have 7, 8, and 9 rush while 11 picks up their man. Players may use a two- or three-point stance. If the ball is caught outside the numbers, the punt returner takes it up the sideline.

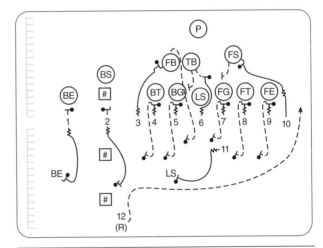

FIGURE 11.11   Field versus twins left.

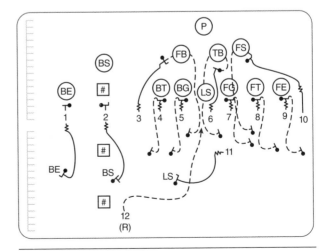

FIGURE 11.12   Middle versus twins left.

Field-Goal Defense: Return Team

This may be one of the most understudied and underutilized phases of the kicking game. Strategically, practicing missed field-goal returns can create a high-tempo environment that gives your team better opportunities to create big returns and can change the outcome of the game. Often, the opposition may employ offensive linemen to protect and cover on their field-goal cover team. This has the potential of a significant athletic mismatch in your favour, as your defensive players will probably be more athletic than their offensive linemen in the open field.

All the skills are transferable between missed field goals and punt return, as well as on defense: covering the eligible receivers, spying the kicker or holder, and defending the fake. Coaching punt-return skills to defensive players can reduce the overlap in terminology and therefore translate into quicker learning and more productive repetitions in practice. This means that for personnel it is often easiest to keep the defensive players on the field, with the possible exception of substituting a dynamic player as the returner and taking out one of your defensive backs.

Figures 11.13 and 11.14 illustrate two options for returning a missed field goal. In figure 11.13, the returner takes two quick steps upfield to draw the coverage unit, then bursts to the field. He uses as much yardage as needed to execute the

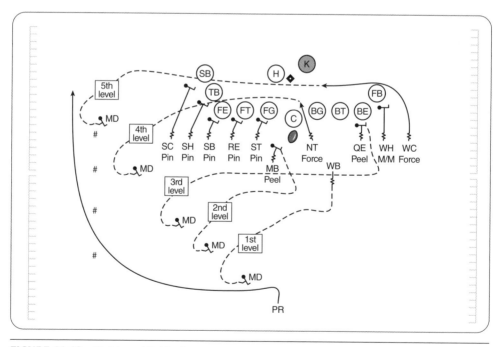

FIGURE 11.13 Field-goal field return.

return. If the ball is kicked outside the numbers, he takes it up the boundary sideline. Field strong. Perform a field-side pin and drive away. The Mac linebacker collides with the centre and forces him to release on the boundary side. The Will linebacker is responsible for setting the return and takes the returner. The quick end must stay with the boundary end for a three count and then release to the wall. The weakside corner is the force to secure the kick then continue to the top of the wall. He looks inside then upfield for threats. All blockers must block the upfield shoulder. Mirror the return if it's from the left hash.

In figure 11.14, the boundary corner secures the kick, then trails behind the first-level player to look for any free coverage players. The strongside corner locks on to the slotback for a four count, then releases inside and trails, looking for any free coverage players. If there is no threat to the returner, he looks for the holder or kicker. Pressure the protection and force the timing as per other returns and blocks. Use punt-return techniques and work to the correct shoulder leverage. The strong-side tackle stays on the shoulder of the centre. If there is no threat to the returner, he looks for the holder or kicker.

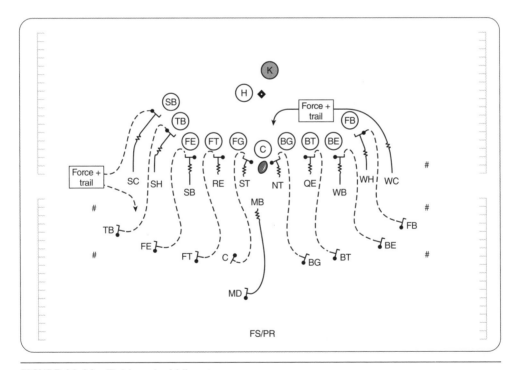

FIGURE 11.14 Field-goal middle return.

Field-Goal Cover

Field-goal cover is a very basic system, so no illustration is provided. As mentioned in the previous section, it may be advantageous to replace your offensive linemen with players, such as defensive ends or big linebackers, who have decent size but are better able to cover and tackle in the open field.

Make sure players line up with zero splits (foot to foot) and emphasize protecting the gap inside of them, as that is the shortest route a defensive player has to block the kick. As on the punt-cover team, the first priority is a safely kicked ball, so they must protect first and cover second.

Convert and Convert Block

These teams are both quite straightforward, and most coaches keep their personnel the same as their offensive and defensive groups that were just involved in the scoring play. There may be some substitutions on the convert team to allow the kicker to come onto the field, and perhaps to replace receivers with bigger-bodied blockers such as fullbacks. Other substitutions may be necessary for specialists such as the snapper and holder.

On the convert block team, there is no need for a returner because missed converts cannot be returned in Canadian amateur football. This allows you to have an extra player pressuring the kicker.

SPECIAL SITUATIONS

Canadian football includes opportunities for unique plays that are not part of the American game. The kick-out or kick-back situation can occur at the end of the first half, but more commonly it's at the end of the game. The defending team is trying to prevent the single point to preserve the victory. This is a key element of the Canadian game and must be practiced; it is a situation that requires flawless communication, observation of the game clock, possible player substitution, and an understanding of the rules if the ball is kicked back (5-yard radius applies after each kick).

Several factors must be considered: number of players to drop back into the end zone (one, two, or three), your returner personnel, and the rush of the kicking team. Regarding your returner personnel, make sure that they can not only field the punt cleanly, but can also punt the ball away. You could even have your punter as a returner. Make sure you and your players are aware of the time remaining on the clock.

Returners must check with the coach for instructions before going onto the field to know what the coach wants them to do.

- First option: catch the ball and run it out of the end zone to maintain possession for your offense.

◆ Second option: catch the ball and punt it out of bounds if it is the last play of the game with no time left on the clock. When attempting to score on a kick-in situation (missed the kick and it is kicked back to you), keep the kicker and two blockers back to secure the ball, and then kick it through the end zone for a single point.

CONCLUSION

In this chapter I have offered you some ideas and sample plays to incorporate the kicking game into your overall team philosophy, and indicated where you can gain an edge on your opponents in the decision-making process. Being good in the kicking game is a key factor in all championship programs. The kicking game is a special part of the game; you need a willing player in every position, 100 percent team commitment, and trust that the system will win games.

Table 11.2 includes some interesting statistics relating the field position that teams start their possessions from and their chance of scoring. This emphasizes the importance of the kicking game, as it includes the greatest changes in field position within a game.

Special teams create momentum changes and can be the deciding factor in many football games. Field position will give your team a chance to win every game.

My coaching career has allowed me the opportunity to work with many outstanding coaches who believed in the importance of the kicking game and overall execution of the special teams. I want to thank all the players who have bought into the system and worked hard to gain an edge on the field. As coaches, players, and spectators, we can all remember games or find examples in the record books illustrating when a game has been won or lost on special teams.

TABLE 11.2 Field Position and Chance of Scoring

Starting field position	Chance of scoring	Percentage
−20-yard line	1 out of 30	3
−40-yard line	1 out of 8	13
55-yard line	1 out of 5	20
+45-yard line	1 out of 3	33
+30-yard line	1 out of 2	50
+20-yard line	2 out of 3	66

PART THREE

GAME WINNING STRATEGIES

12

Scouting the Opposition

Scott MacAulay, Dwayne Masson, and Sean Reader

Most of the chapters in this book focus on what coaches need to do to effectively teach players the right way to execute skills and systems. This chapter focuses on a very important contrasting priority: scouting the opposition and preparing players to be as effective as possible against the opponent's plays. Scouting can give you a distinct edge if you have the time to do it right.

Offensive coaches should study the opposition's defense, defensive coaches should study the opposition's offense, and the various special-teams coaches should study their counterparts on the other side.

In this chapter three coaches provide their perspectives on scouting the three components of the opposition. Coordinators and position coaches may want to focus specifically on their own opposition group, while head coaches may want to familiarize themselves with scouting all three opposition units: offense, defense, and special teams. Each section in this chapter provides different degrees of detail and time commitment for scouting. Don't think you have to do all of them! Start with the basics and then add new details as you pick up steam.

Before reading the following sections, take one bit of important advice: when communicating information about opponents to players, keep it simple enough that your players can learn the material and apply it. A coach who has learned a lot about the opposition may be tempted to try to teach players everything he's learned from his hours of film study and data analysis. Don't do it! Your players will end up tentative and confused. Look for the data that makes a difference; otherwise your scouting will be counterproductive. Make sure your players can line up correctly, identify significant presnap keys, make basic adjustments, and feel comfortable combating the opponent's favorite plays. Most of the details should remain with the coaching staff, to assist them in game planning and play calling. KISS: Keep It Simple, Stupid!

SCOUTING THE OFFENSE

Film study is obviously the best way to scout the opposition's offense. You can scout teams live, but game film is good for detail. If you are scouting a team live, have all of the defensive coaches in the stands so that each one can focus on a specific aspect of the offense. The defensive line coach should chart the offensive line (run blocking and pass protection schemes), the linebackers coach should chart the backfield and run plays, and the defensive backs coach should chart the receiver alignments and pass plays. If you have the advantage of watching game film and using a service such as Hudl, tagging the plays with data (spot, down and distance, play type, etc.) will help you create helpful reports. The more data you input with your tagging, the more you can get out through reports. But useful data is what should go in. Tagging takes a lot of time, so don't bother inputting extraneous data.

As you begin to chart the opposition's offense, the first thing to note is their formations. If you know how the opponent is likely to line up, you can make adjustments to your defensive alignment. Most teams run basic formations, but sometimes you'll face opponents that do the unusual. Your players need to be prepared.

Identifying formations also helps you to categorize plays: which specific plays can they run from specific formations? For example, you know that if the quarterback is under centre, they can't run any kind of run-pass option play. As you look at the plays they are running out of a specific formation, you can begin to anticipate what else they may run that you haven't seen yet. For example, from the I formation, they can run a fullback dive, a tailback lead, a tailback counter, and a pitch. Some logical progressions you may anticipate would be a play-action pass to the fullback from the lead play, or a quarterback bootleg run or pass from the toss sweep play.

You are looking for tendencies. Out of which formations do they usually run? Out of which formations do they usually pass? Sometimes teams have a formation from which they run only one or two plays, so players will have a very good idea what to expect if the opponent lines up in one of those formations. In the end, you want to match the plays they run with the formations they show.

As you chart their formations, also diagram the plays they run out of each formation. Give the plays a name, ideally the same names your team's offense would call them. This makes it much easier if you run a scout period in practice, and your offensive players will have an easier time identifying and running plays.

As you diagram and name the plays, take note of the following details:

Running Plays

- *Favorite plays*. This is a simple tally. Which running plays do they use the most?

- *Ball carrier*. This will help you identify which player(s) is their main running threat.

- *Backfield sets and motion*. As well as diagraming the formation, what presnap motion (if any) does the offense use? This may give your players a good presnap key to know what play is coming.

- *Personnel*. Do they substitute specific players for specific plays? This will probably happen on short-yardage plays if they take out a receiver and bring in an offensive lineman type, but could happen in other situations as well.

- *Down and distance.* As you chart the plays or tag them on the video, make sure to include down and distance. This can help you identify specific plays they like to run in specific down and distance situations. For example, they may like to run the lead on first and 10.
- *Field zones.* This is more advanced, but it may be helpful to know what plays they like to run when they are backed up (inside their own 20), at midfield, or in the scoring zone (inside your 20). A team may like to run special plays such as a slotback counter when they are around midfield. You can decide how you want to divide field zones to fit your team's needs.

Passing Plays

- *Favorite plays.* Again, a simple tally. Which passing plays do they use the most? Look for route combinations that they like, because they will often run the same combinations out of different formations. They may have two-receiver combinations (such as a slant and wheel) or three-receiver combinations (such as a hitch, flag, and seam).
- *Main receiver.* This will help you identify which receiver(s) is their main target and threat to your defense.
- *Formation and motion.* Formation aside, what presnap motion (if any) does the offense use? This may give your players a good presnap key to know what play is coming. For example, both running backs setting up early outside of the right tackle may indicate that the quarterback will be doing a rollout pass to his right.
- *Personnel.* Do they substitute specific players for specific plays? If they take out their fullback and bring in an extra receiver, can you anticipate a pass play?
- *Down and distance.* This can help you identify specific plays they like to run in specific down and distance situations. For example, a team may like to run a screen pass on second and long situations.
- *Field zones.* It may be helpful to know what plays they like to run when they are backed up (inside their own 20), at midfield, or in the scoring zone (inside your 20). For example, a team may like to run all hooks when they are between your 5 and 10 yard lines. You can decide how you want to divide field zones to fit your team's needs.

At a more advanced level of scouting, you can look for other things as you analyze film of your opposition:

- Do they like to use the strong or weak side of the field more for run or pass plays? Some teams may like to run to the weak side and pass to the strong side.
- Do they have any tendencies based on which hash the ball is on?
- Are they a right- or left-handed team? A right-handed quarterback may feel more comfortable throwing to his right (defense's left), so you may be able to key on that.

- Do they move offensive linemen depending on their play call or do they try to run behind their best offensive linemen? A team may have a very good pulling guard, and they move him depending on where they want to run the ball. They may also have a good guard–tackle combination that they flip from side to side depending on where they want to run the ball.
- How do they react to specific defensive formations? For example, do they have audibles that they check to see if the defense shows a high-pressure pass rush look?

While scouting the opposition's offense, look at the defense they are playing against. If you run a 4-3 defense, and the team your upcoming opposition played against ran a similar 4-3, you are getting a good indication of how they'll probably play you. If their last opponent ran a 3–4 front, you may have to look at another game that they played.

Division of labour is very important on a coaching staff. While it is necessary to get help from other coaches if you are scouting a team live, it is just as valuable to get all of your coaches to help analyze film. Everyone sees things differently, so one of your assistants may notice a nuance that you missed. Also, with everybody studying the film, you and your staff can collaborate on the game plan and arrive at a unified approach to presenting the plan to the players and leading practices.

A big challenge for many defensive coaches is consolidating the scouting information for the players. Coaches should have an in-depth understanding of the opposition, but young players won't process everything you've learned from your hours of film study. They're there on the field, with everything happening a hundred miles an hour. "Paralysis by analysis" is real, and players can end up unable to play because they've been overloaded with information. Players don't need every detail; they need the important details:

- Main formations and how they should align
- Key players
- Main run and pass plays and any presnap keys they can focus on

Your job is to decide how to best teach players this information. Several methods of presentation will help. One is film study. Select specific clips that highlight the main formations, players, and plays that the offense runs so players can see how they actually look.

Secondly, do a chalk talk. Diagraming the plays on a whiteboard helps players understand the details that pertain to their positions, as well as the overall concept of the play.

A third method is a scout sheet (table 12.1). Give players a hard copy of the important information they need to know. You can make it more interactive by getting them to copy the play diagrams from the whiteboard onto their scout sheet.

If you do not have access to a film-game service, you can create your own scout sheet to meet your needs, one similar to that shown in table 12.1. A data sheet

TABLE 12.1 Sample Offensive Scout Sheet

Play number	1	2	3	4
Quarter	1	1	2	2
Series	1	1	6	6
Down and distance	1st and 10	2nd and 9	1st and 15	2nd and 4
Down and distance grouping	P10	2 > 7	1 > 10	2 2–6
Hash mark	L	R	R	L
Spot	–30	–31	50	44
Yards gained or lost	1	0	6	0
Play type	Run	Pass	Pass	Run
Result	Run	Incomplete pass	Completion	Run
Personnel	15	15	24	24
Quarterback alignment	Gun	Gun	Gun	Regular
Backfield alignment	High	Heavy	Split	Louie
Receiver set	3×2	4×1	2×2	3×1
Protection	Run	60	70	Run
Opponent's play	OSZ BD			ISZ FD
Field routes		9841 R	44	
Boundary route		2	97	

program such as Excel is also a great way to sort all the information you collect to help find any tendencies.

Information you may find useful includes:

- *Play number.* To help you organize and identify individual plays for reference in film study and meetings.
- *Quarter.* To help you organize when you are scouting based on the period of the game. You may want to write in a comment regarding weather or game situations (i.e., in which quarters the offense had the wind, two-minute offensive situations, etc.).
- *Series.* To know when each new series begins and how many plays each series involves.
- *Down and distance.* To identify tendencies based on certain situations.
- *Down and distance groupings.* To clump certain down-and-distances together, providing a high-level view of possible tendencies.
- *Hash mark.* Note if the ball is spotted on a hash mark (from the offense's perspective) or in the middle. If the ball is inside the left hash mark, but the

left offensive tackle is lined up on the hash mark, you can still consider the ball spotted on the left hash, as there is a definite wide side to the right.

- *Spot.* Note the yard line on which the ball is spotted. We like to have the vertical field position marked down from the offense's perspective.

- *Yards gained or lost.* To easily figure which plays were the most or least successful.

- *Play type.* Note whether run or pass. We use this to break up the run plays from the pass plays. It can be used to find tendencies or easily sorted to take a high-level view of all the run or pass plays in a grouping.

- *Result.* Figure out what happened on each play and sort to find the opponent's most or least successful plays.

- *Personnel.* Figure out which groupings were on the field. In our shorthand, 15 means one back and five receivers, and 24 means two backs and four receivers.

- *Quarterback alignment.* Note the alignment of the quarterback at the snap of the ball. Is the quarterback in gun, under centre, in wildcat formation, and so on.

- *Backfield alignment.* Note the alignment of the backs at the snap of the ball.

- *Plays.* Note the alignment of the receivers at the snap of the ball.

- *Protection.* Note the protection used by the offense for that particular play. Best practice is to use the same language as your offense.

- *Opponent's play.* Note the type of plays that were used for the run game. Use similar play names to your own offense to help prepare your scout teams for practice.

- *Field and boundary routes.* Note the routes used by eligible receivers on both sides of the field. We currently use a numbering system, but you could use the name of passing concepts or your own offense's terminology.

Other ideas for useful columns are penalties and highlights. The idea is a chart or spreadsheet that's as useful as possible in supplying the data needed for you and your staff to prepare for the opposition. You also can use this scout sheet for your own games. If you fill it in as completely as possible during the game, you'll cut down dramatically on the time needed for entering data and tagging your own game film.

The fourth way to present the opposition's offense is on the field in practice during your defense period. During practice one, show them the opposition's formations and get players properly aligned. During practice two, review alignment and then run some of the opponent's main plays. During practice three, review alignment and plays while adding presnap motion. If you have enough time and players, you can also use scout periods (inside run, pass skeleton, or full scout team periods) in which your offense runs the opposition's plays. Again, if you have named the formations and plays using terminology that is familiar to your offensive players, they will be much more efficient in running the opposition's plays. You will still want to have diagrams for the players to look at before each repetition.

Your final step is to prepare yourself for game day. During the week of meetings and practice, you should have taught your players the main formations, players, and plays of the opposing team. You may have also given them a couple of defenses they should audible into if the offense comes out in certain formations. Now you need to get yourself ready for the game. Based on your study of the opponent and their tendencies, you can put together your call sheet or scout sheet. How you do this will be specific to your needs as a play caller. A less experienced coach may want to make a call sheet that lists all his defensive fronts and coverages and then organizes them in lists based on down and distance (for example, based on scouting, what defenses should be called in second and long situations?). A more experienced coach who has a very strong grasp of his own defense may want a sheet that is divided by field zones, lists down and distance and run–pass percentages, and includes notes of specific offensive tendencies. If you are using headsets and have a coach upstairs in the spotter's booth, you may want him to have a list of the opposition's top formations and plays based on down and distance and field zone. He can provide little reminders of likely offensive play calls that you may want to consider before making your defensive call.

Scouting the offense is a big job, but if all of the defensive coaches work together, it can be an efficient process that gives players a big advantage on the field. Nothing shakes an offensive team's confidence more than lining up and having the defensive players call out the play that the offense is running. If you have done your work studying the opposition, prepared yourself for how you want to make defensive calls during the game, and have given your players the right amount of information to play and react confidently and aggressively, your team will enjoy great defensive success.

SCOUTING THE DEFENSE

Many factors are involved in scouting the opposing defense prior to playing them. Most teams will scout an opposing defense, and many methods and tools can be used to do this. Let's touch on a few of the tools and techniques that will come in handy.

Ideally, game film is the best way to scout. If game film isn't available, you may have to scout live at games, using staff coaches to assist in compiling data for each play. Technology can be used to break down the opposition.

I have the luxury of receiving game film that is already broken down into categories (for example, ODK, meaning offensive plays, defensive plays, and kicking plays) and has all the data related to down and distance, field position, play result, and so on. Many coaches have to spend time breaking down the tape into some sort of usable format. Determine what output you want from your scouting process, and keep it in mind when undertaking the process of breaking down film. For example, if you want a tendency based on field position (e.g., red zone), ensure you are including field position in your initial breakdown. We break down all opponents every week to efficiently build a database of all opponents in our league. Obviously, as the season goes on you have more data and tape to compare, and tendencies may become more apparent. Inputting data is time consuming, but the more you put in, the more you can take out.

Some things I consider when looking at the opposing defense are:

- ◆ What are their base defenses versus our formations?
- ◆ How do they adjust to motion?
- ◆ What is their favourite coverage?
- ◆ What is their favourite blitz and stunt?
- ◆ Do we have any individual mismatches we can try to exploit?
- ◆ Are there areas we need to address, plays or moves that we haven't seen much of, or blitzes we can't handle out of our base protection package?
- ◆ Any great players we need to be aware of?

When cutting the tape, I enter all the defensive information for each play as I review it. Those categories include front, stunt, blitz, and coverage. I enter the data in the terms we use for each category (i.e., 4-3 Over G, NT, MAC-A, cover 3) so that players and coaches understand the breakdown when they review the tape. This can take time, and many teams use some sort of division of duties among assistant coaches to make the process go more efficiently.

If you do not have access to a game-film service, create your own scout sheet to meet your needs. Table 12.2 provides an example that includes these categories:

- ◆ *Quarter.* This helps you organize the scouting based on the period of the game. You may want to include comments regarding weather, for example, if the opposition was defending when the offense had a wind advantage.
- ◆ *Series.* This helps you know when each new series begins and how many plays each series involves.
- ◆ *Play number.* This helps you organize and identify individual plays for reference in film study and meetings.
- ◆ *Down and distance.* This gives you a chance to identify tendencies. As you can see in table 12.2, the opposition plays base cover 3 in all three first-and-10 situations.
- ◆ *Spot.* Note the yard line the ball is spotted on. If the offense is in their own end, put a minus sign (–) in front of the yard line. If the offense is in the opponent's end, put a plus sign (+) in front of the yard line.
- ◆ *Hash.* Note if the ball is spotted on the hash mark (offense's perspective) or in the middle. If the ball is inside the left hash mark but the left offensive tackle is lined up on the hash mark, you can still consider the ball spotted on the left hash, as there is a definite wide side to the right.
- ◆ *Offensive formation.*
- ◆ *Offensive motion.* Do any offensive players go into motion prior to the snap?
- ◆ *Defensive front.* What is the alignment of the defensive line and linebackers?

TABLE 12.2 Sample Defensive Scout Sheet

	First quarter						
	Series 1		**Series 2**				
Play number	1	2	3	4	5	6	7
Down and distance	1–10	2–9	1–10	2–4	1–10	2–6	3-1
Spot	–36	–35	–41	–47	+53	+49	+44
Hash	L	L	R	M	R	R	M
Offensive formation	2–2 I	2–2 gun split	3-1 Louie ace	2–2 I	2–2 I	2–2 gun split	DTE diesel F1 R
Offensive motion	FB b	3–3 gun		31 Roger ace		Backs left	
Defensive front	4-3 base	4-3 A	4-3 base	4-3 base	4-3 base	4-3 A	6-2 A
Defensive adjustment	Mac fill	$/W out	$ widen	BH over		$/S to backs	
Defensive stunt		NuT					
Defensive coverage	3	1	3	1	3	0	0
Defensive blitz		Mac B		Will b		MoW A/b	SaW D/d
Comments	Mac filled hard	T fast		S bit on run fake	BH filled hard	W patient on flow away	B gaps open

- *Defensive adjustment.* How does the defense adjust to the formation or motion of the offense?
- *Defensive stunt.* Do any of the defensive linemen fill or rush gaps other than the ones they line up in?
- *Defensive coverage.* What coverage are the defensive backs and linebackers playing?
- *Defensive blitz.* Do any linebackers or defensive backs blitz? Which gaps do they blitz through? Use uppercase letters to refer to strong gaps (A is a strong A gap) and lowercase letters to refer to weak gaps (b is a weak b gap).
- *Comments.* Add any observations about the defense's system or players.

Depending on your needs, you may find other columns useful, such as:

- *Personnel.* If the defense has substituted for an extra box player, cover player, and so on
- *Penalty.*

- *Tackler or playmaker.*
- *Yards gained.*

Not all data is useful, of course. Leave that out and focus on making your chart or spreadsheet as handy as possible for you and your coaches. And remember that the sheet can do more than track the opposition. Fill it out during your own games as well. Do so and it will drastically cut down on the time you need to spend entering data or tagging your own game film.

Once all the raw information is entered, you can begin to analyze. One approach is to compare the opponent's fronts, coverage, and blitz packages versus formations run by your team. Take the trouble to zero in on games where your upcoming opponent's defense faces an offense that's similar to your team's. If the team being scouted is up against things that your offense doesn't usually feature, you may choose to ignore those plays.

In the week leading up to the game, we develop our game plan with an eye to tendencies and percentages we've pinpointed in the other team (I'm fortunate to have a program that assists in generating reports based on some of the criteria we look for). This approach requires a large time commitment for planning scripts and scheduling practices. It is easiest and most effective to do those tasks at the beginning of the practice week, to ensure we don't miss anything. That allows our offense to see the primary defense the opponent runs, any exotics (unusual fronts, blitzes, or coverages) they mix in, and also the opponent's overall tendencies when it runs things.

Self-scouting is a good idea. Check out your own offense and play calling, and your own tendencies, if possible with the help of your defense coaches. Many teams save this job for the off-season, but try it a few times a season if you have enough people. If you're aware that your opponents are scouting you, you have the chance to throw them off. Small adjustments to your offense or play calling may catch the opponent unprepared.

Finally, technology has given us a wealth of scouting data, but the trick is to manage that data. Think about what you pass on to your players. Single out what can actually sharpen and improve their play, and remember that too much data will slow them down. Don't think of information as a cure-all, either. Football is still a sport played between the lines: player vs. player. Yes, information matters. But individual matchups and personal battles determine the outcome of many plays.

SCOUTING SPECIAL TEAMS

Football coaches at every level try to find the edge, the advantage that ups their odds of success. Savvy coaches realize that special teams provide ample opportunities to change field position, cause turnovers, retain possession of the ball, or score points.

Gadget plays, trick plays, or fakes have their popularity, but they can eat up meeting and practice time. Scouting offers a steadier, more reliable advantage, and one that's less demanding of time. It's the same rule as for offense and defense.

Knowing what to expect from their opponents on special teams will allow your players to play faster and with more confidence.

The following are some guidelines regarding scouting special teams, thoughts garnered through many years of coaching.

General Principles

When laying out the data on your opponent, use the same terms that you do when describing your own special teams. This cuts down memorization and increases the players' familiarity with your chosen vocabulary. Your players will be better equipped to communicate with you and their teammates about what they experience on the field.

Special-team coaches can be especially vulnerable to the data-dump temptation. They often feel they don't get enough practice time (and possibly meeting time), so they make up for it by saturating players with every detail about an opponent. Avoid this! Instead chart what's important.

When deciding how much practice time and meeting time a special team gets, look at how much time that team spends on the field. More game time, more practice time. A game of Canadian football typically has more punt covers and punt returns than it has kickoffs, kickoff returns, field goals, and field goal defends put together. Practice time and meetings should reflect that. If your team is scoring a lot of touchdowns, more time should be allocated to kickoffs and field goals or converts. If a team's giving up touchdowns, then time should go to kickoff returns and defense against field goals or converts. Focus your time on those of the opponent's special teams that you anticipate facing most frequently.

Punt cover, punt return, kickoff cover, and kickoff return are the four special teams that are both complicated and very likely to be encountered in play. Therefore, the following sections cover how to scout them. Convert and field-goal kick and defend teams are worth scouting, but they're quite straightforward.

Punt Cover

Of all the special teams, punt cover is the most volatile. Knowledge and preparation can greatly enhance success.

The five key elements in scouting an opponent's punt-cover team are formation, eligible players, alignment and protection, punt direction, and contain and safeties.

Formation

Every formation used by a punt-cover team has pros and cons. For example, a spread punt-cover formation (figure 12.1) allows for maximum downfield coverage but provides short edges and minimal protection. With only seven protectors (five on the line of scrimmage and two upbacks), there is more room to pressure from the outside and one-on-one pressures on the upbacks.

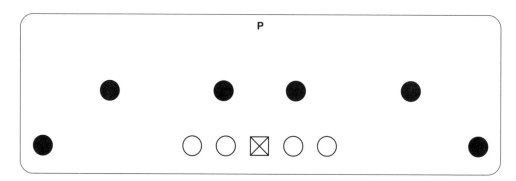

FIGURE 12.1 Spread punt-cover formation.

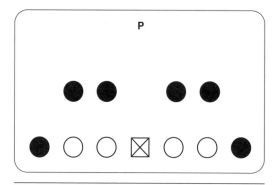

FIGURE 12.2 Max punt-cover formation.

On the other hand, a max punt-cover formation (figure 12.2) provides maximum protection but less coverage strength, due to tight contain men and the bunching together of the players. A punt-return team will be able to pin coverage players inside, thus allowing returners to escape laterally and gain the sidelines more easily. Also, with four upbacks, there's less coverage personnel downfield once the ball is caught, creating more vertical and horizontal seams in the coverage lanes.

Players who understand the strengths and weaknesses of a punt-cover formation can better predict where best to run returns and where to pressure opponents.

Eligible Players

One of the most revealing traits of well-coached and prepared punt-return teams is how they control eligible receivers on the punt-cover team. Identifying where eligible receivers are in the formation and who is responsible for them is key to controlling fakes and gadget plays. Figure 12.1 highlights eligible receivers in the spread formation, and figure 12.2 shows eligible receivers in the max formation.

Alignment and Protection

Many coaches put little thought and time into developing solid fundamentals when it comes to protecting the punter. Scouting these mistakes will create opportunities to block punts or simply disrupt the punter from his normal routine and cause miskicks or shanks.

Study the gaps between the cover players on the line of scrimmage. Large splits give your return team more chance to escape through those gaps and pressure the punt. But larger splits lengthen the edge of the line of scrimmage, making outside pressure difficult. Narrow splits ensure little penetration but make the coverage personnel's release and escape routes more congested, and shorten the edge of the line of scrimmage.

Pay attention to technique. Does the cover team retreat (kick step like an offensive lineman) to gain depth from the return team? Doing so makes running twists and pressure difficult because the cover team has time to see the return team movement and adjust. But it slows down the cover team's downfield coverage. Do they engage and release immediately or do they stay in and block until the punt is delivered? Teams that engage and release are more concerned with downfield coverage, but they'll also be more apt to have punts blocked if return players are released too quickly or the snap is slow or bobbled. Conversely, teams that remain in and block will be downfield in coverage later. What direction do they release? Teams may outside release their cover players in an effort to stop outside returns and ensure their lanes are wide enough to funnel the returner towards the middle of the coverage. In this case, running set returns back into the middle of the coverage are most effective, since all cover personnel are wide and concerned about lateral returns. Some teams will release to the direction of the punt in an effort to shorten the distance the coverage players will run. In this case, running returns wide and away from the direction of the punt is more effective, since to set up your blocks you can use the natural leverage created by the coverage players.

Punt Direction

One of the easiest things to chart is whether a team punts to the boundary or to the field. This information helps your returners anticipate where the ball will land and informs your return team where the coverage personnel will be trying to escape to.

Here are some important steps to take: chart the location (or landing) of each punt, including sidelines, numbers, hash marks, middle of the field, or any other means of delineating location. A percentage breakdown of location based on left hash punts, right hash punts, and middle-of-the-field punts will help your returners anticipate the landing area and make every catch in the air.

Chart the distance of every punt. Returners should know this data going into a game so they can align themselves in the best spots possible. Also, talk to your return team before the game and discuss the impact of the weather. Wind can add or subtract a great deal of distance to a punt. It can also change a punt's trajectory; most punts will sail high into the wind unless the punter drives it low.

Contain and Safeties

If a coach wants to run a return laterally, players need to know who is setting the edge of the coverage lanes. That contain player needs to be blocked early (so the edge is set late and high) and blocked definitively inside (so the returner can escape wide) or outside (so the returner can escape inside the contain and then outside the rest of the cover team).

To score touchdowns, you need to block the safeties or at least identify them so the returner knows who is free. Too many punters make tackles because the return team does not account for them. If you block the punter, block him a little later but not to the ground; too many return players want a highlight reel knockdown block, only to find their cover man getting up and making the tackle late. Safeties need sustained, legal blocking in order to be eliminated.

Punt Return

Like punt cover, punt return can be an explosive, game-changing part of the game. Four key elements when it comes to scouting an opponent's punt-return team are formation, personnel, return type, and pressure type.

Formation

First, identify whether a team is a one-returner or two-returner team. Even if they run their system with both, your players need to know a few things. In what situation do they run two returners or one returner (for example, one returner only in punt-block situations)? What percentage of the time do they run either returner sets? What are the most common pressures (or blocks) they run from these sets? What are the most common returns they run from these sets?

Line of scrimmage or box personnel alignment allows your players to understand who they are blocking and where a punt-return team is pressuring from.

During the transition from protection to coverage, players will know the direction from which their opponent is blocking them; that helps them better avoid the block, preventing knockdown blocks. Also, a cover player gets a chance to feel the leverage that a return team is establishing, giving him valuable information as to the type and direction of the return.

Personnel

Look at the breakdown of players lined up on the opponent's return team. Position and size can give you significant clues as to the intents or ability of a punt-return team.

> *Defensive back, receiver.* Fast and able to slip blocks and rush the punt with speed. Less violent at the line of scrimmage but better able to recover from a successful line release by the punt-cover player.

> *Linebacker, running back.* Fast to the punter and able to slip blocks easily. Violent at the point of attack, has enough agility to maintain a block at the line of scrimmage with size, strength, and speed. Able to recover from a successful line release; although the block may come a little later than if the player is a defensive back or receiver, it will be much more physical.

> *Defensive linemen.* Rushing the punt is more difficult, as a solid block in their path may be enough to prevent them from being close to the punter. But protection has to counter their ability to avoid a block or use strength to

drive a punt-cover player into the punt. Successful line release is much more difficult due to the size, strength, and technical skill development of these athletes. But their downfield blocking takes longer to set up if a punt cover player cleanly escapes them at the line of scrimmage.

Some teams have a set of personnel for returns and a set of personnel for pressures and blocks. Identifying as much, especially by players during the game, not only helps the entire punt-cover team handle pressures and returns, but can greatly undermine the confidence of a punt-return team. Having a block or return called out before the play begins is disheartening.

Return Type

Understanding the different types of returns, how they are executed, and why teams use them provides athletes a significant advantage. Chart the direction and type of every single return. Compare each return with the direction of the kick (boundary or field) so athletes have a better idea where the return team will attack them.

Man returns (figure 12.3) are returns in which a certain punt-return player is responsible for blocking a specific punt-cover player. Cover teams will be

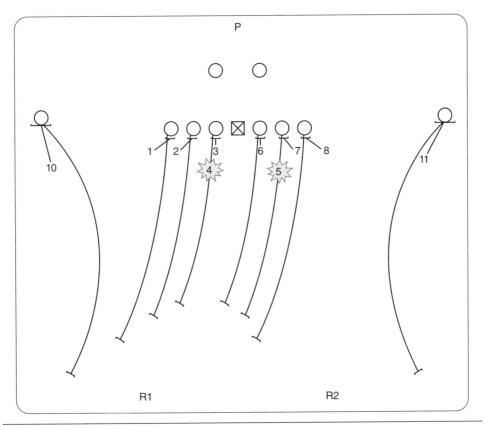

FIGURE 12.3 Man right return. Return is being run to the return team's right.

engaged and held up at the line of scrimmage for as long as possible before being released. The direction released will determine the direction of return. (For example, if the entire cover team is released to the short or boundary side of the field, which is typically where most punts go, then the return team is attempting to run to the wide or field side of the field.) Man returns are easy to run as a system.

Wall returns (figure 12.4) are zone-blocked returns in which a specific number of punt-return players disengage and set up a wall that the returner runs behind. The idea is to pin the cover team inside the wall, allowing the returner to escape. As with a man-blocked return, some punt-cover players remain engaged with punt-return players and will feel the leverage created. Others will disengage and experience a free run down the field to the returner. The key learning point is to have punt-cover players understand the difference between beating their man clean and being allowed a free release. This is exactly what a defensive lineman experiences on a screen, and it may help to have your defensive line coach explain how to read and react.

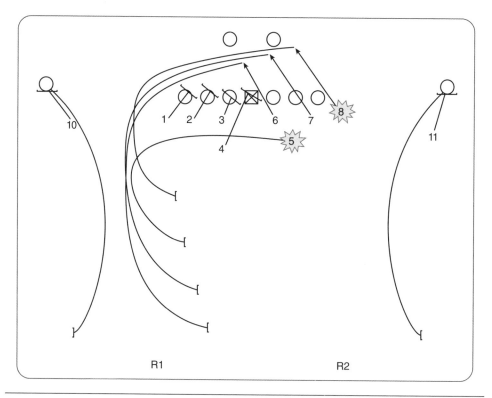

FIGURE 12.4 Wall left return. Return is being run to the return team's left.

Pressure Types

Teams can pressure the punt in a variety of ways from a variety of formations. It is important to understand and relate to players how the pressure works and why they are running it.

It is also important to remember that pressuring the punt is just as valuable as blocking the punt. Punters who feel rushed tend to punt more balls short and out of bounds; cover players tend to stay in a bit longer to ensure protection is solid, which means a less aggressive cover downfield.

Look for keys in alignment, formation, personnel, down and distance, location on field, score—anything that will give your athletes a presnap cue that a specific type of pressure is coming.

A *blitz* (figure 12.5) is a straight-ahead rush by the punt-return team in which every player attacks a gap. The hope is that someone on the punt-cover team misses a block and thereby gives a punt-return player an opportunity to pressure or block the punt.

With *overload* pressure (figure 12.6), outmanning a side gives the punt-return team a free rusher on the punter. Typically, a punt-return team will line up in the gaps and drive straight ahead.

In *twist* pressure (figure 12.7), two punt-return players exchange gap responsibilities (like defensive line twists). Typically, the first rusher is stopped, but the second player looping behind will penetrate the line of

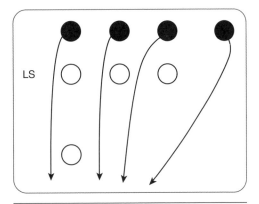

FIGURE 12.5 Inside gap blitz pressure.

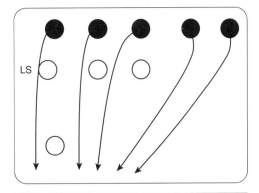

FIGURE 12.6 Overload pressure.

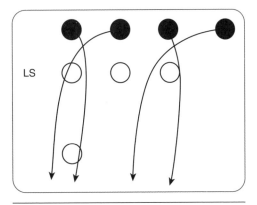

FIGURE 12.7 Twist pressure.

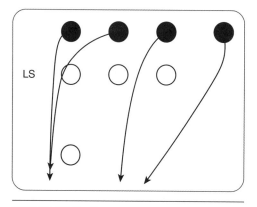

scrimmage and have a free lane to the punter. The goal is to disrupt the protection, especially against punt-cover teams that employ man blocking.

Pony pressure (figure 12.8) is accomplished by sending multiple punt-return personnel through the same gap. The goal is to have one player engaged by a blocker, leaving the other with a free run to the punter.

FIGURE 12.8 Pony pressure.

Kickoff

Kickoff and kickoff return are the special teams' home run hitters. Both of these special teams create opportunities to gain massive amounts of field position or regain ball possession. Most importantly, they can provide a successful team with momentum.

Many coaches spend their time on intricate returns that ensure solid yardage. But most coaches don't prepare their players for the ways that kickoff teams can steal the ball back or make running returns difficult by varying the location and depth of kicks.

The four key elements in scouting an opponent's kickoff cover team are formation, alignment, kick direction, and contain and safeties.

Formation

Players can identify the formation of a kickoff cover team in several ways. Again, use the same language you use to describe your own kickoff cover team. Here are two different methods for counting kickoff cover formations.

Starting from the kicker, count inside out (figure 12.9). Players on the left are labeled L1, L2, L3, and so on. Players on the right side are labeled R1, R2, R3, and so on.

Second, you can use a direction indicator. For example, if the cover team is kicking from the return team's left hash mark, then we count from the left (figure 12.10a). If we are running our return to the right, we count from the right (figure 12.10b).

Formation identification is important for a very specific reason: many teams will kick to a specific side of their formation based on personnel (i.e., the side with the most cover players) regardless of where the team lines up.

| L5 | L4 | L3 | L2 | L1 | **K** | R1 | R2 | R3 | R4 | R5 | R6 |

FIGURE 12.9 Counting inside out.

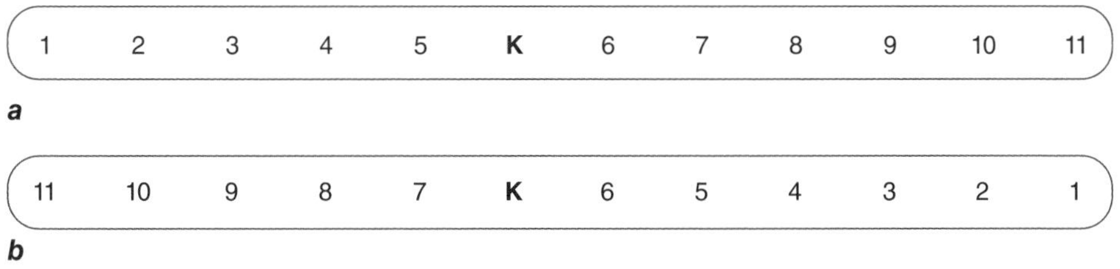

| 1 | 2 | 3 | 4 | 5 | K | 6 | 7 | 8 | 9 | 10 | 11 |

a

| 11 | 10 | 9 | 8 | 7 | K | 6 | 5 | 4 | 3 | 2 | 1 |

b

FIGURE 12.10   Direction indicator: (a) kicking team aligned on the return team's left hash mark, (b) running the return to the right.

Alignment

Alignment refers to the displacement of cover players across the field. Break the field into zones and count the number of cover players in each zone. The simplest form is to use field marks (i.e., sidelines, numbers, and hash marks) and count (i.e., from left sideline to left hash, left hash to right hash, and right hash to sideline). For example, a kickoff team aligned in a 5-4-3 would have five cover players between the left sideline and left hash, four cover players between the hash marks, and three cover players from right hash to right sideline.

The higher concentration of players tends to be in the direction of the kick regardless of where the ball is set up on the field. Deviations in alignment can give substantial clues to altered kick locations or even onside kick attempts. If a team kicks from the left hash and has been using a 5-4-3 formation all season, and then opens their game against your kickoff return team by setting up on the left hash in a 4-3-5, that is a significant indicator that they might be trying an onside kick.

Kick Direction

Much like scouting punt direction, knowing the direction a team kicks gives your return team a significant advantage. It allows you to anticipate a kick direction and landing point so you can make a return call that gives your players the greatest chance of success and allows your returners to set up under the ball early to ensure a clean catch.

Most kickoff teams set the ball to a hash and kick to the boundary; this helps maximize the distance of the kick and cuts down the amount of field to cover. Some teams set up in the middle of the field to try to conceal the direction of their kicks. If you carefully chart the formation and alignment and educate the return team on these tendencies, your players will be able to discern the direction of the kick before the whistle.

Some teams kick only toward their sidelines. This way, if there is a fumble or any turnover, it will be on their side of the field. The choice also brings the hidden advantage of influencing the officials. Nothing seems more intimidating than 40 players, coaches, and staff all signaling that their team has recovered the ball while the officials are trying to sort out a pile of bodies.

Chart the location (or landing) of each kickoff: sidelines, numbers, hash marks, middle of the field, or any other means of designating location. A percentage breakdown of location will help your returners anticipate the landing area and make every catch in the air.

Chart the distance of every kick. Your returners should know this data going into a game so they can align themselves in the best spots possible.

Talk to your return team before the game and discuss the impact of the weather. Wind always plays a part in a kickoff, especially when kicking into the wind. Not only will the kickoffs be shorter in distance, but they will hang in the air longer, giving the kickoff cover team a greater chance to run under the ball and recover it. Ensure your entire kickoff return team understands how to adjust to the wind, typically by moving closer to the ball to help defend a short kick.

Contain and Safeties

Many effective kickoff teams have players form the wide side of the formation (the side furthest from the kick direction) and slide or loop across the formation either before the kick or while the ball is in flight. This can cause a disruption in the blocking scheme of your return.

During the scouting process, diagram the location of the safeties' alignment and, if possible, their jersey numbers. During practice, have those scout team players identified with a helmet pinnie, a different jersey, or something else that sets them apart from the remainder of the kickoff cover team.

How these second-wave players are handled completely depends on the coach. A suggestion is to leave them in your counting scheme and teach players to anticipate their movement relative to the kick. Scout where they end up after the kick is delivered and then renumber the formation.

For example, figure 12.11a shows the formation prekick. The scout sees that, after the kick is delivered, the opponents' safeties slide over and the formation changes to the one shown in figure 12.11b (i.e., 5 slides two spots left and 11 slides three spots left). The coaches rediagram the formation and present it to their players as figure 12.11c. This tells the return team how the formation will look when the ball is in the air.

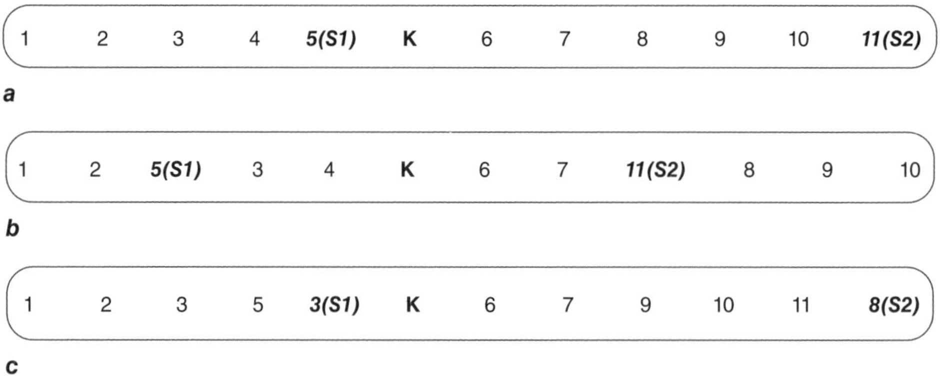

| 1 | 2 | 3 | 4 | 5(S1) | K | 6 | 7 | 8 | 9 | 10 | 11(S2) |

a

| 1 | 2 | 5(S1) | 3 | 4 | K | 6 | 7 | 11(S2) | 8 | 9 | 10 |

b

| 1 | 2 | 3 | 5 | 3(S1) | K | 6 | 7 | 9 | 10 | 11 | 8(S2) |

c

FIGURE 12.11 Anticipating safety movement relative to the kickoff: (a) formation prekick, (b) formation while ball is in flight, (c) reconfigured formation.

Kickoff Return

Many coaches believe the key to a successful kickoff is being able to drive the ball as far as possible. But some other aspects are more important. Focusing on kick hang time (or height) and location are significant parts to limiting a kickoff return. But equally as important is how quickly athletes can dissect what the kickoff return team is running and then swing into an effective response. That takes preparation.

Three key aspects of scouting an opponent's kickoff return team are formation, initial movement of the front row, and angle or tilt of the back row.

Formation

When scouting a kickoff return formation, concern yourself with the number of players in certain areas:

- *Front row.* The more players in the front row, the more time your athletes need to spend on a fast takeoff and downfield avoidance so they can sift through the opposition and collapse on the back row. Having more front players means more obstacles and less room to work downfield.
- *Back row.* Having more players in the back row means your cover team has to be disciplined and collide into the gaps of the back row and not the actual man. With more of your cover team downfield, it takes only a small crack in coverage to let the return burst through to the open field.
- *Outside the hash short.* If the kickoff return team has bunched their players in the middle of the field, there are opportunities to kick short and wide and outnumber them.
- *Outside the hash deep.* The width of the back row can reveal some glaring holes. If a back row is set up hash mark to hash mark, then a high kick landing outside the numbers at their level will either force the returner to track the ball a very long distance (and put him or her outside and possibly in front of the back-row protection) or else the back-row player closest to the kick will recover it.

Look at the depth of each row. A front row that is 10 yards from the kick will have greater difficulty with a fast takeoff by the kickoff team. Also, they'll have less time to process movement or shorter kicks by the kickoff team. The greater the distance between the back row of blockers and the front row, the more of an area there is where high or squibbed kicks can land. If the back row is tighter to the front row, they will have a greater distance to travel to get back to the returner before turning around and making blocks.

Consider the location of the returners. Well-coached returners will adjust to the known kicking distance of the opponent's kicker and will line up at the appropriate yard line. Also, they will adjust to the hash kicked from and the scouted direction of previous kicks. But if returners stay true on their landmarks (i.e., if they always start in the same spots regardless of what the kickoff team does), then there are opportunities to manipulate them with various kick locations, distances, and even heights.

Initial Movement of the Front Row

Determine if the front row of players runs straight back toward the returner before turning to face the cover team, or if they loop away from their blocks and ambush. If they run straight back toward the returner and then turn and face the cover team, they will establish their leverage much later and closer to the point of attack. Your athletes must be more disciplined in their lanes, quicker on their avoidance technique, and much more diligent in reestablishing their coverage lanes postcontact.

If the front line loops away from its blocks and ambushes, your athletes can discern the direction of the return much earlier in the sprint downfield. The challenge is avoiding the collision and block.

For each type of return, diagram the return and show film so the kickoff players can see the angles of attack and speed of collision, or anticipate the location of the opponent who eventually engages them.

Angle or Tilt of the Back Row

Of all the keys to dissecting a kickoff return, reading the back row is the cleanest. Back-row players typically turn their bodies toward the return or even create a perpendicular line toward the direction of the return (figure 12.12). This gives your cover team the chance to work to the play side of the back row.

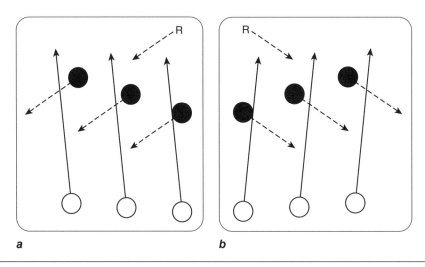

FIGURE 12.12 Angle of the back row: (a) back row left tilt (black circles) with cover team (white circles) working play side, (b) back row right tilt (black circles) with cover team (white circles) working play side.

Using Special-Teams Scouting

Although this chapter touched on only four of the eight special teams, it should become clear how much of an advantage a team can gain from proper preparation and scouting. From rules, to formation strengths and weaknesses, to kick direction and location percentages, to weaknesses in fundamentals, all these things make a difference in two very important ways:

1. Players are able to play with a sense of control and anticipation that leads to faster decision-making and faster play.

2. Players can see what the coach is trying to accomplish in their own special-teams preparation as they install their own system. They will begin to understand the strengths and weaknesses of their own fundamentals, tactics, and grasp of rules. They will begin to anticipate how to nullify any advantages the opponent might seek from scouting.

CONCLUSION

Great time and effort are needed when scouting the opposition. But coaches and players should make this effort for every game, regardless of the opponent. The more you do it, the better you will get. Also, the more you train your athletes to internalize the resulting information, the better they'll get at using it. No, scouting might not be the difference between winning and losing every game. But it could make the difference for the most important game. Isn't that worth the effort?

CHAPTER

13

Developing a Competitive Mental Edge

Jay Hetherington

This chapter focuses on how psychological principles can inform the practice of coaching Canadian football. Psychology is about the workings of the human mind as it pertains to behavior within a given context. In this case, the context is Canadian football as played by children and youth. This chapter is for the community-based coaches who coach these players.

For this chapter, I collected information from a number of popularly accessible places as well as some more scholarly sources. I encourage you to further explore some of the popular literature on the subjects discussed.

This chapter includes thoughts on a wide range of topics, such as putting together a coaching staff, choosing players, teaching effectively, leading positively, and developing focus and mental toughness. One chapter cannot hope to cover the entire breadth of topics in psychology as it pertains to Canadian football. But nearly all aspects of coaching can be improved by understanding how people work in groups, learn, make decisions, and discover how to compete and persevere.

BUILDING A COACHING STAFF

Building a football team begins with developing a working, energetic, and cohesive coaching staff. Basically, a football coaching staff is a specialized type of working group. Understanding the behavior of persons in working groups can be complicated, but we have a great deal of research by organizational psychologists to guide us. Their work can help inform the process of choosing a coaching staff.

I asked a bright young coach to name his main skill and he quickly told me that he was an "organizer of many talented people." This is a great answer. Importantly, it lacks the hubris of coaches who believe they know everything about football. In their book *The Knowledge Illusion*, Steven Sloman and Philip Fernbach

(2017) contend that people tend to overestimate how much they know about subjects. This likely includes football coaches. These authors caution against knowledge hubris and they point out that most great things are rarely achieved though the singular action of a hero. Their work suggests that everything of consequence tends to come from teams working together. This suggests that head coaches who manage good people well will have at their disposal far more knowledge and talent that they themselves can possess.

Who does a coach choose for the coaching staff? Some coaches pick a staff with diverse personalities. These types of coaching staffs tend to come up with creative and well-thought-out solutions to problems, but sometimes friction may result in difficult behavioral outcomes. In the short term, a more homogeneous (similar personality) group will outperform a more heterogeneous (diverse personality) group. In the long term, if a diverse group learns to respect the differences of its members, a heterogeneous group performs the best (Kozlowski and Bell, 2001).

If, as a group, the coaches are high on the personality trait of conscientiousness, they will tend to be excellent planners but less effective at making quick decisions. This is because planners like to study and plan, and making a decision means you need to quit planning, which is, by their estimation, the cool part. In the past, I have described the conscientious type as being a "ready, aim, aim, aim" coach. If you pick coaches who have extraversion as their primary personality trait, they will have a great impact on team effectiveness in communication and decision-making. They may be less motivated by the detailed-planning piece. Extraverted types can be characterized as "fire, ready, aim" coaches. It is easy to see that a mixture of these personality types will make for a balance between detailed planning and a willingness to decide on a course of action.

Like many typologies in psychology, neither of these positions tends to exist in the extreme. Extraverts plan, they just don't prefer it. Highly conscientious types can make great decisions; they just are more interested in the planning (Kozlowski and Bell, 2001).

When choosing assistant coaches, is there an optimal size for a coaching staff? Predictably, the answer is this: it depends on the task at hand. Researchers say the size of a working group (coaching staff) has a curvilinear relationship to performance (think of an inverted U on a graph). Too few coaches, and the task is too large for good work to get done. Too many coaches and individuals on staff may feel that their efforts don't count; responsibility is so dispersed that motivation drops (Kozlowski and Bell, 2001).

Research has come up with some suggestions that match common sense. If there is a large, complicated task that requires many hands and a diverse skill set, a large coaching staff is appropriate. Think about large U Sports teams such as Laval University or the University of Saskatchewan. But either Laval or a small youth football organization needs to have a staff that is just big enough get the job done and lean enough that all coaches know they contribute to the mission.

PLAYER SELECTION

The psychology of decision-making can help coaches make better decisions about the selection of players, the next big job after the staff has been put together.

Several years ago, before learning about the work of Amos Tversky and Danny Kahneman, I was already interested in errors in thinking in regard to team selection. This was because, in Alberta, we were interested in fairness and accuracy in the choosing of players for our Football Canada Cup provincial team. The process was shaped around eliminating some possible inadvertent sources of cognitive bias. We looked at how we tended to act when we made selections.

The first source of bias that became evident was really a function of memory processes. People have a tendency to remember what occurs first and last in a series of events. The things in the middle often are given less weight or simply forgotten. This is called the primacy and recency effect. This effect is prevalent when a coach watches a series of players taking their turns to perform skills in a player selection drill. To combat this effect, we asked our selection coaches to do some simple things:

- Mentally take special note of the players who were performing in the middle of the line of players.

- Keep a simple record of the evaluation of their performances throughout the tryout.

- Minimize distractions for the duration of the observation period because this bias is strengthened when the observer's attention is interrupted.

The halo effect is another problem. Coaches can give too much importance to a single trait, basing their general impression of somebody on that one element— for example, deciding that a player has the look of an athlete and therefore must have the talent. Instead the coach should examine the person's specific abilities, such as speed and agility. The original general impression of the player could be refuted or confirmed by making a decision based on tangible measures.

Then there's negativity bias. That's the tendency to recall and be influenced by negative past experiences, and to weigh negative information more heavily than positive information when forming an opinion. Negative data needs to be taken into account, but it shouldn't be your exclusive focus. Be sure that you also record what players are doing well, and don't let one negative event or catastrophic episode eliminate a person from consideration. Develop a system that will capture a picture of players who are consistently skilled performers over the entire selection process.

Once people form an opinion, they are inclined to look for evidence that confirms it. This is confirmation bias. Of course, football coaches don't live in a vacuum. Often they'll have prior knowledge of how a given player performed in his respective local leagues; if they don't, plenty of coaches and parents will fill them in. But when selecting a team, it's best to keep an open mind as long as possible. Look for evidence that refutes your currently held opinion, not just confirms it.

Eventually, the evaluating coaches meet to make final team selections. At this point, watch out for groupthink. This is the tendency to seek consensus just so a group can stay cohesive. The coaches should pick a devil's advocate, a coach who gets the job of challenging the group's decisions. If possible, the coaching group should meet a second time, to determine if opinions about player selections have changed. The aim is to base decisions on observable facts, not group mood.

The selection of your team is important. Therefore, making better decisions about player selection is important too. As Thaler and Sunstein (2009) state in their book *Nudge*, "Human behavior can be improved by appreciating how we systematically go wrong." A system of selection predicated on evidence-based psychological principles is well positioned to be as fair and effective as possible. Simply being aware that we think in imperfect ways should encourage us to slow our thinking process from a rush to judgment to a more evidence-based, controlled, and deductive method of decision-making.

COACHING AS TEACHING

In his most despondent moments, Vince Lombardi used to say, "I must be a lousy teacher" (Kramer and Schaap, 1968). He knew that the essence of coaching was teaching, and that coaches were in a weekly teaching competition with their counterparts on the other side of the field. Lombardi seemed to understand the importance of coaches knowing aspects of educational psychology and its use in their weekly on-field preparation.

Likely the most important bit of advice for every coach is to become very familiar with the curriculum of your sport. Football Canada has many excellent resources for coaches at the youth and high school levels. Each coach needs to decide what skills are to be taught over the course of a season and which skills to emphasize weekly and daily. This list of skills to be taught can be thought of as the scope of your team or unit's football curriculum. Understanding the learning needs of your players will help you decide on the sequence of the skills being taught and the frequency with which they will be repeated to solidify the automaticity of the skills that your players need to learn.

Every learner has a preferred way of taking in information. Football coaches tend to rely heavily on demonstration as a method of instruction. People who learn best from demonstration are called visual learners. Not everyone, however, learns best through observation. Auditory learners may learn best though lectures. People who learn by doing are referred to as tactile or kinesthetic learners. A coach may prefer one approach or another, but a good coach uses a variety. An in-depth understanding of learning styles can be complicated, but the essence of this three-factor model is that a group of players will benefit from receiving a similar message in a single lesson (meeting or practice) in all three learning styles.

A good learning experience needs a good beginning. In educational psychology, this good beginning is called the anticipatory set. It is a brief activity or event at the beginning of the session that effectively engages all players' attention and focuses their thoughts on the learning objective. It could be as simple as letting players know what you are trying to teach them in a certain set of drills by relating it to a theme such as "hustle and heart." The anticipatory set gives the activity or lesson that follows the appropriate cognitive framework for player engagement. Research shows repeatedly that a positive expectation and learning climate starts at the beginning and tends to energize a player's learning.

A common approach to teaching skills is the whole-part-whole approach. The coach presents a representation of the whole skill, including how that skill fits into the strategy of the team and benefits the players. Explaining the big picture provides continued support to the motivation introduced in the anticipatory set. In the part section of this process, the coach deconstructs or breaks down a skill. This may require a working understanding of biomechanical principles, such as summation of forces and centre of gravity. Good coaches tend to take an interest in the details of skills, such as correct footwork and body position. Even better coaches are able to deconstruct whole skills into their constituent parts. The constituent parts of a skill are then taught in a progressive manner. The coach then begins to link these skills in a chain that eventually represents the complete skill. Research into learning tells coaches that, for players to achieve mastery, the athletes need to acquire the component skills and practice integrating them into a complete or whole performance.

In *Peak* (Ericsson and Pool, 2016), the authors speak of the importance of deliberate practice, meaning a practice that is both purposeful and systematic. While this concept is not exactly a paradigm shift for coaches, Ericsson's emphasis on feedback and vigorous systematic correction marks a difference in his approach that coaches should find useful. In his view, practice does not make perfect. Perfect practice makes perfect.

At graduate school, I had the pleasure of studying with a Franciscan friar who was fond of saying "man is a meaning maker." In my experience, players seem to learn better when what is being learned has meaning for them. When connections in knowledge structures are actively and meaningfully organized, players will be better able to remember and apply the things they have learned in practice. So it is important that they know why they are learning the skills you are teaching at practice and how it all fits into being a good football player on game day.

I am fond of saying, "What is vigorously practiced passes into habit." This saying seems to have great utility in explaining how people develop their habitual way of doing things. Whoever coined this phrase knew that learning physical skills required the laying down of neural pathways through repeated performance. This is still a standard practice when teaching physical skills. Football coaches need to allow time for enough skill repetition so that what is learned passes into habit. At the beginning of the season, coaches should focus on mastering the basics of positional skills, and then continue to build on them throughout the season. For example, at the beginning of the season, introduce the skills of the Safe Contact program relating to blocking and tackling (see chapter 4). As players master the basic body positions and movements through drills, you can begin to integrate them in one-on-one drills and other full-speed scenarios. Once players can perform individual skills effectively at high tempo, you can begin to integrate other skills, such as having them defeat a blocker and then perform a tackle on the ball carrier. In the end, with careful purposeful practice, players will perform their basic skills with unconscious competence.

Following a repetition-filled learning session, the coach needs to provide time for closure. Closure is a natural end point in the lesson, when the drill's relevance to the objective is reviewed and reinforced. Closure keeps the big picture in view. It ensures that the objectives of the practice are met.

Not all lessons on the field are planned. These teachable moments should not be wasted. The teachable moment is the unplanned moment in a practice when something of educational importance occurs. Doug Hargreaves, the former head coach of the Queen's University Golden Gaels, was a master of this technique. He'd stop practice and quickly give the players his insight into what they'd just seen, then dive back into practice. The immediacy of this technique lends emotional emphasis to whatever is being learned, so that recalling the information later is likely to be enhanced.

If you sense that you have come to a teachable moment, don't hesitate to stop the practice and take advantage of the learning opportunity. In the long run, it will be more valuable than skipping the teachable moment to stay on schedule, or trying to come back to it when it is no longer highly relevant in the players' minds.

POSITIVE LEADERSHIP

Coaches must be good teachers and positive leaders. To this end, a coach should provide age-appropriate attention to players in his unit. For example, acknowledge as many players as possible in prepractice meetings or as players begin warm-up. While coaching with a midget football team, I observed that the head coach asked the players and coaches to shake hands at the end of practice. It was a ritual that the players seemed to enjoy. This simple exercise was also a symbolic gesture of peacemaking and a powerful example of culture building. When a coach creates a positive learning climate for players, they begin to understand they are valued and it increases the likelihood that players will be willing to "buy in" to the coach's instruction.

At the same time, it is important that the coach also maintain a certain amount of professional distance. You are being friendly. This is not to be confused with being the player's friend. Blurred lines between friend and coach sets up a conflicting dual relationship that may become confusing and problematic.

Generally, an effective coach strives to increase the number of positive interactions with his or her players. A good coach is skilled at noticing when players behave in a manner that is to be encouraged (catch them doing something right). The coach should respond with positive reinforcement. Football coaches should strive for a ratio of at least four or five positive interactions to one negative utterance. Educational psychologists have used this ratio to improve teacher effectiveness and encourage desired behavior.

So as the coach moves around players while in a drill, the coach is actively giving praise. The praise is distributed precisely and it's about specifics. "Good job" and "way to go" don't tell the player what specifically to continue doing. The coach looks for what each player is doing well and describes it, calling the player by name and praising the action of that person in a voice loud enough to be heard by other players in the immediate area. The coach does this right when the action happens, because that's when reinforcement is most powerful. The aim is to develop a style of rapid-fire positive feedback with observations that emphasize the learning taking place.

The coach names the player and singles him out for praise during the drill for two reasons. First, the player is named so others may look to see what that person is doing. Second, identifying that person as a temporary exemplar encourages others to seek praise by doing what the first player did.

Over time, as players gain competence and improve, the comments can be adjusted so that players are gently led to more closely approximate near-perfect performance. This is an example of leading players through positive feedback toward constant improvement of skills.

Finally, as part of the closure to a current drill or the anticipatory set of the next drill, the wise coach will remind players what they did well in the last drill.

A good example of the power of positive interaction occurred with the Alberta Under 18 provincial team. Team Alberta has a proud history of achievement at the Football Canada Cup National Championship. But in the 2010 Canada Cup, the team finished a disappointing last place. Bryan Brandford, the head coach of the team, spent that long prairie winter thinking about his experience. One day, as he was in traffic in Calgary, he noticed a bumper sticker that said simply, "More Wag Less Bark." It occurred to him that the poor finish of that past year might have been partly due to the coaching staff's tendency to be more critical and less positive than they would have liked.

Coach Brandford proposed to the Football Alberta board of directors that they needed a fundamental change of approach. He wanted to make the message from a dog owner's bumper sticker the theme for our team. Our provincial association was a little concerned. The 2011 Canada Cup was being hosted in Alberta. We wanted a good showing, and "More Wag Less Bark" sounded a little fuzzy. Would this approach fit our tough, no-nonsense team of young cowboys from Alberta? But we knew our man was a great coach and a master educator. If he wanted "More Wag and Less Bark," he had our total support.

Coach Brandford worked hard to make positive interaction a team policy. In 2011, I witnessed a much-improved Alberta team defeating the first-seeded team from Saskatchewan. Alberta then went on to meet Quebec in the national final. A highly skilled and deserving Quebec team was crowned champion, but I think "More Wag Less Bark" turned out to be a brilliant coaching intervention.

Positive leadership and interventions get results because players see leadership in action. The ability to lead by example takes a certain moral and social courage that is often seen in the best football coaches. Positive leadership can create a cascade of positive effects, all flowing from this one small but fundamental change. The mechanism of change is known in psychology as social learning theory. The method of learning is called observational learning.

Albert Bandura was the first to study this type of learning (Hergenhahn, 1984). His work on this type of learning made him one of the world's foremost psychologists. He explained that much of what we learn occurs through the natural process of observing the behavior of others. Observational learning does not require reinforcement or rewards. It does require a social model, someone who can be observed and emulated.

Our coach was a good social model. His positive attitude had a cascade of effects that flowed throughout the team culture. His coaching staff took their lead from him and in turn the players developed a more positive expectation of success and were willing to risk and compete with unbridled enthusiasm. Just like their coach.

Observational learning can help build peer leadership potential on your team. But for young players, being just like coach may seem too large of a step. Learning about exemplary behavior through social stories can be another powerful way to help players become leaders.

People are natural storytellers. We may have always been this way. Joseph Campbell (1982) noted that "the fundamental themes of mythological thought have remained constant and universal, not only throughout history but over the whole extent of mankind's occupation of the earth." According to Campbell and other thinkers, stories have always carried social meaning in the form of mythology. The purpose of this social meaning was often to serve the psychological need for generativity, the human need to make your mark on the world through accomplishing things that make the world a better place. Erik Erikson (Hergenhahn, 1984) originally thought that generativity was a need found only in adults, but later writers such as Karen Frensch (2000) have recognized this altruistic behavior in youth as well.

Stories in human organizations can teach people how to behave in socially complicated situations. Football teams need to teach team-specific prosocial behavior. Psychologists regularly use social stories to teach children how to behave in a prosocial manner. Football coaches hand out game balls and helmet stickers while talking about the laudable exploits of the players involved. Football teams that have long histories often have stories of former players that serve as exemplars for generations of other players. We had just such stories on teams that I coached. Those stories were well known by the veteran players and told religiously to the rookies. The stories transmitted team expectations about what was the standard of behavior expected of players.

The stories also helped players develop a template for leadership behavior with the team. Leadership requires knowledge of how to lead, a propensity to lead, and an opportunity to lead. All three must exist for leadership to occur. If a team has provided exemplary models to emulate (coaches and players) and has carefully told social stories of good people doing good things, players will learn what leaders do. If players on the team have been encouraged to leave their mark on their small piece of the world—the team—their natural propensity to step up and lead will be nurtured. If the wise coach creates small opportunities to show leadership to a wide range of people on the team, there will be opportunity to lead. When these three conditions are met, positive prosocial leaders will emerge at the confluence of knowledge, propensity, and opportunity. Great things will occur.

BECOMING WILLING AND ABLE: BUILDING SELF-ESTEEM THROUGH SELF-EFFICACY

In a mature individual, self-esteem is just that: the value that the person decides to affix to him or herself as an individual. The mature perspective is that people have inherent self-worth as human beings. Coaches usually are not dealing with persons who have a mature viewpoint regarding self-worth. We tend to deal with young people who are in various states of maturity. Football coaches often have a substantial amount of influence on the people they coach. Therefore, what we say or do matters a great deal. Use this influence wisely. Be consistently positive and respectful in your interactions with athletes.

In case you think that self-esteem is an abstract concept that does not affect the football bottom line, you should understand that a player with fragile self-worth most likely won't risk damage to it by taking chances on the field. By contrast, players with high self-esteem tend to be bold and decisive. They have a positive expectation of success. Football coaches should want players with high self-esteem.

Self-esteem answers the question "Am I worthy?" Self-efficacy answers the question "Am I able?" As a coach, I have noticed that self-efficacy seems to be the high road to self-esteem in young players. Right or wrong, young people seem to link competency with worthiness. It is because of this apparent link that I have come to see working on building efficacy through skills as an intermediary step to improving self-esteem in young people.

It is likely not an accident that Scouts Canada has had such a long run of success with young people. I remember as a Cub Scout the importance of earning merit badges as affirmation of my growing competencies. Young athletes who begin to play football are very interested in doing something well. As they feel the success of growing competence in football, it should positively impact their self-efficacy and by extension their self-esteem. The combination of athletic competency and the expectation of a positive outcome should be such that they will be willing to risk open competition. In many ways, a player's self-esteem is the measure of an effective coach.

DON'T WINK AT THE RULES, JUST COMPETE

Doug Hargreaves wasn't just a master of teachable moments. The great coach of the Queen's Golden Gaels gave a talk that included one of the best pieces of wisdom I have ever learned in this game. In his forthright manner, he told a room full of coaches, "Gentlemen, we should never wink at the rules." This sounds so quaint by today's standards, in a coaching world where some may harbor a counter opinion: "If you aren't cheating, you aren't trying." But Coach Hargreaves had it right. He knew that every time we play this game, we enter into a kind of agreement, an unwritten contract that binds us to the rules. It has become clear to me that deviating from or disregarding this contract will make any victory hollow and devoid of honor. Coach Hargreaves also knew that the players watch a coach's every move, and he took his responsibility to lead seriously. Yet, within the framework of the rules, he said there is ample latitude to encourage vigorous and fiercely competitive play.

When football coaches talk about competitive play, they are usually thinking about good, clean, hard play. They are thinking about football played within the rules and with vigor and enthusiasm. In this context, competitive play means trying hard and performing to the best of your abilities. Coaches want their players to feel free to compete in an unreserved manner. Executing skills with a high degree of tempo and emotional vigor wins games.

Players need to believe that they can be successful through competitive play. The Roman poet Virgil said, "They are able because they think they are able." This aphorism applied to human performance 2,000 years ago and it applies now.

As a coach, your first pillar of competitive behavior is to focus on helping your players being physically able to compete. Increased physical fitness has a positive effect on a player's ability to perform. The good coach helps players perceive that they are getting better physically. This perception of an increased fitness makes it more likely that a player will risk a full effort to compete.

Second, as players become aware of their increased technical competence in football, they will increase their competitive engagement with other players. The psychological key is to bring their progress in learning skills into their awareness. This act of noticing their positive growth is called "giving news of difference." If the coach can demonstrate in some way, either through film or verbally, that there is growth, the player will feel that he has the second pillar, the technical ability to compete. The third pillar of ability is having license to compete. Giving a full and honest effort should be rewarded. It is important for players to know that the entire organization supports highly competitive fair play. Coaches need to be tracking selected observable behaviors such as hustle, second effort, and enthusiastic defensive pursuit to reinforce vigorous competition. In this way, coaches can encourage a culture of trying hard and playing hard

UNCONSCIOUS FOCUS: MAKING GOOD RECEIVERS GREAT

Timothy Gallwey has never written a word about football, yet his book *The Inner Game of Tennis* (1977) explains a lot about why athletes or football players have difficulty and why they excel.

Gallwey has a clear and simple way to look at life and the connection between consciousness and human performance. He conceptualizes the nature of self as an active dichotomy between what he calls Self 1 and Self 2. He sees Self 1 as the teller and Self 2 as the doer.

Self 1 is the active voice that we sometimes hear inside of our heads. It is like the running commentary of a critical observer. Self 1 is the critical self that tends to try to talk the athlete through a performance. It is as if the commentary is meant to guide the player from a position of conscious competence to conscious incompetence. The inner commentary itself hampers performance. If the athlete listens to the inner dialogue, it slows reaction time. According to Gallwey, it "produces muscle tension and conflict within the body."

Self 2 can be thought of as being the wisdom of the body. Self 2 has no voice. It speaks through action. It does the performance to the degree to which it has been trained. I often think that it is the pure expression of muscle memory. This kind of intelligence seeks to take the athlete's performance from the state of conscious competence (hampered by the constant criticism of Self 1) to the performance state of unconscious competence. Occasionally, a well-trained and liberated Self 2 can bring the athlete to a transcendent state of performance, commonly called the zone of peak performance. This concept is best described by Mihaly Csikszentmihalyi's concept of flow states (Csikszentmihalyi, 2007).

There is really a three-step process to using this technique. The first thing is to quiet the mind. When Gallwey was working with tennis players, he would occupy Self 1 by giving it something to do. He would ask the tennis player to describe what she saw. For example, she was asked to describe the path of the ball coming toward her. She might say "bounce" to describe the action of the ball in her side of the court. She might describe her trained reaction to the tennis ball by saying "hit" as she executed the volley. Giving this simple description task to Self 1 left no room for criticism. With receivers, the mantra of "look-look-catch" has worked for my players. I am sure the reader can be more creative. The important thing is to occupy Self 1 with a useful descriptive task until the athlete can learn to empty the sound of criticism from his mind in a meditative fashion and just let Self 2 use its wisdom.

The second pillar of this technique is to drill and train the muscle memory in biomechanically sound ways that build the neural pathways in the brain specific to the performance required. Start slowly so that the receiver can observe, experience, and feel the required movements in their entirety. Many repetitions of the required movement give Self 2 the education it needs without criticism from Self 1.

The third and final pillar of Timothy Gallwey's approach is, in my opinion, the key to turning a good receiver into a great one. The concept is simple. Everything in football and life coming toward you can be viewed as an opportunity or a threat. The decision is yours. The results of the decision can be profound.

A receiver who is burdened by Self 1 criticism and negative past experience may view an approaching football as a threat. The result of this decision would be a half-hearted attempt at catching the ball. Conversely, if Self 1 is silent and Self 2 is trained, the receiver will enthusiastically approach the opportunity to catch the ball.

After my son went to the University of Alberta to play receiver for the Golden Bears, I could not find my copy of *The Inner Game of Tennis*. My son had taken it with him, and he read and reread the book until it fell apart. Now he is a high school football coach in Edmonton and all of his receivers learn about the inner game.

GOAL SETTING FOR COACHES AND PLAYERS

Stephen Covey (1989) said that you must always "begin with the end in mind." This is very true, especially when setting goals as an individual or as a group. A clearly articulated objective, combined with a close emotional bond to that objective, is the key to goal setting.

It is natural for people to have goals. Goal setting harnesses this natural proclivity and takes conscious charge of the process. The first thing to do is to define clearly your ultimate goal. Where do you want to be? What would it look like and feel like to be in that end state? How would you act when you got there? It is important to define clearly your final goal—intellectually, emotionally, and some say in a sensory manner as well.

A clear long-term goal inspires athletes. This inspiration can continue over the long haul of one or more seasons, with the big prize being the fruit of sustained efforts. Unfortunately, goals that are of high benefit and in the distant future are not as motivating as smaller-value goals that are nearer in time.

That is why it is hard to stick to a distant goal of fitness when it is immediately rewarding to watch football on television (Hergenhahn, 1984). The answer to this problem is more goals: well-thought-out intermediate steps that lead you to the big prize. The process of keeping your eye on the prize is largely the function of setting short-term daily and weekly goals. The eventual attainment of your long-term goal depends on the successful completion of your short-term and intermediate goals.

Many people are familiar with the acronym SMART as a guide to setting effective goals. There are different interpretations of what each letter stands for, but here is one example:

- *Specific.* Goals should be written precisely. For example: "My goal is to bench-press 250 pounds" rather than "My goal is to get stronger."
- *Measurable.* Goals should be objective, evaluated based on data such as numbers or clear achievements, rather than subjective, evaluated based on

opinions or feelings. For example, "My goal is to improve my current maximum bench press by 5 percent in the first 60 days."

◆ *Attainable.* Goals should be realistic in relation to the individual's current level of performance and the time available for goal achievement. For example, it is probably not realistic for an untrained 15-year-old athlete to make the provincial under-18 football team. Goals should be very challenging but realistic.

◆ *Relevant.* Goals should be suitable to the individual's performance area. For example, it is probably not a relevant goal for a high school quarterback to bench-press 300 pounds. That level of strength (and the time required to develop it) is not related to being an outstanding quarterback. Also, goals in one area of life should coordinate with goals in other areas of life, and should be consistent with a person's values.

◆ *Time-bound.* Goals should have a set time frame to help the individual have the required level of focus and for the individual to know if he has achieved his goal in the set time. Short-term goals could range anywhere from a goal for that practice to a goal that may take a few weeks. Intermediate goals will require the achievement of a number of short-term goals and may take weeks or months to attain. Long-term goals will require the achievement of many short and intermediate goals and will take months, years, or even decades to accomplish.

MENTAL TOUGHNESS

Like many Canadians, I have marveled at sports heroes such as Terry Fox, who had the determination to attempt to run on one leg across the second largest country in the world, a challenge that most Canadians with two legs would never consider. I have wondered what special qualities the canoeist Silken Laumann possessed that allowed her to remain committed to representing our country in the Olympics with a barely healed broken leg What deep well of confidence empowered Paul Henderson to leap onto the ice to score the winning goal in the iconic 1972 Canada–Russia series? Where did they get the mental reserves to fuel their great achievements? These people exhibit a quality of grace under pressure combined with certain clarity of purpose, and this sets them apart. They demonstrate a quality called mental toughness.

Researchers at Hull University in Great Britain became interested in the difficult-to-explain concept of mental toughness (Clough, Earl, and Sewell, 2002). They looked at resilience (the ability to withstand stressors) and hardiness (the interrelation of a desire for challenge with a need to control and a commitment to persevere). They believe that mental toughness exists as a universal human quality that everyone has to one extent or another.

At one end of the continuum is mental toughness. The person who holds this extreme position does not seem to be bothered by psychological stress. At the other end, a person displays a high degree of sensitivity to stress. A person at that end will be somewhat rigid, and a person at the other will be quite flexible. It should be noted that this type of toughness is evenly distributed between the genders. That is why Silken Laumann could be just as mentally tough as Paul Henderson.

Each person has a preferred style of interaction with the world, and this style determines their level of mental toughness. But people can change and become more mentally tough. This is done by challenging and manipulating certain mental constructs to allow people to become more able to handle psychological stress.

The result of Dr. P. J. Clough's work is a framework that includes the interplay of independent factors of control, commitment, challenge, and confidence. (Descriptions of the factors are in table 13.1.) Control and confidence are broken into two subcategories: life and emotional control, and interpersonal confidence in one's abilities.

Dr. Clough developed a measure of the factors that comprise mental toughness. His model indicates that a person's general style of performance under stress can improve by the use of various interventions that build competency in each particular area. The following sections provide examples of some activities that coaches can use with players.

Coaches who have players who require growth in the area of control may wish them to learn what things can reasonably be expected to be controlled and also understand what can't be controlled. Coaches should help players become technically competent in their sport so that they have a high degree of sport-specific self-efficacy. Coaches may wish to help players be aware of their emotional state when experiencing challenging competitive situations or learning to interact effectively with teammates. Coaches need to help athletes be aware of their optimal state of arousal for competition. This refers to the individualized balance between relaxation and activation that puts a performer in his ideal performance state, or "the zone."

TABLE 13.1   Components of Mental Toughness

Component	Description
Life control	Degree of control over what the athlete considers the important aspects of his or her life
Control of emotions	Degree of control of the athlete's emotions under stress
Challenge	Tendency of an athlete to seek opportunity and take on new challenges
Commitment	Degree to which an athlete is committed to a task regardless of pressure
Confidence in abilities	Degree to which an athlete feels that he or she has the abilities to make a difference
Interpersonal confidence	Degree to which an athlete is assertive and able to resist intimidation

If players require growth in the area of challenge, get them to deal with the unexpected. Many coaches employ disaster drills, the simplest of which is the fumble drill. A more complicated scenario involves a punting duel, that rare but exciting part of Canadian football in which teams punt the ball out of the end zone to prevent the scoring of rouge. The coach should help players embrace change and develop an optimistic outlook that inspires them to search for chances to reach their goals in any situation.

If players need growth in the area of commitment, coaches may want to help them set clear, achievable personal goals that align with the team's goals. Make sure that the goals have short and intermediate targets on the way to the big-picture goal. A goal could be something like completing all school assignments and homework on time each week so the players are eligible to practice and play. Coaches also may have players become involved in team-building activities that foster cohesion, either through shared work or by social interaction such as team meals, a position activity, or a team community service activity.

For players requiring growth in the area of confidence, banish negative self-talk and replace it with positive self-talk. Focus on the basic fundamentals of the game until players feel competent. Also focus on fitness. An improvement in fitness levels usually correlates positively with personal confidence. While this can happen during the season to an extent, the off-season is the optimal opportunity for significant personal fitness improvements. Give each player an opportunity to contribute to the narrative of the team. Improve interpersonal skills between team members so that you can build your team while you build leaders. This can be done informally or formally. Informally would mean team workouts or pregame meals. Formally would be training camp player introductions and other icebreaker activities, or team leadership meetings in which players learn about leadership and get to discuss team issues.

CONCLUSION

Games tend to be a reflection of the spirit of the peoples who create them. In 1874, McGill University students took the beginnings of just such a game to Harvard and in so doing helped invent football. From that day on, our game evolved in parallel to that of the Americans. Canadians kept pieces of the game that spoke to who we are. That is why our football is about fair play and hard work, with unlimited motion. It is a game writ large on a big frozen field. It is like the people and country that made it.

REFERENCES

Campbell, J. 1982. *Myths to Live By*. New York: Bantam Books.

Clough, P. J., K. Earl, and D. Sewell. 2002. *Mental Toughness: The Concept and Its Measurement*. In I. Cockerill (ed.), *Solutions in Sport Psychology*. London: Thomson Learning.

Covey, S. R. 1989. *The 7 Habits of Highly Effective People: Power Lessons in Personal Change*. New York: Simon and Schuster.

Csikszentmihalyi, M. 2007. *Flow: The Psychology of Optimal Experience*. New York: Harper Collins.

Ericsson, A., and R. Pool. 2016. *Peak*. Toronto: Viking.

Frensch, K. 2000. *Prosocial Behaviour and Adolescent Generativity: A Question of Moral Orientation and Parental Example*. Paper, Guelph University, copyright National Library of Canada.

Gallwey, T. 1977. *The Inner Game of Tennis: The Classic Guide to the Mental Side of Peak Performance*. New York: Random House.

Hergenhahn, B. R. 1984. *An Introduction to Theories of Personality, Second Edition*. Englewood Cliffs, NJ: Prentice Hall.

Kozlowski, S. W. J., and B. F. Bell. 2001. "Work Groups and Teams in Organizations." Retrieved 6/20/17 from Cornell University, ILR School site: http://digitalcommons.ilr.cornell.edu/articles/389/.

Kramer, J., and D. Schaap. 1968. *Instant Replay*. New York: Random House.

Sloman, S., and P. Fernbach. 2017. *The Knowledge Illusion: Why We Never Think Alone*. New York: Riverhead Books.

Thaler, R. H., and C. R. Sunstein. 2009. *Nudge: Improving Decisions About Health, Wealth, and Happiness*. New York: Penguin Group.

14

Evaluating Performance

Jim Barker

An often overlooked but crucial facet of coaching is understanding how to evaluate players and to choose schemes that will give them their greatest chance to be successful. At most levels of football, a coach had better implement systems that complement the type of players he has. For example, I coached at Alberta's Drumheller High School, which was looking to reestablish a football program when it had an inexperienced coaching staff and a very limited number of available players, all of whom had relatively limited skill sets. Rather than employing a normal spread or two-back offense, we opted for an easy-to-understand and effective double-wing offense and a slanting 5-3 stack defense, which the high school continued to run for the next seven years with great success. As with any program, understanding the strengths and limitations involved, including those of the coaches and players, is critical to taking any less-than-ideal situation and turning it into a success.

This chapter provides guidelines and tips on how to test athletes. Also, and more importantly, it offers some insight into identifying their strengths and weaknesses. That's one of the most important things we can do to help each athlete reach his maximum potential, mentally and physically. The tests discussed in this chapter, together with the athlete's training in these specific areas, will directly translate into success on the football field. Additionally, it is important to understand how to utilize different types of athletes at various positions, and how to continue evaluating athletes throughout the season. Understanding the basic principles of football is crucial, and so is learning the schematics that are applied to all phases of the game. But don't overlook evaluation. Sizing up, the ability to see what each athlete is about, allows you to get the most out of your players.

EVALUATING PHYSICAL SKILLS

Here are some tests that I've found easy and reliable. Each of them should be accurately timed or measured, and the results should be recorded and evaluated against those of other athletes in the program. Ideally, do the comparison with results from other programs too; provincial team combines or tryout camps are good places to check. Be aware that times can vary a lot depending on who does the timing. That's why I try to get my watch on every athlete.

These tests will help athletes locate their areas of performance that need improvement. The tests also hone competition and motivation as the athletes see their results.

Size

Each player's height and weight should be recorded at regular intervals through-out the season and off-season. Pro football records heights to the nearest tenth of an inch. We should too. First, weight loss is a tendency for players, especially in training camp, and it can be substantial. Look for dehydration and other issues when it occurs. Second, close monitoring can motivate those players who are trying to gain or lose weight, and it provides feedback regarding which weight actually works best for a given player on the field.

There are times athletes should be pushed to gain weight or lose weight based on performance. Normally, an underweight athlete may have durability issues due to size or an inability to physically perform a required task. Gaining weight is tricky because the athlete has to gain the weight in a manner that will make him quicker, faster, and stronger. Since muscle weighs more than fat, adding muscle will help the athlete maximize his ability. Losing weight is normally needed when an athlete cannot move well enough to execute. Losing fat, and in some cases muscle, usually gives the athlete increased flexibility, and with that an ability to move faster and with less stress on his body.

Speed

The 40-yard dash (figure 14.1) is the most utilized speed test in North American football. When administering this test, do not assume the field markings on the football field are correct, as many fields are lined incorrectly (of course, artificial turf surfaces should be correctly lined). Measure the field yourself in order to standardize the test, record accurate results, and analyze a player's top-end speed.

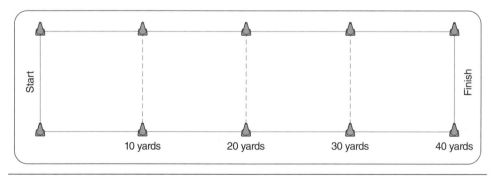

FIGURE 14.1 40-yard dash.

The athlete has to run 40 yards, not 39.5 or 41. Otherwise, the test results can't be precisely compared.

The player should always start from a three-point stance with his hand on the starting line. The timer focuses on the player's down hand and uses it as the guide to begin timing the run. Use your index finger to start and stop the watch; it's been proven to be more accurate than the thumb. The stopwatch should begin on the runner's first movement from the hand on the start line, and it should end as soon as any part of the athlete's body crosses the finish line. The 40-yard dash is an important test of an athlete's speed, so a great amount of focus and attention should be placed on the science of timing.

While the 40-yard test is being administered, 10- and 20-yard splits can be timed as well. To accomplish this, place additional timers at 10 and 20 yards and follow the same timing guidelines set out in the 40-yard dash.

This test will accurately measure the player's ability to get off the line quickly. In professional football, this test is used mostly for offensive linemen because they have to quickly set or get out of the stance and block a linebacker. Additionally, as athletes continue to learn how to run the 40-yard dash, these splits can help gauge the type of start they are having and whether it needs improvement. The splits can also help evaluate defensive backs, who never move forward from a stationary position. Measuring their speed from 10 to 40 yards will provide an accurate measure of top-end speed, which is more important than a start-to-finish 40-yard dash for a defensive back.

Strength

The bench-press test is the most common test used in football to measure an athlete's strength. At the professional level, the player is evaluated on the number of times he can correctly bench-press 225 pounds. College teams often require 225 pounds as the weight linemen have to lift, and 185 pounds for wide receivers and defensive backs. High school teams would do better to use an established weight-repetition chart or app that calculates the single repetition maximum (1RM) based on how many times the player lifted a lower weight. Another option is to use a formula. This formula is quite accurate based on the player choosing a weight that he or she can lift 6 to 12 times:

$$\text{reps} \times 0.03 \times \text{weight} + \text{weight} = 1\text{RM}$$

If a player lifted 185 pounds 9 times, the result would be

$$9 \times 0.03 \times 185 + 185 = 234.95 \text{ pounds}$$

Measuring and analyzing a player's bench-press test over the course of a year helps to gauge the player's motivation and discipline, and also allows monitoring of any changes in his strength. For example, the East-West game for U Sports football players takes place every May, and the players are evaluated using tests such as those described here. Invariably, a few athletes post very low results for the bench press. Once a 6′6″, 315-pound offensive lineman benched 225 pounds only 8 times, which is very poor for his position. I told him if he did not double his result by the annual CFL Evaluation Camp, we would not consider him as a potential player to be drafted. He had the choice of improving this phase of his profile or not. Later, at the combine, he benched 18 repetitions. And he proved that he took football seriously, that he was motivated to improve his results and do something for his draft position. Our team didn't draft him, but another took him and earlier than was projected. The test results played their part in that. Weightlifting is a discipline, and if a player is motivated to hone this aspect of his game, he will improve daily and give his confidence and play a boost.

Explosiveness

Football is an explosive game. The vertical jump, even more than the 40-yard test, has become a critical measure of a player's eventual football success. Off-season, a football player's workout should have a key focus on building explosiveness and core strength. The vertical test will gauge an athlete's development in these areas. It's worth a program's while to buy a Vertec stand, which is specifically designed to calculate a player's vertical jump. But you can also adhere a measuring tape to the wall (with 0 at the floor) and do the same reach and jump measurements.

The test's first step is for the athlete to raise his hand above his head while keeping his heels firmly on the ground. This lets the recorder determine the athlete's reach, meaning the highest point his hand touches. Then the athlete must keep one foot stationary and take only one step into his jump. The recorder measures the highest point where the athlete touched, and then subtracts the athlete's reach height; this determines the player's vertical.

While this test utilizes the player's quadriceps and hip flexors more than the hamstrings, the results will be a good indication of whether a young athlete needs to adjust his workout regimen to maximize his explosiveness and core strength.

The standing broad jump test also examines an athlete's explosiveness and should compare closely with the vertical jump. This test utilizes more of the hamstrings and should correlate with a player's top-end speed. The standing broad jump is tested on a flat surface. The athlete jumps from a standing start; he doesn't run, walk, or do anything else beforehand. The recorder measures from the start point to where the back of the athlete's heels land. A weak result indicates the player needs hamstring work. That will improve his test result and his top speed.

Change of Direction

The short shuttle (figure 14.2), commonly known as the 20-yard shuttle, evaluates an athlete's quickness and ability to change direction. These are vital, especially for defensive backs and running backs.

The athlete starts in the middle of a measured 10-yard distance with a hand on the ground. Time begins on his movement as he explodes in either direction for 5 yards to touch the premeasured line with his hand. Then he runs 10 yards in the other direction to the opposite line, making sure he touches it with his hand. Finally, he turns to finish through where he started. It is important to have individuals, aside from the timer, at each line to confirm that the player has touched the line. This will help to standardize the test and give accurate, comparable results.

The three-cone drill test is used at most evaluation camps to evaluate a player's overall agility, change of direction, quickness, and fluidity of movement. First, arrange three cones in a right angle, with the cones 5 yards apart (see figure 14.3). At the start line (the first cone), the athlete begins with one hand on the ground. He runs to the middle cone and touches it. He then reverses back to the start, touching the line again with his hand. He again turns, running toward the middle cone. He turns around it, continues in a figure-eight around the final cone, and finishes back at the original starting line. Once the participant crosses the original start line

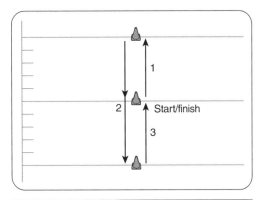

FIGURE 14.2 Short shuttle.

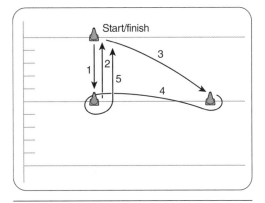

FIGURE 14.3 Three-cone drill.

after the approximately 30-yard drill, timing stops and the time is recorded.

Flexibility

The sit-and-reach test measures the flexibility of both the lower back and hamstrings. Players with tight hamstrings have an increased chance of being injured, not to mention impairment of their overall agility and athleticism.

The athlete sits on the ground with the toes pointing straight up and the backs of the knees on the ground. The athlete reaches over his toes as far as possible, and the distance from the bottom of the feet to the tip of the fingers is measured. If the athlete cannot reach the toes, the score is recorded as a negative measurement from the bottom of the feet to the fingertips. Athletes who test in the negative had better work on their flexibility.

Fitness

Testing cardiovascular fitness at the beginning of training camp is always a challenge. It is important to see what shape athletes are in, but don't work them out too much before they begin training camp. Dave Wright, trainer for the Toronto Argonauts, came up with what I have found to be the most effective test of cardiovascular fitness: the cardiovascular stress test. It produces minimal stress on the athlete's legs, but gives a firm number indicating the kind of shape he's in.

The start line can be any yard line on a football field. If you aren't on a football field, place tape down and use a measuring tape to make sure the distances are correct. At the sound of a whistle, the player runs 35 yards and returns to the start, staying in his assigned lane. Subsequent runs begin every 30 seconds, inclusive of the time to run down and back, with the test facilitator providing a 5-second warning before each 30-second start. The difference between the start time and the time it takes the athlete to run down and back is the amount of recovery time prior to the next run. For example, if a lap to 35 yards and back takes 14 seconds, the athlete has 16 seconds to recover prior to the next run. Players complete a total of 6 repetitions, with the entire test lasting a total of 3 minutes. Timers record all interval times for each player. To determine the individual fatigue index as a percentage, simply divide the athlete's best run time by his slowest time.

The idea is to establish a reporting level of fitness while using an energy system directly related to football. The results determine how quickly an athlete will fatigue and develop lactic acid, a substance that impairs physical performance and increases risk of injury. We want our athletes to understand that the one element any athlete can control is his own personal level of fitness.

EVALUATING EMOTIONAL STABILITY

Gauging emotional stability is often overlooked at younger levels. But acquainting young football players with these types of evaluations helps them develop a solid foundation of emotional stability. That's key, since the ability to learn about our actions and be accountable for them, both on and off the field, becomes progressively more important as players become old enough for more competitive levels of football.

Personal History

Regardless of a player's age, coaches and mentors should have a grasp of his basic background. A coach can be an important person in a player's life, and knowing about the player will help the coach make sure this importance has good results. Use more than one method and source to get a good idea of what's going on.

Interview

Sitting down with each individual may be time-consuming, but the benefits will be far reaching. A conversation with an athlete regarding his background and family life, his goals, and aspirations for the future on and off the field, can be as important as anything you do as a coach. It doesn't need to be formal, just a conversation. The time a coach devotes to an athlete one-on-one is what counts. Listening, taking a real interest in the athlete, will pay dividends for both of you. For many young athletes, football is the only real structure they know. Being part of something bigger than themselves is very important to them, and they learn the discipline and work ethic that success requires.

Academic Records

Whether you coach in a high school or grade school or in an organized youth program, you should have access to a young person's academic records. These can give insight into a player's learning ability and focus, and many other factors that may become issues. Behavioral problems in school can often be defused by a coach, but only if the coach knows about the problems.

Social Background

It is very important to understand the type of social background your athletes come from. My first high school job was at a school where the athletes all came from very low socioeconomic backgrounds. Eighty-eight percent of the players on my team came from single-parent homes. The temptation and fear of gang life was a part of their everyday lives. For many of those young players, football was their main outlet and the one place they felt they could escape to a life they truly loved. As their coach, I became the most influential male in their lives and they often came to me for advice. Later in life, many former players have told me that they learned many positive characteristics from interacting with and observing me daily. I didn't have any idea of this influence, but it is something you should be very aware of as a football coach. On the other hand, I have also worked at an elite university where most of the athletes came from affluent and influential families. Many had strong, influential fathers, and sometimes this led to issues—different issues than the ones I'd faced before. As I continued to recruit most of the athletes there, it became clear how necessary it was to be cognizant of the social background of all the athletes. I became better equipped to aid them when issues came up, and that translated into more success on the field.

DEFINING GOALS AND EXPECTATIONS

The next step in helping an athlete attain a high level of performance is to set up a specific plan in order to guide the athlete to a higher level of success. Some say that to be a successful coach, you must take athletes to levels they could not otherwise reach on their own. I've found that, to do this, a coach must learn to identify a given athlete's physical and mental attributes and shortcomings, and in turn put a plan of action in place. This plan should include detailed short- and long-term goals and should be shared with each athlete and the team as a whole. By sharing the expectations of the coaching staff with individual players, an exchange of accountability on both sides is created—a covenant. Ultimately, combining the individual goals and the covenant will create an important foundation, the kind that I have experienced with every program with which I have been involved. That foundation provides the winning edge.

Each week I ask every player to give his position coach a goal card (figure 14.4) that outlines his personal and team goals for the week. As a position coach, I

	This week's goals	Obstacles
Individual		
Group and team		
Practice		

Name _____   Week _____

FIGURE 14.4 Individual goal card.

would often take the time to sit down with each athlete in my group and discuss that week's goals. These goals deal with individual on- and off-field goals, team goals, and even weekly practice goals. I've always made a point of including in these talks the physical, mental, and emotional characteristics and concerns discussed in this chapter. Alongside each goal we also write and discuss what challenges the athlete may face that may keep him from attaining his desired goal. In order to maximize the effectiveness of the goal card, I meet with the player and discuss the previous week's goals, whether they were attained or not, and any unforeseen challenges the player faced prior to reestablishing new goals each week. As a result, the player can recognize areas he may need to work on, and as a coach I am able to monitor progress throughout the year.

UTILIZING EVALUATIONS

Once the testing is done, how do we make use of the results? This section covers each position, the type of athlete we look for, and the mental and physical skills required to excel at the respective positions. The key component of coaching, in my opinion, is getting the most out of each athlete every day. Evaluation of the player talent a coach has to choose from will give the information necessary to help athletes and the team excel.

Quarterbacks

While this position may be the most difficult in all of sport to play, there are certain talents and characteristics we have found to be consistent with quality quarterbacks at all levels of football. The higher the level at which a player plays, the more important intelligence and rational decision-making become. As athletes move up the football ranks and offensive systems become more complex, more importance is placed on a player's ability to reason and organize thoughts.

At all levels, a quarterback who possesses great leadership qualities will experience success. The only way to evaluate leadership is through the interview process and through discussions with people who have been around the athlete and can attest to his character. Leadership can be learned to a point, but much of it is inherent. When I first arrived at Drumheller High School, we did not have a single player with any quarterback experience—or, more importantly, the ability to throw. We did have a young man with great confidence and leadership qualities that were evident from the first day of practice. This young man used his limited athletic ability, his above-average intelligence, and his fantastic leadership skills to direct the Titans to a playoff berth.

In Canada, a quarterback's athleticism and speed are more important than in the American game, where his throwing strength is more the focus. But intangibles, things that are difficult to test, play the biggest role of all. Look for confidence, toughness, and leadership, and then build your offensive system around the player who has them.

Offensive Line

Traditionally, this is the position for players who are not athletic enough to play at any of the other positions. Many professional teams have moved to smaller, more athletic offensive lines to counteract the tendency of teams to place their smaller and quicker defensive linemen up front. In youth and high school programs, you don't recruit. Who you pick depends on who tries out. A larger youngster who isn't the most athletic probably belongs on the offensive line. While at Drumheller, we had a great kid play for us who was about 5′9″ and weighed over 350 pounds. He was not in very good shape and he had very limited athletic ability. But with only 15 players, we made him our centre in the double-wing offense. He competed, and eventually he became a team cornerstone. The trick was to have an offensive system that didn't require him to move a lot. Your plans have to fit your players. A pro sports organization can scout players to fit the coach's schemes. In youth and high school football, the coach has to adapt.

The bench-press test and the short shuttle are the most important tests for evaluating offensive linemen. The bench press is not only a test of an individual's upper-body strength, but also of his commitment to improving himself. When watching a college player, I will often challenge him to sizably up his bench-press repetitions between his second and third years. The gain indicates how much importance he places on professional football, and often that factor—his desire—will decide if he succeeds as an offensive lineman in the CFL.

The tests mentioned in this chapter can also help to gauge an offensive lineman's athletic ability. The short shuttle can be interpreted as an indication of how quickly he can gain an advantage in pass protection. The 10-yard split is often used to gauge a player's ability to get off the ball; many coaches consider it more important than an offensive lineman's 40-yard dash time. Finally, if your centre is called on to make a lot of calls, an offensive lineman with intelligence is ideal. Numerous test results can be used collectively in order to place players in positions where they can contribute the most to the team's overall success.

Running Backs

Traditionally, teams have different types of running backs, based on a given team's offensive philosophy and scheme. In high school and youth programs, the running back is often the fastest, strongest athlete in the program. Generally, passing games are difficult to execute at younger levels, so the running back becomes the focal point of most offenses. The idea is always to get the ball in the hands of the best athletes. If this player happens to be a big, strong, physical player, the offense may consist of more of a downhill running game that will allow a running back to get a head of steam and find a running crease between the tackles. Throwing screens and checkdowns to this type of player can be effective, especially if there is a big size discrepancy between the running back and the defenders. The bigger running backs can also double as tight ends, as they can often be coached to be good blockers. Another type of running back is the small, agile, and very fast athlete. This player will likely have the fastest short shuttle and one of the faster 40 times on the team. Generally, he is able to make defenders miss in the open field, and he has the ability to start, stop, and change direction very quickly. This type of back is great in the passing game because he's very elusive in the open field. The best small back is usually a tough player who will slash hard inside and have the ability to cut and make guys miss outside.

The problem with smaller running backs becomes evident in pass protection, since typically they won't be as big as the players they're blocking. When looking at a smaller running back for pass protection, review his bench-press test result. A solid result means he'll probably be fine. Of course, overall athleticism and size at the running back position will be factors as coaches plan their offenses. Regularly using the short shuttle, the 40, the vertical jump, and the bench press—along with other tests described in this chapter—will keep you on top of your running backs' progress and capabilities.

Wide Receivers

Receivers come in a variety of heights, weights, and athletic ability levels. Some successful professional wide receivers have run 4.8 in the 40-yard test, which is slow for the position; others have run 4.3, nice and fast, but have been busts. Even so, speed and explosiveness are two of the most important physical qualities a wide receiver can possess (the third being eye-hand coordination). One key component that is difficult to measure is the receiver's natural ability to catch the ball, although this is critical in predicting success.

In evaluating receivers, we've found that the 40-yard dash, the vertical jump, the short shuttle, and the three-cone drill give us a great picture of an athlete's ability to be a successful wide receiver. The numbers help an offensive coordinator place his athletes in the positions he needs in order to design an effective passing game that best utilizes his players' talents. Having at least one fast receiver who can stretch the defense is extremely important, and you need a tough, solid receiver who can block and be effective in the intermediate areas on the field. When watching receivers on film, we also look for a receiver's ability to play the ball in the air. Developing young players to be great wide receivers essentially comes down to three areas of focus: a player's basic physical tools, whether he has consistent hands, and his knack for playing the ball in the air. Luckily, all of these can be honed by practice.

Defensive Line

The physical qualities required to be effective on the defensive line vary greatly depending on the defensive scheme. Again, plans must fit players, especially in youth and high school football. If the players on the defensive line are very big and do not run well, the coach should run more of a static defense, allowing the linemen to use their size to neutralize blockers and their strength to push the pocket with a "bull rush" attitude. If the players are smaller and quicker, a slanting and movement type of defense would be preferred.

The vertical jump, the 10-yard split, and the short shuttle are the most important physical tests for this position. Cam Wake, the greatest pass rusher in CFL history and a star pass rusher in the NFL, had an incredible 46-inch vertical jump even though he weighed 245 pounds. This incredible explosiveness, as revealed through his vertical jump, was the key to his success as a pass rusher. Additionally, a good defensive lineman usually possesses enough "fast twitch," or explosiveness, to get off the ball very quickly on movement, to continue moving through or around a blocker, and to change direction effortlessly. Having a great motor and relentlessly pursuing the ball can be learned and coached.

When evaluating a defensive lineman on film, we look for specific characteristics: his quickness when getting off the ball on the snap; his ability to play low with his knees bent, which transfers from his explosiveness; his ability to play relentlessly to the ball, refuse to be blocked, and sprint all the way until the whistle blows; and his quickness to his top speed when changing direction.

Linebackers

The best linebackers have great instincts, which is a very difficult trait to test. In the professional game, we look for cover linebackers and tackle-to-tackle linebackers.

The cover linebacker must have more speed and athleticism than other linebackers, as he often is asked to cover a receiver or running back in the open field. On the other hand, a tackle-to-tackle linebacker must be very physical and strong enough to handle offensive linemen, yet agile enough to make plays anywhere on the field.

In youth and high school settings, linebackers are normally the best football players, though not necessarily the best athletes. They are typically the toughest, most instinctual players on the team. In most amateur settings, the linebackers are the team leaders, the individuals who lead in the weight room and when coaches are not around. I have found that linebackers are typically not the most gifted athletes, but just have an incredible love for the game and a passion for hitting opponents.

When watching film, we look for a player who "plays downhill," meaning he can attack the line of scrimmage because he has the ability to diagnose and trust what he sees. A linebacker with explosiveness translates into a player who blitzes well; usually he possesses a great 20 time, which allows him to play in space very well.

Linebackers and quarterbacks are the two most difficult positions to evaluate through physical testing, but they're the easiest to evaluate from watching players in action. Both of these positions involve numerous intangibles and leadership traits that can't be measured by physical tests.

Defensive Backs

The joke goes that at the youth and high school level you take the best athletes who can't catch and put them in the secondary. For a defensive back, athleticism is the most important factor, though the best players at the professional level also have tremendous ball skills. To play in the secondary, a player must have very good top-end speed (10- to 40-yard dash) and explosiveness (vertical jump). His ability to seamlessly change direction and transition from a backpedal to a sprint are also very important and can be assessed through the short shuttle and the three-cone drill. The best defensive backs also have a certain swagger and confidence that allow them to recover after being beat on a play. Players who lack confidence in the secondary ultimately play scared, which makes it very difficult to succeed. Defensive back coaches and coordinators who can help their athletes feel this confidence will have a group willing to take chances—to play an aggressive game, not the reactive game of making tackles after the receivers make the catch.

The more athletic a team's defensive backs are, the more man-to-man defense a coordinator is able to play. On the other hand, a secondary who is not athletic forces a coordinator to use more zone defenses, therefore making it more difficult to be aggressive. The more zone coverage a team plays, the more instinctive a secondary must be.

ONGOING EVALUATIONS

An important part of coaching is providing feedback to players about their progress and performance so they understand what is needed to succeed at a higher level. Here we outline some of our methods for doing this, and also share tips on how to make evaluations and feedback most effective for the athlete.

Individual Goal Card

Ongoing use of the individual goal card is vital. A coach can't sit down with each athlete every week. The goal card allows the athlete to self-evaluate his goals, performance, and areas of needed improvement. The card also gives the coach an opportunity to let the athlete know whether or not he accomplished his goals from the previous week, and to provide feedback about what is needed in the upcoming week to improve his performance. The more time a coach chooses to put into this task, the more thought and time the athlete will commit to it as well. The coach's comments do not need to be elaborate, just well thought out and concise. That way the athlete fully comprehends what needs to be improved in order to maximize his performance on the field.

Game Grades

At the professional level, where film is readily available and there is a position coach for each group, grading players is one of the most important parts of the teaching process. Each position coach watches the game tape and gives each player a grade—usually plus (+), minus (−), or zero—for technique, and additionally will assess a grade for effort. The player then can watch the film on his own and see the mistakes and corrections the coach would like him to make.

The grading process also gives the coach a picture of what each player is doing in the game and an ability to monitor how the player's game performance is doing from week to week. Using a video service such as Hudl makes it very easy to add grades and comments to every play clip.

At the youth level, sometimes film quality doesn't allow adequate evaluation of a player, and there may not be enough coaches able to make the time commitment for grading. One solution may be for the coach to put the clearly positive and negative plays on a team grade sheet. This will give the team some understanding of what they might need to improve. If no film is available, coaches should learn to take notes throughout the game, which will help not only in making game adjustments, but also in providing feedback to players about what should improve in the following week. Grading performance on a game-by-game basis is another important but often overlooked part of coaching football.

Point Systems and Individual Recognition

While football is the ultimate team sport, getting great individual effort in a collaborative team setting is the coach's underlying goal. Chris Jones, a very successful CFL coach, created a point system that is customized for each position and allows a player to accumulate points for important factors selected by the coaching staff. Each position coach establishes the criteria for his group to be awarded points, based on the factors critical to the players' success at that position. This allows an offensive or defensive lineman, who may not have numerous stats, as much an opportunity for points as a running back or linebacker. Collectively, the coaches establish different levels of achievement, and players are awarded different T-shirts for their different achievement levels. Of course, the shirts don't just give the coach info. They double as motivational tools. It's amazing to watch professional athletes work to get points so they can move from a white to a gray T-shirt, then from a gray to a blue, and finally from a blue to a black.

CONCLUSION

Thank you to Football Canada for the opportunity to present some of the ideas and systems we use in evaluating football players. The differences between professional players and youth players can be immense, but the coach's goal remains the same: create an environment that allows athletes to achieve at the highest possible level for their skill set, and provide an avenue for them to improve those skills. Evaluating your players, knowing what they've done and what they're doing, makes it easier to build what they're going to do.

15

Preparing for a Tournament

Lee Barette

Coaching football is complex and challenging. The game has evolved over time and is usually played in a regular-season format with approximately seven days between scheduled games. The one-week lead time has become the norm, both because players need it and because it helps with scheduling and promoting professional games. Also important: coaches get ample time to scout their opponents, as discussed in chapter 12, and to prepare.

Tournament football is a completely different reality for both coaches and players. In tournaments such as the Football Canada Cup, teams play three games in seven days, so the physical, mental, and emotional demands are far more intense than in a normal season of play. The level of competition and the importance of the games are also much higher. Coaches do not have the normal time to prepare a complete game plan and have to make adjustments quickly, a circumstance that can get to even the most experienced coaches. In my years of coaching Team Ontario East at the Football Canada Cup, I learned some valuable lessons on the peculiarities of coaching a team for a tournament. Taking unique steps to manage the physical, mental, and emotional energy levels of your players is also a critical consideration. Competing in tournament football requires a high level of planning in order to put together your team, prepare them for the tournament, and compete effectively.

Tournament Playing Factors

- The team is usually an all-star team compilation of the best players available.
- There is a limited amount of time to prepare for the tournament (including tryouts).
- There are three days or less between tournament games.
- All offensive and defensive positions are covered by individual coaches or coordinators.

OFF-FIELD PRETOURNAMENT PREPARATION

As always, preparation is key. But prepping a tournament all-star team has challenges that aren't found during the regular season. Not all these challenges are football related, so a wise coach and sponsoring organization will put people and structures in place to manage the off-field details. That way the coaches can focus on the players and on-field details.

Marketing

Football coaches and administrators are likely not professional marketers. Even so, marketing every aspect of a program is very important. Players and parents do not have the awareness or information that the coaches and administrators have. How well known is the program to prospective players and their parents? Is the program competing against other football teams or other sports? How do you make sure the best players attend your team tryout?

Get your message out using your website and social media, and communicating to as many coaches and prospective players as possible. Be clear and concise, and if there is a fundraising component to your program, give the players the tools to begin fundraising as early as possible. Ideally, this job should be done by the organization or team management, because coaching and prepping a tournament is a big enough job. But make sure someone good is doing the marketing and promotion.

Tryouts

Schedule and announce tryouts months ahead of time. Again, this should be the responsibility of the organization or team manager. Players and parents need to schedule these events in their calendars, and the longer the lead time, the more awareness will spread. Try not to schedule tryouts against statutory holidays, spring break, Mother's Day, Father's Day, other team tryouts and games, and so on.

And go where the players are. Even great players can be insecure about trying out for an all-star team. Going to them, holding tryouts in the geographical areas of all players, is one of your strongest marketing tools. Make the first set of tryouts in a variety of geographic areas.

Be sure facilities are booked ahead of time. Many sites are reserved months in advance, so you must be proactive. Don't forget that you're booking change rooms, meeting spaces, and trainer's areas as well as the playing field.

Identification and Recruiting

Every coach would like to have a team full of superstars. When identifying players for an all-star team, you have a chance of getting the best players in your designated area. Contact potential players directly. Call them up with details of the tournament and let them know they're wanted at the tryout. Everyone likes attention, so give some. Depending on the player's age, of course, be sure to engage the parent or guardian as well.

When identifying players for an all-star team, watch these players in a game situation, preferably in person. Knowledge of a player's performance in game competition is key. Some players may perform well in tryouts or combines but not in game situations (or vice versa). The character of a player on the field or the sideline is a crucial element of the selection. A negative, disruptive player can quickly become the distraction that limits a tournament team's chances for success, whereas an enthusiastic teammate or strong leader can be the ingredient needed to bring a tournament team together.

Expectations

Our first year of tryouts, the number of athletes who showed up came to just a little more than our final roster. Apparently, the low turnout created a sense of entitlement among some of the players. At least that's the year we had the most trouble with parents. But as turnout picked up, we managed to build an all-star program, not an entitled one.

Probably the best addition in the second year was a one-page document that parents or guardians had to sign and return at registration. This one-page form was extremely positive in nature, congratulating the parent and player for having the courage and confidence to try out for this elite program. It also highlighted the fact that none of our coaches were player parents or affiliated with any team of the same age group as the players attending tryouts. We also stated the team would be chosen based on who we thought were the best football players, leaders, and potential teammates. The most important highlight stated this was an elite team and that playing time would not be equal. Setting player expectations and, more importantly, parent expectations, was extremely important for our program.

Our playing philosophy was simple. We wanted to win the tournament through great team defense, by minimizing the opposition's best players or plays, through great special-teams play that highlighted our best players, and by incorporating aggressive play calling where appropriate. Our offense was based on getting the ball in the hands of our best players in as many different ways as possible, taking what the defense gave us, and accounting for their best players if possible.

Make sure the players, coaches, administrators, and anyone else directly involved with the team understands how they should conduct themselves when at the tournament and at all training camps and team events. Interaction with other players, meal hall behaviour, respect for tournament representatives, and a nighttime curfew and room check are part of the many things to be established and communicated. Every player should know he is representing himself, as well as representing the team, the coaches, club or high school team, community, parents, former coaches, and so on. Also, since football players tend to be easily noticeable due to their stature compared to the general population, players must understand that they are being watched and judged at all times. It is also important that the players and coaches have fun, take in the entire experience, and enjoy as much as they can in this limited amount of time.

Budget

Do you have funding for the tryout process? If not, participants will need to pay a tryout fee. This fee may also be incorporated in the overall fundraising for the program. Make sure you understand your budget, and if you have administrative support, make sure that the administration understands all of your potential costs. Always account for miscellaneous expenses that may occur, like having to replace a bag of footballs that goes missing or purchasing team water bottles because they were forgotten at home. Major expenses include travel, accommodation, meals, team clothing, team equipment, registration fees, team building events, and so on. The organization and manager should take care of all of this.

Hydration and Nutrition

Assume players know nothing about proper hydration and nutrition, an assumption that probably will be confirmed. I recommend tackling the hydration issue first. Our rule was that, at every team function, players had to have in their possession their team-issued water bottle filled with water. We mandated that, during a meal, three-fourths of their liquid intake had to be water. Electrolytes are useful too, but we stressed water because players will always resort to their sugary ways on their own.

Nutrition counseling happened as well. Simplicity and balance were the theme. We ensured that the players were always getting a balance of proteins (food that used to swim, walk, fly, or run) and carbohydrates (things that grew). We can't change players' eating habits in one to two weeks, but we can definitely help.

Athlete Investment

It is very important to invest in athletes. This means purposely building into the players to be successful now and into the future. If you have a fair tryout process, your program will have a good reputation; if you develop a player's skill level and marketability, you are investing in the athlete's current and future success; if your program is first class and professional, athletes (and their parents) will want to be a part of it. If your program has a great reputation, you have a great opportunity to invest in the athletes. To keep this process as simple and conflict-free as possible, it is wise to keep parents out of the process; their role should be to watch their child practice and play, and to support their child and the team.

ON-FIELD PRETOURNAMENT PREPARATION

Design the tryout process around principles that will allow it to be most successful. Before every tryout practice, give players a simple, consistent, and encouraging message. First, congratulate them for attending and having the courage and confidence to attempt to make the team. Second, make clear that the coaches will teach them drills and skills that may differ from those the players know. It's not that one is right or one is wrong. But on your program, here's how it's done. Third, let players know you're looking for fast learners. This isn't a season and time is short. They have to listen hard and process the instructions quickly. Fourth, tournament football is unique. There is no room on a team for players who cannot play hurt. Training camps are physically taxing, and they're mentally and emotionally intense.

Finally, tell the players to enjoy the day and to work hard in every aspect of practice. And remind yourself of something too. When the games start, the physical intensity must go way down. But the players' mental activity (learning and studying) and emotional intensity (pressure of games so close together) go up.

Tryouts With Large Attendance

In years three and four of our program, we had approximately 150 players attend our general tryout. Handling these numbers can be a challenge. Preparation, appropriate facilities and equipment, and an adequate number of coaches are critical for success.

The first item—ideally, this is another job for your manager—is to make sure players are easily identifiable. Each player should have a jersey number that corresponds with a camp roster available to all coaches. Of course, it will increase efficiency greatly if the offensive and defensive players are wearing contrasting colours. Furthermore, attach player names to the front of their helmets (it is up to you if you prefer first or last names) so coaches can address them by name during the tryout, something that makes the players feel that they are noticed as individuals.

The practice plan has to be perfect and it has to account for the total number of players. The players have paid for a fair opportunity to showcase their skills and make the team. A tryout is all about getting the players enough repetitions so you can evaluate them, and so they and their parents feel they had an appropriate chance. Competitive drill locations also have to be well planned, as travel time to drills can eat into the time for practice and competitive drill.

An entire football field, including end zones, is the absolute minimum field size needed for a large tryout. Even better: two fields, or else a field that has an area where the defensive and offensive linemen can practice on the side (hopefully adjacent to one another, so competitive drills can be done close by). Make sure you have enough footballs and other field equipment for this large group. You may have 10 quarterbacks at the tryout who all need footballs, and other positional groups needing balls as well.

It is important that you have enough assistant guest coaches. Especially at the first tryout, the guest coaches can be the ones explaining the drills, allowing your tournament coaches to evaluate and interject where they feel appropriate. You cannot run drills with an inordinate number of players and evaluate at the same time.

You are going to have some positions with a very big number, and you may have to split that group in order to get enough repetitions. Also, you may have a group of defenders (e.g., linebackers) whose unit number far exceeds the offensive counterpart (e.g., running backs). Have a backup plan. You could use some of the defenders as offensive players in some of the drills, or divide the players into two groups and have mirrored drills (back-to-back drills with two different groups). This is more intense and challenging for coaches, but it allows more evaluation and quality repetitions.

If you have a large tryout number, be prepared for it. The greater the number, the more difficult it is to execute the tryout and evaluate the players.

Identification of Impostors and Gamers

In our first three years of tournament competition, some players tricked us during the tryout process. Two, three, or four players who looked great in tryout and combine situations did not perform well in game action (and we could assume the opposite was also true). In our fourth year, we finally rectified this issue. A new facility had opened, giving us access to a field in early spring (new artificial turf). But also we finally got smarter as a coaching staff.

What we did was have a 30-hour minicamp. We brought in 70 players to compete for the 40 roster positions and the 8-player taxi squad. Around noon, players registered (with their fundraising completed and fee for the 30-hour minicamp). Following that, we would begin with the player and parent meeting, and then would break into offensive and defensive groups to introduce our systems to the players. By midafternoon (after a snack), we were on the field for a power practice, meaning back-to-back practices that are approximately 90 to 120 minutes long and are separated by a 20- to 30-minute rest and nutrition break. The point was to get the players ready for the scrimmage the next afternoon. We wanted to give players the tools they needed and to put them through an atmosphere like training camp and the tournament. After the power practice, we had a team meal and then again had meetings. The players were housed at dorms for the one night.

The next morning, the players had breakfast and attended brief meetings, then took part in a long but low-tempo practice focusing on skills and systems. After the practice, the players ate a lunch and then rested until it was time for the scrimmage.

The scrimmage also had clearly set goals and philosophy. The coaching staff already had an idea who the top 20 to 25 players were, so we put them all on Team A, as we wanted them to develop some cohesiveness and have some success together. Players 26 through 55 were put on Team B, so we could see how they reacted against great competition. We conducted offense, defense, punt cover, punt return, and a nonlive field-goal team during the scrimmage. With those three special teams, we could evaluate potential specialists and special-teams players, and see how the potential nonstarters performed. The scrimmage did not include kickoff or kickoff return.

The result of the scrimmage was exactly what the coaching staff wanted. Our potential starters began to build some cohesion and confidence. Three or four players who looked average in the tryout process made the team on their great scrimmage performance. All of these players went on to play an important role on special teams, and one became a starter on defense. If we did not have this scrimmage, none of that would have happened. With a 40-player roster, and three games in seven days, these players may have made the crucial difference for us.

Releasing Players

This is the hardest part of picking an all-star team, but we can do it well. Congratulate all the players who try out, whether they make it or not. Shake each player's hand, look him in the eye, and thank him for his efforts. This is professional, respectful, and appreciated. The rejected players can use the encouragement, especially if they're young, and some may be a factor on next year's team. Most of all, it takes courage to do what they did.

When you have a lot of players to cut, the process can take time. We did it this way. After a scrimmage or at the end of a tryout, we made sure the players did not leave the field and go meet their parents (you can avoid any drama and miscommunication this way). I, as head coach, addressed all the players, usually congratulating them and outlining the process that would now occur. The players would go to their positional groups; the coaching staff gathered at midfield to decide which players we were carrying to the next tryout, or which were going to be our top 50 players and chosen as roster and taxi squad players. Most of these decisions had been made earlier based on overall camp performance, but we made some adjustments after watching the scrimmage video. After that, the positional coaches gave a general message to their group. I would then point to a position coach, and he announced players who should stay with the positional coach; the rest of the players were to meet me at centre field. The position coach would congratulate the players in his unit who had made the team or were going through to the next tryout. At centre field, one by one I would shake the hands of the players who had been released and gave them a quick message if appropriate.

An alternative process is for the position coach to meet briefly with each individual so each player who did not make the team gets some specific feedback, positive and negative.

Parental Feedback After a Player Is Released

Every year we had parents who asked why their son had been released. We handled this in a professional way. The position coach and coordinator gave the head coach feedback on the boy, and the head coach e-mailed the parents with a set of reasons. Most parents appreciated the feedback. Two factors helped the process: none of the coaches had children on the team, and none of the coaches had students of theirs on the team. There were no perceived biases and every player had an equal chance.

OFF-FIELD TRAINING CAMP PROCESS

Training camp may be the most critical phase of your team's development. During training camp, you want to set and build the team culture, insert all of your systems, and push the limits of your players. It is a physically, mentally, and emotionally challenging and intense time. If you are going to push the players beyond their perceived limits, this is the time to do it. Of course, this is a delicate balance. You want to push players beyond what they think they can deal with (i.e., fighting through two-a-day practices in hot weather, sleeping in uncomfortable dorms, learning new systems and techniques quickly, etc.). But you don't want them to break down. Keep your finger on the pulse of the players by listening to your assistant coaches and a few leaders among the players that you trust.

Reestablish player behavioral expectations. You went over this in tryouts, but do it again. Go over the team expectations now that the roster is set and the tournament is about to begin.

Take time to review the team philosophy that was presented during tryouts. We are playing to win. Not everyone will get equal playing time. Player roles and play calls are designed to help the team be successful.

ON-FIELD TRAINING CAMP PROCESS

With time short, great planning is demanded. Put players in a tournament atmosphere as soon as possible; we highly recommend a training camp that's away from the local city and other distractions. Bring your offense in earlier than your defense. The offense is always behind the defense, so it is important that they get a chance to even this out. But don't leave the defense out for too long; you want your team culture and chemistry to take shape.

Bring the quarterbacks and the offensive line in first. These two positions are the most complex and require the highest amount of communication and pre-game preparation. Put the quarterbacks to work on play calling, cadence, and basic physical movements. Put the offensive line to work on techniques, protections, and communication. Then bring in the running backs and receivers. That way the offense can begin to work as a group, and you can begin to work on ball handling by the quarterbacks and running backs, and pass-play execution by the quarterbacks and receivers. Quarterback and centre exchange is built into every prepractice and practice.

If you do a remote training camp, consider scheduling a day or so for the players to go home for a break before departing for the tournament. This allows them to eat mom's cooking rather than dorm food, and sleep in their own bed rather than on a dorm mattress. It also gives them a bit of a social break from the team and a chance to reconnect with their families. A week of tournament life is a grind, and players (and coaches!) can become homesick.

Don't be afraid to get away from your regular-season methods. Tournaments are different, so think differently. You will probably have more meeting time compared to the regular season. Once games start, you will want to cut down the level of contact significantly; practices will probably be just in shoulder pads and helmets, or just helmets.

Remember, you're preparing for only a few games, not an entire season. You won't implement your whole playbook. Focus on implementing basic systems that players can understand and execute with confidence. Then build on this as needed, based on the competition.

You won't have film of your game-one opponent, but it's worth showing your team game film from the previous year's tournament. The players may be different, but if the coaching staff isn't, there's a good chance a lot of the same systems will be in use. Your team also picks up a small but significant benefit from seeing the opponents' uniforms; a bit of familiarity will give your players that much more confidence.

ON-FIELD TOURNAMENT STRATEGIES

After all that time, effort, and preparation, it's very exciting to finally arrive at the tournament. Much of what happens will be out of your control, so be proactive in taking control of what you can. Make sure your players understand that things will not always go as planned, and the best thing they (and the coaches) can do is roll with the unexpected events and frustrations, and handle them with patience.

If you can, arrive a couple of days before your first game, especially if there's a significant change in time zone. The team can get used to the new location, adjust their sleep schedule, and get settled in. Hopefully, you can visit the game field and maybe even have a practice on it.

The first game is a big coaching challenge. You don't know your players, especially if you weren't fortunate to have an exhibition game or scrimmage. You can't go through every game situation with your team, let alone assume that everybody will remember their particular responsibilities in pressure game situations against what may be the best competition they've ever seen. Manage player emotions, as you do not know how they will react to game pressure. Manage the communication breakdown between coaches who may be working together for the first time. Manage the reality of not knowing what system the other team is employing, and the chaos of adjustments in the first quarter and at halftime. Above all, manage the game by keeping it simple for players.

After the first game, you can start to scheme for opponents, scheme for players, and potentially outcoach your opponents. The big messages I would give our coaching staff came down to this: outcoach our opponents, not ourselves; don't overestimate what a defender will recognize regarding play-action or putting our best player in a variety of positions; and keep it simple but have enough plays to defeat your opponent. Remember, a tournament is a very short period of time to prepare and develop a cohesive team. By the end of a tournament, usually you'll feel your team is ready for regular-season action. A tournament is like a training camp with games. Highlight your best players, minimize what your opponents' best players can do, and when in doubt, scheme to stop a great player, not a great play.

Avoid the temptation of changing and rechanging your playbook. Yes, make adjustments to deal with specific unique looks and plays. But leave it at that. Unnecessary change unsettles your players and doesn't give them the chance to master their roles in your systems. Focus on getting better at what you already have, not on reinventing your team in two days.

OFF-FIELD TOURNAMENT STRATEGIES

Teenagers tend to be on the go and don't think about conserving energy. We constantly told our players not to be on their feet or in the sun for any prolonged period of time. Reminding is a challenge, so equip the players to monitor things that you are better off letting them monitor.

Through experience, we learned that less was more in classroom meeting times. We gave our coordinators a time limit for meetings. But we did incorporate impromptu walk-throughs (on-field meetings, basically). Our players would literally show up in sandals, and we walked through all the plays, special scenarios, and so on, sometimes on a small patch of grass. Sit-down meetings were good when time was short and we had to incorporate different learning methods. Players learn, process, and embrace teaching methods differently. Showing video, diagraming on a whiteboard, speaking, and walking through scenarios can all play a role.

Given the extra pressures of tournament play, helping your team get away from it all can be a good idea. Have your team manager take them to a local outdoor pool for an hour, or to a movie theatre to watch a matinee (they will probably fall asleep!), to interesting local sights, or to a professional football or baseball game that's at the tournament location. Team activities build cohesiveness, give players a break from tournament preparation and stress, and provide them with unique memories and experiences. Also, the events give your coaching staff the option of taking a break from the players and either resting or doing some extra film work and meetings.

POST-TOURNAMENT REFLECTION

Coaching a tournament is exhausting. When you finally get home, the thing you will want most is to get away from football and just relax. But take a little time to reflect on the experience. It's a golden opportunity to improve yourself and your staff as tournament coaches, and to ensure the continued success of your program.

Debrief to improve. Every year between the next-to-last and last games of the tournament, our coaching staff met for an hour with a script. Everyone gave feedback on what was done well this year, what we could improve for next year, and so on. This was always our most important meeting of the year, with ideas being written down and (if possible) put into practice for the next year. Here's an outline of our meeting agenda:

Review and Suggestions

- This year's top three challenges (on-field or off-field)
- This year's top three successes (on-field or off-field)
- Suggestions for next year (afterward I went through these to rate them and determine if they were possible)
  - Program promotion
  - Budget
  - Tryout process
  - Training camp format
  - Team building
  - Tournament practice plans
  - Tournament meetings
  - Tournament nonfootball events
  - Coaching roles
  - Support staff and roles
- Possible schedule and format for next year
  - Tryouts
  - Training camp
- Other comments or suggestions

If your coaching staff is together for only one tournament, it is imperative to create a written report to pass on to your organization and the next coaching staff. Check your ego at the door, help the future coaches, and realize your experiences can and should help the next coaching staff. It is a privilege to coach these teams, so for the next generation of players and coaches, pass on your knowledge to better their experience.

One of the most rewarding experiences that we had after coaching so many great players and coaching with so many great coaches was seeing them on football fields and at various functions in subsequent years, or just hearing about their progress.

One athlete who played for us returned to his minor team a few months after the tournament, and I received this feedback from his coach: "I don't know what happened to him; he was a kid who gave us trouble but now he is one of our strongest team leaders." We received this feedback from another player's coach: "I am not sure what you did but he is an entirely different player. Great job guys."

I attended a playoff game where each team had five or so players who had played for us. One team used some plays that had worked for their players back on our team. To me this was amazing, since coaches have egos and it can be tough to say, "If that worked for you in this situation, let's try it." Despite being the underdogs, that team won the game handily.

In 2009, after helping us win a Football Canada Cup under-17 championship in the summer, two of the coaches from that staff led their CIS team to a national championship victory in the fall. I was fortunate to attend two of their home playoff games, and they were some of the best football games I have ever witnessed.

In 2010 and 2011, we had our first two players drafted in the Canadian Football League, and we had many, many more go to CIS and NCAA teams across North America.

CONCLUSION

All-star teams can bring the football community together. The camaraderie shared by players, on the same team and across teams, does the football community tremendous good. Foster that camaraderie and share in it. Compete on the field, but cooperate in the board room. The players just want to play and have the best opportunities to do so. It is all about the players. It is all about the game. Respect the game.

It was an honor and privilege to be involved with so many fine players, coaches, administrators, fans, supporters, and parents during my time as head coach of Team Ontario East. Many great relationships stemmed from this process, and it is these relationships that I most value. I know all the players and coaches learned a lot about themselves during this venture, but none more so than me.

16

Managing the Clock

Ryan Hall

Clock management should be a priority all during game day. Many coaches only think of managing the clock in the final minutes of a half, but they're missing an advantage. A good understanding of the rules, a quick pregame look at the hourly weather forecast, and ongoing adjustments to the ever-evolving situation of the game may make the difference between winning and losing.

The head coach has a lot to do, so delegation is key. The head coach should be focused on accepting or declining penalties, taking time-outs, going for it or not going for it on third down, and giving input to coordinators for important play calls. And, while thinking about all this, he should be thinking about how to manage the time clock.

The clock is almost exclusively controlled by the team on offense, including offensive special teams such as punt cover and field goal cover. For that reason, the head coach and offensive coordinator must work closely together on game planning, including how to manage the clock. Of course, there are situations when you can stop the clock on defense as well.

PREGAME PREPARATION

The head coach's first clock-management decision has to do with the pregame option of receiving the kick, kicking off, choosing a side, or deferring to the second half. In Canadian football, the second and fourth quarters are significantly longer than the first and third quarters due to the timing regulations of the final three minutes of each half. As all coaches know, significantly more plays are run in the second and fourth quarters than the first and third quarters.

If wind is a factor, consider the advantage of having significantly more plays with the wind in the longer quarters. Several factors affect the decision.

◆ *Do you have the choice to start the game?* In some leagues, a designated team (home or visitor) has choice. If you know you will have choice to start the game, you can choose your option well before the captains' pregame meeting with the officials. If the decision is based on the coin toss, have your plan set and communicated to your captains for both a winning and losing coin-toss call.

◆ *Have you checked the forecast?* In most places in Canada, an hourly weather forecast can be found online. Look at what it has to say about precipitation and wind speed. Are winds expected to gradually build, die, or remain consistent?

◆ *How important is momentum?* While it is true that you will get more snaps with the wind at your back in the second and fourth quarters, going against the wind in the first or third quarters gives your opponent an advantage when starting the half. This may not matter if your defense is strong enough to deal with giving up field position due to the effects of the wind on kicks and throws. But if your team needs an early-game advantage to build momentum, you may want to take the wind to start the game. Keeping the opposition pinned in their own end for an entire quarter is bound to hurt their confidence. But giving the opposition the ball and the wind to start the half gives them a distinct advantage in starting the game, since you'll be kicking into the wind and they'll be starting with possession and probably good field position. Your decision-making may change at half time, depending on the state of the game. For example, if your team has a good halftime lead, you may want to take the wind in the third quarter to put the game out of reach.

Choosing the ball is often a good option. If your opposition wants the wind in the long quarter, that leaves you with the ball and the wind to start the half and build momentum. If they don't want to give you both, they still have to give you the ball to start the half, and then you get the wind in the long quarter.

RULES AND STRATEGIES

You want the clock to run as much as possible in the quarters when you are going into the wind or when you are protecting a lead. Conversely, you want the clock to stop as much as possible when you have the wind or when you need to score. The rules governing clock management in a game can be found in *The Canadian Amateur Rule Book for Tackle Football*. They deserve close study. The timing rules usually don't change much, but check to be sure. The rule book is updated every two years, and this article is based on the 2016–2017 version.

Here is a summary of the rule book's relevant sections and some ideas for manipulating the clock to your advantage.

Clock Starts

Rule 1 deals with game conduct, with section 5 dealing specifically with timing. According to section 5's first article, the clock begins to run

- after a kickoff, when the ball touches an inbounds player of either team,
- when the ball is ready to be scrimmaged (meaning that the officials have allowed time for the ball to be spotted, for substitutions to be made, and

for the chains to be moved if that's necessary, and that they have then blown the whistle for the 20-second play clock to start),

- when the ball is snapped after a time-count penalty (a time-count penalty occurs when the offensive or kicking team does not put the ball into play before the 20-second play clock expires), or
- when the ball is snapped following a requested team time-out.

Several timing rules are specific to the time period after the three-minute warning signal has been given for either half:

- The clock starts when the ball is snapped following an incomplete pass or when the ball is carried out of bounds.
- The clock starts when the ball is snapped immediately after a play during which possession changes.
- The clock starts when the ball is snapped on a play following a kickoff, a kick from scrimmage, a return kick, or an open-field kick.
- The clock starts when the ball is snapped after the application of a penalty. The nonoffending team may decline the penalty and permit time to resume as though the foul had not occurred.

When play is stopped due to a procedural penalty after a time-out or the three-minute warning, the game clock starts on the snap of the ball whether the penalty yardage is accepted or not.

Note that, in many cases, the clock does not start until the ball is snapped. In those situations, nothing can be done to manipulate the time. But when the clock is running prior to the snap, the offense has significant control over how much time runs off. If you want to save time, the offensive coach can signal the plays from the sidelines; if you want to run the clock, use a player to run the play call to the huddle (all this is before the three-minute warning signal). The quarterback, for his part, can call for the snap quickly or he can take his time and use up most of the 20-second play clock.

Clock Stops

Rule 1, section 5, article 2 covers when the clock is stopped during a game. The clock stops

- when a team scores, and remains stopped throughout any convert attempt,
- when a live ball goes out of bounds,
- after an incomplete forward pass,
- when a penalty needs to be applied,
- when three or more players are substituted at the same time or when a player is injured,

- when time expires at the end of a period,
- on a dead ball after the three-minute warning signal for either half,
- when a field official recognizes a request for a time-out or the referee feels it is necessary to suspend play (to take a measurement, for example),
- after the end of a play in which there is a change of possession, or
- at the end of all kicking plays.

In 2014, some modifications were made to article 2. For any game shorter than 48 minutes, such as a youth game or a game within a tournament, it is recommended to stop the clock when first-down distance is made. This allows for more plays to be run within a shorter game.

Some leagues modify the rule to stop the clock in situations such as a long first-down play or a long incompletion. This gives the officials time to spot the ball and move the chains (if necessary), and allows the teams to get into position for the next play without running significant time off of the clock. Find out if your league has any of these rule modifications.

Note the situations that cause the clock to stop. Avoid these situations if you want the clock to run (to protect a lead, for example). But if you want the clock to stop, consider taking the ball out of bounds or using one of these other strategies.

Incomplete Pass

Typically an incomplete pass isn't a positive offensive play. But if the alternative is a short gain in the middle of the field that may result in precious seconds ticking at the end of the game, the quarterback may want to throw the ball at the receiver's feet to stop the clock.

Substitution of Three or More Players

This may be the least-used method of stopping the clock. It's found most often with special teams, but it can also be effective in an offensive or defensive situation. If you have the player depth to replace three offensive or defensive players, doing so gives your team a chance to gather themselves and prepare for the next play while delaying the start of the 20-second play clock or stopping the game clock.

This strategy likely won't help the defensive team kill the clock after the three-minute warning signal has been given, as the offensive team still has the full 20-second play clock to run down in a clock-running situation. It does give the defense an opportunity to slow the tempo of the offense, though.

First, make sure the officials will stop the clock for substitutions of three or more players. They may be accustomed to doing this for special-teams plays only, not other plays.

Injury

Of course it is not ethical to have a player fake an injury, but the coach can remind his players to take a knee, rather than run off the field, if they need a substitution due to injury or equipment problems. While a player taking a knee will stop the clock, it also means that the injured player has to sit out three plays. Again, this won't be any kind of advantage to the defensive team after the three-minute warning signal has been given, as the offensive team still has the full 20-second play clock to run down in a clock-running situation.

Time-outs

In Canadian amateur football, teams are given two time-outs per half. Unused time-outs cannot be transferred to the next half. Because of the clock-stoppage rules of the final three minutes of each half, the importance of saving time-outs for the end of the half may not be as important in Canadian football as it is in American football.

Consider using time-outs in these situations:

- If you have a late defensive substitution on second or third down (a player goes onto the field after the "gate" has gone up from the sideline official, which will lead to an illegal substitution penalty). Taking a time-out makes the substitution legal rather than giving the offense a first down. The penalty for illegal substitution is 10 yards; if it is third and 10 or less, and if the other team is in punt formation and you have an illegal substitution, take a time-out rather than risk the penalty.
- If you do not have enough players on the field on an offensive play, a punt, or a field goal. You won't get a penalty for having too few players (remember that rule 4, section 3, article 2 states that if the offensive team has fewer than 12 players on the field, the team may reduce the equivalent number of players on the line without penalty), but you have a much higher risk of a quarterback sack on offense or a blocked kick or punt on special teams.

If the 20-second play clock is about to expire but the play isn't ready to be run, and if the loss of 5 yards is not a significant disadvantage, instruct players to not snap the ball and take the time-count violation penalty instead of using a time-out.

Don't waste a time-out if you are missing players on a convert attempt; tell players to not snap the ball, take a time count penalty, and get 12 players on the field. The 5 yards on the convert attempt or the ensuing kickoff are likely not as valuable as a time-out, unless you feel the wind is a major factor on either of the kicks. If you are yelling instructions to your players on the field, try not to say "Take a time count!" because they will often mishear you and think you said "Take a time-out!" Rather, yell to them "Don't snap the ball!"

Measurement or Other Official's Time-out

If the spot of the ball is close enough to raise the question of whether it is a first down, request a measurement if you want to stop the game clock. This is an especially relevant request on natural grass fields, since their painted lines aren't as accurate as lines on artificial turf.

20-Second Play Clock

Rule 4 applies to scrimmage. Section 2 and article 4 of rule 4 apply to the time count for the method of scrimmage. After each play, the referee allows 20 seconds for players to line up before the ball is put into play, and the referee is the sole judge as to when the 20 seconds starts and ends.

Often the referee will discuss the application of this rule during the pregame meeting with the head coach and will ask the head coach if offensive plays will be signaled in from the bench or if players will run them into the huddle. As mentioned, signaling from the bench saves time, whereas running plays in takes time. The first move can make sense when you have the wind, and the second when you don't. Of course, this strategy won't make a difference in the final three minutes of either half, because the game clock does not start until the 20-second play clock starts.

END-OF-QUARTER SITUATIONS

As you are nearing the end of the quarter on offense, think carefully about your play calling if wind is a significant factor. If you may face a kicking situation (punt or field goal), you want the wind at your back. Instruct the quarterback to slow the tempo if you are going into the wind at the end of the first or third quarters. At best, you can continue your drive with the wind; at worst, you will be in a situation to kick or punt with the wind behind you. Conversely, if you have the wind at the end of the first or third quarters, pick up the tempo. At best, you will get more plays with the wind; at worst, if you have to kick or punt on third down, you can do it before you have to change ends.

LOPSIDED GAME SITUATIONS

Rule 1, section 5, article 5 is called the Mercy Rule. Any time after the first half, when a team has a lead of 35 points or more, the clock will run for the remainder of the game (with the exception of injury time-outs, scoring plays, or time-outs called by the coaches or officials). Use these situations as learning opportunities for your team. Get coaches and players to use good clock-management techniques, even if they don't actually affect the game clock in this situation.

GAME PLANNING AND CLOCK MANAGEMENT

All good coaches put together a game plan for the upcoming opponent. Here are a few situations in which play calling and clock management directly relate to game planning.

If you are playing a team with an explosive offense, and your offense is not suited to a shoot-out, don't run a lot of pass plays that will stop the clock and create a lot of two-and-outs. Instead, your game plan should include a healthy dose of runs, play-action passes, and high-percentage passes that will keep the clock running and hopefully keep the chains moving. Explosive offenses like to be on the field, not on the bench, so eating up time will make it harder for your opponent's offense to get into a rhythm.

You may need to adjust your game plan midway through the game to compensate for an injury or to give a player a break. If one of your best defensive players gets injured, but he looks like he'll be able to return after some treatment on the sideline, the offensive play calling may need to change to focus more on ball possession to move the chains and run the clock. Similarly, if one of your key players needs a rest due to special-teams activity or playing both offense and defense, the coaching staff may need to quickly collaborate to adjust the offensive play calls to give this player a break.

PRACTICE IT

A prudent head coach will anticipate situations in which clock management is important and will integrate them into weekly practice scenarios. These scenarios are best if they are competitive (although they don't need to be full contact), and there must be a coach or manager who keeps time and announces it regularly for both the offense and defense to hear (unless you have a time clock at your practice field). There should also be a coach or manager on the whistle to end plays and whistle in the 20-second play clock. It will help players, especially the quarterback, to understand the situation better if the clock-running status is announced ("The player was tackled inbounds, so the clock runs on the whistle" or "The pass was incomplete so the clock will hold on the whistle"). In each scenario, the head coach should give the hypothetical score, start the offense at a position on the field to march, and tell both the offensive and defensive teams how many time-outs they have.

The goal for these drills is to not only put your players in situations in which time is a very important factor, but also help them understand the importance of clock use throughout the game. The quarterback, in particular, should be cognizant of time use and check in with the head coach or offensive coordinator to find out what tempo he should use for the next series. He should be thinking of the same things the coaches are: wind, score, and overall game scenario.

Here are some common drill concepts to practice.

Four-Minute Drill

The scenario is that the offense has the lead. Its goal is to use as much time as possible: by using the full 20-second play clock before snapping the ball, and by keeping the ball inbounds, throwing only complete passes, and getting first downs. The defense needs to make a stop or at least try to stop the clock by forcing the ball carrier out of bounds.

(continued)

Four-Minute Drill   *(continued)*

You'll need a coach to keep track of the clock and to whistle in the start of the play clock. To educate your players, the timer coach can announce the situation. For example, before whistling in the 20-second play clock, he may announce, "The ball carrier was tackled inbounds on the previous play, so the clock will run on the whistle." The coach then starts and stops the clock as appropriate during the scrimmage. If the offense gets a first down, the timer coach should remember that the stick crew would need time to get the first down chains moved, so he should allow time for that. If the defense forces the offense into a punting situation, the drill ends and the timer coach announces how much time the offense ran off the clock on the drive. It's a big win for the offense if they are able to sustain a long drive and then finish it by adding to their lead.

Three-Minute Drill

The scenario is that the offense is trailing, but time is not a major concern, unless they are trailing by more than one score. The goal for the offense is to score. Three minutes in Canadian football is enough time for several changes of possession to take place. Again, the defense needs to make a stop to protect their lead.

Like in the four-minute drill, you will need a timer coach to manage the clock and the whistle. The offense wants to efficiently move down the field by snapping the ball soon after the 20-second play clock is whistled in, and to take the ball out of bounds at the end of the play. The defense tries to tackle the ball carrier inbounds. The timer coach should keep in mind the time it would take for the stick crew to readjust the chains after a first down. If the defense stops the offense, the coach announces how much time is left, and if you want to continue the drill, you can take a minute off the remaining time (assuming the other team would run only a couple of plays before punting) and then give the offense the remaining time. This may now put the offense into the one-minute drill.

One-Minute Drill

The offense is trailing, and time is a major concern. The goal for the offense is to score quickly, because there is only a minute left on the clock. Besides using the clock-management techniques described earlier, the offense can also practice their "hurry-up" mode. Along with needing to make a stop, the defense needs to adjust to the offense's hurry-up tempo by lining up quickly, and then efficiently communicating their play call.

As in the previous drills, the timer coach will control the situation by managing the clock, whistling in the play, and announcing if the clock will run or hold when the 20-second play clock is whistled in. If the offense scores, they win; if the defense stops them (there is no point in punting, so the offense would use all three downs), the defense wins.

CONCLUSION

Away from the game, it's easy to think and talk about time management. On the sideline, with dozens of other things running through the head coach's mind every minute of the game, it is much more complicated. Just as players get better through practice and repetition, coaches can improve clock management through practice. Besides working on the use of time with the players in practice, a proactive coach also takes advantage of nonstressful game situations (lopsided score, exhibition, etc.) to work on the finer points of managing the clock.

As you go back through your game film, analyze the decisions you made relating to clock management, including the choices you made in the first- and second-half options. Keep notes on things like:

- How many plays were run in each quarter?
- How did your combination of pre-half decisions (defer, ball, wind) work out in this game? Do you think the decisions would have worked the same against a stronger or weaker opponent or a stronger or weaker wind?
- Did you have situations in which you could have made good use of a time-out?
- Relative to wind conditions, how well did you manage offensive play calls at the end of the first and third quarters?
- Were there any situations you or your players were not prepared for that you can integrate into practice?

Clock management is one of the intangible skills that distinguish the highly competent coach from the ordinary coach. By learning the rules of the game related to timing, and by practicing different scenarios with your players during the week, you will prepare yourself and your team for game situations when time is a big factor. In football we're always looking for an edge, so "take time" to get better.

17

Preparing to Play U.S. Competition

Brad Collinson

Canadian and American football have their differences: the size of the field, the extra down, and different rules and fair catches, to name a few. The game is still football. North or south of the border, it's played with an oval ball made of pig skin, on a rectangular field marked off by four white lines. But internationally it's played with American rules. And in football, mastery of the rules counts for a lot. Canada has been participating in international competition for a number of years, from the International Bowl and the International Federation of American Football world championship on down to cross-border high school games. If your team is headed into international play, here's what you should know.

First, the differences:

- *Field size*. In American football, the field is 100 yards long by 53 1/3 yards wide. The end zones are 10 yards deep. In Canadian football, the field is 110 yards long by 65 yards wide, and the end zones are 20 yards deep.

- *Goalposts*. In American football, the goalposts are set on the end line. In Canadian football, they are on the goal line.

- *Hash marks*. In American high school football, the hash marks are 17 yards, 2 feet, and 4 inches from the sideline; in American college football, the hash marks are 20 yards from the sideline. In Canadian football, the hash marks are 24 yards from the sideline on all fields.

- *Players*. In American football, there are 11 players on the field per side; Canadian football has 12.

- *Number of downs*. In American football, an offense has four downs to get a first down; in Canadian football, it's three downs.

- *Distance on the line of scrimmage.* The distance between the offensive and defensive lines is 11 inches in American football, whereas in Canada you must give 1 yard between the offensive and defensive units.
- *Fair catch.* Returners in the American game can decide not to return a punt or kickoff by signaling a fair catch. To do so they must wave their hand above their shoulders while the ball is still in the air. If the returner signals a fair catch, the defenders covering must give space for the returner to field the ball. The play is then blown dead at the spot where the returner fielded the kick. In Canadian football, there is no fair catch in any kicking situation, although on punts and missed field goals you must give 5 yards between the returner and the players covering the punt or kick.
- *Presnap motion.* In American football, only one player on the offense can be in motion prior to the snap. The player in motion can move only laterally; he cannot move forward. Also, players who are on the line of scrimmage must not be in motion prior to the snap. They can move laterally but must be still for a full second prior to the ball being snapped. In Canadian football, every eligible player can be in movement prior to the snap of the ball.
- *Play clock.* Depending on the competition, the play clock can vary. For American high school games, the offense has 25 seconds to get the ball in play once the referee whistles in the play. If the competition uses NCAA rules, the offense has 40 seconds to snap the ball once the referee whistles in the play, or 25 seconds after a timeout or if there was a penalty on the previous play. In Canadian football, regardless of the level, you have 20 seconds to get the ball in play once the referee blows the play in.

Not only is preparing for the American game a challenge for coaches, it is also a challenge for players. Most likely they've been playing Canadian rules for their entire career, so playing internationally requires a period of adjustment. Coaches should include a detailed document at the beginning of all the playbooks outlining the rule differences.

OFFENSIVE GAME PLANNING

Game planning can be tedious, sometimes overwhelming, and that's especially so if you are playing by different rules. Simplify and don't overthink. Probably there's no game film to look at, since most likely you're preparing for a tournament game, an all-star game, or a preseason cross-border exhibition game. If you do have film, break down fronts, coverages, blitzes, and stunts just as you would against Canadian competition, and look for tendencies in the opposing defense that are vulnerable to attack.

First you have to look at the types of defenses you may face. Figure 17.1 shows four basic defenses.

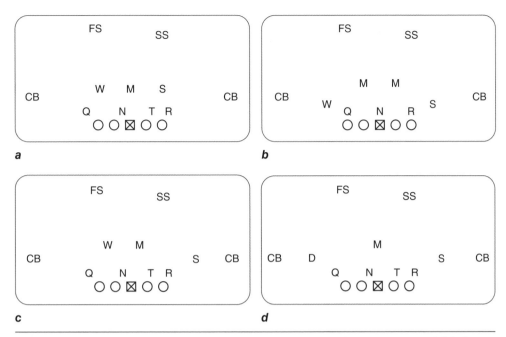

FIGURE 17.1 Common defenses in American football: (a) 4-3, (b) 3–4, (c) 4-2-5 (nickel), (d) 4-1-6 (dime).

These four are the basic defenses you will have to prepare for. Of course, there are variations and additional defenses you might see. But the four here are the most common.

Next you must look at the different coverages the American game has. Since the American game is played with two safeties, the coverages are a little different. Figure 17.2 shows the basic coverages you will need to prepare for.

Those are the four basic coverages most teams play. Again, there are further variations, but these are the most common.

Once you understand the fronts and coverages, you can start designing an offense to attack them. Canadian plays will work fine; you just need to take out a player, tweak the alignments of the receivers, and eliminate the motions. Remember this is four-down football, so you have that extra down to work with. For an offensive coordinator calling an American rules game, this is a dream come true. That extra down lets you be a bit more creative on first and second down, so installing more run and play-action plays may be a good move. The coordinator must also be aware of the size of the field and passing windows. The throwing windows close much more quickly and are not as big as in the Canadian game, so it will be an adjustment for the quarterback and the receivers.

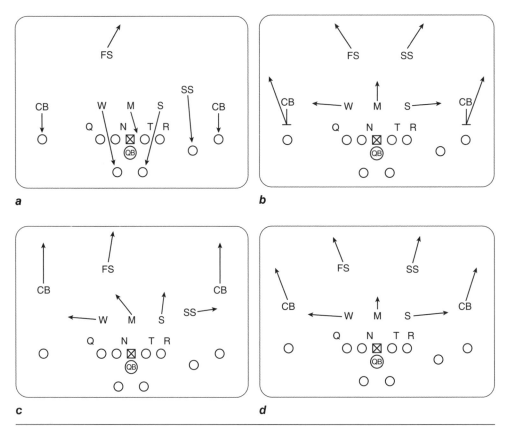

FIGURE 17.2 Common coverages in American football: (a) cover 1 (man-to-man with a free safety in the middle), (b) cover 2 (zone with two deep safeties), (c) cover 3 (zone with three deep players), (d) cover 4 (zone with four deep players).

DEFENSIVE GAME PLANNING

You'll break down your opponent the same as you normally do. First, identify the formations. Tight ends play a much bigger part in the American game, and preparing to defend against tight ends isn't as easy as it looks. Ask yourself:

- Do we play the tight end with the defensive end aligned inside shade and the linebacker stacked head up?
- Do we play the tight end with the defensive end aligned outside shade and the linebacker playing between the defensive end and the defensive tackle?
- Do we play the tight end with the defensive end aligned inside shade and the linebacker on the line of scrimmage jetted (on the line of scrimmage) outside shade of the tight end?

All these questions need to be addressed, and there is no right answer. It all depends on your defensive personnel and how you want to attack the opposing offense.

The fun thing is that there is no multiplayer motion. There are shifts and players do move around, but they all must be set for one second before the snap. So defensive backs and linebackers get a clear presnap picture. There may not be motion, but American offenses attack defenses by formations. They want to create a one-on-one matchup to take advantage of a particular player versus a particular defender. Figure 17.3 gives a great example.

How would you defend this? Play the single receiver man-to-man and shift your safeties to the three-receiver side, or play a cover 2 contour in which your isolated corner has help on top? These factors are the same as in a Canadian rules game; the only difference is you may not have film on your opponent.

An American offense usually features a lot more run plays than a Canadian offense does. Because of the extra down, offenses tend to run the ball more to set up the pass with play action or straight drop back. From what I've seen in preparing against U.S. teams, our players and coaches lack experience in defending against this heavy running attack. With three-down football, we play a passing game. When it comes to fitting gaps and defending the run correctly in U.S. play, we have to make an adjustment.

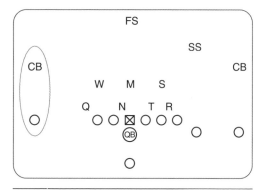

FIGURE 17.3 Creating a one-on-one matchup.

In U.S. play, defending the passing game is simpler. Your presnap image will be static, and the field is smaller. Defenders have less ground to cover, so we tend to see much more spot dropping in zone coverage by the linebackers and defensive backs. If all your players drop to their designed area, the field will be covered. The opposing quarterback will have tighter windows to throw into, which results in more knockdowns and, hopefully, more interceptions. Figure 17.4 gives an example of all the zones that are covered when playing a zone defense.

When designing zone coverages, you must be aware of the zones you need to defend. But man coverage in U.S. play is the same as in Canadian.

Keep defensive game planning sound and simple so that your athletes can fly around and make plays. Overthink it and your players start turning into robots instead of hitting their potential. By keeping it simple, you'll get better results and make things much easier on yourself and your team.

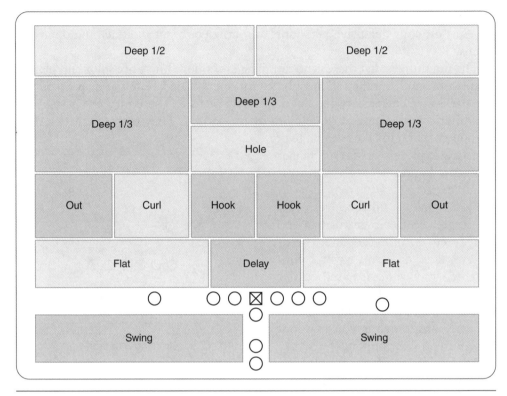

FIGURE 17.4 Pass coverage zones.

SPECIAL-TEAMS GAME PLANNING

Make your special teams a priority. Time will be short; it usually is when preparing for international play. Even so, never lose sight of this topic. U.S. and Canadian play have a lot of differences regarding special teams, and your side has to master them.

Kicking Field Goal or PAT

First, all converts and field goals must be kicked from the ground, without a tee or block (Canada was allowed a tee in the International Bowl series, but not the World Championship). This is a significant difference, and you only have a week or two to get your kicker used to it. You need to allocate prepractice and postpractice time so your kicker, holder, and short snapper can work on the mechanics of kicking from the ground.

In Canada, we return all missed field goals out of the end zone so that we don't give up a rouge (single point). In the American game, the field-goal defense can decide to have a returner (on a long field-goal try). But this is rarely done, since a missed attempt gives up no points and the ball is returned to the original line of scrimmage. As in the Canadian game, the centre can't be hit when his head is down, but he can be jumped over. Schemewise, you can use the same techniques that we teach in Canada; you just need to adjust your diagrams for 11-man football.

Field Goal Defense

This is probably the unit that is the easiest to adapt. Since there are rarely any field-goal returns, you only have to install a safe (defend the fake field goal) and block scheme. As in Canada, the centre can't be touched; you also need to cover all the eligible players in case of a fake. As mentioned, returning a missed field goal is rare but it's permitted. If the situation does happen, have a return scheme ready (see Auburn versus Alabama in 2013).

Kickoff

This unit is very similar to the Canadian game, but the differences count. First, alignment: all players except the kicker must be 5 yards from the line of scrimmage. When timing their run-up with the kicker, Canadian players have to get used to that space and no more. Focus on this procedure during practice so you don't have any offsides. Another difference: if the ball is kicked in the end zone, the returner can take a knee (touchback) and the ball will be placed at the 25-yard line. Unlike in the Canadian game, the kicking team doesn't get a point.

On onside kicks, the kicker must kick the ball differently than in the Canadian game. Since the American game has the fair-catch rule, the kicker must kick the ball on the ground before it reaches the return team. If the kicker does not kick it this way, the return team will signal for a fair catch and the kicking team will not be able to tackle or make a play on the ball. As in the Canadian game, the ball must travel 10 yards before the kicking team can touch the ball. When installing your kickoff schemes, you can use the same ones as in Canada.

Kickoff Return

This unit is the most similar to the Canadian game, but there are still some differences you have to know. The return team must align 10 yards from where the ball is being kicked. You may fair-catch any kick that has not touched the ground right off the tee (see Kickoff). The returner may take a knee in the end zone to take a touchback, and the ball will be spotted on the 25-yard line. There are no single points for not returning the ball out of the end zone, and none if the ball goes out the back of the end zone. As in the Canadian game, if the ball does not touch a player and goes out of bounds before the end zone, there is a penalty. The return team has the choice to make the kicking team rekick 5 yards back, take the ball at their 35-yard line, or take the ball where it went out of bounds.

Scheming a kickoff return is like in the Canadian game. You will have either a middle or sideline return in your playbook. You will also need a "hands team" prepared in the event of an onside kick.

Punt

Canadian schemes work fine for punts in American competition. A man scheme, zone scheme, or shield punt can all be used. The alignment of the punter from the long snapper can be the same as well; you usually set your punter 14 to 15 yards from the line of scrimmage.

The differences show up in the coverage part of the unit. These aren't major, but they need to be addressed and practiced. The biggest is the lack of a "no yards" rule; the cover team does not have to give a 5-yard cushion to the returner. Players need to know that that the returner can signal for a fair catch, which means you cannot interfere with the returner catching the punt. What happens a lot in the American game is the returner will signal for a fair catch and let the ball go over his head, hoping that the ball will go in the end zone for a touchback. Your cover team needs to have someone run past the returner and be prepared to down the ball as close to the end zone as possible. The opponent's offense will then scrimmage from where the ball was touched by the kicking team.

Punt Return

This unit is probably the most challenging one for the returners. In Canada, our returners are in a relatively stress-free environment when fielding punts, since we have the "no yards" rule of 5 yards. In the American game, the punt cover team does not have to give any yards to the returner to catch the ball. You must teach your returners to make sound decisions when fielding a punt. First, they have to be able to see the ball kicked and locate where it will land. Second, they have to decide if they are able to return the kick. Third, if they decide not to return the kick, they need to either give the fair-catch signal (wave an arm above the shoulders) or get out of the way. And all this must be done in a few seconds. Needless to say, you need someone with nerves of steel and the ability to make quick decisions. That is the most challenging aspect of the punt return, since the scheme aspect is very similar to the Canadian game.

The game of football is changing, and because of that you won't see any wall returns, since players are penalized for any blindside blocks and the player has the potential of being thrown out of the game. You will need to have a few variations of a man-return and a block-punt scheme in your playbook.

CONCLUSION

Because the United States is recognized as the home to the best football in the world, it is an exciting opportunity for your coaches and players to take on a team south of the border. While it is important to educate your players on the differences in the game, and to remind your coordinators of the different mindsets they will need to deal with the extra down, the game being played is still football. Blocking and tackling are universal, and the team that does those skills the best, as well as takes care of the football, will likely end up winning the game. Work hard to find the balance between enjoying the uniqueness of the experience of playing U.S. competition, and the fact that it is just another great opportunity for you and your players to compete and get better. Go Canada!

PART FOUR

INNOVATIVE AND EFFECTIVE PRACTICE SESSIONS

18

Planning and Running an Effective Practice

Christian Audet

There are many ways to get the job done, and in the search to find our own way, we try new things, we adjust, and we analyze what works and what doesn't. As an NFL offensive coordinator once said, "If you can't adjust and improvise, your winning percentage will not increase." With that in mind, this chapter provides information that may be different and that may help you in the creation of your practice plan. A creative nature and improvising skills are most important in day-to-day planning, which will inevitably change due to injuries, temperature, absentees, and other factors outside of your control.

Preparation is the key to a solid performance on the field, and it all starts with a plan. The head coach's responsibilities include the planning and running of practices, which should include the physical, psychological, technical, and tactical preparation of both athletes and coaches. Time is always key, and a plan will help keep it from being wasted. Considering the ruggedness of the sport, a yearly plan should be prepared and executed for the athletes' physical preparation. The psychological aspect should be integrated into all phases of coaching. The technical section is dictated by the skills and progression of athletes. The tactical portion should be organized with offensive, defensive, and special-teams systems preparing for the most important part of season: the playoffs. The development of each individual player and the units within the team (offense, defense, and special teams) will affect the time spent on the different segments in a practice Every second must be utilized efficiently. The synchronization of these elements is the goal of practice planning, and the guidance in this chapter will help in planning and running an effective practice.

IMPORTANT PRINCIPLES OF PRACTICE

Athlete safety is an important factor when planning a practice. Football is a collision sport, and the body can take only so much physical abuse. Fatigue triggered by heat or the duration of certain exercises can cause injury and mental mistakes.

The brain can also reach a saturation point. Depending on the level of fatigue, an athlete's capacity to take in information and execute techniques properly is maxed out at 120 minutes (for a mature athlete). Younger athletes can practice effectively for shorter periods than that. The physical health status of the athletes has a direct effect on concentration levels. The planning of the physical preparation and conditioning of the athletes is important. Also, reducing the amount of effort and energy strains at the beginning of practice may result in a better focus at the end, when the need for execution and concentration is typically most demanding.

After you've covered safety, there's enthusiasm. Your leadership and energy will determine the flow of your practice. Start each practice with an enthusiastic welcome and introduction. Coaches are responsible for the enthusiasm on the field, in meetings, and in relationships. In general, the psychological part of coaching has a great influence on the way a practice is executed. Our choice of words, tone of voice, and the timing and situation of our critiques affect the perception by which the players receive and assimilate the information. Words can tear down or build up. The preparation of these hearts is our responsibility, and what the players are feeling inevitably shows up in their performance.

Confidence is the main ingredient to great performance, and as coaches, it is our role to implement plans, exercises, techniques, and schemes that heighten the confidence of each player. To do this, we need to maintain our individual confidence and level of enthusiasm.

Players imitate coaches and seek our approval. A coach's attitude, his level of stress, and his positive energy will influence the whole team. The best way to lead is by example. Barking out orders and directions can irritate people; stepping in front and guiding them is much more efficient. For example, if a one-minute water break is called, the head coach should be the first guy running to the water station, which results in everybody running. In the end, we control the effectiveness of a practice with our attitude.

Assistant coaches also have a huge role in this display of energy; they are the fuel in the engine that propels the team. They must be in sync, and they must understand the importance of communicating and leading players through the practice plan with the energy needed to keep intensity where it has to be. Keeping the energy up will have a positive result on any practice.

The selected drills can also heighten the level of intensity and fun. Having fun while doing conditioning drills will lead to better effort and attitude from players. Sticking to the set time allocation will accelerate transitions and add repetitions in the execution column, so put somebody in charge of timekeeping. That's critical in the execution of the plan.

To cut time consumption, teach players who aren't taking part in the actual play that's being run. This allows for a better communication environment and less stress than trying to provide feedback quickly between repetitions. If the coach needs to communicate specific observations, he should take the athlete aside and correct him while the drill continues with the other coach and athletes. If you have the benefit of filming practices, that reduces the stress in getting the information to the players. By being positive in critiques, and being brief and precise in teachings, coaches have a great influence on running an effective practice. When players are having fun and the energy is up-tempo, the atmosphere is game-day realistic.

The technical components of a practice are fundamental in preparing athletes to perform on game day. The drills used to perfect techniques should be efficiently organized to save time. For example, an offensive line coach may ask his players to line up in a huddle, and have them break the huddle and run to the line of scrimmage to set up their stance and takeoff on a predetermined cadence and play. In a stance-and-start drill, the coach will have implemented four skills that will be executed every play on game day.

A high number of repetitions is not always beneficial if the repetitions are not executed with proper technique. One good repetition is worth more than five bad ones. The emphasis on good repetitions is essential in the pursuit of the full potential of a team's success. Dr. Richard A. Schmidt (coauthor of *Motor Learning and Performance*) states that it requires between 300 and 500 repetitions to develop a new motor pattern, and it takes about 3,000 to 5,000 repetitions to erase and correct a bad motor pattern. If this is true, we have no time to erase bad patterns that have been created. We must strive to teach the good pattern from the start.

Asking an individual to do something that is physiologically impossible for him will deteriorate his confidence and your credibility. Demanding a certain technique from athletes before teaching it puts them in an uncomfortable situation. If they are told to do something, but their muscles send the message "not possible" to their brains, they will not be able to perform the action. They need to see it. They need to try it. They need to feel good doing it and have success executing it to build confidence. Valuable time can be saved by understanding this dynamic, and the progress of the athletes can be accelerated.

Filming is probably the most helpful tool for a coach in this day and age. Technology allows us to see every action of a skill in fractions of seconds. We can isolate movements, techniques, and reactions without missing anything, and offer the players the opportunity to view themselves. The use of tablets, cellular phones, and cameras on-field is becoming common for football practice. The recording of drills also enables coaches to take care of smaller details in the reviewing process. Although this is time-consuming, it is worth the effort. A film session can be very productive if the right people are involved and the right angles are shown. For team drills, two angles are generally used: the tight (tackle-to-tackle) end zone angle for the run portion of the game, and the wide sideline for the passing portion, capturing all the receivers and the defensive personnel in the coverage. The results will provide for a better performance analysis for each athlete in the next practice, thus saving valuable minutes in coaching.

The tactical portion of the practice plan correlates directly with the playbook insertion schedule. The schemes developed in the off-season are applied for the first part of the season and the first game. Then the schemes evolve with each week's opponent. Every week, teams go through adjustments to perfect their play. With the evolution of offensive football, defensive coaches have a lot more work on their hands to stay on top of the tactical threats. The practice plan has to include synchronizing the new strategies and skills necessary to counter challenges such as defending the read option and six-receiver sets and adjusting to all the motion. Also, selecting and utilizing the same personnel for the service and scout teams makes it easier for the coaches and increases the amount of good repetitions of opponent plays. Finally, your greatest time-saver will be picking the right individuals to execute the schemes. If you are running a reverse, only one or two athletes can run it; if they can't, don't use it.

Good communication will help with consistency of player performance during practice. A wide run shouldn't be called a sweep by the offense and a toss by the defense. No time should be lost on trying to convince someone that you're talking about the same thing. If offense and defense—meaning coaches and players—use the same terminology, you can simplify and accelerate the exchanges in meetings, practice, and urgent game situations. Use the off-season to get everyone on the same page about this.

Player substitution should also be looked at. Groups can be prepared in advance, and a chart with each player's name can be posted in the locker room and distributed to all coaches. If a player is hurt, any coach can make the substitution and no time is lost. When the receivers are included in a pass shell or 12-on-12 period, they can be replaced every play; that saves waiting for their return in the huddle. With this approach, more repetitions are performed and the groups evolve faster.

PRACTICE OBJECTIVES

We work so hard toward winning that sometimes we forget our top priority, which is to motivate human beings. A team mission or vision will guide everyone involved and set the key principles of the team. Team goals, coaching goals, and individual goals are all essential in the motivational process (see chapter 3 on coaching philosophy and chapter 13 on mental preparation).

Every week is different, and plans and objectives will evolve. Setting practice objectives will create a day-to-day motivation that will offer all team members a target for which to aim. This is an example of a practice goal: Thursday is a No Drop Ball practice. For each football that is catchable and dropped, a sprint is added at the end of practice. Receivers, running backs, returners, and defensive backs will get better at receiving, and your team cardio sessions are in their hands. A year-round motivational plan to provide incentives for getting better (off-season training) can also be developed. Players will enjoy the challenge and rewards, and at the same time they'll help the team's performance.

IMPORTANT FACTORS OF PRACTICE

The principles we've discussed will help develop an effective practice strategy. The following factors need to be clarified to build the foundation of your plan:

1. *Objectives.* What important goals (individual, group, unit, team) do you have for today's practice?

2. *Practice length.* How much time can you allocate to each period and drill, and how long can your players remain focused and intense?

3. *Required space and equipment.* How will you allocate areas of the practice field and coordinate the use of bags, sleds, balls, and so on?

4. *Coach-to-player ratio.* What role will each coach play during each period of practice?

5. *Hydration.* Based on physical intensity and weather conditions, how often should players take water breaks?

6. *Collisions and levels of contact.* What level of contact is required to achieve the goal of each period and drill? (See chapter 4 on safe contact.)

7. *Enthusiasm.* What team or competitive drills can be inserted to maintain attention span and motivation?

With all these factors, a breakdown of the yearly schedule of competition will enable you to organize your practice timetable, including the different needs for each period.

A football year (with a fall season) is separated into four segments and each has its own priorities:

1. *Off-season (January to May).* In this segment, the emphasis should be on the physical preparation of athletes, including neuromuscular and overall athletic development. (For many youth and high school players, this should include participation in other sports. See the introduction for a discussion of long-term athlete development.)

2. *Preseason (May to August).* In this segment, the emphasis should be on the position-specific physical preparation of athletes, including agility and cardiovascular, neuromuscular, technical, and tactical development.

3. *In-season (August to November).* In this segment, the emphasis should be on the tactical preparation of athletes, including cardiovascular, some neuromuscular, technical, and tactical development.

4. *Post-season (November to January).* In this segment, the emphasis should be on the physical preparation (active rest and recovery) of athletes, including cardiovascular and some neuromuscular development.

PRACTICE PLANNING

For the purpose of this chapter, we will focus on the preseason and in-season segments. In the preseason and during the training camp period, the emphasis is on developing skills and techniques. As the season progresses, more emphasis on tactical (systems) is necessary. These factors can be predetermined before the preparation of your practice plan:

◆ Objectives for the season and for each week
◆ Themes for the season and for each week

- The number of practices (preseason and in-season)
- The number of practices in full pads
- The number of practices with helmets and shoulder pads
- The number of practices without pads
- The hours needed for the preparation of the offense before the first game
- The hours needed for the preparation of the defense before the first game
- The hours needed for the preparation of the special teams before the first game
- The time needed in a week for the preparation of the offense for the following game
- The time needed in a week for the preparation of the defense for the following game
- The time needed in a week for the preparation of the special teams for the following game

Depending on the time, personnel, equipment, and facilities available, a practice should include many of the following periods, though it is not possible for one practice to have all of them.

Prepractice meeting. Before practice, explain the practice schedule, the drills to be executed, and the schemes to be inserted, including time frames and a reminder of the week's theme. Even if the meeting is only five minutes, athletes will know what, where, and why, and that will help in the logistics of the practice. Ideally, this is a 15-minute period with a review of the practice from the day before and the viewing of a selection of film clips.

Warm-up. The warm-up should be short and efficient. A dynamic routine is ideal as it activates muscles athletes will use during practice. Here is a sample dynamic warm-up:

Sprint. Seventy-five percent effort for 20 yards

Ankle hops/jumping jacks. Jump off the balls of the feet and don't allow the heels to contact the ground; perform 15 repetitions

Frankenstein walk. Keep legs straight and kick target (hand) for 15 yards

Walking quad pull. Pull leg and opposite arm back to effectively stretch hip flexors for 15 yards

Walking knee hugs. Pull knee into chest to stretch hip extensors (gluteus maximus) for 15 yards

Sprint. Seventy-five percent effort for 20 yards

Walking lunge twist. Bend the front knee approximately 90 degrees, keeping the back leg extended with the knee an inch off the ground; push hips forward and rotate trunk to one side, alternating sides, for 15 yards.

Sumo squat. Go through a full range of motion with a wide stance (feet wider than shoulders) to stretch groin muscles for 15 yards

Spider-Man. From a push-up position, bring one foot to the hand, attempting to touch the ankle to the elbow or the ground next to the hand, hold briefly, continue for 10 yards

High knees. Quick contacts off the ground, keep heels from touching ground, continue for 15 yards

Butt kicks. Attempt to kick butt with foot rhythmically for 15 yards.

Carioca. Quick, fluid movement at the hips for 20 yards

Backpedal. Athletic position, back flat, looking straight ahead, sitting into position and staying on the balls of feet for 20 yards

Full sprint. Hundred percent effort for 40 yards

Walk-through period. Offense and defense insert new tactical schemes on the field. This should be performed after the warm-up period because of the physical demands of each position. Though it is called walk-through, it usually ends up with players running at almost full speed.

Specialist's period. Pinners, kickers, punters, returners, long snappers, and blockers practice their skills. This period includes every athlete on the team (offensive line and defensive line point after touchdown block); a circuit can be developed where athletes may perform more than one skill (blocking, tackling, ball security, etc.).

Individual skill period. Technique training for all position groups.

Mesh period. Groups work on related skills; for example, quarterbacks can hand off to running backs or linebackers doing zone coverage drops with defensive backs.

Unit period. The offense and defense work on system implementation, such as the offense running plays or the defense practicing pursuit. This may also include a service or scout team giving the offense or defense a look at the opposition's plays.

Special-teams period. The special teams work together on system implementation. A service team may also take part, to give the special team a look at the opposition's plays.

Offensive priority inter-position period. The offense selects a skill to work on; for example, receivers can practice releases against pressing defensive backs (one-on-ones).

Defensive priority inter-position period. The defense selects a skill to work on; for example, defensive backs can practice taking on crack blocks from receivers (one-on-ones).

Offensive priority inside-run period. The offense (OL, RB, and QB) practices their run plays versus the scout defense (defensive line and linebackers), which is playing the opposition's defense.

Defensive priority inside-run period. The defense (DL and LB) practices versus the scout offense (OL, RB, and QB), which is playing the opposition's run plays.

Offense priority pass-shell period. The offense (QB, RC, and RB) runs pass plays versus the scout defense (LB and DB), which is playing the opposition's defense.

Defense priority pass-shell period. The defense (LB and DB) practices versus the scout offense (QB, RC, and RB), which is playing the opposition's pass plays.

Offensive priority 12-versus-12 period. The offense runs their plays versus the scout defense, which is playing the opposition's defense.

Defensive priority 12-versus-12 period. The defense practices versus the scout offense, which is playing the opposition's plays.

Team drills. Short, high-intensity, competitive drills to increase energy and enthusiasm.

Cooldown. Some light jogging and stretching.

Weekly coaches meeting. Prepare the following week's practices (schemes to be inserted and techniques to be reviewed).

The number of hours needed for all of these aspects should determine the amount of practices needed in a regular season week of preparation. They can't be done in one day, so organize them to set a progression through the week. "Going back to basics" is good, but a successful team doesn't lose sight of the fundamentals in the first place. Emphasize blocking and tackling skills so players are equipped for the collision aspect of football. The safety of athletes is a priority, and teaching the fundamentals does help reduce the amount of injuries (see chapter 4 on safe contact).

As players progress, the mesh periods can also be used for competitive drills between two opposing positions or more (one-on-ones, inside run, or pass shell). The team drill sections bring the energy up and also serve as a fun conditioning period. For example, do team burpees with a vocal signal for the start of each burpee, fake signals to test concentration, penalties for breaking concentration, and early water for the most successful athletes.

SAMPLE PRACTICE PLANS

Table 18.1 is an example of a youth practice during the preseason. Table 18.2 shows a sample three-practice weekly plan for the in-season. For this schedule, a pregame walk-through could be added the day before or the actual morning of the game. This 45-minute session would cover all the sideline procedures, special-teams substitutions, turnovers, halftime and end-of-game procedures, and exceptional situations such as kick-backs, quick punts, overtime, and so on.

All periods need to be planned and prepared in advance. Include a script of the plays to be run and the time spent on each hash with down and distance for all walk-through, inside-run, pass-shell, and 12-on-12 periods. An inside-run period can be efficient if plays are scripted (with the same play possibly executed 5 times in a 15-play period) and include both offensive and defensive schemes for each play. Service periods with plays scripted and drawn up in a binder in their executional order will help you get 1.5 plays for every minute of a period. Table 18.3 shows an example of a script for two 12-on-12 plays.

TABLE 18.1 Preseason Youth Practice Sample Plan

Time	Period	Notes
3 min.	Meeting	Welcome, practice plan, practice goals
7 min.	Warm-up	
10 min.	Walk-through	Offensive plays versus air, defensive systems versus bags
4 min.	Team drill	Three-on-three punt drill
1 min.	Water	
15 min.	Individual	Position skills
10 min.	One-on-ones	Blocking situations (OL vs. DL, RB vs. LB, RC vs. DB)
1 min.	Water	
15 min.	Individual	Position skills
10 min.	One-on-ones	Passing situations (OL vs. DL) live; (RB vs. LB, RC vs. DB)
1 min.	Water	
15 min.	Mesh	OL/QB/RB—run plays 8 min. versus bags; QB/RB/RC—pass plays 7 min. versus air* LB/DB—man-to-man responsibilities 8 min. versus bodies; DL/LB run responsibilities 7 min. versus bags/bodies*
15 min.	Unit O/D	O: selected plays versus bodies D: formation, motion, and play communication 7 min. versus bodies; pursuit 8 min. versus rabbit
5 min.	Cooldown	

* Groups not involved have extra individual time.

TABLE 18.2 Sample In-Season Practice Plan, Three Practices a Week

Day 1		
Time	**Period**	**Notes**
3 min.	Meeting	Welcome, practice plan, practice goals
7 min.	Warm-up	
5 min.	Specialists	Kickers, snappers, returners, and blockers (field goal and punt linemen)
10 min.	Walk-through	Offensive plays versus air, defensive systems versus bags
15 min.	Individual	Position skills run emphasis
1 min.	Water	

(continued)

Table 18.2 *(continued)*

Day 1		
Time	**Period**	**Notes**
10 min.	One-on-ones	Blocking situations (OL vs. DL, RB vs. LB, RC vs. DB)
15 min.	Individual	Position skills pass emphasis
1 min.	Water	
10 min.	One-on-ones	Passing situations (OL vs. DL) live; RB vs. LB; RC vs. DB
15 min.	Unit O/D	O: selected plays versus bodies D: formation, motion, and play communication 7 min. versus bodies; pursuit 8 min. versus rabbit
1 min.	Water	
15 min.	12 versus 12	Scripted plays
10 min	Special teams	Punt and field goal at the same time
5 min.	Cooldown	
Day 2		
Time	**Period**	**Notes**
3 min.	Meeting	Welcome, practice plan, practice goals
7 min.	Warm-up	
5 min.	Specialists	Kickers, snappers, returners, and blockers (field goal and punt linemen)
10 min.	Walk-through	Offensive plays versus air, defensive systems versus bags
15 min.	Individual	Position skills run emphasis
1 min.	Water	
10 min.	One-on-ones	Blocking situations (OL vs. DL, RB vs. LB, RC vs. DB)
15 min.	Individual	Position skills pass emphasis
1 min.	Water	
10 min.	One-on-ones	Passing situations (OL vs. DL) live; RB versus LB; RC versus DB
15 min.	Unit O/D	O: selected plays versus bodies D: formation, motion, and play communication 7 min. versus bodies; pursuit 8 min. versus rabbit
1 min.	Water	
15 min.	12 versus 12	Scripted plays
10 min	Special teams	Punt return and field-goal block at the same time
5 min.	Cooldown	
Day 3		
Time	**Period**	**Notes**
3 min.	Meeting	Welcome, practice plan, practice goals

Day 3		
Time	**Period**	**Notes**
7 min.	Warm-up	
10 min	Specialists	Kickers, snappers, returners, and blockers (field goal and punt linemen)
10 min.	Individual	Position skills run emphasis
1 min.	Water	
15 min.	Unit O/D	O: selected plays versus bodies D: formation, motion, and play communication 7 min. versus bodies; pursuit 8 min. versus rabbit
10 min.	Individual	Position skills pass emphasis
15 min.	Unit O/D	O: selected plays versus bodies D: formation, motion, and play communication 7 min. versus bodies; pursuit 8 min. versus rabbit
1 min.	Water	
15 min.	12 versus 12	Scripted plays offensive emphasis
1 min.	Water	
15 min.	12 versus 12	Scripted plays defensive emphasis
20 min	Special teams	Punt return and field-goal block at the same time
5 min.	Cooldown	

TABLE 18.3 Sample Script for Two 12-on-12 Plays

Play	Offensive group	Hash	Offensive play	Defensive group	Defensive play
1	1	Right	23 Thunder Jailbreak	Service 1	43 Cut weak, hold strong Sam extend, Mike A strong
2	1	Middle	32 Apache	Service 1	34 Man, Twist Sam C strong

Table 18.4 shows a weekly plan that covers pretty much everything that needs to be taken care of during the season, excluding the physical preparation. Some minor details may vary, but the main plan is there. Most of you may not have the time or resources to follow such a plan, let alone the personnel to execute it. But sharing this plan provides both extremes and offers you the freedom of adjusting to create a unique plan. As I advanced in my coaching career and wanted to become a head coach, I read Bill Walsh's book, *Finding the Winning Edge*. In it, he shared the 49ers' practice plan, and that plan enabled me to set a base and aim higher.

TABLE 18.4   Sample Weekly Practice Plan

Sunday	
Time	**Activity**
60 min.	Coaches meeting (game analysis)
20 min.	Team meeting
30 min.	Postgame meeting (individual video)
120 min.	Coaches meeting (next opponent game plan), player physical-training session

Monday	
Time	**Activity**
30 min.	Meeting (offense and defense, new game plan)
45 min.	Dress, taping, and getting to the field
10 min.	Warm-up
10 min.	Specialists
15 min.	Individual period
20 min.	Pass offense/inside run defense period
20 min.	Pass defense/inside run offense period
15 min.	Punt and field goal
10 min.	12-versus-12 offense period
10 min.	12-versus-12 defense period
5 min.	Conditioning
5 min.	Cooldown
30 min.	Showers
30 min.	Postpractice meeting (individual video)
30 min.	Coaches individual practice analysis
30 min.	Coaches meeting (preparation for the following practice)

Tuesday	
Time	**Activity**
30 min.	Meeting (offense and defense, adjustments to game plan)
45 min.	Dress, taping, and getting to the field
10 min.	Warm-up
10 min.	Specialists
15 min.	Individual period
20 min.	Pass offense and inside-run defense period
20 min.	Pass defense and inside-run offense period

Tuesday

Time	Activity
15 min.	Punt return and field-goal block
10 min.	12-versus-12 offense period
10 min.	12-versus-12 defense period
5 min.	Conditioning
5 min.	Cooldown
30 min.	Showers
30 min.	Postpractice meeting (individual video)
30 min.	Coaches individual practice analysis
30 min.	Coaches meeting (preparation for the following practice)

Wednesday

Time	Activity
30 min.	Meeting (offense and defense, adjustments to game plan)
45 min.	Dress, taping, and getting to the field
10 min.	Warm-up
10 min.	Specialists
10 min.	Individual period
15 min.	Pass offense/inside-run defense period
15 min.	Pass defense/inside-run offense period
15 min.	Kickoff and kickoff return
15 min.	12-versus-12 offense period
15 min.	12-versus-12 defense period
5 min.	Conditioning
5 min.	Cooldown
30 min.	Showers
30 min.	Postpractice meeting (individual video)
30 min.	Coaches individual practice analysis
30 min.	Coaches meeting (preparation for the following practice)

Thursday

Time	Activity
30 min.	Meeting (offense and defense, adjustments to game plan)
45 min.	Dress, taping, and getting to the field
10 min.	Warm-up

(continued)

Table 18.4 *(continued)*

Thursday	
Time	**Activity**
10 min.	Specialists
10 min.	Individual period
10 min.	Pass offense and inside-run defense period
10 min.	Pass defense and inside-run offense period
15 min.	All fakes, short kicks, and how to defend
20 min.	12-versus-12 offense period
20 min.	12-versus-12 defense period
5 min.	Conditioning
5 min.	Cooldown
30 min.	Showers
30 min.	Postpractice meeting (individual video)
30 min.	Coaches individual practice analysis
30 min.	Coaches meeting (preparation for the following practice)
Friday	
Time	**Activity**
45 min.	Dress, taping, and getting to the field
10 min.	Warm-up
10 min.	Specialists
20 min.	Review all special teams
10 min.	Offense and defense unit periods (separate)
10 min.	12-versus-12 offense period
10 min.	12-versus-12 defense period
15 min.	Game-day review (from walking on the field to all different scenarios, change-ups, turnovers, last two minutes, and kill the clock)
5 min.	Cooldown
30 min.	Showers
20 min.	Overview of personal equipment and preparing gear for the game
Saturday	
Time	**Activity**
Travel	Eat three hours prior to kickoff
120 min. before kickoff	Meetings, dress, taping, and getting to the field
60 min. before kickoff	Warm-up on the field

Saturday	
Time	**Activity**
25 min. before kickoff	Back in the dressing room
10 min. before kickoff	Back on the field
30 min.	Eat after the game
Travel	

CONCLUSION

I have attended different practices at different levels, and the one that impressed me most was at the New York Giants training camp. We all know how boring a pursuit drill can be: the entire defense running after a rabbit (ball carrier) and getting to a spot on the field to wait until the whistle is blown. The defense was executing a pursuit drill with gamelike intensity and it stunned me. Those professional athletes knew where to go. They'd been doing this drill since they were kids; now, with contracts worth a lot of money, they executed the drills with enthusiasm and intensity. That attitude on the part of the players came from the coaches who demanded it and brought it themselves. Everybody ran on the field at water breaks, transitioning from drills, and from the huddle to the line of scrimmage. Too much emphasis on performance and winning can create a negative environment, because of the pressures imposed by the athlete himself and because of outside pressures. Having fun, even at the professional level, is mandatory for success. The love for the game is something we can transfer through our teachings.

Congratulations to you for making the effort to be the best coach you can be. Our passion for helping athletes to reach their highest potential is our motivation, and this flame remains ignited because we are contributing to the development and education of young athletes who look to us for guidance. We are a great influence on the players who admire us, and our responsibility is to offer our best. Reading articles and attending clinics can only help us become better coaches and people. Planning and running effective practices is a very important piece of the football coaching puzzle.

19

Maximizing Player Abilities

Ryan Hall

A coach's job is to help people be the best they can be. But when you get honest answers from many coaches about why they do what they do, you'll probably find that their primary goals are to win, to gain notoriety or respect, or to advance their own position. In short, coaching for many is about ego. But ego-boosting results should be viewed as by-products of fulfilling your real and primary role. Great coaches don't view players as pawns or tools there to serve a coach's ego. They view them as individuals who can grow and mature in many ways, and who can do it best with positive leadership and mentorship. As you honestly consider your motivations as a coach, I hope you will make the development of your players your first priority.

While this chapter is mainly intended for youth and high school coaches, there will be some ideas that apply to higher-level coaches as well. As we look more closely at maximizing player abilities, we will focus on some key mechanical areas of athletic development, but we'll also consider some character-related intangibles. Any experienced coach can cite many examples of players who had significant physical abilities and tons of athletic potential that went to waste because of character flaws. The following strategies will help you to teach and train your athletes to be the best that they can be, which will naturally contribute to the competitive level and success of your team.

GIVE PLAYERS A CHANCE TO SHOW THEIR SKILLS

At the start of the season, you may get a crop of athletes who are completely new to you, or you may have a combination of returning players and rookies. Many youth and high school coaches devote the first practice or two to rotating the entire team through a circuit of positional stations. That way they can introduce a wide variety of basic football skills, and they see what the players can do. Usually six stations work well: blocking (on the line and in the open field), block defending, tackling, ball carrying, passing and receiving, and pass coverage. Position coaches can go through the same progressions with each group, and they can identify players who seem well suited to specific positions. Assigning players to their positions should be done in cooperation with all coaches, to ensure a balanced team in all positions.

During training camp, devote significant time to developing team skills, the skills that every player has to perform: blocking and tackling. All players (and coaches) should go through a skill-development progression for blocking and tackling at the beginning of the season, based on Football Canada's Safe Contact program (see chapter 4). This not only lets you develop their body positions and movements, it also gives you a great opportunity to teach important concepts such as using pursuit angles, working for effective leverage or angles on an opponent, and working with teammates to block and tackle.

Throughout the season, it is helpful to put the team through a skill circuit in practice at the beginning of every week. In a skill circuit, each coach does a drill that focuses on blocking, tackling, or ball security from a variety of offensive, defensive, and special-teams perspectives. Each station should be done for around four minutes. This allows your coaching staff to work with all players on the team; as players improve their skills, they may catch a coach's eye in a drill and earn an opportunity to move up the depth chart or get on a special team.

MAKE SKILL DEVELOPMENT THE FOCUS OF PRACTICES

Many coaches decide to use individual positional-skill periods as extra warm-up time, and then spend large amounts of time scrimmaging. Scrimmages are by far the least effective setting for players to develop their skills. There are 24 players running around, and the coaches are probably putting most of their focus on what is happening around the ball. The majority of players on the field get little or no feedback. Rather than putting so much emphasis on systems, put a significant emphasis on individual skills.

This starts with great individual periods. An individual period is only as good as the coach leading it. The position coach must have a good understanding of the important skills players need, and the progression of drills that will help the players develop their skills.

Many great books can give you a deeper understanding of effective teaching strategies and practice techniques. Some I recommend: *Peak, Practice Perfect, The Talent Code, Talent Is Overrated,* and *Outliers.*

Most of these books are based on the research of psychologist Anders Ericsson (the author of *Peak*), who is one of the world's leading authorities on high performance. Ericsson's theory is that it is not just practice that leads to improvement and excellence, but *purposeful* practice. Purposeful practice depends on the mindset and mental focus of the person who is practicing, but the coach plays a key role in facilitating it. Here are the main aspects of purposeful practice:

- ◆ The individual has "ignition," passion for the activity and intrinsic motivation to improve.

Learn From the Best

Peak: How to Master Almost Anything by Anders Ericsson and Robert Pool, Houghton Mifflin Harcourt, 2016.

Practice Perfect: 42 Rules for Getting Better at Getting Better by Doug Lemov, Erica Woolway, and Katie Yezzi, Jossey-Bass, 2012.

The Talent Code: Greatness Isn't Born. It's Grown. Here's How by Daniel Coyle, Bantam, 2009.

Talent Is Overrated: What Really Separates World-Class Performers From Everybody Else by Geoff Colvin, Portfolio, 2010.

Outliers: The Story of Success by Malcolm Gladwell, Back Bay Books, 2011.

- Practice is planned by an expert (the coach), someone who can help the individual improve existing skills.
- Practice is planned with a specific focus and goal for improvement.
- Individuals know exactly what skills they are trying to improve, and the coach has designed a plan to help them improve.
- The individual had been given a clear "mental representation" of what the skill should look and feel like through explanation, demonstration, viewing video, and so on.
- The individual is putting intense mental focus and concentration into a specific aspect of performance.
- The individual will be in the challenge zone (operating beyond his current abilities), not the comfort zone (operating within his current abilities) (see figure 19.1).
- Mistakes will be common, and the individual will go back and work on correcting his mistake as quickly as possible (mistakes should bother the individual enough that they are motivated to correct them).
- To work toward realization of the mental representation, the coach provides specific feedback to the individual after every repetition to describe what was done well or what needs to be done better or differently and how to do it.
- It is not "fun"; it is challenging and mentally tiring.

A full two-hour purposeful practice is too mentally demanding for players and demands too much input from the coach. Even performers who are highly trained in implementing purposeful practice hit their maximum at 60 to 90 consecutive minutes. Young athletes will need much shorter time periods, but they should get more adept as the season goes on. Many segments of a football practice would not be considered purposeful practice (warm-up, many conditioning drills), and

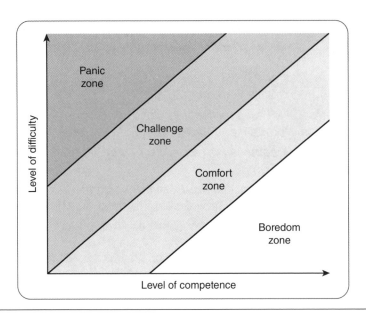

FIGURE 19.1 Zones of performance in practice.

individual players get many breaks from mental focus with water breaks or waiting out drills that don't involve them.

After an individual period in which athletes work hard to develop their existing skills and learn new skills, the next progression is to put them into one-on-one competitions. These drills should give the athletes a chance to take the skills they were working on and use them in a full-speed, competitive environment. This is another great opportunity for coaches to give specific, individual feedback. This does a lot more for individual improvement than putting everyone into a scrimmage, where most of the players aren't observed or given feedback. One-on-ones can definitely be done with a purposeful practice approach.

The ball can be the biggest distraction from skill development. As soon as a ball is involved, players tend to lose focus on everything but the ball. This is especially true for receivers, defensive backs, and quarterbacks. Consider having players in those positions run through drills without a football when the focus should be on technique: footwork, changes of direction, throwing technique, finishing, and so on. Legendary basketball coach John Wooden used this approach with his national champion teams at UCLA for years. Even pass one-on-ones can be done without a ball, leaving defensive backs to focus only on excellent footwork and eye discipline, receivers to focus on great route running and turning upfield after the catch, and quarterbacks to execute perfect pass drops and throwing technique. Try spending one third of the one-on-one period without a ball, and then bring the ball in when the players have demonstrated good focus on skills.

As you continue to more gamelike simulations (pass skeleton, inside run, special teams, scrimmage), you can prepare athletes by using high-tempo and gamelike circumstances. Keep the repetitions happening quickly so that the players have to remain focused and have a sense of urgency. As the season progresses, coaches (especially offensive ones) should get out of the huddle and use the signals or substitutions they will use in games to call plays. You can assign a coach to be the timekeeper and to whistle in the 20-second play clock to force the offense to stay within gamelike parameters. Remember that high tempo does not have to mean high contact. Make sure to manage the levels of contact throughout your practice because injured players are immediately unable to improve.

Another gamelike aspect you can train is different time and score scenarios (the following drills are described in more detail in chapter 16, Managing the Clock). If your team is leading late in the game and you want to teach the players on offense to use as much time as possible, put them into a four-minute drill. If the offense is trailing by a score but there are still a few minutes left in the game, put them into a three-minute drill so they speed up but don't panic. If the offense needs to score and time is running out, put them into a one-minute drill so that they do everything they can to conserve time and gain yards. These drills not only teach situational football and time management, but they also increase the intensity of the practice. If players understand how to play in these different situations, they will be much more equipped to use their abilities effectively to help the team. Athletes should be able to approach simulations and situations with a purposeful practice mindset.

Using backup players on scout teams can give them a good opportunity to show what they can do. The depth chart can become static, sometimes with the result that starting players grow complacent and backups lose motivation. By encouraging backups to show their skills and effort on scout team, you give them a good opportunity to show what they could do with more playing time.

If you have younger, less experienced players on your team who are not benefiting the team with their participation in these simulation drills, you can use one or two of your position coaches to take those players aside to do additional skill development. Rather than keeping them standing on the sidelines for a 10- or 15-minute team period or scout period, get them actively engaged in working on specific positional drills or basic team skills.

Another smart move is to get beyond "bag running" with the conditioning period. Put the players in high-intensity situations to work on football skills. For example, the defense can do high-tempo pursuit drills, or the offense can do high-tempo hurry-up offense with a 25-yard sprint on every play. You can do special-teams drills for kickoff coverage, or punt return and coverage for conditioning. You can even change your bag sprint concept from just running the players' "bags" off to a shuttle where they run out, tackle a bag, and then run back to tag the next person in line. Of course, they should be working on proper tackling technique on the bag. Use your imagination and you can get the players working very hard without their realizing. They'll be busy working on skills, possibly competing, and probably having fun.

THINK OUTSIDE OF THE BOX

The right position is often the key to maximizing a player's abilities. In most cases the match is obvious, but sometimes an athlete doesn't fit where you think he should. The player's a good athlete and in good shape, but he isn't working in the position that logically seems right for him.

A grade 10 student came to our high school spring camp a few years ago. He was about 5'7" tall and loved the weight room, so he had strength. He also had several years of good playing experience from minor football. We tried him at defensive back, but he lacked the footwork to cover receivers. We moved him to linebacker, but we found he couldn't react; he was lost and confused by the offense. He wasn't dumb (in fact he was quite a strong student), but he just didn't process things on the football field. Plays didn't stay in his head. We decided to move him to fullback in the fall. There, our thinking went, he'd know the play coming out of the huddle.

He remained a backup for the year. In the winter after his grade 11 season, he was working out after school. I looked at him working hard, and I was frustrated that we hadn't found a place for him to excel. I thought about his traits—strong, fast, but not adept at decision-making—and I tried to think of what position could use them. The answer that came to me (and maybe to you too) was defensive end. There aren't many 5'7" defensive ends in high school football, but it seemed to be my last hope. I proposed the position change to him, and he enthusiastically agreed. To make a long story short, he ended up having a great season as our starting rush end, was a league all-star, and helped our team win a provincial championship.

Make sure you don't get blinded by the look test. A player may look like an obvious match for a particular position. He may look like he could never do some other position. But be ready to think outside the box. Our program has had a lot of success with players whose body type proved less important than their skills and attributes. They became very effective players after we found positions that called for their key traits, not their superficial ones. Of course, "inside the box" thinking has some value, and doing physical testing at least twice a year (at spring camp and fall camp) gives you data on your players' physical abilities and their levels of improvement (or lack thereof), which reflects their "outside the box" abilities, such as commitment and work ethic. Here are some traits that you may consider inside the box, followed by some that are more outside the box:

Inside the Box

- ◆ Size
- ◆ Speed
- ◆ Strength
- ◆ Quickness, reaction time, and agility
- ◆ Coordination (eye-hand or foot-hand)
- ◆ Power

Outside the Box

- ◆ Toughness (physical and mental)
- ◆ Decision-making and reacting
- ◆ Leadership
- ◆ Communication
- ◆ Work ethic
- ◆ Tenacity and determination

Substitutions can also benefit from outside-the-box thinking. At elite and professional levels of football, situational substitutions are common, but in youth and high school football, often the only situations that include substitutions are for short yardage. This can be an effective way to maximize player abilities by putting the best-suited players on the field for certain situations. In a pass defense situation, you can insert a backup player who is a skilled blitzer or cover player to replace a player who specializes in run stopping. If your receiver just had a big run, you can substitute a backup; likely the defense kept the same defensive back on the field and he will probably be tired, so you may want to go after him with your fresh player.

Special teams are another context to think outside of the box. Sometimes you will have players who aren't good enough to start on offense or defense, but they flourish on special teams. Again, running weekly skill circuits and conditioning drills that involve special-teams skills and situations will help you identify these players and utilize their skills extensively in the kicking game. Once they get comfortable performing on special teams, their building confidence may help them move up the depth chart on offense or defense as well.

Two-way players provide another opportunity for thinking outside the box. Many coaches utilize the same star players on both sides of the ball, and many players view playing both ways as a badge of honor. In my coaching philosophy, this practice is directly counter to maximizing player abilities. Two-way players get, at most, half of the amount of skill-development time in practice that one-way players get. Also, every two-way player on the field is keeping another player on the bench, forcing him to sit out the chance to develop in a game situation. The coaches who go that route want to improve their chances of winning, not help the athletes develop. A better way to utilize the two-way player concept is to get good players involved in special teams. The players who aren't as skilled, but who have earned a spot on special teams, can reach a higher level if they play alongside the more developed players.

GET THEM IN THE GAME

While practice is the prime opportunity to develop player abilities, there is no substitute for getting them in a live game. The speed, intensity, and pressure reach a level that can't be simulated in practice. If you want your team to be successful, you have to find ways for your backups, not just your starters, to experience game situations.

A wise coach will use preseason games to get meaningful repetitions for the backup players, because every team loses starters to injury, illness, or other factors throughout the season, and the backups should be prepared to step in. When you plan an exhibition game, make sure to discuss substitutions with the opposing coach so that you can monitor matchups effectively.

Midseason exhibition games are also a great idea. If you have a bye week, planning an exhibition game will keep your team focused on practice (something that is often challenging during bye weeks). It also gives you the opportunity to put backup players into starting roles for the week, and forces them to assume the responsibility of a starter. Your regular starting players can mentor the other players, which deepens their own understanding of their skills and playing responsibilities.

Another way to get more players into the games is to substitute them, as mentioned previously. Besides the situations already described, you can run your play calls into the huddle with substitute players.

Finally, there's the lopsided game. Whether you are winning by a lot or losing by a lot, this is a great opportunity to get many players into the game. Communication with the opposing coach is advisable here, as both teams can make substitutions to try to have balanced matchups.

MAKE USE OF THE OFF-SEASON

In youth football, you may not have access to your players in the off-season, but if you are a school coach, your players are with you throughout the winter and spring. As we all know, the football season is very short in comparison to the off-season, so not taking advantage of those off-season months is a huge lost opportunity.

Encourage athletes to be involved in other sports. Research proves that, for youth athletes, involvement in a variety of sports is far more beneficial than specializing. Every year, more and more youth sports encourage (or demand) young athletes to stay in their sport year-round. In hockey, there is the fall and winter season, followed up by spring travel teams and summer three-on-three leagues. In soccer, the spring and summer seasons are followed up by indoor fall and winter seasons. High school volleyball and basketball seasons sometimes seem minor compared to long club seasons and summer programs. Hopefully, we in the Canadian football community can continue to facilitate multisport participation along with excellence in football.

There are many sports that have great crossover benefits for football. Basketball helps players with footwork, eye-hand coordination, and moving without the ball. Wrestling teaches players individual toughness and competitiveness as well as using physical leverage. Track and field events help players with speed, power, and running technique. Hockey utilizes angles, physicality, and leverage that are similar to football. And there are many other sports that help develop athleticism and skills that are valuable for football. Exposing players to different coaching helps too. There's a lot to learn from experiencing a variety of viewpoints.

Strength training during the off-season is also a good idea. For younger players who haven't finished their growth spurt yet, body-weight exercises are sufficient. As you develop an off-season program for high school–aged athletes, you should utilize a progression of training phases. Start with strength endurance (medium weight with higher repetitions), then move to hypertrophy (high-volume training to increase size), strength (heavy weight with lower repetitions), and speed strength (powerful movements with lower weight and low to medium repetitions). Most high school–aged athletes can participate in weight training, though players in their growing years should focus on strength endurance training, not heavy strength training.

Of course, football isn't all about being big and strong. Athletic movement skills can be developed off-season with the exercises in the NCCP Prevention and Recovery module (this is one of the multisport training sessions for NCCP Competition-Development certification; see Prevention and Recovery Reference Material, National Coaching Certification Program, Coaching Association of Canada Version 0.5, 2013).You can also utilize plyometric training with athletes who have a good base of strength and balance. Speed training is valuable as well. Start with coaching athletes on proper form and running technique, and then drill them on acceleration and speed drills. You can also train agility with speed ladder training or other footwork drills.

Great football opportunities also present themselves in the off-season. Many U Sports teams or provincial football organizations offer skill-development camps in the winter, spring, or summer. These camps usually run for a weekend or a week, so they are not a significant time commitment, but they should expose players to more quality coaching. For top players, provincial or select teams are a great developmental opportunity. These teams participate in short-term competitions such as the Football Canada Cup Under 18 tournament, an experience that typically includes several weekends of tryouts as well as intensive training camps (see chapter 15, Preparing for a Tournament). Trying out gives a player the chance to play with the best players, with top-quality coaches, and against tough competition. Some communities operate spring or summer football leagues. These can be very worthwhile, but your players should remember there's such a thing as too many football games. Because of the physical nature of the game, Football Canada's long-term athlete development plan cautions athletes against playing football for extended periods of time. Practicing and training are different than playing, where contact and risk of injury go way up. For more detail regarding these strategies of athletic development, see the introduction to the book.

FOCUS ON CHARACTER

For athletes to maximize their abilities, they have to be in good standing with the team, school (if it is a school team), community, and home. That means your coaching has to go beyond physical and mental performance—you have to coach character as well. The steps here represent the main ways of training character:

1. Describe the expected behavior and give examples and nonexamples of the expected behavior.
2. Make the desired behavior part of the team's goals and ethics.
3. Make sure the coaching staff models the behavior that is expected of the athletes.
4. Praise players for exhibiting the expected behavior and correct players if they do not exhibit the expected behavior.
5. Implement consequences for players if they continue to fail to exhibit the expected behavior.

It's up to you to decide what ethics you will expect from your players. There are several character traits that I consider foundational for my teams.

Respect is crucial for effective team functioning. Players must show respect for their coaches by looking at the coach when the coach is speaking, and by responding in positive ways (nodding their head, "Yes, Coach," etc.). Behaviors such as eye rolling, huffing, or "showing the coach their hands" (a term I learned from Coach Justin Ethier of Laval, describing a player holding his hands palms up and out to the side) should not be tolerated. Players should be able to communicate respectfully with their coach at all times, even when there is a disagreement. Of course, coaches must model respectfulness as well. When coaching youth teams, I also expected my players to be respectful of their parents anytime their parents were at practices or games. That was something the parents really appreciated.

Gratitude is another trait we train with our program. We have developed a team culture where it is common for players to stop and shake hands with their coach after practice and say thank you. At our team windups, parents and school administrators are blown away by the articulate tributes our graduating players pay the coaching staff and support staff. When people outside of our team watch our players leave off-season training sessions and stop to thank me for opening the training centre, they are very impressed. One thing we tell our players at the beginning of the season is that there are a few words that are impossible to say too often: please and thank you. In a culture where so many young people grow up with an attitude of entitlement, it is rare to see this kind of attitude of gratitude.

A countercultural trait we train and expect in our players is **humility** and a team-first attitude. Coaches talk about humility, but the idea is nothing unless it's effectively modeled and reinforced. Players should be humble in their interaction with coaches, teammates, opponents, media, and family. They should be willing to sacrifice personal preferences and aspirations for team success and goals. To help the players understand this, I quote Mr. Spock from *Star Trek II: The Wrath of Khan*: "The needs of the many outweigh the needs of the few . . . or the one."

Related to humility is **coachability**, a willingness and eagerness to learn and improve. Coachable players make an effort to take feedback and implement it immediately (see the section on Make Skill Development the Focus of Practices). Coachability goes beyond skills and systems; it also includes a willingness to be corrected on matters of character, and being willing to make the necessary effort to change.

Positive leadership seems to be rare these days, so that is another trait that we try to teach and encourage. We have a team leadership group, and any players who meet team expectations on and off the field can be a part of the group. The group meets in the off-season, and we talk to them about different characteristics and demonstrations of leadership. The beginning of leadership is service. When the players get an idea of how hard their coaches work for them, and all of the unglamorous jobs coaches do (fixing equipment, lining the field, washing uniforms, etc.), they get an understanding that leadership doesn't start with telling people what to do—it starts with doing what needs to be done. Of course, working hard and exhibiting positive character are other keys to establishing a position of leadership among teammates.

Accountability is another trait we reinforce. Players show leadership by keeping themselves and their teammates accountable, and this takes personal humility and a respect for the team. When a player fails to exhibit the character expected by the team and is called to account for his behavior, he has the choice of how to react. He can react with pride and arrogance and refuse to change or make amends for his behavior, or he can respond with humility, apologize to any team members who were affected, and change his behavior. It is amazing to see the effect a heartfelt apology has on a team. Even if a player has shown a serious lack of character, a humble apology will bring the team closer as they choose to forgive and help the individual exhibit more positive behavior. This release of guilt and the resulting team support often have a significantly positive effect on the individual's on-field performance, while the prideful refusal to genuinely apologize often results in an underperforming athlete.

The philosopher Heraclitus said, "Character equals destiny." To maximize player abilities, character really does count.

CONCLUSION

Hopefully, these strategies for maximizing player abilities will help you to enhance your approach to your role as a coach. Whether you are in practice, a game, or the off-season, there are a multitude of opportunities to help players be the best they can be. Throughout all of those times, don't forget that positive character is something that should become more and more engrained in their behavior on and off the field. This will ensure that they avoid situations such as suffering through team discipline, being grounded by parents, or being on academic probation, situations that keep athletes from getting the best out of themselves on the field.

Coaching is a serious role. You are the most significant catalyst in the development of your players. As you consider this responsibility, remember that you are working with young people. Yes, they want to get better as players, but most of all they want to have fun. Demonstrate passion and an infectious love for the game in your coaching. Develop a positive relationship with players by getting to know them and their aspirations. Remember that they are people first and athletes second. Make sure to have some fun with them while you are teaching, challenging, and driving them to be the best that they can be.

20

Watching Game Film

Marcel Bellefeuille

Watching film is an art. In fact, game film has so many aspects that you can get lost watching it. Know exactly what you're trying to accomplish when you look at film. Some of the best coaches and players have made this phase of their preparation a clear and concise process. Doing so makes all the difference in efficient use of preparation time. Another point: different readers, depending on the level of football they coach at, will have different levels of resources. Extract from this chapter the information that matches your needs and resources.

GENERAL INFORMATION

Every time we turn on the film, we have to know what we're looking for. We don't watch with blinders on, but we do maintain our focus. Some of the many reasons to watch film include data input, game review, practice review, self-scouting, offensive game planning, defensive game planning, special-teams game planning, player evaluations, player development, and preparation of meeting cutups. We also use a variety of film angles, among them wide angle (which is from a high vantage point and encompasses all of the action), tight angle (which is shot from a higher angle behind the end zone and focuses on the line play), and field level (which is taken from a handheld camera on the field behind the area being focused on).

DATA INPUT

Before we start analyzing film, we do the breakdowns (sometimes called tagging the video). This will make the job of filtering what we want to see much easier. It's now possible for most levels of football to invest in some sort of video-editing program, such as Hudl, VidSwap, or DVSport. Prices have come down, the programs can adapt to most computer systems, and finding people to work with the systems has become much easier as computer skills spread.

Create your filters based on the information you want to look at. The good news is that most video-editing systems will also create the scouting report breakdown that you will need. Be sure to include the following baseline filters in your system: play-by-play data (down and distance, field position, hash mark, run or pass, etc.), offensive breakdowns (personnel groupings, formations, motions, play type, etc.), defensive breakdowns (personnel, front, dogs, blitzes, coverages, etc.), and special-teams breakdowns (play type, formations, etc.).

SELF-SCOUTING

Before we start breaking down our opponents each week, we have to know what our own team is doing. Whether focusing on offense, defense, or special teams, we want to watch the film from our opponent's point of view. There are three specific things that we look at.

First, we want to watch ourselves to verify whether our reports are accurate about our tendencies. If our reports tell us that we have 100 percent called runs in second and 1–3 situations, and that our conversion rate is 98 percent, we want to see how we converted. Did we get the line of scrimmage blocked as we designed the plays? Is our running back making yards after contact in blitz situations? Did we call a pass and it ended up in a run? This will help determine what we might change in our game plan in this particular situation.

Second, we want to watch our players. Are they showing our opponents tendencies that might be exploited? Usually, we can find these answers from their alignment, stance, and takeoff. Offensive linemen who are pulling will sometimes cheat their stance back and tighter to the player next to them. I can remember two teams I coached against whose offensive linemen gave away run or pass; you just had to look at whether they were in a two- or three-point stance. We had calls on the field to take advantage of the tell. Another team, one that we played multiple times in one season, had a linebacker who gave up the blitz tendency. From the depth of his alignment, we could tell if the cover 0 blitz look was real or for show. Our quarterback knew whether to throw hot or play out his reads.

The third aspect we want to look at is our schemes. Are they effective or are our players making them effective? For example, we may have a pass play that is not being credited with a positive conversion rate. Did we have a dropped ball? Did the quarterback miss a wide-open receiver? Was there a breakdown in protection? Perhaps the play just isn't that effective in the situation where it was called. Sometimes a good player makes a poorly designed play work because of his individual ability.

Regardless of whether you are looking at your own tendencies in play calling or your players' execution of the schemes, self-scout film is important. Watching your own players' tendencies will take away any advantage your opponent may have from their film study. Understanding not just what you are calling, but how you are converting will help you adjust your game plans from week to week.

PRACTICE FILM

Viewing practice film is probably one of the most comprehensive football activities that players and coaches execute during their weekly preparation. This is where coaches and players work collectively to implement a game plan. The following are some key areas that should be focused on:

- *Schemes*. Does the scheme translate from the whiteboard to the field? This will tell you if there needs to be an adjustment.
- *Execution*. Are the players able to mentally and physically execute what was drawn up? This will tell you if you should run the new schemes.
- *Technique*. Are the players using proper and effective technique? Fundamentals win football games.
- *Effort and tempo*. The speed at which you practice will show up on film. Find examples to show your players what the correct speed and effort are at practice.

Note: Any use of film is critical to your success. If you are limited, a handheld video camera in the stands can give you a sideline view. You can use a handheld camera on a stepladder from the back of the play to film a tight-angle shot from tackle to tackle. Utilize a tablet on field level to film individual players (i.e., quarterback, kickers, offensive line versus defensive line, one-on-one periods).

OPPONENT SCOUT

Whether you are viewing offense, defense, or special teams, this is an area where you will need to decide how your time will be spent. I truly believe that viewing cutups (film spliced by down and distance or formations) is the best move. But you have to decide what works best for you. Most times your reports will tell you what cutup filters are most important. Having said that, I always liked to go back after viewing cutups and watch full linear (chronological) clips to get a feel for the flow of the complete game. It is important to try to show the players and coaches the film by both cutups and linear clips.

Before selecting the filters to watch opponent film, know what you are going to delete. When the score is one-sided late in the game, the film may not be helpful unless you find yourself in that situation (i.e., a Hail Mary pass, or giving up a safety at the end of a game). That becomes a special situation. Teams that play completely different styles of football may not give you film that is as valuable in this area. For example, as an offensive coordinator preparing for a defense, watching opponent film of that defense against a wing T team may not give you what you are looking for. Therefore, you may need to add a different game to the opponent breakdown, one that more closely resembles your style of offense.

As a general rule, your cutups will include your opponent's last three games. If this does not apply to your level or film availability, find what film you can to evaluate. You should also have a cutup of any games your team has previously played against your current opponent. The following is a suggested starting point to splice your film:

◆ *Field zones.* Include backed-up, move zone, and score zone (red zone). The yard lines you use when backed up and in the score zone are determined by when the offense, defense, or special teams in your league play differently than in the move zone.

◆ *Down and distance.* Cut up the film by your preferred down and distances. Typically, you will have at least these filters in Canadian football: first downs, second down and medium, second down and long, and all short-yardage situations.

◆ *Personnel.* Regardless of whether it is offense or defense, there should be a personnel filter. Defensive coaches use this filter more because of the multiple personnel groupings that offenses deploy. The various uses of tight ends, receivers, running backs, and extra offensive linemen on every down are important when dissecting what tendencies a team may have. Offensive coaches will also want to see how defenses are deployed versus these personnel groups, and they'll want to see what different defensive personnel may be used. For example, offensive coaches may want to know how much man coverage defenses play when they have tight ends in the game. Defensive coaches may want to know what the run-pass tendencies are for offensive coaches who deploy tight end packages.

◆ *Formations.* Formations give excellent information in all three phases of the game. They dictate how teams cover down (who lines up over the eligible receivers) and align on defense. Offenses may give some tendencies by formation, and special-teams cover down and alignment rules change significantly by formation (some offenses may only run or pass the football out of certain formations).

VIEWING THE FILM

Now that you have your filters, you can begin to watch the cutups. Cross-reference the cutups by all four filters: field zone, down and distance, personnel, and formations. For example, you may begin watching first and 10 in the move zone versus base personnel in all balance formations (whatever that is at your level). This will be the most intensive portion of your film study, one that supplies much of your game plan. This is where you will study your opponent's tendencies, schemes, personnel, and formations.

◆ *Tendencies.* When you watch the film, your study and reports will reveal your opponent's tendencies. Now you can study the different alignments and movements that are played out on the film. For example, if they are a man coverage team, what is their defensive backs' depth and alignments? Do certain tendencies only fit versus different personnel groups?

◆ *Schemes.* What schemes do they play? For example, how do they block a play? Do they zone-block only? Is there a weakness that can be exploited? You will also have to draw up these schemes for practice and meetings.

◆ *Personnel.* When you look at the personnel, what matchups are most favorable? For example, how do you get your best receiver aligned over the weakest secondary player? Who should you line up over their best kickoff cover player? Do certain players give away scheme with their alignments? Know what your physical mismatches are.

◆ *Formations.* This will be a key to see how your opponent aligns in formations and how they play against your formations. Many of your offensive schemes will be designed from your multiple formations. For example, your opponent may play "9 techniques" (wide defensive ends) versus your tight-end sets. This could be beneficial information when selecting or designing run plays versus these fronts.

SPECIAL SITUATIONS

Watch all the film you can to prepare for an opponent. When you study special situations, you may have to go into the archives. It's worth it to get the best possible idea of what you may see from your opponent. Viewing these types of plays are the same as your regular opponent scout. Some of these situations are:

◆ *Hail Mary.* This is at the end of the half or the game.

◆ *Sudden change.* What your opponent does after a turnover.

◆ *Catch and kick.* Throw, catch, and kick situations at the end of the game or the half.

◆ *Freeze.* The opponent tries to draw you offside without any attempt to snap the football.

◆ *Two-point convert plays.*

◆ *Quick kick plays.*

◆ *Trick plays and gimmicks.* Prepare a tape of all trick plays and gimmick formations. It should be easier to identify these tendencies by both personnel and formations.

◆ *Special-teams fakes.* When watching special-team fakes, you can usually identify keys by checking personnel and alignments. The subtle alignment changes make it easier to get presnap tendencies. Field zone and distance to go on third down are also excellent barometers. When you're devising fakes from watching film, your opponent's cover down rules in special teams will be a critical indicator of whether you can get off a fake.

PLAYER EVALUATIONS

The player evaluation process has many aspects. In my estimation, film study is the most important and heavily weighted component. When evaluating players, recruits, free agents, or draft-eligible players on film, there are some baseline criteria to watch:

◆ *Physical attributes.* Size, speed, and agility show up through testing. But does the player have good game speed? Does he play with leverage? Does a big player play big? Is the player athletic? Does he move well in space?

◆ *Technique.* There are two areas to look at here: position-specific technique and football fundamentals. For position-specific technique, watch the film to see if the player has good technique that relates to his position. Does a defensive back have good footwork? Is the technique specific to how we play? Does an offensive lineman have good footwork? These are completely different to evaluate. When evaluating football fundamentals, watch the film to see if the player has good basic football fundamentals. Does the player block or tackle with good technique? These skills are required for most positions.

◆ *Intangibles.* Does the player have great effort? Good instincts? Does he play to the whistle? Does he pursue hard from the backside when not in a position to make a play? Does he take a lot of penalties?

◆ *Playmakers.* Note if the player makes the plays that are available to him. If he has only 2 opportunities in a game, does he make both plays? If he has 12 opportunities, does he make 8 plays? What do these numbers mean to you? Does he make plays in critical periods in the game? Look to see if he is winning one-on-one matchups. Evaluate the quality of the players he is working against to give your film study better perspective. If it is an offensive lineman, does he make blocks at the point of attack? These are just some of the things we can extrapolate from watching film.

CONCLUSION

Watching film has become an integral part of preparation for both players and coaches. We all get caught up watching hours on hours of film. My advice is: have a plan. Structure your time viewing film and understand what you want to achieve. It's part of being detailed and will define your approach to the game. Clarity will help your coaches and players focus and internalize what you are trying to achieve.

PART FIVE

PROGRAM BUILDING AND MANAGEMENT

21

Building a High School Program

Mike Circelli

Hard work makes all the difference. I've found success coaching high school football that way, and I've surrounded myself with others who are also committed to success. As a coach, I've helped reinstate and improve the pride and sense of tradition at the high school where I was a student, and I continue to learn about my chosen field by working with other coaches who can teach me more.

My parents showed me all about hard work. They immigrated to London, Ontario, from Italy in 1955, wanting to better provide for their two sons. Peasant farmers who manually laboured in the southern wheat belt of Italy, they could see no chance of any improvement without a drastic change, so we joined extended family living in Canada. My parents had no English and very little money, but they worked hard and found opportunities for success. They believed that good things happen to those who work hard, and so it came to be for them.

School is where I learned about football. Several teacher–coaches had a passion for the game that inspired me to follow in their footsteps. They taught and modeled the value of hard work, in school and football, and they motivated me to be the best player I could.

After graduating from teachers college, I started my teaching career at a small school of 400 students, with only 80 to 90 boys. I tried to start a football program. After a two-week camp with borrowed equipment and great interest from the male students, administration vetoed the proposal of a varsity team. I was still determined to coach! My alma mater, Catholic Central High School (CCH), hired me back to London, to teach and to coach football and wrestling. Under the leadership of Mike Tucker, the physical education and athletic department head, I began a plan to strive for excellence. As assistant coach, I was allowed to start making changes. I recognized that the best football teams had solid offensive and defensive lines, with the best athlete as quarterback. It was necessary to teach fundamentals to all the positions, as opposed to incorporating numerous schemes and thereby eating up practice time. Too many high school coaches make that mistake. It's more important to master a few offensive plans and select key defensive schemes that players can handle.

My first season coaching the Crusaders was in 1984. After it was over, I realized that we had to work harder. Coaches and players had to make greater commitments to our becoming a top-level program. As I thought about that, I began to integrate some principles that helped me lead our program to consistent levels of success for many years.

TEAM VERSUS PROGRAM

Many coaches run a high school football team, but not as many coaches run a high school football program. Basically, a team operates during the football season, and its sole focus is football (skills, systems, and wins). A program usually operates beyond the competitive season, and it focuses on the overall development of the team members: physically, mentally, socially, and emotionally. Leading a program is a big task; that's especially so when, as is often the case in Canada, the person doing it is a volunteer who's also holding down a full-time job. Chapter 1, Responsibilities of a Coach, provides more detail about the wide variety of things head coaches do, and it supplies ideas for using other people to share the load.

EXPECTATIONS

Players need expectations to follow. At my high school, the new season began every February with a meeting at which coaches learned which players were returning and players learned what was required from them for the next four months. The calendar was set for weight-lifting tests, spring and summer camps, and the upcoming season schedule. Each prospective player received an official summary of the team's timeline, goals and objectives, registration forms, and fundraising initiatives. The players needed to know that two-a-day workouts began one week prior to Labour Day.

In late August, the team reconvened and the rules for the season were presented. I was never fond of having many rules, as each one required set consequences. I tried to keep things simple to avoid time-consuming meetings with administration, parents, and players. The players were to respect these rules:

- You must attend all practices, even if you are injured. You should be ready to help with basic team tasks or rehab your injury.
- Call the head coach if you're going to miss school or practice.
- Tobacco, drugs, and alcohol are not allowed during school.
- Foul and obscene language is not tolerated.
- Good academic participation and effort are expected.

I tried to handle all issues with as much consistency and common sense as possible while staying true to the values of our program.

COACHING DEVELOPMENT

I started to educate myself more in coaching and mentoring, using books and videos and attending coaching clinics. My biggest challenge was to instill my philosophy in my coaches and players (see chapter 3, Establishing a Coaching Philosophy). I wanted them to know that I would be firm but fair when making decisions. The coaches needed to become role models. Cursing, including by coaches, would not be tolerated; 25 push-ups on the spot was the simple punishment. A student doing push-ups in the hall demonstrated the fact that discipline was expected beyond the football field. As a football coaching staff, we collectively pushed our athletes to achieve their best and to be prepared for the next level of football by having clear standards and high expectations. During my years at CCH, more than 70 players went on to the CIS and eight went to the NCAA.

You are only as good as your coaches. After I became department head of athletics and physical education, I would ask our school administrators to hire new teachers with the ability to coach. Full-time teachers in high school receive fair wages, and most teacher–coaches take pleasure in giving to their students what someone gave to them.

Without enough teacher–coaches, it was necessary to bring in volunteers from the community. I'd search for the most qualified people, and I'd make the work enjoyable for them to ensure they would continue with the team. With a budget from student council, I purchased clothing items that would serve as our game-day coach's uniform, acknowledging the team staff. I treated teacher–coaches with respect, but community volunteers deserved even more esteem; often they'd leave work early to be present, or they would juggle their university timetables to fit the midafternoon practice time. Former players, with their pride for the tradition of CCH, were passionate and eager to volunteer, especially those who saw their careers as being in education. In 2005, while preparing for the OFSAA Bowl at the end of a very cold November, I supplied parkas and toques with the CCH insignia to my coaching staff (two teachers and six community volunteers) to show them my appreciation. You are only as good as your coaches.

There are always opportunities to improve for coaches of all levels. Attending clinics for professional development with the entire coaching staff is an effective means of improving the levels of knowledge of football tactics and techniques. Through the years, the Crusader coaching staff attended university clinics at Western, Michigan, Notre Dame, and Penn State, as well as the Nike clinic in central Michigan and the Football Canada clinic in Burlington, Ontario. Clinics during the off-season are also an excellent way to build relationships with coaches from outside the community. If this is not economically feasible, a coaching retreat for your staff can be useful for exchanging X's and O's, and debating systems based on personnel.

SCHOOL SUPPORT

At CCH, I had to rely on various staff to help me throughout the season. The secretaries were instrumental as they ordered buses, organized banquet tickets, prepared fundraising programs, and helped with other details. The custodial staff and the school maintenance staff were also incredibly supportive. Despite the mud that was tracked in from the field throughout hallways and dressing rooms, the custodians were always accommodating (and if they needed help with a big job, they knew they could count on us). The maintenance staff was efficient as they repaired the field, the equipment shed, or broken lockers that held player equipment. Capable student managers were assigned to handle everyday tasks, such as cleaning the equipment shed, handling water bottles, making minor repairs to equipment, taping players for games, and so on.

School administration and most teachers were proud of the association with a championship-quality team, but if players displayed inappropriate behavior or were doing poorly with their schoolwork, I would be called on to help solve the issues, both during the season and after. Discipline was another responsibility I had to contend with, but I did appreciate that both teachers and principals gave me the opportunity to help quickly resolve problems. More serious issues regarding drugs, alcohol, and property damage consumed much more time and energy on my part. When you are dealing with high school–aged people, you are going to encounter these situations no matter how hard your program works to develop good school citizens. Don't be discouraged when these frustrating situations occur; stick to your program's values, and help be a part of resolving the situation and helping the young person learn from his mistakes.

FINANCES

Money was vital. Through fundraising, including bingos, garage sales, discount cards, pop machines, and participation fees, we raised the money we needed to enhance our program. Revenue can also be generated by the formation of parents clubs, inclusion of night games, and pursuit of alumni support. After my retirement, some of these endeavors were implemented with great success. Now the program had spots for 50 to 60 players whom the coaches felt would benefit from the football experience. The equipment inventory was improved and Crusader football became the most important sport program at CCH, both because of the number of students involved and the direction our program was taking. The players were required to give a full commitment, to focus on their schoolwork, their families, and football. It was essential that each player become a quality citizen.

ROSTER DEVELOPMENT

As head coach in 1985, I made more changes. The Crusader team usually carried 40 to 45 players, and many of them were seniors. With 60 students showing interest, it was imperative to make a balanced roster that would help us build a successful program year after year. In order to compete for a championship every year, it was more beneficial to have a large number of returning players. We encouraged younger players to try out for the team, and we made room if we felt that being on the team would be a good developmental experience for them. Often, a younger player who spent a season primarily as a backup would learn and develop enough to step in and be a starter for his final couple of seasons.

The player is an essential element of a successful team. When I took over as head coach, I assumed that the athletes would just sign up. I soon learned that, no, I would need to search the school for athletic prospects. The physical education classes were my audience as I spoke about the importance and value of involvement in all athletics and club opportunities provided at the school, not just football. In addition to an in-school campaign, coaches and players would visit our elementary feeder schools. The incoming grade nine students were the target, but all the students would benefit from participation and the development of school pride. This is how Ryan Thelwell, a volleyball and basketball star, was convinced to try football in grade 12. Upon leaving CCH, he received a full scholarship to the University of Minnesota in the Big Ten. He went on to become a seventh-round pick of the San Francisco 49ers and moved on to a 14-year pro career with the BC Lions.

At our school we experienced a reality that is becoming more and more common in Canada, especially in urban centres. Our overall enrollment declined, but our percentage of newcomers to Canada increased. Many of our students had no cultural connection with football, so we developed a plan to introduce them to the game in as unintimidating a way as possible. Participating in a basic football orientation camp gave some of these students the confidence to attend our spring camp. Of course, our coaches had to adjust their approach to this new reality, and to make sure that their delivery was appropriate to students who were new to football and didn't speak English as their first language.

PROMOTION

The road to success isn't traveled overnight, and the journey involved a strong work ethic. The team needed to be reminded of their achievements, the legacy of our program, and the tradition that had become Crusader football. I developed an official CCH football letterhead for all communications so we would be more professional.

Before it was the norm, I decided that I needed film. Chapter 20 focuses specifically on using film, and many of the chapters make reference to it. In this day and age, using game and practice film is not only normal, it's necessary. One great use of game footage is to create yearly highlight videos for your team. These were very popular at our season-end windups, and these days they can also be viewed on the Internet. I was fortunate that my brother, Sal, unfailingly performed the task of creating a quality highlight video. When the season ended, highlight clips were used to create an outstanding record of the achievements at the awards banquet. To this day, many football alumni continue to request copies.

Developing and promoting team tradition is also very important to promote your program. Team photos and player action shots from the many years of your program's existence are very popular with current players and with alumni who return to the school. If you have room in your dressing room, hallway, or office, put up as many photos as possible to represent the history and tradition of the team. If you can, highlight the players who went on to significant levels of success playing football beyond high school. That gives your current players a significant aspiration.

Instilling and maintaining the pride and tradition from year to year was critical. On entering and exiting the dressing rooms, the players would see phrases like this: "Play like a champion today" (with our championship years listed below), "To you from failing hands we pass the torch; be yours to hold it high" (from "In Flanders Fields" and used also in the Montreal Canadiens' dressing room), and then simply "Tradition," "Pride," and "Excellence."

Team clothing counts too. Having a traditional melton-and-leather football jacket year after year binds your current players with the alumni. Yearly team clothing is also a great promotion for your program. Whether it is a sweatshirt, jacket, hat, T-shirt, or shorts, players love wearing team gear because it gives them a sense of identity and belonging. Do what you can to have unique and attractive team clothing. If you don't have that sense of style needed to create designs, find someone who does.

On game days, it is important to promote your team within the school Make sure that the players are all dressed the same to let everyone know that it is game day. Some teams have their players wear their jerseys on game day, while others get their players to dress in a shirt and tie, or to all wear the same team clothing. Go with whatever works best for your players, but make sure they look sharp.

A strong tradition is built from doing similar good things year after year. Team bonding events are very important, whether they take the form of an annual retreat, a rivalry or homecoming game, or even a nonfootball event such as a preseason paintball day or a New Year's Eve pond hockey game. These events create memories that players will cherish for years.

One more very important way to promote your program and build on tradition is to have a strong alumni connection. Use social media, mail-outs, newsletters, and local media outlets to let former players know what is going on with the team. Invite them to events (games, gatherings, etc.) as often as possible. Encourage them to stop by a practice, and when they do, introduce them to the current team and tell the players a little bit about the alumnus.

PUBLIC RELATIONS AND MEDIA

The media has always been important to help keep fans and alumni informed of our season. The local newspaper, radio, and television report the games and standings for our league. Athletes should be guided for interviews, preparing them with appropriate answers in order that they not appear boastful or uninformed. Remind them that if they get interviewed, they should come across as humble and to emphasize the good things their teammates and coaches are doing. They should also be careful to be respectful and complimentary to their opposition and the officials (this is good advice to coaches too!).

Social media calls for the same principles and then some. Players need to be cautioned strongly about posting anything football-related on social media. They need to protect their team, avoid giving "bulletin board" material to their opponents, and refrain from making the program look bad in public.

OFF-SEASON TRAINING

The top programs in the league had stronger, bigger, more athletic players. Therefore, year-round training became an integral part of our program. A weight-room area was established with a 15-station global gym set in an empty classroom, along with free weights and two cycling machines. We emphasized hard work year-round.

Early-morning workouts for athletes involved in other school sports were not well attended. With cooperation from the other coaches, we launched Sunday evening workouts so that training could benefit students in all of their sports. From February to May, for an hour and a half in the evening, the team came together to improve the program. Agility and speed work were the focus of the first half hour, followed by weight training with a focus on specific lifts. The remaining 30 minutes might involve touch football, tug of war with a rope, or obstacle course competitions. These activities were beneficial to all the football players and started to attract other students in the school.

FAMILY SUPPORT

Since my retirement as teacher and head coach, I am often asked about my years at CCH and I reflect on the events and memories of which I am most proud. First and foremost, I must give credit to my wife, Gini, who supported my coaching duties at CCH. She sacrificed more than anyone so I could be generous with my time. Having had the opportunity to coach my two sons, Jean-Paul and Joseph, and having my daughter, Jenna, serve as manager were life highlights that cannot be measured.

CONCLUSION

The best rewards any coach could ask for are the relationships made with other coaches and players. At times I cannot remember where I put my car keys, but ask about a football event in the last 30 or so years and I will always remember those teams. Through the years, I have been included in the wedding celebrations for many players and have even coached their sons. Conversations regarding the teams that players were a part of never get old. I am proud to see how my players have grown into outstanding citizens, that being the true reward of having coached.

Work hard. I embraced my philosophy and applied it to my coaching career as best I could, and I feel satisfied that I did help reinstate and continue the pride and tradition that is London's CCH Crusader football.

22

Building a CEGEP Program

Alex Surprenant

For the non-Québécois coaches reading this book, let's begin with a brief definition of CEGEPs and a rundown of the major differences between the Québec
educational model and those of other provinces.

In French, CEGEP stands for Collège d'enseignement général et profession-
nel. It's the stage that falls between a Québec student's time in high school and
university. High school ends with Secondary 5, which is the equivalent to
grade 11 in the rest of Canada. By our rules, a football student-athlete has eight
years of eligibility following his high school diploma. As a result, the athlete finishes his football years later than in the rest of Canada (unless the athlete else-
where in Canada plays CJFL or takes redshirt seasons in U Sports), as you can see
in table 22.1.

We work with athletes between the ages of 17 and 20. This results in a higher
caliber of play than with high school football, especially in division 1, and that
advantage allows us to better prepare our players for the university level. The

TABLE 22.1 Player Ages in Québec and the Rest of Canada

Age	Québec	Rest of Canada
16	Secondary 5	Grade 11
17	CEGEP	Grade 12
18	CEGEP	U Sports or CJFL
19	CEGEP	U Sports or CJFL
20	CEGEP or U Sports	U Sports or CJFL
21	U Sports	U Sports or CJFL
22	U Sports	U Sports or CJFL
23	U Sports	U Sports (if the athlete previously redshirted or played CJFL)
24	U Sports	U Sports (if the athlete previously redshirted or played CJFL)

majority of our athletes have made the decision to concentrate solely on football. They can focus on the game 12 months a year. Player development in CEGEP is a major factor in the success the RSEQ (Réseau du sport étudiant du Québec) has experienced since the first championship won by le Laval Rouge et Or in 1999.

DEVELOPING RELATIONSHIPS WITH OTHER FOOTBALL ORGANIZATIONS

St.-Jean-sur-Richelieu, as a CEGEP, forms a stepping stone between high school football and U Sports. For that reason, we maintain good working relationships with both levels. We are also part of our provincial and national football sport governing bodies, so those are additional relationships that need to be cultivated.

High School Programs

Separate the local schools from those outside your region. In our case, we have maintained a high level of success over the past five years in recruiting outside of our sector. Few CEGEPs use this type of recruitment to build their program nowadays. With a weaker local system, it was the only way for us to improve our recruiting classes. Whether it be in Outaouais or the North Shore of Montreal, we have sustained success in developing contacts throughout the province. We must now separate the strategies in our recruitment between local and nonlocal programs.

As a local program, we can see the players and coaches regularly. This allows us to offer these programs different ways to help them. An example would be allowing these programs to use our field, and even giving them access to our offensive and defensive meetings during both our spring and summer camps. It is an opportunity for them to observe our methods, technical or tactical, and provides something similar to an NCAA coaches clinic. We also have our Géants Focus Camp, which was created in 2013, my first year as head coach. It is a summer speed camp that allows the young athletes to prepare themselves for their high school season. Every year we have around 20 kids that participate in this camp. Occasionally, coaches from these local schools contact me to talk football, whether it be about our playbooks, team management, or team philosophy.

Finally, I participate in local clinics, sharing my knowledge and experience with fellow coaches on specific subjects that can help a coaching staff get better.

Concerning the teams outside of our region, our strategies vary due to the distance and the limited contact we have with the coaches and players. Sometimes we are able to land a certain player even without any prior relationship with the program. When a player visits our school, our amazing facilities, great coaching staff, and recent success allow us to rapidly build confidence between the players, the parents, and our program. In other cases, we have developed great relationships with coaches who respect our program and become ambassadors who help us find talent from all over Québec. These relationships are valuable and must be kept up annually. At St.-Jean-sur-Richelieu, we do it to uphold the interest and respect that we have toward the high school programs that produce talent year after year.

We also offer a football camp that is open to all of Québec. This one-day camp allows high school players to focus on the technical aspects of the game. In order to minimize injury risk, this camp has no equipment and no contact. The day includes two on-field sessions of two hours, and two one-hour sessions of video. Overall, this day is a great opportunity to display the knowledge of our coaching staff and the quality of our facilities, including our top-notch stadium and locker room. Finally, we get a chance to develop the local and nonlocal football players.

Recently, the RSEQ implemented an annual recruitment calendar that significantly limits the contact between its players and us. This major change will reinforce the importance of our relationships with the high school programs and coaches. With limited access to the players, we must focus more than ever on our relationships with coaches and parents.

U Sports Programs

High school programs feed good players to CEGEPs, and CEGEP programs feed good players to the universities. Accordingly, university programs want to stay in touch and on good terms with CEGEP programs. This allows me to meet with different U Sports coaches to stay up-to-date regarding all the new strategies, trends, and techniques used at the next level. Going into 2013, with no offensive experience, I used these relationships to improve my knowledge of the game. I was fortunate to work with Carl Brennan, offensive line coach of le Laval Rouge et Or, to get more comfortable with concepts I was less familiar with. I regularly try to meet with U Sports coaches every winter, and have gone to several spring camps. It is always interesting to see other programs in their day-to-day routine. You can always learn something.

Another part of my relationship with the university coaches would be my participation in the selections of the Québec under-18 team as a guest coach. In Québec, CEGEP coaches are not permitted to be part of the provincial team coaching staff. I have been around the team for several years. This is a great opportunity to assist quality U Sports coaches like Olivier Turcotte-Létourneau, who is now the defensive backs coach at the McGill University and for our provincial team. This is another chance to develop relationships in the football community, while seeing U Sports coaches with the next generation of young athletes.

I also had the chance to be chosen by Football Canada to observe the Canada Junior National Team (under-20) coaches as part of the new mentoring program. The team traveled to Orlando to face the United States in the North American Championship. It was a great week due to the company of coaches I had never met before. Not many CEGEP coaches work with Football Canada, but my recent participation has been a privilege and it's something I look forward to doing again.

Football Québec and Football Canada

When I take part in the federations, I always learn things and become a better coach, and I do so while developing my contacts within the province and the country.

I have participated in many selection camps for Team Québec and one selection camp with Team Canada. I also participated annually in the Tim Hortons All-Star Game, which invites all the best grade 10 football players in the province.

I have also been a course conductor for Football Québec since 2013. With the implementation of the Safe Contact program, Football Québec needed help in the teaching of hundreds of coaches in Québec.

I am also in training to receive my certification in NCCP Competition Development (the certification intended for postsecondary level coaches). The recent changes in the NCCP allowed us to receive different training over the last couple of years. Eventually, certified coaches will be responsible for training the coaches that are taking the NCCP Introduction to Competition course.

In 2015, our institution partnered with Football Québec to host the Football Canada Cup in our facilities. This was a great opportunity for our city to be the focal point of the Canadian amateur football community. We also took the opportunity to ask our players to volunteer during the event. The tournament kickoff was the Spalding Cup finals (the championship of community programs from across Quebec), which started the festivities. Overall, it was a great 10 days of football in Saint-Jean-sur-Richelieu.

COACHING A PROGRAM WITHIN AN ACADEMIC INSTITUTION

For our team to be successful on the field, we need to be successful in the classroom. There are academic eligibility standards that must be met by our student-athletes, so it is our job to provide a structure and support system to help them be successful.

Academic Support

Part of a coach's job description is to maximize the number of students who graduate. Our team offers very substantial academic support and employs the best academic learning methods found in universities. Nearly 75 percent of our players come from outside the region, and many are away from home for the first time. Guiding these young students is our responsibility, on the field and off.

The foundation of our team's academic system is that every week, all throughout the year, players have to put in two study periods of two hours each. These are run by a teacher from our CEGEP who's assigned to follow the students' progress throughout the year, and they take place in highly equipped classrooms where each student has his own workplace. The players use the study periods to stay up to date with homework. Good classroom synergy allows the best students to help those that have more difficulty. Meanwhile, the teacher in charge of academic support uses these periods to acquaint himself with the students' motivation and preparation.

To coach them in time management, the students are required to fill out a weekly schedule that forces them to determine their obligations from 8 a.m. to 10 p.m. We also ask them to prepare an evaluation chart that allows them to predetermine which weeks of the session their upcoming assessments are due. Following the syllabi handed out by their teachers at the beginning of the session, they fill in their calendars accordingly. These two methods allow the students to better prepare themselves and learn the importance of time management in their day-to-day lives.

Relationship with CEGEP Professionals

We have a variety of professionals who can be in contact with our players if any issues arise. The first level of intervention would be our athletic director and our academic supervisor. These two important authorities intervene daily to help with a variety of issues. The athletic director is responsible for everything that concerns our league (RSEQ). Eligibility, rules, and all finances are linked to his or her job. Our academic supervisor ensures that, through conversations with the teachers, our players conduct themselves according to our team values. Different situations can lead us to work with financial aid specialists, psychologists, special education staff, and many others. For example, a student-athlete who comes from a less wealthy family may go to the financial aid office in order to get loans and scholarships from the Québec government's student-support program. Tutoring is another very important resource that we are fortunate to have. Whether it be in French, English, math, or philosophy, our players have access to teachers and tutors to help them with any difficulties they may encounter. All these services are free.

We also have counselors (conseillers en aide pédagogique individuelle) who can guide our players in academic decisions within their programs. For instance, before the beginning of their first semester, our players meet with their counselor and plan their academic future. Our students studying in pre-university programs will complete five sessions at our CEGEP (two and a half years) instead of four sessions (two years). This is strategic for our players, not only academically but also athletically, because their workload during the session is reduced and they can play three full seasons with our team. Student-athletes can enter university in January, allowing them to commence their U Sports career with the whole off-season to get in tune with their new team.

Compliance and RSEQ Rules

To compete at the CEGEP level means having a high school diploma. In certain CEGEPs, Saint-Jean-sur-Richelieu being one, it is possible to start playing while still missing six credits or fewer, but the student has to get those courses done before mid-February.

The student-athlete is required to pass eight classes before being allowed to play the following season. For a rookie coming off a poor first session, the number may be reduced to four classes in the winter session. But there are no other exceptions. These rules force the athletes to prioritize their studies at an earlier age to continue playing (you may notice some differences here with sports, like hockey, that are run by nonacademic leagues).

Player transfers also have a rule. When an athlete decides to transfer, he will be automatically suspended for half of the upcoming season (five games). In order to avoid a suspension, the player must receive authorization from his former team. The idea is to limit player transfers annually. Unfortunately, we still see multiple transfers every year. There are a number of situations that lead to a player asking to transfer, but most commonly it comes down to the player not being happy in his new environment. It is very difficult for a teenager to properly evaluate his options at the age of 16. We can understand that certain players will regret their choice and transfer after a season or two. In our case, we will typically have between two and five players transferring to our team each year.

BUDGETING AND FUNDRAISING

Besides the obvious football and academic responsibilities we have in CEGEP, we also have a role in the very important matter of raising money for our program and making sure the money is properly managed.

In 1987, les Géants were experiencing many problems. The CEGEP made the decision to no longer support the team financially. For lack of players and money, the team did not take part in the following season. Following these failures, a group of alumni and businessmen created "la corporation du club de football les Géants." This corporation pursues the sole objective of financially supporting our team. Excellent progress has been realized over the last 30 years. With an annual budget of $250,000, our program is one of the most financially stable programs in the province.

All of our major revenues and expenses are approved by a board of directors that manages the day-to-day operation of the team. I am employed by the corporation and not the CEGEP. Our structure is unique in Québec and it allows us to compete with the top teams in the province. It is a great example of synergy between the private and public sectors. All of our fund-raisers are organized by our corporation. Here is a list of the biggest fund-raisers:

- Golf tournament in partnership with the CEGEP foundation
- Annual lottery (1,200 tickets at $20 per ticket with prizes from $100 to $2,250)
- Alumni club ($50 per year for two season tickets and access to our Alumni Tailgate)
- Corporate tickets

- Team program (selling advertisements)
- Game sponsors
- Uniform sponsors
- Wall of team photos (each team photo is sponsored for $250 per year)

Our rich history and the support of our city greatly help the success of our program. A few hundred Géants alumni still live in the city and this contributes to our game-day crowds, which are by far the biggest in the league.

Concerning our budget, we have monthly meetings where all the financial decisions are made. When it comes to a major expense, like a change in uniforms, the board of directors must approve the expense. Around the table, there are a variety of alumni and business people that vary between the ages of 30 and 60. Multiple generations of players are represented within the group. Two members of the CEGEP are part of the board of directors in order to ensure that all decisions respect the values and rules of conduct of the institution.

SPORTS FACILITIES

Overnight, our program at Saint-Jean-sur-Richelieu transitioned from the league's worst facility to the best. This happened during the 2011 season. Thanks to the efforts of our program and its friends, we inaugurated our new stadium, le Stade Alphonse-Desjardins. The major investment of $5 million allowed for the construction of a 1,500-seat stadium, a synthetic game field, lighting for the stadium, and an adjacent grass practice field. We also have a team building that contains our beautiful locker room, the coaches meeting room, our physiotherapy room, and the head coach's office.

These new assets are major playing cards that are frequently used in our player recruitment. The players have the luxury of living their CEGEP career in university-level facilities every day. Each year, the parents and players who visit our facility are very impressed. The quality of our facility allowed us to attract major events like the provincial championships (le Bol d'or) from 2014 to 2016, and the Football Canada Cup in 2015. These big events were all great publicity for our city and our program.

Our board of directors is very active and is always on the lookout for new projects. The ultimate goal of everyone in the program is to improve the lives of our players during their time with our program.

TEAM STAFF

As with any other high-level football program, a CEGEP team requires many committed experts to make it successful. These experts are necessary both on and off the field.

Coaching Staff

In 2013, I became our program's first full-time head coach. Having someone full-time, our program can now put in more time and effort toward recruitment, supporting our players, and giving a helping hand in the financial support of the team.

In 2016, we hired a second coach, who spends three days out of his working week fully committed to preparing defense. This is another addition that has allowed us to be more competitive in the highest level of CEGEP football in the province. We have started discussions with our board of directors about hiring a second full-time coach.

Over the years, we have always put together a quality group of coaches. When hiring, I look for individuals who have played at the university level and who completed their university degrees. One good reason for this is that coaches are role models; another is that having the right experience helps us help our players through their college difficulties.

If possible, I prioritize the young men who played for our team in the past. But the unfortunate reality is that there isn't a long list of ex-players waiting to be coaches. And, of course, building a great coaching staff is one thing. Maintaining the staff is another, and it's up to me to take the steps to fill spots when a coach decides to leave our program.

Volunteering is no longer as popular as it once was. It is becoming more and more difficult to find coaches who will commit to investing so much time for little compensation. People's passions have become second to their jobs and family life. I am always impressed when I speak to coaches who spent 30 to 40 years of their lives as volunteer coaches without any financial compensation in return. These coaches are role models for our generation because they spent the majority of their lives contributing to the development of our youth. In this day and age, we must find the balance between being demanding of our coaches and respecting their limits and their level of involvement. Some assistants have more time than others, and it is my job to divide the team's needs according to each coach's involvement.

Our organization encourages professional development by investing annually in the training of our coaching staff. We use this opportunity to learn in the United States at clinics like Nike Coach of the Year and Glazier. It is always interesting to listen to our southern neighbors share their team philosophies, strategies, and techniques. My assistants and I always come back with information that allows our program to take the next step. Also, I believe that these clinics are a source of motivation when we come back to Québec.

Support Staff

We are lucky to rely on a great team that includes physical training coaches, medical staff, and equipment managers. Our level of stability in all these categories is very impressive.

Our head trainer is very passionate. His salary does not represent his value to the team. Year in and year out, our program and our training vary with his latest finds. Our players have the opportunity to take part in two supervised runs and four gym sessions per week. Since we compile the results in our physical tests, we can notice that our team is getting stronger and faster. These gains allowed us to win two provincial championships in division 2 and be competitive in our first season in division 1. In my opinion, the investment of our program to improve our physical training supervision was a vital part of our success.

Our medical team has been led by la Clinique Acti-Sport for the last 15 years. Like the majority of the teams in our league, we have a physiotherapist present at all our practices and games. In addition, we plan to pay for an extra block during the school day, a period when players can receive treatment for free (considering how expensive treatment can be, this should provide a great addition for our players). We also have access to a doctor and an orthopedic surgeon in Saint-Jean-sur-Richelieu. These contacts allow us to accelerate the process of getting appointments for our injured players, and avoiding the costs that come with seeing someone in the private sector. Finally, we use social networks to communicate the medical reports on our players to all of our coaches.

Our program has also been lucky in our long-time equipment manager. This type of work seems simple, but any coach will agree that having a good equipment manager makes our lives so much easier and allows us to concentrate on coaching proper.

COMMUNITY INVOLVEMENT

In the past, our presence in our community was not always a strength. In 2013, we focused primarily on the finances of the team by including our players as much as possible in our fund-raisers. After four years, I felt that we were ready to take another step and have our players be part of activities in the community. The first objective was to allow the kids in our region to spend time with our players. For these kids, our players represent a level of excellence on the field and in the classroom.

The second objective was to improve the reputation of the team. Even if we have a rich history, we should still work toward maintaining a positive presence within the community. Furthermore, we want people to see our involvement in the community so that they will want to support our program. With more of a positive presence within the city, we will have more fans at our games and more businesses interested in sponsoring the team.

Here's how we accomplished our objectives. At the start of May, our players organized football-based drills for the kids at a nearby elementary school. During a 90-minute period, over 100 kids had fun during their introduction to the game of football. The following week, they participated in the warm-up for a group of kids who were taking part in a run at another elementary school. The players even handed out snacks to the kids after the event. These gestures seem very simple but were appreciated by the young kids and the teachers

CONCLUSION

As you can see, coaching and leading a CEGEP program has a multitude of challenges. It is important to develop positive working relationships with a wide variety of people, including coaches and support staff, school instructors and administrators, the team board of directors, coaches at other levels of football, administrators at Football Québec and Football Canada, sponsors, and people within the community. While there are always challenges, it is very rewarding to be an integral part of the development of so many student-athletes, and to see many of them go on to excel at the university and even professional levels, and to also see many of them go on to outstanding educational achievements and roles within the community.

Building a CJFL Program

Tom Sargeant

I have been very fortunate to have played and coached in the Canadian Junior Football League (CJFL) for more than 25 years, all with the Saskatoon Hilltops. Junior football is a great opportunity for young men 18 to 22 years old. It develops football skills and understanding, and it builds men who have the character and desire to perform to their full potential on and off the field. Because of volunteering, the junior league also provides tremendous opportunities for coaches, not just players. This chapter provides a game plan that will allow you to have success in leading a CJFL football program.

First, you'd better love what you're doing. Realize that's what it takes if you're going to commit the hours and energy needed to being a good coach. A coach must be an instructor able to teach skills, and a first-rate analyst able to look at game film and see how players can be put in the right spots to make plays and understand what the opposition is up to. Because of the hours you'll spend away from home, you need to communicate clearly with your family to create understanding; you also have to prioritize wisely and decide what needs to get done now and what can wait. Find ways to integrate your family into your football life, and make sure to set aside family time away from football. When your family gets on board with your passion, that's when you can fully immerse yourself into coaching.

A coach cannot cut corners, so putting in the time in the off-season doing film study, recruiting, planning practice, and connecting with outside agencies (sponsors, provincial organizations, etc.) is critical to success. The coaching role evolves. Do not be outworked and always have a clear vision of where you are headed and how you are going to get there (see chapter 3, Establishing a Coaching Philosophy). Make sure you articulate the vision to your coaches, players, directors, and media so everyone understands the significance of what you are trying to accomplish. When you are interviewing for the head coaching job, one of the key ingredients the hiring committee will be looking for will be the passion and energy that will motivate the players and the community.

COACHING STAFF

The most important job of a head coach is to hire and recruit the best coaches to lead young men. Do not settle for second best. Be patient, do interview prep so you can ask specific questions, and develop a plan for how everyone will fit into the staff. Set roles and parameters for each coach. All staff members must understand how they are expected to conduct themselves and what their roles are in practice and on game day. They must be excellent teachers, students of the game, great communicators, and great listeners.

Coaches play a critical role in the success of a football team. They must work in a cohesive fashion so the rest of the team sees the loyalty among the staff. The head coach should always look for ways to bond, planning get-togethers with coaches and their families. Challenge them to seek coaching development opportunities, and create an open coaching environment in which everyone has a voice. Sometimes the head coach must exert his influence on a decision, and the support of the coaching staff is critical. Follow the old saying, "You do not have to agree with me, but you must accept the decision." When assembling a coaching staff, remember that you do not want clones; you want people who have a solid football background, good character, and a passion for coaching. These ingredients will allow you to develop a football team ready for success.

BOARD OF DIRECTORS

With any junior football team, there will be a board of directors, and its members will be volunteers giving their time and energy. In running your team, honor and respect the role of the board and work closely with it. Players need to understand how hard directors work at fundraising; create opportunities in which the players have to give back as well, because having more hands in the pile does make a difference. And always be in contact with the directors on the state of the team. Topics such as fundraising, recruiting, scholarship money, and the number of players to keep should all be discussed and understood before the year begins. Discipline issues, such as off-the-field transgressions, are also handled with the board. In high school, handling a discipline issue means connecting with your administrators to work out a response. But at the CJFL and U Sports levels, the media takes an interest too. The board of directors has an executive who deals with tough situations like this and problem-solves with the head coach.

The manager is usually a director who volunteers to take on the role. The right manager, one who works closely with the coach, allows the staff to focus on football. Handling the registrations, planning for home and away games, and working as a liaison with parents, directors, and the team, the manager tackles these things and frees up the coaches. The position is sometimes paid, but even then the manager's focus should stay on organization.

I'm proud to say that when the Saskatoon Hilltops are fortunate enough to win a championship, the directors get championship rings along with the players and coaches. We're all in this together. It is the board of directors who make junior football what it is today, and it will be the same group that continues the game 100 years from now.

RECRUITING

Recruit, recruit, recruit. This is key to your team's success. Identify the characteristics you want to see in players and the types of athletes you need for your systems. The realities of junior football are that you must have a keen eye for talent and not always fall for the stud athlete who won't be in your program long. Some players may move to university football after a couple of seasons. But, over the years, the team that wins the championship is the one with loyal 21- and 22-year-olds. This can lead to conflict with university sport teams. Solid relations with U Sport coaches are important, especially if there is a university program in your community. But the success of any team in the CJFL should be on the shoulders of its fourth- and fifth-year players. Keeping your players is vital, and the way to do it is to show them they'll continue to develop and grow as athletes and leaders in your program. We always talk about winning a championship for our fifth-year players, and we hold weekly leadership meetings with them because it's their team and they need to make the key decisions. I have learned that usually it isn't the star player who becomes the leader. It's the player who has to work very hard, and who becomes both a fine athlete and someone who cares about the team.

Don't exhaust yourself trying to recruit a given player, but be ready to go up against other teams and universities if a prospect looks worthwhile. Meeting with families and individual players is certainly a good recruiting scheme, and there's the global approach of meeting with a high school team's eligible players and giving them your pitch. Connecting with high school coaches goes a long way to selling your program, and treating players right sends a positive message back to others. Texting and e-mail are a good strategy, especially with today's young athletes. Quick communication can be very encouraging to young players and helps build trust.

Develop a recruiting system that works closely with the high school coaches in your area. Communicate often and be visible in their schools and at their games so the players know you are interested in them. Set up information nights at your clubhouse, go to team banquets, and invite players and coaches to your banquet; do whatever you can do to communicate and sell yourself and your team.

The most important part of recruiting is to be honest. These are young athletes, many of whom are moving a far distance from home. Do not mislead them or disparage another program down the road. We need to create an atmosphere in which players decide through our interactions what will be the best fit for them. I still believe the best teams win, so look for 15 to 20 new players each year to upgrade your team and put yourself in a position to win with 21- and 22-year-olds. At some point, you may have to decide to release a player who isn't making a significant on-field contribution after an opportunity for development. Many coaches see the third year (20 years old) as the make-or-break year. The best way to release a player is to sit down with him and give him the bad news. Always focus on the positives and try to help him find another place to play if he still has the desire. There have been many success stories in which athletes have turned a negative into a positive and have become starters for other teams. A change of scenery can make a world of difference, so be proactive and keep developing your young players. Sometimes, of course, a player who doesn't do well on-field can still do a lot for team culture off the field. Maybe he can stop being a player but stay with the team in another role.

MARKETING

Media people should be viewed as royalty, not the enemy. Make yourself and your players available to the media, and be cooperative and friendly with them. Send press releases or event invitations if that's what it takes to get coverage. Local media is an important ingredient to gaining a solid fan base and building energy in the community. Everyone gains so much when positive press is on board to support players and coaches.

Sponsorship is important, because money is an essential ingredient in giving the best for your players. The directorship needs to drum up contacts to create an energy and momentum that junior football is a worthy product and these young men need to be supported. There is a variety of models out there to attract businesses, so look for the model that fits your program and actively pursue them and get them on board. If you are just starting, target businesspeople you know in the community, or parents of your players. Networking is very important, so establish a few key sponsorship relationships and get additional potential contacts from them.

Be sure your players know that they're ambassadors for your program. Players should be your best marketers, so utilize them as often as possible. Whether it be reading to schools, participating in parades, getting involved with local charities, or helping with kid sport activities and minor football teams or events, your players can do the critical job of showing the public the value of your team's culture. All athletes need to give back—both to help people feel good about the process, and more importantly to bring teams closer together and allow the athletes to grow as individuals.

BUILDING THE FOUNDATION

Coaches must know what they stand for and how they are going to create a winning attitude. When beginning a new program and becoming the face of the team, start with integrity and positive energy. This is a critical aspect of coaching a successful program. Focus on how to be a great team and always set high goals such as winning a championship every year. When that is not realistic, reestablish your goals and work hard to attain them. Remember, if you shoot for the moon and miss, you'll still be among the stars. Setting player and team goals is essential to challenging and motivating athletes to reach their full potential.

Recruiting motivated athletes is a key ingredient to winning a national championship. Off-season morning workouts, speed sessions, and lifting sessions demonstrate which players have the desire to make themselves better. The ones who show up are the ones you want in your future. The Hilltop motto is "Champions Commit," and that is paramount to creating a culture where second place is not good enough.

Coaches need to set goals as well so they can be accountable to their players and challenge them to constantly strive for improvement. Even though you are dealing with young adults, you will still need on- and off-field rules and expectations for players. A leadership council made up of veteran players is very beneficial in helping make decisions that are best for the team. Players appreciate the opportunity to provide feedback and to be involved in decisions, and I have always found that they will be very hard on teammates who are jeopardizing their chance to win. But remember: the more rules you have, the more headaches you deal with. I have learned to keep the rules to a minimum, because you do not want to constantly deal with issues that take you away from winning and improving as a team. If you have a team that is respectful toward themselves and others, that understands work ethic, realizes the importance of curfews, and abstains from illegal substances, you should be in great shape to be successful.

PURSUIT OF KNOWLEDGE

As a young coach, I quickly immersed myself in the National Coaching Certification Program and realized how important these opportunities were to my development as a coach. Not only did these courses focus on football specifics, they also looked at nutrition, sport psychology, training, ethics, team building, and a variety of other topics that help create a complete coach. I was fortunate to be chosen to attend the level 4 certification, and it was one of the best professional development activities I was ever associated with in football. I connected and networked with two delegates from each province, all with the same passion as me. The presenters had a high degree of knowledge and insight and shared their successes from the professional ranks and the university level. Through the outstanding support of Football Canada and Football Saskatchewan, I became the type of football coach I wanted to become. Today, the new NCCP coaching program allows for more initiative from coaches and helps them be more specific in their training. The competition development stream for postsecondary coaches is designed specifically for leading elite-level athletes and working in highly competitive environments. Still, the course is collaborative and provides a great chance to learn from peer coaches from other programs and even other sports. It also helps my assistant coaches to focus on their teaching and reflect on good practices. Every coach who wants to excel in the game of football needs to begin with the NCCP, because it provides a solid foundation of knowledge and builds confidence for leading players on the field.

In general, coaches need to seek knowledge, to get the tools to coach skills and drills more effectively and to develop a better understanding of schemes. Send coaches to any local clinics, have them present in clinics, and have them regularly dialogue with high school coaches to uncover any trends. Head south and spend a few days with a college program; sit in on their meetings and attend practice sessions. I have found our American neighbors to be extremely gracious, and my coaches have found these trips to very beneficial in their development.

The head coach needs to spend time talking about philosophy and challenging assistant coaches to read books, articles, and coaching manuals to create a healthy environment in which learning the craft of coaching is ongoing. As soon as you think you know it all, it is probably the time to leave coaching. I personally have developed my knowledge through reading many books on coaching styles, attending many coaching clinics, having conversations with other coaches, and learning many lessons on the field, both good and bad. Today, there are many ways to gain knowledge, but remember the key is to get the most out of athletes and have them all work towards a common goal.

When setting up your in-season and out-of-season programs, maximize your time with the athletes and minimize distractions. You need to have great focus and follow the plan you set at the beginning of the year. During the season, you need to make sure you allot the proper time for film study, field practice, conditioning, mental training, nutrition, and rest. Your athletes are extremely busy during the season with work, school, or life, so you need to keep them engaged and energized for the grind of a football season. Keeping meetings down to 30 minutes does a lot for retention and to combat boredom. Also, as it gets colder outside, you need to find ways to shorten your practices while keeping them effective. In the off-season, we do Topper Tuesdays; we meet with players for play install and film study to make our players smarter and more knowledgeable regarding our schemes. This is an excellent way to keep your team together and to keep sharpening their focus.

CONCLUSION

When I look at the growth of the many players I have coached over the years, I realize how lucky I was to be connected to them. They have gone on to much bigger things in life, but I know their football experience between the ages of 18 and 22 was important in their development as young men. If you believe in making a difference, there is no more exciting and challenging task than coaching a football team. Bring passion, energy, knowledge, and commitment if you are going to be successful. Understand sacrifice, work ethic, criticism, and patience if you are to guide a team over a long time. At the end of the day, if you are a part of a vibrant, successful football team, the rewards will last you a lifetime. Happy coaching!

Building and Maintaining a U Sports Program

Blake Nill

When I explained to a colleague that my family and I had decided to accept a new position at the University of Calgary, he asked, "Do you think you can make it work there?" This colleague knew what made me tick and what motivated me to be a university football coach. After all, I was leaving my tenure at Saint Mary's University, an eight-year period in which we won two national championships and restored the Huskies to a symbol of Maritime pride. My response to this assistant was sincere: I told him I was confident in my approach and knew that, if I applied it correctly, it would get results for the Dinos.

My approach isn't the only way to run a program. But it's worked for me, and I've developed it over years of experience. That includes working with such established coaches as John Stevens (St. Francis Xavier University) and Larry Uteck (Saint Mary's University). Of course, I'm also willing to adapt. I'm quick to adopt tactics from coaches all over Canada, from any sport, given the right circumstances.

The Dinos position was the third time I came into a program as a head coach or part of a coaching change. Following my time in Calgary, in 2015, I was named head coach at the University of British Columbia and went on to win the Vanier Cup in my inaugural season with the Thunderbirds. When taking over a program, a coach faces an endless list of responsibilities that need to be accounted for, both on and off the field. Time is a key factor; a well-thought-out plan of attack is necessary, and you must be able to prioritize and work within a structured time-line. My strategy through this process of renewal has always centred on four fundamental components: proper team culture, recruiting strategy, development strategy, and alumni plan. These areas all need attention in the short term to ensure your efforts are productive, and each is critical to sustaining your program at or near the top. The components work together because their values mesh. But focusing on each as a distinct entity allows for more detailed effort as you work to make your program truly a reflection of yourself.

CULTURE

Nothing puts the head coach's stamp on a program more than the culture he builds and allows to exist while in charge. Through my experience in football, I have concluded that a coach's football program is simply an extension of his individual personality.

When a coach enters a new program, he brings with him a set of core values or principles he feels are important. Where do these values come from? They are developed through the entire life experience of the coach. They are principles that he was taught by his parents, teachers, and former coaches, as well as experiences he has had that have influenced his belief system. This is where core values originate. These values have been instilled in the individual through time. They can't be artificially replicated just because they worked for another coach (see chapter 3, Establishing a Coaching Philosophy). There is no shortcut.

My upbringing was in a small town, and I was raised by two parents with an agricultural background. Hard work was a big part of what my parents instilled in my belief system. It was in this same environment that I learned to compete by playing various sports. After completing high school, I was fortunate enough to go to university and discover the value of education. My formal education lasted until I was almost 40, when I completed my master's degree. No matter if I am addressing a team, meeting with a recruit and his family, or having lunch with a potential sponsor, it won't be long before you hear the words *compete* and *work ethic* come from my mouth. At the same time, my belief in the value of lifelong learning makes education a big component of my recruiting efforts and my strategy for retaining student-athletes. These three values—work ethic, lifelong learning, and the most important of all, competitive instinct—are what drive me. They are who I am and how I coach.

The coach aside, two other components play a significant role in developing a team's culture. The first is time. Professional football and the major U.S. college programs have always had limits to the time available to show success or improvement. Such constraints are now becoming evident in Canadian university football (U Sports) as well. Athletic directors have less patience for allowing a coach to learn on the job, and that means university coaches now have less time to instill their core values in their players. A new coach must be aware of his time and prioritize his core values accordingly. Failure to do this ultimately may cost him the opportunity to implement his full plan, as he will simply run out of time before a coaching change is made. For some athletic directors, winning is the most important priority of the program.

The second influence is the school environment. What does a school environment include? Faculty programs, entrance requirements, geographic location, funding, and student demographics are all examples of school influences that should be considered by any incoming coach. You will need to find ways to develop a team culture that fits the culture of the university.

Saint Mary's University in Halifax, Nova Scotia, is an outstanding option for any student-athlete with a strong tradition of academic and athletic success.

Because Saint Mary's is a smaller school, athletics plays a major role in its identity and that of the city. Generally, athletes recruited to the east coast are older and somewhat more mature, as parents are more likely to support this arrangement only after their children have had a few more years of life experience. You can see the difference in the environment when you compare it to the University of Calgary, which is a larger research school. Athletics, although viewed as important, is certainly not the only profile of the school. Typically, more than 50 percent of my recruiting classes at Calgary came directly from high school. These young men started the university stage of their lives by remaining at home, as most came to me at the age of 17 or 18. Despite the reality that there will be age differences in any recruiting class, you must remain steadfast in your expectations. I expect accountability, good decision-making, and a level of personal motivation to succeed (both academically and athletically) whether players are 17 or 22 years old.

I am confident that my core values remained intact as I left Saint Mary's to join Calgary and then the University of British Columbia (UBC). However, adjustments were necessary to account for the differences in school environment, primarily the demographics of the athletes recruited. Younger athletes meant more involvement with parents, both in the recruiting stage and after. Structure in all aspects of the Dinos program increased, taking away a lot of the decisions our 17-year-olds may not have had the maturity to make correctly. Examples of structure for younger players include heightened supervision regarding academics, nutrition, and training, and perhaps even logistical issues such as finance and travel arrangements.

Culture in the sport of football is everything. It effects every decision, plan, and effort, in every aspect of the program. In the spring of 2012, Dinos Athletics adopted a mission statement with the words "Build championship culture," highlighting this overriding priority.

RECRUITING

This is the second critical component to building and sustaining a college football program. In fact, a program's success hinges on recruiting. Look at the resources and significant man-hours every university football program invests in the process. Recruiting is a year-round process that dwarfs the time element of even regular season preparation.

How do you ensure success as a recruiter? First, realize that recruiting will parallel your core values as a coach—who you are is who you will attract. You must also understand your target market (admissibility is key here). What about the profiles of potential athletes in your market? I consider myself to be a home run hitter. I typically go after the top athletes across the nation, competing fully for every recruit. My success rate, consequently, is not as high as if I focused on those athletes not in the spotlight. Many coaches have had successful careers bringing in tier 2 athletes and developing the players' potential.

Finally, recruiting is a dynamic process, a pathway that is continuously evolving. Your ability to keep up with this progression will certainly play a role in your success as a recruiter. Social media is the most obvious illustration here. You must also consider what potential recruits now deem important. Some programs have chosen to highlight flashy uniforms; others are fortunate to have modern team facilities. Many coaches still feel the fundamental attraction to their programs lies in more traditional features, such as quality university programs and academic support.

As I mentioned earlier, the word *compete* is a fundamental depiction of how I view my role as a football coach. Recruiting motivates me as a competitor; I look forward to challenging other coaches and programs in a bid to successfully attract top athletes. I am driven to outwork my competition. Like football itself, recruiting has a series of highs and lows. In fact, the successful recruitment of a blue-chip or highly touted athlete brings with it much the same level of satisfaction as victory on the field. The opposite feeling is also true when a young man chooses another program over yours.

During my tenure at the University of Calgary, I had the good fortune of getting to know Coach Peter Connellan, the former Dinos head coach. With four CIS national championships to his credit, Coach Connellan was recognized as an outstanding recruiter who understood the concept of one's target market. As a recruiter, he was a specialist; his potential athletes came from a select group of young men with specific criteria. By staying within the measures of his criteria, Coach Connellan recruited athletes who best fit his core values and ultimately gave him the greatest opportunity for success.

My approach prior to coming to the University of Calgary was much more diverse. With the Huskies, I recruited from all areas. My recruiting classes were a mixture of high school athletes and CJFL football players, and there were always a couple of transfers from other programs thrown in as well. Since I had no real target market, I worked extra hard to cover all fronts, often feeling overwhelmed by the extraordinary number of potential athletes. Working with such numbers, I found it difficult to efficiently research the athletes or get to know them as well as I should. Inevitably, some athletes brought into the Huskies program did not match my personality as a coach. This added to the workload, as I struggled at times to teach my core values to a variety of young men with different values and mindsets.

My discussions with Coach Connellan convinced me that I needed to hang my hat on a more defined group of athletes. When I got to Calgary in 2006, I became an almost exclusive recruiter of high school athletes, primarily in the province of Alberta. While I still considered some prospects from junior football or even transfers, it was with noticeably less frequency and certainly more prudence. What did this change in approach mean to my recruiting efforts? First, I felt I had an established set of criteria for the athletes I looked at. Knowing my target market, I have been able to become more efficient timewise, attracting athletes who I believe best fit my core values. I also have time to grow my market by working with and supporting local high school and minor programs as much as possible. Dinos football was involved in the lives of these young men and their families earlier than ever. When I arrived in Calgary, the biggest challenge I had was to recapture our backyard. When I left, I could confidently say that Dinos football was once again the program of choice for our target market of athletes.

An increasingly significant component of recruiting is managing the rules and regulations, which are changing yearly as U Sports deals with the complexity of governance. The implementation of blackout periods for recruiting is a good example. A blackout period is simply a time when recruits may not be contacted by coaches or schools. When first introduced, this rule created some heated discussion among U Sports coaches. Many were openly opposed to the idea of being told when they could recruit. Nowadays, these blackout periods are part of the structure that comes with U Sports football. Coaches must respect these periods or face discipline.

Lastly, success as a recruiter means evolving with your target market. In my 20-plus years in the CIS (now U Sports) program, I've spent plenty of time on extended road trips, identification camps, and phone calls. But now I also use social media and special software designed for recruiting. I still prefer the old-fashioned face-to-face approach and feel confident in that setting. But the way we now interact, at least initially, continues to change. Success as a recruiter will always depend on my ability to reach my target market. If their preference in communication changes, so must mine.

PLAYER DEVELOPMENT

I first became involved in Canadian university football when I started playing in 1980. Much has changed in the game since then. Entering athletes now come to university programs in better physical condition than ever. Not only that, they are more prepared to deal with the stress of academics, and they better understand the need to make mature decisions. At the same time, the expectations placed on athletes have never been higher. What has remained constant is the need for athletes to be given the opportunity to develop through their university years. This is when young individuals develop the skills that allow them to go from dependent adolescents to independent young men.

I have always evaluated university football programs by their consistency. Their ability to remain competitive on the field year after year is a clear sign that the program is being run correctly and the player-development strategy is working. What components are critical in player-development structure? Here are the three I focus on: time (longevity), academic support, and coaching (primarily strength and conditioning and positional skill sets).

Time is the first priority. An athlete can't have the opportunity to reach his potential if he isn't in the program long enough. Few recruited athletes have the skill sets necessary to compete when they first arrive. These competitive skills are developed through long hours of training, practice, and study. A coach has no chance at constant, ongoing success unless he can keep athletes in the program. The key elements of retention are academic success and compliance with the expectations of the program.

While I was at the University of Calgary, I was approached about the opportunity to add another full-time member to our coaching staff. I was thrilled at the prospect of having my workload reduced, but I thought long and hard about exactly how an extra person could best serve the team. Eventually, I decided to forgo the opportunity for another on-field coach and instead hired a full-time academic adviser. Looking back at the decision, I would have to say it was one of my best. When Sandra Wigg came into the Dino program in 2010, things changed. Her role as the coordinator for academic success created a cultural shift in our program.

I have never met a coach who does not understand the importance of having an efficient academic strategy in place to support his student athletes. When implementing these strategies, the problem once again becomes resources, time chief among them. Keeping track of athletes is a challenge at the best of times. It gets harder during the off-season, when you don't see them regularly and you're out recruiting instead of in the office. By delegating academic support to one individual, I could rest easy. I knew we'd be on top of any issues that our athletes faced in the classroom. In addition, we became a progressive program academically. This included holding seminars to teach athletes the necessary skills associated with success in the classroom. The bottom line is that our productivity in the classroom was never better, and we had fewer academic casualties than ever before. Athletes stayed in the program and had the time to develop into productive athletes, and that meant they could develop into productive citizens. One of my core philosophies is that success on the field always lines up with success in the classroom, that our student–athletes need to use the same skill sets in each setting, that they need to compete in the classroom.

Strength and conditioning have always been an important part of my life and who I am. Going back to my upbringing, I have always believed that if you can outwork a competitor, you have a big advantage. My first year at Calgary and in the Canada West Conference, my athletes were not physically ready to play at this level of football and be successful. It was a tough year. As soon as it was over, I approached a booster about the need to hire a strength and conditioning specialist. The individual we hired was a strong advocate of team training, in which the entire team trains together. I had tried the approach at Saint Mary's, with only mixed success. But Coach Mac Read felt this was what our program needed, both for physical development and for player commitment. He figured that team training would show us which athletes would make the team successful.

Coach Read's logic was simple and direct. The players who invested in our program by committing to our team training were the ones we needed; those who could not discipline themselves would not help us reach our team goals. In January 2008, we began a year-round structured program under Coach Read that included 16 weeks of 6:00 a.m. workouts through the winter months. It was difficult on the athletes at first, especially the early-morning starts. But over the years it became who we were. Our athletes were bigger, faster, and stronger than ever before. Strength and conditioning were an important part of our evaluation process and helped us tremendously in recruiting. The most telling statistic though was our on-field record. When we adopted the concept of team training, our program went 41–7 in the regular season and 15–6 in the playoffs.

ALUMNI DEVELOPMENT

When I first heard that the University of Calgary had relieved their football coach of his duties, I thought it would be wise to go on vacation for a few weeks. I knew what was in store. Sure enough, within the hour I started receiving calls from former Dinos players inquiring if I was interested in the position. The calls kept coming all night, each from a different individual. It was clear that the 5th Quarter Association (Dinos football alumni) had taken an active interest in recruiting the next football coach. Reputed to be one of the best varsity alumni groups in Canada, and possibly the best outright, the 5th Quarter was launched during the era of Coach Connellan. They are very active within the program: generating scholarships and operating endowments, providing recruiting assistance, and opening up networking opportunities for current graduates of the program. There is no question they are well organized, and their efforts play a significant role in the operation of the Dinos.

Early in my tenure with the Huskies at Saint Mary's, I felt I had enough on my plate without worrying about former players. Alumni could be somebody else's responsibility. A conversation with Coach Uteck one afternoon changed all that. He explained to me that alumni development was an integral responsibility of any coach. More importantly, he opened my eyes to the fact that football alumni are simply lifetime members of the program. Some of them will go on to affect the program even more than when they played, perhaps by making financial contributions or initiating change in the program. A strategy needs to be in place to grow and foster alumni development, a strategy that starts when the individual is an active player and continues after he leaves the program. I acted on that advice, at Saint Mary's, University of Calgary, and University of British Columbia.

When you look at the size of current U Sports football programs, many keep upward of 90 players and 30 support staff. You'd think that would produce large numbers of alumni. In reality, a big roster can create numerous issues, with the head coach trying to keep everyone satisfied with their roles. Small gestures that acknowledge significance are important investments. Recently, I had a young offensive tackle come to me who'd been with the team for five years. He explained that he was leaving the program. This young man had never seen much playing time, but he hadn't missed a practice, meeting, or training session. My response to him was sincere: I acknowledged his effort and attitude. More importantly, I explained to him how his role within the team (no matter how inconsequential he felt it was) made us better. My hope was that being genuine with this young man would allow him to feel good about the time he spent with the Dinos. In the future, he may become an active alumnus.

A similar approach must be taken with players who have been out of the program for some time. Acknowledgment is critical. Coaches who want the support that alumni can offer must find ways to engage these individuals. Invite them to special events; welcome them at team practices and introduce them to the current team. Yes, it is another task, but one that only the head coach should be responsible for.

CONCLUSION

Taking over a U Sports program is certainly a difficult task, and more so if you are building from the ground up. Maintaining the program at a competitive level can be just as challenging. You must be confident and not intimidated by the past. When I arrived at the University of Calgary, the first thing I saw was that the Dinos had lost their ability to compete. The culture was no longer one of excellence. Mediocrity had become the norm. I had a similar experience years later when I moved to the Thunderbirds.

Three primary decisions had to be applied. First was the choice to move to a high school–based recruiting platform. This allowed us to focus on a more select target group and better research the athletes we wanted to bring into the program. Fewer recruiting mistakes were made, and our athletes developed more quickly and efficiently than ever before. The second was to move to a team training concept. Team training allowed us to develop the necessary physical skills to compete in the tough Canada West football conference. Where we were once dominated physically, the Dinos were able to play a faster, more powerful game. Team training teaches accountability and provides an opportunity to invest personally in the program. This vested interest is then taken onto the playing field and applied. Like most forms of training, team training is simply hard work and dedication. It became a large part of the culture at the University of Calgary. Finally, the decision to bring in a full-time academic adviser rededicated our academic support system. The support avenues we provided ensured a greater opportunity for academic success, which is necessary for on-field success. Our young men were staying in school, and this gave us more time to work on their development plans.

When I have come into a program, I have been part of a superior support network that made the task less daunting and taught me the necessary skill sets. John Stevens at St. Francis Xavier taught me to recruit on the merits of the program. Recruiting for the X-Men can be a challenge, but we were able to go from a single victory in 1992 to the Vanier Cup in 1996. Coach Larry Uteck (athletic director at Saint Mary's University) was an inspiration to us all as he battled Lou Gehrig's disease. Coach Uteck's knowledge about the game of football was incredible. Bringing him a Vanier Cup in 2001 is a highlight of my career. In Calgary, the support of our 5th Quarter alumni was there from day one. This group is a prime example of what can be done when former athletes are organized and encouraged to remain in the program in some capacity. At UBC, the support of the university, alumni, and a great coaching staff allowed us to win the Vanier Cup in my first season there. My hope is that, wherever I am, I can find a great people to collaborate with to develop a quality, competitive program that the university deserves.

About Football Canada

Football Canada is the national governing body of Canadian amateur football, which represents tackle, touch, and flag components, including players, coaches, officials, and administrators. Football Canada's mission is to initiate, sustain, and encourage programs, services, and activities targeted at all levels, from the novice to the elite, that foster safe and ethical participation in amateur football.

Football Canada's National Coaching Certification Program (NCCP) provides coaches the opportunity to develop their skills and knowledge of coaching tactics, player development, strength and conditioning, and leadership. Football Canada's membership of nearly 7,500 Canadian coaches participate in the NCCP and its Safe Contact program.

Contributors to this book are among the most respected and renowned coaches in Canadian football. Each contributor has been carefully selected by Football Canada and is recognized as an authority on his respective topic.

About the Contributors

Ryan Hall has spent several decades as a high school teacher (English, psychology, and physical education) and football coach. Hall has coached at every level of the sport, from youth flag football to Football Canada's under-20 junior national team. He has coaching experience with organizations such as Football Saskatchewan, Football Canada, the Saskatchewan High Schools Athletic Association, and Regina Minor Football. Hall is also a National Coach Certification Program (NCCP) master learning facilitator in the areas of competition introduction, competition development, and safe contact. In 2015, he received Football Saskatchewan's Darcy Busse 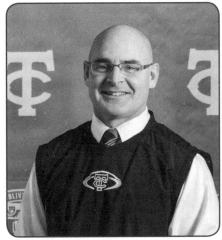 Award for lifetime contribution to coaching in Saskatchewan. In 2007, he garnered the Outstanding Coach Award from the Saskatchewan High Schools Athletic Association.

Tom Annett had an unexpected turn in his career when he incurred a serious spine injury. He was forced to leave competitive football, and his life changed forever. His passion turned to coaching—specifically, safe tackling methods to ensure that what happened to him would not happen to other up-and-coming football athletes. Due to his intense focus and knowledge of safe practices, Tom drove the development of the Safe Contact program in conjunction with Football Canada and the NCCP, and it is now a required module in the NCCP.

Christian Audet, a certified NCCP level 3 coach, has helped many athletes surpass mental barriers while providing them with the tools to help them reach their full potential. Audet, who has a degree in sports administration from Durham College of Applied Arts and Technology, has presented numerous clinics, conferences, and seminars on topics such as football, leadership, and motivation. In 2015 through 2016, Audet was assistant coach and recruiter for Bishop's University. Previously, he was head coach for the Cégep Beauce-Appalaches (2009–2014) and an assistant coach with the University of Ottawa (2006–2008).

Lee Barette is CEO and publisher of CanadaFootballChat.com, an amateur football news and recruiting website. During his coaching career, Barette coached at Acadia University and Ottawa University, and he coached in the Football Canada Cup tournament from 2006 through 2009. His Team Ontario East teams were undefeated in medal games and won the gold medal in 2009. He also guest coached with the Hamilton Tiger-Cats and McGill Redmen.

Jim Barker began his long and illustrious coaching career in the college ranks in 1978 at San Francisco State, with subsequent stops at Occidental College, New Mexico State University, University of Nevada at Reno, and Pomona-Pitzer. His Canadian Football League (CFL) coaching career began in 1996 as a member of the Montreal Alouettes coaching staff. The next year, he was named the Toronto Argonauts' co–offensive coordinator and offensive line coach. In 1999, he was named head coach of the Argonauts, becoming the youngest head coach in the CFL. In 2000, as offensive coordinator of the XFL's Los Angeles Xtreme, Barker coached quarterback Tommy Maddox, who was named XFL Player of the Year and who later earned NFL Comeback Player of the Year honors with the Pittsburgh Steelers. In 2002, Barker again joined the Montreal staff as offensive coordinator and quarterbacks coach, leading the Alouettes to the Grey Cup championship. The next year, he became head coach of the Calgary Stampeders, and in 2005 he became general manager of the team. After two years at the helm, he moved into the position of senior vice president of football operations and director of player personnel. In 2010, Barker returned to the Toronto Argonauts for his second stint as head coach. After leading the Argonauts to the playoffs for the first time since 2007, he was named 2010 CFL Coach of the Year. That same year, Barker assumed the role of general manager, a position he held until 2017. In 2012, with some off-season personnel moves coordinated by Barker, the Argonauts won the CFL's 100th Grey Cup.

Marcel Bellefeuille is currently the wide receivers coach for the BC Lions. He has been a collegiate and professional football coach since 1995. His previous CFL coaching experience includes head coach of the Hamilton Tiger-Cats and offensive coordinator with the Montreal Alouettes, Saskatchewan Roughriders, and Winnipeg Blue Bombers. He has coached in the Grey Cup championships, conference championships, and numerous playoff games. Prior to coaching in the CFL, he was a successful head coach at the University of Ottawa, being named OQIFC Coach of the Year in 1999 and culminating in a Vanier Cup championship in 2000.

Scott Brady is the head coach of the Mount Allison Mounties—the first in the football program's recent history who is both a Mount Allison University graduate and former player for the Mounties. Brady has been on the Mounties coaching staff for six years. After a four-year playing career as a running back and receiver (2006–2009) and Academic All-Canadian, Brady became the defensive backs coach and special teams coach in 2010. In 2011, he was promoted to defensive coordinator. In 2013 and 2014, he helped lead the Mounties to back-to-back AUS championships. In 2014, Brady served as the defensive backs and special teams coach for the U-18 National Team, which defeated Team USA 53-9 in the International Bowl. Earlier that year, he also served as the defensive coordinator of Team East in the 2013 CIS East-West game in London, Ontario; as the defensive line coach for the IFAF World Development Team in Bradenton, Florida; and as defensive coordinator for U-18 Team New Brunswick. In 2015, Brady served as a guest coach (defense) for the Winnipeg Blue Bombers; in 2011, he was a guest coach (defensive line) with the Toronto Argonauts.

Mike Circelli is the president of the London Junior Mustangs Football Club, part of the Ontario Provincial Football League. Circelli coached football at Catholic Central High School in London, Ontario, for 30 years (1984–2014). For more than 10 of those years, he also coached for the London Minors (1993–2000) and London Beefeaters (2001–2004). Most recently, Circelli was the defensive line coach at Western University in London, Ontario (2007–2015).

After **Brad Collinson** signed as a free agent with the Montreal Alouettes in 2003, he helped the team reach the Grey Cup championship. Collinson started his coaching career with his alma mater, Concordia University, where he served from 2004 through 2009. He continued his coaching career with Laval University, where his teams won four Vanier Cup championships (2010, 2012, 2013, and 2016). Collinson also was head coach of U19 Team Quebec, winning three Canada Cups (2012, 2013, and 2015). He also was head coach of U18 Team Canada, winning two International Bowls (2014 and 2016). He also was running backs coach for U20 Team Canada in the summer of 2014; the team finished second at the World Championship in Kuwait.

Joe D'Amore is the head coach of the University of Windsor Lancers, a position he has held since 2011. Widely respected as one of the top young coaches in the country, D'Amore was named the 2011 Tuffy Knight Coach of the Year and the Ontario University Athletics (OUA) Football Coach of the Year and was a finalist for the Canadian Interuniversity Sport (CIS) Football Coach of the Year. Prior to joining the Lancers, he served as the offensive coordinator, special teams coordinator, and defensive backs coach for the Essex Ravens in the Ontario Varsity Football League. D'Amore coached at the high school level with the Villanova Wildcats and Sandwich Sabres. He played wide receiver for the University of Windsor (1996–2000), where he started all 40 games of his career and was team captain for three seasons. Following his college career, he played professional football with the Carolina Rhinos in the Arena Football League (AFL2) and played two seasons with the Fursty Razorbacks in the German Football League in Munich, Germany. D'Amore got his start in coaching in 2000 when he worked as a graduate assistant with the Lancers.

Tim Enger has served as the associate executive director of Football Alberta since 1989. During his tenure, he has served as Alberta's Provincial Team head coach and led the team to six Football Canada Cup gold medals. He has also spearheaded the creation of Football Alberta's Senior Bowl and Bantam Bowl as well as participation in the Alberta Summer Games. Enger also serves as an instructor of sports administration at MacEwan University in Edmonton.

Scott Flory is the head football coach for the University of Saskatchewan Huskies in Saskatoon, Saskatchewan. Prior to taking the head coaching position, Flory was the offensive coordinator for the Huskies for three seasons. Scott played for the Huskies in college and then went on to enjoy a successful career with the CFL's Montreal Alouettes. In his 15 years with Montreal, he won three Grey Cup championships and was named All Star 11 times. He also received the CFL's Most Outstanding Offensive Lineman award twice in his career. After retirement, Scott joined the Huskies coaching staff.

Jay Hetherington has had a lifelong interest in helping people reach their full potential. He has practiced psychology in and out of the school system. He has worked with athletes and has a passion for football. Jay is a member of the College of Alberta Psychologists, the Psychologists Association of Alberta, the Canadian Register of Clinical Hypnosis–Alberta and the Canadian Association of School Psychologists.

Neil Lumsden was named director of athletics and recreation at Brock University in St. Catharines, Ontario, in 2016. His career highlights as a player include winning the Vanier Cup with the University of Ottawa in 1975, being nominated the eastern conference's Most Outstanding Rookie in 1976, and winning three Grey Cup championships with the Edmonton Eskimos (1980–1982). After retiring from professional football in 1985, he enjoyed a highly successful career in sport management. He worked for the Ottawa Rough Riders before joining the front office of the Hamilton Tiger-Cats, where as general manager, the team won the Grey Cup in 1999. Lumsden spent five years on the coaching staff of the University of Guelph Gryphons, winning a Yates Cup in 2015. Lumsden was inducted into the Canadian Football Hall of Fame in 2014.

Scott MacAulay started coaching in the Regina High School Football League in 1996 while playing junior football for the Regina Rams Football Club. After finishing his junior playing career with the Regina Thunder, he went on to coach linebackers and help coordinate the defense under Randy Shaw. He later served as defensive coordinator for Team

Saskatchewan and was part of the national championship teams in 2009 (under Ryan Hall) and 2010 (under Mike Humeny). In 2010, he rejoined the Regina Thunder as linebackers coach and special teams coordinator under Erwin Klempner. In 2013, the year he took over the team as head coach, the Regina Thunder won the CJFL national championship.

Greg Marshall is currently the defensive coordinator for the Edmonton Eskimos. He began his coaching career in 1994 in the CFL with the Saskatchewan Roughriders. From there he moved to the Eskimos as their defensive line coach, and later to defensive coordinator. In 2005, he served as the assistant head coach for the Ottawa Renegades in their final season of operation. Marshall made his way to Winnipeg to work with the Blue Bombers as their defensive coordinator for three seasons and then went on to hold the positions of defensive coordinator and assistant head coach for the Hamilton Tiger-Cats. In 2013, he returned to the Edmonton Eskimos, and he remains on their coaching staff.

Dwayne Masson is currently the running backs coach with the University of Regina Rams. His extensive coaching background includes time spent with the Regina Thunder (CJFL), Campbell Collegiate, Sheldon Williams Collegiate, and Regina Minor Football. He was also an assistant coach for Team West in the CIS East–West Bowl (2014 and 2015). Masson remains very active in the Regina football community by assisting in the Regina Minor Football Spring League as well as presenting at various coaching clinics.

Blake Nill has coached Canadian university football for more than 20 years, the majority of which as head coach. Since 2015, Nill has been the head coach at the University of British Columbia. His prior head coaching stints were with Saint Mary's University (1998–2005) and the University of Calgary (2006–2014). He has led his programs to the national finals on eight occasions, winning in 2001 and 2002 with Saint Mary's and in 2015 with British Columbia. His career record stands at 144 wins and 53 losses. Nill was named university football Coach of the Year in 1999 and was a finalist on six other occasions.

Jay Prepchuk is the quarterbacks coach at the University of British Columbia (UBC). His coaching career boasts two long tenures as high school coach (1984–1998 and 2002–2016). In between, Prepchuk was head coach at UBC (1999–2001). In 2002, he served as a guest coach for the BC Lions. He has run football camps in western Canada since the mid 1990s. In his playing days, Prepchuk was quarterback at Simon Fraser University (1979–1982).

Sean Reader has a coaching career that has spanned two decades, two provinces, and five teams. His experience includes 4 years at the University of Alberta, 14 years in Canadian Junior Football (4 years with the Edmonton Wildcats and 10 with the Regina Thunder), 3 years at Dr. Martin LeBoldus High School, and 3 years at St. Gregory Elementary (touch football). A certified NCCP level 3 football coach, Coach Reader's main areas of expertise are special teams, receivers, and strength and conditioning.

Tom Sargeant played for the Saskatoon Hilltops and, after his playing days were over, he got into coaching. He was head coach of the Evan Hardy Souls, winners of three city championships and two provincial championships in his seven years with the team. In 1990, he joined the Hilltops' coaching staff, where he remains today. He served as assistant coach for his first seven years with the team and has been head coach ever since. His teams have won 13 CJFL championships, 10 of which while he was head coach. Sargeant has a master's degree in educational administration and level 4 coaching certification.

Alex Surprenant is head coach and offensive coordinator for Les Géants du Cégep Saint-Jean-sur-Richelieu, a position he has held since 2012. Prior to moving to Division 1 in 2016, the team won back-to-back Bol d'Or (Golden Bowls) in 2014 and 2015 in Division 2. Surprenant is an alumni of Laval University, where he was defensive back, with his team winning two Vanier Cups (2006 and 2008). He was named an All-Conference player in 2009. After graduation, he was assistant coach at Saint-Jean from 2010 to 2012.

Patrick Tracey is currently the defensive coordinator at the University of British Columbia, a position he has held since 2016. His extensive coaching experience spans 30 years, having coached teams at all levels: university (Guelph University and Queens University), Team Ontario, Team Canada, Canadian Interuniversity Sport (CIS/U Sports), and CFL (Hamilton Tiger-Cats and Winnipeg Blue Bombers). During his coaching career, Tracey has served as defensive coordinator and special teams coordinator.

Clint Uttley is a high school teacher and coach at New Westminster Secondary School. He previously spent 14 years as a university coach, most recently as the head coach at McGill University (2012–2014). He spent a total of seven years at McGill, following stops at Acadia University and University of British Columbia (UBC), where he held defensive and special teams coordinator roles. Clint has also been a guest coach at the training camps of several teams in the Canadian Football League (CFL), most notably the Toronto Argonauts (2003, 2005, and 2008) and Calgary Stampeders (2011). He played collegiately at Acadia University (1996–2000), where he was a four-year starter and team captain in his final two seasons.